The Winner's Circle

THE WINNER'S CIRCLE

Triumph of Jesus Christ

K. R. Jones

VANTAGE PRESS
New York / Washington / Atlanta
Los Angeles / Chicago

1-88

FIRST EDITION

Published by Vantage Press, Inc.
516 West 34th Street, New York, New York 10001

Manufactured in the United States of America
ISBN: 0-533-07092-9

Library of Congress Catalog Card No.: 86-90128

gift
author

The winner's circle always contains the one who sacrifices the most. Here Jesus Christ endures the Cross and it becomes a victory symbol.

It is the first step in the long road or vision of the future or new government. One must set the example in order to construct a new road or in the ordering of a new character composed of a new body and then a new spirit, both of which will mold the new personality.

What this book is about is one-third of the circle. Government, Philosophy, and Religion are the three columns to support the scaffolding of the whole universe. As my niece puts it, "We have tried government of today, which is not very successful, so why not try all of them mixed together to find out how it fares?"

So this book is the religious side of the circle.

PREFACE

The basic three-thousand-page manuscript that served as the foundation structure for the condensed five books, which included *Textbook On Character*, *The Role of Perfection*, and this fifth book, titled *The Winner's Circle: The Triumph of Jesus Christ*.

This original manuscript was titled *Jesus Christ—The Perfect Man*. The manuscript was surveyed or reviewed by different publishing firms or individuals as noted below:

Editor G. Chattham of Exposition Press writes:
"This is a most unusual work on Jesus Christ. It is impressive in its content, too. I find this contains a readable, fresh and stimulating approach to the true spirit of Christianity.
"There is a compelling logic in the presentation of the Christian story; the author has delved deeply into character delineation and motivation, adding modern psychological light to painstaking research. There is a wealth of Scriptural quotations to prove points. This book amounts to an indictment of traditional Christiandom."

Editor Seth Richards of Pageant Press writes:
"I have never encountered such a forthright, logical, highly readable story and interpretation of Jesus Christ, particularly in regard to the 'mysterical aspects of His life and influence.' Your refutation of the liberal and scientific objection to the supernatural elements of the famous story is eminently convincing on a purely intellectual level."

Editor of Carlton Press, Inc. writes:
"K. R. Jones' mammoth manuscript, JESUS CHRIST, is not only clearly and forcefully written, but thoroughly organized in its incorporation of factual, traditional, interpretative, and critical commentary on the life of Jesus."

The book of *Textbook On Character: The Miracle of Perfection*:

From the Sacramento Bee the following Book Review said:

"*Perfection* is topic. Jones states man can free himself from chaotic confusion through developing a character based on the life and teachings of Christ."

Robert C. Perm, Team Coordinator for Billy Graham at one time, says about the same book:

"You have really achieved something in freshness of style, which always makes reading much more enjoyable. And you have reminded us again of many of the age-abiding truths that are so easily forgotten, particularly when we always read them in the same literary style."

CONTENTS

Contents of the Frontispiece

The Winner's Circle

FRONTISPIECE

EXPLANATION OF THE LIFE OF CHRIST

This is merely an exposition or explanation of the life of Christ. The book itself explains the latter part of Jesus's life. This exposition following gives hints in regard to the addition of the Cross which now makes his name, Jesus Christ, the son of God. This is the conversion to the life of the Holy Spirit.

This is the fifth volume on his life. Volume one was titled *Textbook on Character—The Miracle of Perfection*. This fifth volume is the important part of his life and since I may never get the other volumes published, I give you this drama, which can be adapted to oral or movie video.

This book is actually an anthology of over one hundred authors, so consequently it is more pertinent and persuasive than other books on his life.

Effecting a Unity

What we attempt to do is what the Bookshelf of the Sacramento Bee explains. "Jones states man can free himself from chaotic confusion through developing a character based on the life and teachings of Christ."

I realize that the Bible says that those accepting the Kingdom only need to turn the key, need only have faith, and that works are not required. That is for now; later it is my belief that for the world of perfection we are going to need works which are developed by perfection and character. Of course, having new minds and new bodies will facilitate the job.

As I told my evangelistic friends, we must try to find a Unity way for all in the everlasting Kingdom. What we are attempting to do is to set up a unity response for all religions to follow. He awaits us as *The Host*.

THE BIBLE IS PRACTICAL

(The Guidebook of Life)

We teach the Bible. We look for the good in all religions.

Whereas modern educators revise their methods and textbooks to keep pace with our changing world, the Bible, on the other hand, has remained unchanged for thousands of years. Instead, it warns about, "not to add to or take away from the words written therein." (Prov. 20:5, 6; Rev. 22:18, 19)

Can the Bible be accepted as a practical guide for our modern day? What we notice is that the Bible is not the product of man's thinking; the Bible is not man's word but God's. This cannot be overlooked because God's knowledge is not restricted by time and circumstances, as is man's, nor is it subject to change.

For proof or support on this: Despite the increased knowledge, man's basic needs and makeup have not changed. Inwardly we are still the same, having the same drives as our forefathers, in every phase of life, in every area of morality, economics, and health.

The Bible's standards are not Victorian but relative to today. In order to save money the Bible advocates that we refrain from drinking, drugs, and smoking. We become in debt because of our habits costing a fortune. Those who adhere to the Bible principles are prized by employers for their honesty, integrity, and industriousness. (Cl. 3:22, 23; Eph. 4:28)

The Bible is accurate and up-to-date on matters relative to medicine and health. This even though it was written at a time when superstition abounded. They work toward improving our mental health. The Bible recognizes the effect that attitudes and emotions have on the body. (Prov. 14:30) So it directs us away from damaging attitudes and emotions, and it helps us replace them with positive, uplifting qualities.

What happens is that wrong ideas impose self-will—you arrive at a state where you cannot escape from sin. You fall into sin and lose the sense of joy. False ideas creep in and require a restoration back to peace.

Yes, the Bible stresses a change from a destructive, hurtful personality to the new, healthful Christian personality. (Eph. 4:20–24; Cl. 3:5–14) It helps us to manifest the fruitage of God's spirit "love, joy, peace, long-suffering, kindness, goodness, faith, mildness, self-control." (Gal. 5:22, 23) The Bible provides healthful food on which the mind and the heart can feed and be at peace. (Prov. 3:7, 8; 4:20–22; Phil. 4:6–8)

4

In addition, those who abide by *Bible regulations* do not become involved in crimes, riots, uprisings, or other things that result in bodily injury. They have a good conscience, which greatly contributes toward maintaining a happy disposition and good physical health. (I Pet. 3:16–18)

However, those who apply the Bible's counsel enjoy a warm, rewarding happy homelife, together with peaceful relations with others.

Jesus compared the Spirit to the wind, or air, and no better illustration can be found. The subtle "air spirit" quickens the inanimate flesh. Jesus breathed on them and said, "Receive the Holy Spirit." (John 20:22) This act by Jesus shows the intimate relation between the *word* and the *breath*.

What happened was that Jesus had purified the soul and made contact with Spirit until His word and the Holy breath were one. Those who are open and receptive can receive it and in turn have insight and spiritual ability like the Master's.

Jesus proclaims or decrees, ". . . the *words* that I have spoken to you are spirit and life." (John 6:63) He gives *creative* capacity to His words and they lay hold of all the forces necessary to the fulfillment of His ideals. As Paul puts it, you have to have the mind of Christ. "I can do all things in him who strengthen me. (Phil. 4:13) You must demonstrate your faithfulness in applying the power of your words and prayers to the achievement of their ideals.

So shall my word be that goes forth from my mouth, it shall not return to me empty, but it shall accomplish that which I purpose. It shall prosper in the thing for which I sent it. (Isa. 55:7–11) Exaltation is assured when you proclaim words founded in Spirit. You will be amazed at the results.

THE WORD IS POWERFUL

We now want to call your attention to the machinery or equipment set up in our book *The Tools of Learning: A Storybook Dictionary*. Here the whole world is to be studied through this microscope of the thirty-five classifications. The world will be sorted out.

According to various persons:

Jerry Falwell says,

"We are anointed."

Dr. Schuller says,

"Talent comes from visualization. You image it. Emotional response is an important part of the limbic system. And emotions are the bridge between thinking and acting. Thinking is not enough. A thought must be followed by an emotion if there is to be action."

James C. Lewis of Unity says,

"If one wants to go beyond average ability, it demands more determination."

Tom Watson, golfer, says,

"It requires more hard work."

The word is all powerful. With right ideas and right words Jesus Christ portrayed power and joy. The word is more powerful than the sword. It becomes dynamic when emotion instills motivation. Jesus Christ showed the way when he accepted the Cross. You cannot dream or visualize its power. You must be willing to die for a cause.

TEN STEPS OF GAINING SUCCESS (TALENT) (FIRST OF ALL YOU MUST BE WILLING TO DIE!)

1. SACRIFICE
2. HARD WORK
3. VISUALIZATION or Imagination
4. IDEAS—Image
5. EMOTION—Determination
6. PLANNING—Goal—Thinking
7. ACTION
8. WORDS AND LANGUAGE— An approximation of our thoughts.
   Communicate the meaning of life.
9. GOD TELLS YOU WHAT TO SPEAK

Stand Firm in your faith—Have trust in God.—FAITH is the key.

Faith working in spiritual substance accomplishes all things.

This is the faith that cooperates with creative law.

Marcus Bach on Writing: What you express is uniquely yours although, at times, you have the wonderful

6

feeling that you are a channel for expressions inspired by this
higher self.

The best advice is to put your heart into it, be con-
structive, believe you have something to share and that you
are working with an inner guide or coach who is creative and
involved with you in your corner.

10. RIGHT WORDS IN THE MIND—Gives you dynamic power.

You channel wisdom and power of God.

How to Live a Christian Life

Peter gives seven steps.
See Peter 2:1–7.
1. Faith
    Desire
    Virtue
    Knowledge
    Diligence
    Self Control—Fruit of Spirit
    Patience—Perseverance—Endurance
    Kindness—Love
2. Enduring Abundance—Begets Productive Life
        Even through trials

TO UNDERSTAND

Jesus Christ promoted the premise that to truly understand you had to
receive the *Spirit of God*, termed the *Holy Spirit* or Holy Ghost. In his last
few days on earth he called it the Comforter.

If you didn't have this God Spirit then you as an average person
could not really see, hear, or understand the truth. In other words, the
truth would escape you. Your eyes and mind would be clouded over
so as to prevent understanding. This was the explanation given out to
the world in the past.

Now "The World Tomorrow," the church of Herbert W. Armstrong
(recently deceased), has given the subject a new twist. This Spirit is a
bridge between the men of nature and the spirit of God. To receive this
spirit of God was presented as a conversion experience. All men in the
beginning are governed by this nature man—they wear the tunic of this

ungovernable nature which Satan sells wholesale.

It was Jesus Christ who brought about a recognition of this bridge. The acceptance of this connection was seen because of his overcoming of all temptations and his ability to live the life of perfection.

The Winner's Circle

Lurking behind the title of *The Winner's Circle* is the idea of the circle including God, the Son of God, and the Holy Spirit or Comforter. Their cabinet is probably composed of the Apostles or other talent.

Now we inaugurate or set forth the Ten Steps of Gaining Success, or how to achieve talent.

The Neophyte

THE FIRST DEGREE

Jesus, as the young child, is the neophyte taking His *first degree* in the mysteries of life.

How it all began. It was John the Baptist who was the symbol of man in his animal or *natural degree of development*.

BETTER UNDERSTANDING

What we all need is a *better understanding* of the *law of soul growth*. Man has floundered in his *ignorance* long enough. The *devils* of parables represent *error* states of mind that had been quickened by *Truth* and were *repentant*.

ESCAPE FROM THE MATERIAL WORLD

What is now sought is an *escape* of the soul from *ignorance* and *materiality*.

PROBLEM OF RULING OVER OTHERS

When in the wilderness, Jesus was tempted by the *adversary*, or personality; but with His *superior understanding* He withstood the *deceptive*

8

promises made. The last straw was when the personality suggested that Jesus make *substance out of matter,* use His *power to rule over others,* or do marvelous things to prove His *mastery.*

Many people try to gain this *control* through personal *ego power.* This is the heavy yoke, the *burden of living,* with which Jesus wanted to help them. This is the constant planning and attempting to *manipulate people* and events for *personal gain or benefits* or even just to eke out a meager living. Jesus suggested an easier way.

SELFISH PERSONALITY

The *selfish personality.* Jesus pointed him out. "Fear him who *can destroy* both soul and body in hell." Jesus also warned that the *kingdom of heaven* had been taken by violence and force.

LOOK TO THE PHASE OF THOUGHTS

Every *phase of thoughts* that the soul passes through was depicted by Jesus in allegories, parables, comparisons, and physical experiences. *His life,* as recorded in the Gospels, covers every point that the individual may experience spiritually, mentally, or physically. This life was the exemplar.

HOSANNAS AND JOYFUL OBEDIENCE

The *hosannas* of the rejoicing multitudes represent the *joyful obedience* and *homage* that all the thoughts in one's consciousness give when an *error state of mind* is *overcome.*

KILLED THE LIFE OF THE BODY

Moral selfishness and ignorance have *killed the life of the body* since the time of Adam's disobedience and selfishness.

RESTORATION OF ETERNAL LIFE

Now the way is opened for the *restoration of eternal life.* Eternal life is gained by thinking about life until life itself springs forth as a living

9

thing that energizes and *thrills with gladness* and satisfaction *every function*.

TEMPTATION OF PLEASURE

Temptation of pleasure as part of living confronts the *neophyte*. All the pleasures of life must come under the discipline of the Lord of *wisdom*. Pain will only follow more pleasure. The pleasure you will name *"good,"* and the pain *"evil."* Do not annihilate *desire and sensation*, but transmute them to spiritual ideas. You balance all things.

EXPRESS THE SPIRITUAL BEING

One must seek to encourage greater expression in the *spiritual being*. "God is Spirit," taught Jesus, and man is the Son of God. He is then the infant Jesus begotten by the *Holy Spirit* and hero of the virgin, pure *Truth*.

The *wise men* from the East, who bring gifts to the young Child represent the wisdom that *experience* in past lives has *stored up* in the inner resources of the soul.

Worship in the Temple represents the efforts of the wisdom of the soul to sustain a *right mental attitude toward God*.

THE CHRIST MAN

This is the son of man who is to be "lifted up," transmuted, into *a higher type* of man when the divine or *Christ man* asserts his dominion.

CAST OUT AVARICE

After this victory over willfulness, Jesus entered the Temple and *cast out avarice* (money changers) and all those who sold doves traffic in *innocence* and *purity*.

THE CROSS OVERCOMES CARNALITY

Jesus on the *Cross* demonstrated in its finality the complete *overcoming* of carnal consciousness. Carnality is the "adversary" that possesses us all.

10

How One Gains Wisdom and Understanding

Thoughts, feelings, words, and actions are timely and in order.
Have to have a *firmness of faith* in Christ.

With the Spirit you can be filled with power.

You affirm that you are *protected and guided* by the Father.

Today's peace and understanding are like a pyramid. They build on themselves.

To pursue a goal until it is attained you use *determination*.
You have to have *faith-filled determination*
God strengthens one.

Lead a life worthy of the calling.
You must put the ingredients in or the cake will not bake.

Have trust in God, then you will be guided aright.
He directs one in all ways.
Acknowledge him and he will make straight your paths.

Stand firm in your faith
Hold to positive thoughts
They will create a positive environment.
Nothing in the outer has power over one.
Fear is cast out with *faith in God.*

All things work together for good.
The Lord is good to those who wait for him.

There are no endings, only beginnings. There are no closed doors.

○   ○   ○

It is my belief that I believed in God and Jesus Christ back along history route as much as or more than anybody else.
I was more loyal to his standards and beliefs
Today is different.

FAITH IS THE KEY:
What you put in is what you receive.

From a firmness in faith and a great determination to overcome my lack and doubt—
   Inferiority Complex

I received power, joy, guidance, wisdom, understanding,
direction, positive thoughts

You must be willing to give up the flesh and denounce the
world.

The object is to focus your attention upon the *ideas* that are
   Life-giving and faith producing.

This is a method for channeling wisdom and the power of God
   Into your problem or channel.

Whatever your personal challenge, here is a surefire spiritual technique for getting help beyond your human resources.

The Bible says you must count the cost first—before going ahead
   You pay the acceptable price
   This is no hoax.
      You just pay the cost or price and
         You can be assured of results.

Faith Thinking (Super Thinking)

   I think Charles Fillmore portrayed or delineated most of the aspects
of our own super-thinking system as shown in our Part II of *The Tools
Of Learning*. The *faith thinking* of Charles Fillmore is similar to our super-
thinking. We have condensed his words to the following exposition.

   We have available infinite expansion but cannot discern but
   a sector of the circle. We become involved in a universe of correlated
   faculties.
   We all are an expression of an *infinite idea*. Since there is but
   one God, there can be but one humanity. Each individual is a part
   of the universal humanity. We draw mental or physical from Christ.
   There is but one fount to draw from. Each one's relation is the
   same. Similar variations are repeated. Attributes of humanity are
   in consciousness focused in infinite combinations. The harmonious

12

man such as Christ Jesus was produced in certain combinations. What we seek is that we can grasp the mind of Jesus Christ. What we find are weaknesses in some coordinating faculty.

Talents are suppressed by excessive egotism. What we lack is not being able to venture into the *spiritual*. Some perceive the Truth but do not carry out in detail. From within oneself He gave forth the doctrine of the Christ. Externally He stood for perfected humanity. Even though we act a *separate part* we blend into the one *harmony—perfection*. In order to control our powers and bring them into unity of action, we must know their places on the staff of consciousness.

Our most important power is the original thinking faculty. The original thinking from which we send forth thoughts. In the present external world we live an average life and never have an original thought.

Faith thinking is done only by one who has caught sight of the inner truths of Being and who feeds his thinking faculty upon images generated in the faith center. Of course faith thinking is not merely an intellectual process based upon *reasoning*. Instead of comparing and analyzing he draws conclusions from divine premises. His thinking gives form to ideas that come straight from the *eternal Fount of wisdom*. His perceptions impinge upon the spiritual, and he knows.

The faith faculty in us makes us free agents, because it is our creative center; in and through this one power we establish our consciousness—we *build our world*.

In the past the power of thinking has fed upon the illusions of sense. All imaginations of the thoughts of the heart brought *evil* continuously. Humanity has been feeding his thinking faculty on evil, instead of true thoughts from God.

Jesus of Nazareth connected the thinker with the *true source of thought*. Sloppy or random thinking brought about a deplorable condition. Our only salvation lies or depends upon again *joining our consciousness* to that of the Christ. He builds the foundation of his church on the *acknowledgement of faith*. Instead, society has tried to build conditions of harmony without making the right connections between the thinker and the *true source of thought*.

Without recognizing the spiritual you drift in the darkness of sense. *Ideas* are the *food* of the thinking faculty. All things are *generated* in the *laboratory* of mind and are your *Tools Of Learning*. With these new powers you begin to do the *works of the Spirit*. Acknowledging the Christ gives you an *inside track. This because he is the corner-stone* of the building and has *"the keys of the kingdom of heaven."* The keys are the *thoughts* he forms, the *words* he speaks. (WORDS are the main item in our book, *The Tools Of Learning—A Storybook Dictionary.*) Words are the fount of wisdom and knowledge. Whatever you bind on earth shall be bound in heaven.

"When the thinking faculty attaches itself to the *things of earth* we limit or bind the free ideas. You lose the desire for higher things. Through the creative power of the thinker you are required to *arrange yourselves* according to *His word* in order *to succeed.*

In other words you cannot do what the Father has set before you unless you discipline your powers. (My article, "The People Must Be Disciplined," expresses it well. This requirement of course overrules any assumption of natural purity and son of God theme which many metaphysical students proclaim.) Unsifted thoughts prove an unruly servant and produce discord.

You have to touch with the infinite *storehouse of wisdom.* Like Peter the faith thinker wanders; he doesn't always stay with the *Truth,* hence needs *disciplining.* One has to look both ways. He must be equalized or balanced. And those who say that *concentration* is not necessary to perceive spiritual truths are wrong. Concentration and discipline are both necessary as *partners* to get *perfection.*

Summary

Let us now make a comparison between Charles Fillmore's recipe for "Faith Thinking" and the supermind thinker of the Superman.

Here in the digest of Charles Fillmore he talks about such things as: [The Superman's code or arrangement is bracketed]
1. Available Infinite Expansion
   Yet lacking in discernment or demonstration
   Becomes over involved in too many correlated activities
   [The Superman is unlimited]
2. We express an infinite idea—One God
   There can be but one humanity
   There is only one fount to draw from
   [For the Superman still to be structured
   There eventually becomes an elite condition
   When he is made new in mind and body]
3. There are infinite combinations to draw from
   The harmonious man such as Jesus Christ

14

Was produced by fitting together certain combinations
[The harmonious man was formed by the Superman
Acting as ambassador of Jesus Christ]
4. Talents suppressed by egotism or pride
Within is the doctrine of the Christ
Outwardly he stood for perfected humanity
We both act the separate part and blend into the one harmony
[We no longer act the separate part
Because we no longer accept the mundane world
Of the Earth-Universe]
5. Thinking the Inner Truths of Being
This thinking is not
An intellectual process based on reasoning
Not based on comparing and analyzing
Instead he draws conclusions from divine premises
[Inspiration, imagination, and intuition
have always been the tools of the Superman
Its doctrine is above reason
He draws from Eternal Wisdom
He knows directly]
6. Through Faith We Build the World
No longer feed upon the illusions of sense
We do away with evil which humanity
Has Been Feeding Upon
[The Superman builds his world also on Faith]
7. Jesus Connected The Thinker With The True Source of Thought
Random thinking brought about a deplorable Condition
We join our consciousness to Christ
We build the foundation of the Church with Faith
Society has tried to build harmony erroneously
We have not recognized the Spiritual
You drift in the darkness of sense
Ideas come to their own.
[The Superman stresses the powers of the idea or ideal
Coming through a Connection with Christ]

THE DIFFERENT FORMAT

All of this above statement is approximately the same as the Protestant religion.

We merely relate a few of the differences that might vary from the Unity School of Christianity expounded here. This statement is a condensed version of Unity, and since it relates in part to our own views and the Christian belief, we have used it to explain the metaphysical miracle.

Superior Understanding

Yes, it is true that Christ had *superior understanding* and so was able to overcome the deceptive promises by the Adversary. Unity sticks to the script and that man can do the same thing: secure superiority. The difference for us is that intellect is no longer a priority resource—that the easier way is through faith and grace derived through repentance.

Error State Overcome

For Unity it is the *error state* of mind which is *overcome* by thoughts. For us it is only possible to overcome errors by first accepting the new birth. Without the new birth one can never gain the better life, let alone have eternal life.

Mortal Selfishness Kills

For Unity it is *mortal selfishness* and ignorance (the same as Herbert W. Armstrong of Ambassador College holds) that *kills* the life of the body. Soon we will be able to overrule it and accept the new sphere of existence. For us the Kingdom of Heaven can never come about or exist by just getting together with your fellow man (such as the Baha'i Faith proposes or Herbert W. Armstrong directs and teaches).

Accept Christ As Ruler

It will have to come by *accepting Christ as the ruler*. This is exactly the opposite of what H.B. Armstrong tells us. He thinks that we stress too much the worshiping of Jesus Christ when the new testament gospel only preaches what the Kingdom of Heaven is.

Is Christ The Son Of God?

Unity stresses happiness and prosperity for this life, whereas the Evangelists stress the next life to come. The Evangelists of the Protestant religion stress pain and learning and that all things work for good. Lately, Unity is stressing the pursuit of the *Truth,* and this is the metaphysical way. They do not call themselves a religion. Unity stresses that Christ was a "Wayshower" and that man can be the same. Mr. Armstrong says Christ is the ruler, which is essentially the same. Neither of them say he is the "Son of God."

Is God Just Spirit

Now they divert from following the theory that *"God is just Spirit"* but advise you to accept desire and sensation as part of the spiritual idea. They no longer want you to do away with the body completely. This must indicate that the body can be spiritual too. They say, do not annihilate desire and sensation.

Unity advocates, along with H. W. Armstrong of the Worldwide Church of God, that man is reaching for a higher type of man. This will come about when the Christ man asserts his dominion which will be soon. Unity of course stresses the idea that the *Christ spirit is within* oneself hence can do the same as the miracle man Jesus Christ Himself.

The Cross Expurgates (Expurgis)

The Cross is most important for the protestant religionists. It is not so important for Unity or H. W. Armstrong. The cross is the means for achieving or overcoming avarice and selfishness. You go through the processes of justice that cannot be offset by any flim-flam by the Adversary or opposition. You are granted a purity standard, a medal because of his blood-letting. Carnality is overthrown so as to gain perfection and eternal life.

The Highest Motif
Overcoming the Perplexities

There are two ways of having awareness. One is a simple natural process of childlike acceptance. All things reflect this truth, even words of poems, works of art, religions, and philosophies. What is stressed though is to know, feel, and believe. But be cognizant that it is not a matter of patterns of behavior handed down through the ages. It is something that is not an organization. It is not learned in school or from books.

Oh, how they all seek to escape from any organization. The escape is from rules and regulations. The Christ is merely a phenomenon or happening who comes only once in a millenium. The difficulty is that this simple truth has been made complex. Men insist on practicing division and anonymity, they say.

Organization and rules or disciplines are out of order and nearly obsolete. They say that Truth is available to all, that character is of no consequence. Only doubt of ourselves needs to be feared. They want us to beware of those who teach the opposite and that Truth is open to only a chosen few.

Yes, creeds and denominations are not to be trusted. We agree that when you lean toward a leader or group you are deceived. But that still does not say you can claim your divinity as being the reason you deny.

They object to religious leaders and groups that try to chop up Truth and label it. Yes, there are so many different kinds of labels: political, artistic, academic, philosophical, sociological, economic, national, ethnic, racial, and gender labels. Yes, we agree that it is a losing process. It creates division, confusion, envy, greed, hate, and conflict that lead to war and destruction.

Trying to divide and label Truth makes no sense unless it is labeled by the heavenly trademark or by God through the cross. They insist there are no labels or divisions because everything is One. Yes, there eventually is only going to be One. But that will come or be only after the era of *Choice* by men and women is over. And when Choice is taken away that includes the taking away of man claiming an erstwhile semblance of Divinity.

The claim is made that we are all endowed with the power to see and know. But does that enable us to see the best or truth when our minds are so conditioned by the secular world of form and excito? It is this individuality they say which supports the universe and gives it existence. Humans err when they support sermons, arguments, differences, conflicts, denominations and divisions. Yes, it is the error that we must see that comes from dividing and labeling. We object to our brains being engraved with pseudo-education and ego-sophistication.

The claim is made that these are appearances only, and returning to the innocent child state, the pure and perfect self will eliminate all these nonsensical items. It is like someone going to see the doctor. It is interpreted as a wordless guidance that comes in the form of feeling. Let all things dissolve into simplicity. Intuition becomes the teacher. Now divisions are cast away along with tags, denominations, barriers, condemnation, denial, rejection. The child that lives in us does not see divisions because it lives on faith. They insist that all the *roads that lead to God are good* because the *One* concept cannot be ignored. All substance is molded into beauty, Truth, God.

The Shadow

We list these things to show you the slavery which Christ overcame, and why it was necessary for him to come to earth as a God-man.

We can describe *the shadow* as a "clump" of undigested energy, which at this point might erupt as negative behavior, destructive behavior, destructive appetites, and cravings, and distorted opinions and attitudes. The shadow is made up of whatever is ugly in us. They are distortions in our larger expression as a dynamic, loving creation of God. Another name used by some is limitation.

Seemingly there are two views we can have of this shadow. It can

18

be an enemy to be denied, hated, or avoided, or may we say it is a stimulus for growth. It seems the further we travel into Light and healing, the greater the challenge and *opportunities* presented by our shadow. The shadow is needed to uplift and cleanse. It requires perseverance and the inpouring of infinite Light in order to transform life conditions and limitations.

Yes, we can use the shadow as just being elemental and primitive and not evil. Our lives need refining and expansion so that our lives might become expressions of harmony, balance, and divine purpose. The expression as here illustrated is that if you deny any shadow it will grow inside you. If you ignore it, it will become more assertive. It is better to redirect and redeem it. Nothing can be covered up—all things are revealed. The dark shall be disclosed in the light.

Without condemning, denying, or condoning the shadow, we can uncover our ugliness and distortions. We work toward upliftment and contact true healing. *Light and purification* come into the dark recesses and brings on the beautiful. An ideal activity becomes more interesting than the allurements of the shadow. Replacement seems to carry more weight than willpower. What does one seek for, perhaps it is a part of you that resists progress or it releases a destructive habit; or you may be afraid, have anger and unforgiveness.

We feel and see what needs attention, direction, and firm but loving upliftment. It is possible that you can see impulsiveness, impatience, and outbursts of temper which are destructive. The *shadow affects your energy field*. The area of desire connects to energy "leakage." Such can make you feel listless, aimless, depressed, or irritable. You redirect your energy.

You can no longer rationalize the making of excuses for destructive actions. You cannot follow the *thinking patterns of other people.* No longer can we blame others for our own unattended issues and problems. No longer can we show a repression of our problems by ignoring them. We must cast away manipulation by using others for our *own ends instead of God's purposes.* Instead we seek to focus the mind toward more fulfilling purposes and results. Under direction the shadow works in *union* with our high purposes. Undirected it is destructive.

We are to pursue creativity and imagination, which nurture brotherhood and global unity by acts of commission. *Unselfish surrender* evolves into a greater *attunement of oneness* with the Divine. You live for the greater *possibilities of humanity* and service to the race.

We now turn our faults into strengths. A loss of freedom can be turned into—*from anger into*—*higher experience.* Fear is replaced with knowledge and intuitive insight.

Revenge can be replaced by working for justice. You must realize it is important to love what you don't like in yourself or others. You raise and transform the negativity. Resolute conviction or willpower is important. We seek change and cleansing.

In this writing it states you must insert the whole psychological premise of "sublimate, do not repress." Yes, "genuine sacrifice opens the shadow to *wholeness.*" In other words, shadows originate and spur the ongoing onslaught. *The Light of the Christ* enfolds and vitalizes the earth. It is asserted that if you become absolved in shadows you bury or *give up your gold*. Their talents lie undeveloped. They do not take over opportunities or responsibilities.

The reason for inserting this part of the prologue is that you will have a better view of why Christ died—it was to chase away problems that show up in shadows. Also the substance of difference in thinking of 2000 years ago and of today is shown more clearly.

For them apperances tell convincing lies. They proclaim that they live the awareness of their Truth and do not have to explain what they do. The ideal then must be to find one's own unique kingdom.

In our method you are not qualified to judge, you must be born again—then you become as a child. A new creature is made of you. We are not going to try patching you up. By nature we are all children of wrath. The unsaved cannot see God—they are conscience seared. Grace is the only vehicle through which you can be saved. Jimmy Swaggert tells it like it is.

If you want Unity and Peace you cannot go the way of obstreperous behavior. You must either conform and know that you need forgiveness or else choice of decision destroys. If you want Justice and equality, you cannot go the way of CHOICE.

There are then these two ways to go: the child life of feeling and faith or the life of discipline, character, rules, regulations, and dogma. There has to be a balance here somewhere where thought, will, brainpower and action has its story to tell, too. Assuredly an analysis must be made.

SUCCESS, IS THAT THE WORD?

WHY DREAM THE DREAM?

We hope for the dream. It is simplistic. We acknowledge and affirm our inner world before we can succeed in our outer world.

The inner world encompasses overcoming. When we err, life can become fragmental. We become sick at heart, in body, and spirit. Yes sin is self-inflicted nonsense. It is inane.

Yes, there is a recovery formula. When we recognize our mistakes and repent, God forgives and heals. Wholeness returns. When behavior is harmonized with God's design, health, happiness and peace are ours. We abhor the outer world and implore your compliance to not paying too much attention to it or else you will regret it. You will surely absorb its attributes such as becoming misled, confused, anxious, and even physically ill.

All is not entirely lost. Since we learn more from failures than from successes, these challenges have served a useful purpose, so you can even learn to laugh or smile at your own pratfalls. What has to occur of course is the unifying of the spiritual, mental, and physical aspects of activity. When doing this, you go all the way and your interests are broadened from self to larger concerns of society. This is found to be the beginning of wisdom.

You learn that the strongest feelings are those of security, gratitude, and being productive. You have to meet or face up to your purpose in life. Of course you have to let go of effete or exhausted substance or energy. In its place you install the new, pure reliance of God—it becomes manifest in one. Because you are open to the splendor of the kingdom of God within, a flood of plenty overcomes a lack of prosperity.

But what takes the prominent place is as Shakespeare says: "The poet's pen . . . gives to airy nothing a local habitation and a name." You know that our world is composed of what we have idealized, makes you more mindful or watchful of the activities of our minds. You see that you cannot harbor our evil thoughts by adding fear in our minds.

And as Mr. Fillmore says there is this one panacea. That is what we have always suggested. You have to install a new economic system (no-profit), in which human greed is eliminated. It will have to be supported by men and women who have overcome greed in themselves and who will harbor the thought of giving to all humankind, which of course requires loving. You simply deny selfishness under the umbrella of "the splendor of the kingdom of God within," and a flood of plenty follows.

You turn the turntable to God's pattern of perfection. It is expressed as the opposite of all negativistic thought. You acquire health and wholeness in mind and body. All of God's resources are now made manifest in your own ideals, activities, and affairs.

(This above is the nuclei, core, or focal point of the Unity movement.)

ONE CHURCH NEEDED

(Published to All Humanity in *Reno Gazette-Journal* on May 1, 1984)

There should be but one church. In Ireland, Catholic is against Protestant; in Islam, Iran is fighting Iraq; in Lebanon, Christians and many Arab factions preclude the possibility of having peace. If we want health and peace, there just cannot be scattered churches or scattered individuals, each church claiming its way as the only way or each claiming his own viewpoint or opinion as being the truth or right. There just cannot be schism or division in the body. All should think alike or agree.

Further, sometimes I think there should not be this adherence to separation of state and church. They are actually one. Church and state are aligned as closely as religion and philosophy. The concept of unity is what perhaps will bring more happiness. We cannot hope to have a paradise for men and women to live in if we back the separation of church and state.

The dream for all of us is that health and peace, laws, creeds and philosophies and all the religions will be merged into one singing chant. Can we not hope to turn society or the world around by merely turning the button of getting to the one of giving? Then no more will there be such thoughts as, "I want to do my own thing." Following your own idea is not correct.

What is needed is the balance wheel of the church with its uplifting influence.

All humanity has been sentenced to being cut off from God! That is, except the few called for a special mission. The apostles as Jesus proclaimed the gospel—the GOOD NEWS of a coming BETTER WORLD. The PURPOSE of the CHURCH is not to "get the world saved NOW!"

The PURPOSE was dual in a world CUT OFF from God. It was to provide a united body of Spirit-led believers to back up the apostles and evangelists. Second, it was the overcoming of Satan and the development of the body of the Church and build righteous CHARACTER in them so they can qualify to sit with Christ on the throne of earthwide government.

The distinction between GOD'S GIVING way and SATAN'S way of self-advantage is outright hostility to God's way and Church. It is proclaimed by some that to get salvation for the SELF is NOT God's WAY.

Christ is to come in supernatural POWER AND GLORY! Satan will be banished! And then all shall be resurrected to a MORAL status. All then will be called to God's salvation and eternal life! Even saints will inherit the transcendent human potential. There will be a BEAUTIFUL CREATION THROUGH THE WHOLE ETERNAL AND ENDLESS UNIVERSE—in happiness, joy and GLORY!

JESUS CHRIST IS THE RIDER ON THE WHITE HORSE

And he carried me away
  In the power of the spirit
Into a wilderness
  And I caught sight of a woman
  Sitting upon a scarlet-colored wild Beast
    That was full of blasphemous names
  And that had seven heads and ten horns.

—Revelation 17:3

The heads of the beast represent governments (Jeremiah 51:25)
The seven governments involved are Egypt,
                                   Assyria,
                                   Babylon,
                                   Medo-Persia,
                                   Greece,
                                   Roman Empire—Sixth power,
                                   Britain—Anglo-American world
                                   power

The beast had ten horns
  (Ten kingdoms who have not yet received a kingdom
    They do receive authority as kingdoms
      They have a short time with the wild beast.
        They give their power and authority to the wild beast.

  The beast is the disgusting thing
    It is the United Nations that is disgusting
      The Pope showed error in backing the United Nations)

The Rider Of The Beast
  There was a "woman" riding it
    She is identified as the worldwide empire of false religion

23

She is Babylon the Great, the mother of the harlots and of the disgusting things of the earth.
Christendom is trying to guide their course through the religions of Christendom

They promote the progress of the human family on earth.
They seek the message of the Gospel which is heavenly to become earthly.
Their instrument or machine of the United Nations
Does not enjoy good relations with God's Kingdom
Its supporters oppose that Kingdom

The Ten Horns will battle with the Lamb
The Lamb being Lord of lords and King of kings will conquer them.
The chosen, called and faithful also will do so.
The nations have constantly battled with the Lamb
They have opposed and persecuted those who act as ambassadors of his Kingdom.
The servants on earth who preach the good news
Will conquer all with the Master
And this despite bannings,
Imprisonments, and even death.

The United Nations could never be a force for real peace.
It has the wrong Rider
Its rider, "Babylon the Great," is one of the wicked war makers in history
She is drunk with the blood of the holy ones
(I told President Johnson once to avoid having blood on his hands.)
The wars of those nations supporting the United Nations
Have soaked the earth in blood.

Satan the Devil, "the great dragon," is no peacemaker
Mankind will never enjoy security as long as those entities exist
They will have to be removed.

Who is the Rider On the White Horse?
He who sits on the horse is called Faithful and True
He judges and carries on war in righteousness
Ranged against him are the political nations of the earth
Along with the image of the beast

The result of the war is
  Destruction for the peace destroyers
    There is only one great obstacle to peace

An angel comes down out of heaven
  With a key of the abyss
  And a great chain in his hand
    He seizes the dragon, the original serpent
      Who is the Devil and Satan
        And bound him for a thousand years.

Peace lovers urged to "get out of" Babylon the Great
  Those who submit to God's Kingdom
    Must avoid having the mark of the beast.
      A great crowd of righthearted ones will "come out of the great tribulation."

Those calling For Peace & Security
  Paul the apostle foretold
    "Whenever it is that they are saying:
      'Peace and security.'
    Then sudden destruction
      Is to be instantly upon them.

    "Thus they be grateful that Jehovah has enabled them
      To discern the significance
      Of the significance of the 'image of the beast'
      And the disgusting thing that causes desolation."

  The great tribulation will be
    A shocking surprise to mankind in general.

  Keep awake, then,
    All the time making supplication
      That you may succeed
        In escaping all these things
          That are destined to occur.

  Submit to God's Kingdom
    Enjoy peace even now
      "The God of peace," is with them
        And gives them

"The peace of God that excels all thought."
They look forward to the not-too-distant time
When the whole earth
Will enjoy the fulfillment
Of Isaiah's beautiful prophecy:

"The work of the true righteousness
Must become peace, quietness and security
And my people must dwell in
A peaceful abiding place
And in residences of full confidence
And in undisturbed resting places."

This will be security on a worldwide scale
And it will be real peace because
Jehovah himself will be its author.

THE DISGUSTING THING

The power of the wicked ones—this includes the United Nations

The task of bringing peace is just too difficult for the United Nations. The United Nations will never be more moral than the individual nations that make it up.

When the religious leaders of Christendom identified the United Nations with God's Kingdom and the gospel, that was idolatry.

Hence, early in this world's time of the end "the disgusting thing" appeared, warning Christians to flee.

A UNIVERSAL CHURCH

Letter to Nephew

I am glad that Alfred asked me about "what church I belonged to." I told you when you were here something to the effect that listening on TV to five or six Evangelists was more productive.

To be direct, what I am trying to do is to establish *a universal church,* or one church and one language. To accomplish this I must contact the more powerful and successful ministers. Consequently, any single minister or church cannot be of much interest to me.

This question brought out of the closet my letters in the newspaper. I am sending them to you. One is termed "One Church Needed," the other "Why The Church?" After this first letter, "One Church Needed," the Baha'i religion people called me to get me to join their church or organization. They stress one church or one religion.

Since Alfred asked this question I am mentioning two letters in my new book, plus putting two other letters in the book headed "The people have to be disciplined." Elma Lawlor, activist, says, "is the greatest article she ever read" and "Voting vs. Economics."

In this last letter I am setting up standards in Economics to be established for all time, for the world tomorrow and for the New Government.

Of course what I am trying to do is to set up textbooks for religion, government, and philosophy. As my niece (in-law) says, "The present government has not been too successful so why not try your mixture of religion, government, and philosophy?"

You cannot go on with all this division of churches. If you consent to just a temporary life you can agree to various opinions. Jesus Christ fought for *one church* (Jew and gentile together) and one language and eternal life. That means, as he says, *"Follow me."* With these standards or principles there will be no division, argument, or problem. All the efforts of people who now exist are futile and useless.

All futility versus the *one church.* Jesus Christ said, "I will build *my church* on a rock. Peter will be the leader."

CONTENTS—SUBJECT MATTER BY SCENE

28

(The Laws of Sacrifice)

31

Play V

Subject Matter by Scene

ACT I. The Inward Struggle (He Had a Struggle to Make)

Scene 1. The Heritage of Union with God Is Restored

32

1. He Had the Infinite Intellect of God Which Knows All Things
   Sees the Past and Future as Present
2. Jesus Interceded with His Father
       Submission and Resignation
           The Divine Became Human
               Stooped to the Dust of Earth
               Subject to the Law of Death
                   Death Confronts Him in Hideous Nakedness
                   If He Died as the Son of God the Sacrifice
                   Would Be Negligible
                       He Would Have to Suffer Much More
                           His Sufferings Were More Than a Mere
                           Man
                               In Addition to Having a Human Intel-
                               ligence He Had a Divine Intelligence
                                   In Obedience to His Father's Will
                                       Took Upon Himself the Iniquities
                                       of the World and Became the Sin-
                                       Bearer
                       He Felt the Agony and Torture of Those Who
                       Deny Guilt
                           Sin with Impunity and Do No Penance
                               The Burden of Sin Is as Natural as the
                               Clothes They Wear
                           He Looked to All the Past and Future Sins
                           Which Man Had Ever Committed or Would
                           Commit
                                       Every Open Act and Every Hid-
                                       den Thought
                   The Dreadful Desertion Which He Had to Endure
                       He Was Treated as a Sinner
                           He Would Pay His Father's Justice
                   He Pulled the Whole Guilt of the World upon
                   Himself
                       He Pledged the Last Full Payment of His Loy-
                       alty
                           It Was More Sensitive to Pain Than Human
                           Nature
                               Human Nature Calloused by Cruel Emo-
                               tions and Evil Experiences
                                   Conditioned by the Past (What Has
                                   Happened)
                       Sensitivity to the Hate of His Enemies

Sensitivity to Moral Evil and Sin
Physical Pain Was Not Predominant
Far Greater Than That of a Man
Who Lives without God
A Deep Personal Communion with God
A Majesty of Moral Purity
Enveloped by Deep Sorrow
The Agony (Hard to Accept Death)
(His Human Nature Recoiled from Death)
The Contradiction is Shown between God and the
World
Between the Divine and the Human
Two Wills Struggling within
We Resent the Necessity of Suffering
Unwillingness to Endure the Suffering
The Supreme Contact with the Powers of
Evil
The World Outside Alien and Hostile
No One Comprehended His Purpose and
His Struggle
No One to Share His Spiritual Experi-
ences
The Handicaps of the World Field
The Inadequacy of Man
The Calumny and Hostility with Which
His Cause Was Greeted
The Loneliness of His Soul
Fights out His Battle Alone with God
Prayer Is the Soul's Endeavor to Open
The Way for God to Do His Divine Will
We Should Not Expect God to Change His
Plans to Suit Our Whim
He Overcame the Temptation to Reject the
Cross and to Seek Refuge in Flight
He Conquered the Temptation to Yield
to Doubt and Despair
Had to Conquer Evil and Sin from the
Inside and Not the Outside
He Associated Himself to the Evil
of the World
He Had to Make the Choice between
the World and God

34

Made It for All Mankind
    He Had to Suffer Being Rejected
    or Cursed by the Father
Faith Threatens to Give Way under the
Weight of Doubt
  How Can One Believe in God If In-
  iquity Triumphs
    Sees the Prosperity of the Wicked
      May Fall into Bitterness and Si-
      lent Hatred
        That Way You Let in Death
    We Cannot Measure God's Thoughts
    by Our Thoughts
    We Cannot Make Our Faith De-
    pend upon God's Doing What We
    Wish
He Endured Every Injustice
  Injustice Gains the Victory
The "Cup" Was the Sense of Failure and
Apprehension for His Cause
  The Justice of God Cannot Allow the
  Sacrifice to Be Evaded
    He Must Taste Death for Every Man
    This Allows Men to Gain Eternal
    Life through Conflict and Suffering
    Two Elements Bound Together
    —Sin-Bearing and Sinless Obedi-
    ence
The World Outside Alien and Hostile
Salvation Is Forfeit If the Injustice Which
Weighs upon Us Gains the Upper Hand
  Is It a Temptation Which Will Work Our
  Ruin
  It Is the Trial Which Will Prove Us Right
    Must Accept the Will of the Father
    Need God's Guidance
    No contempt toward Men
    Who Cause the Injustice
      The Power of the Injustice Is Broken
      Commit Oneself to Him Who Judges
      Righteously
      The Bitterness Which Seeks to Poison

The Killing of Supreme Goodness,
Truth, and Love
The Weakness of the Flesh
The Natural Will Had to be Subdued by the
Higher Will
He Accepted the Father's Will
The Hard Road of the Father
There Was No Other, Easier Route
An Agony of Suffering Is Laid
When Fear Is Piled upon Fear
Blood Poured Forth from the Redemptive
Blood of Christ
Sin Is in the Blood
Jesus Vanquished the Agony
Through Prayer He Had Been Refreshed
The Need of Inward Purification against
the Crushing Circumstances of Life
He Had Regained Strength and Courage
He Came Away Victorious
Christ Emerged a Victory
Scene 2. Christ, the King of Heaven, Is Set Up against Caesar, the
King of Earth
3. He Is Betrayed into the Hands of Sinners
1. The Hour Planned for Had Struck
He Submitted Himself to Death
Love Fettered Himself to Unfetter Man
2. Those Bent on Evil Cannot Recognize Divinity
Even Though the Light Shines in Darkness, Darkness
Does Not Comprehend It
Unbelieving Minds Are Blinded by the God This
World Worshiped
3. The People Were Awed and Frightened
Calm and Dignity Were Beyond the Borders of Their Ex-
perience
They Know and Felt His Miraculous Power
His Glory Flashed Forth
Never Is There Humiliation without a Hint of Glory
4. The Lips of Treachery Simulated Love
When Wickedness Would Destroy Virtue It Prefaced
the Evil Deed by Some Mark of Affection
Deny and Compliment with the Same Lips
The Answer Still to Judas and the World Is "Friend"
Concerned Only with the Pitiable Failure of Judas

and the World, Not with the Bitter Wrong Done to
Him
    Stands Not as a Helpless Prisoner but as a Giver
    of Bounty
5. Blind Anger and Force Is Not the Way to Save The World
    Will Restore any Harm Done to Men
        Stands Not as a Helpless Prisoner but as a Giver of
        Bounty
        The Meaning of Life Is Service to Divine Love
    All They That Take the Sword Perish with the Sword
        Resist Not Evil
        Those Who Resort to Arbitrary Violence Would Feel
        That Violence Itself
            Revenge Brings Its Own Punishment
        The Contrast of the Cup and the Sword
            The Sword Wins by Slaying, the Cup by Submission
            Not the Impatience of the Violent but the Patience
            of Saints Is the Way to Win Souls
        The Cup is Accepted Voluntarily
            You Are Not Forced to Undergo Your Passion
            You Do It Out of Love for Man
6. He Was Submitting Voluntarily and According to Plan in
    Accordance with Forseen and Predicted Developments
        Not an Involuntary Bowing to a Fate
        A Voluntary Surrender of Some of Your Rights for
        the Sake of Those Who Seem Weak May Be Divine
        He Had Power at His Command
            Don't Oppose Those Who Seek to Capture You
            He Turns the Other Cheek and the Blow Falls
            on the Heart of His Persecutors
            One Blow in Return Would Destroy the Cause
                He Refused Their Weapons and Used His
                Own
            He Willed His Fate
7. The Power of Darkness Has Its Hour
    Evil Could Turn Out the Light of the World
        Evil Has Its Hour, God Has His Day
            A Monetary Triumph in Which the Blind Would
            Think They Had Gained a Victory
                Darkness Would Soon Lose Its Power at the Res-
                urrection
            All Was Planned Beforehand
                Sin Required Atonement or Reparation

He Acted In Man's Name
8. His Disciples Were to Save Themselves (Run) by Any Means
while
Spreading the Kingdom of God
To Save Their Faith They Were Not to Endure Abuse or
Humiliation
Now He Would Tread the Wine Press Alone
All Other Men Were to be Allowed to Go Free
He Never Wavered in His Purpose and Passion
Self-Sacrifice Seeks No Vengeance
Only One Concern, That of His Own Sheep
They Were Not Yet in a Spiritual Condition to Die with
Him
Later On They Would Suffer and Die in His Name
They Could Not Suffer for Christ Until Jesus Had
First Suffered for Them
All His Disciples Forsook Him and Fled in the Darkness
They Make No Attempt to Rescue Him
They Betray Him
They Knew Jesus Was Determined to Submit
They Forgot the Glory of the Messias
All Was Written
He Had Acquitted Them Beforehand
9. Jesus Did Not Call Himself Defeated
He Was a Success though Apparently a Failure
Learn to Be Content in Whatever State You Are
The Truly Successful Man Is the One Who Can Enjoy
the Life of God
If You Allow Suffering to Affect You, You Can Do
Nothing
Have Zeal
God Takes Advantage over Your Despair over Fail-
ure
Through Power of God You Can Rise up Again
Success Will Then Compensate Your Failure
10. He the Pure One Fell (Seized and Bound) into the Hands
of Sinners
Jesus Stands over against the World as Redeemer and
as Judge
He Was Able to Present Himself as Such because
There Was Not the Slightest Burden on His Consci-
ence
He Was in No Need of a Redeemer

This Is Why He Knew He Was the Deliverer
Came to Seek the Lost World of Men
He Was Confident He Could Transform All
Men
Because He was Secure He Dared to Set Him-
self Up as the Judge of All Mankind
He Won over Insult and Threat
He Made No Effort to Escape Pain
Love Is an Agony
Passion Is Suffering Not to Escape Suffering
Makes Itself Redemptive
The Unique Quality of Human Life Is the
Capacity to Make the Tragedy of Life Re-
demptive
He Was Put in Chains for His Testimony to the
Truth
They Said He Was Not the Messiah because
He Used No Power to Destroy Them
Just Another Faker under Arrest
Time Had Caught Up with Him
What Chance Had a Nazarene Magician
Who Was Not a Real Prophet

ACT II The Outward Struggle (The Trials before the Sanhedrin)
Scene 1.
2.   Both Divine and Human Natures Were on Trial
1. On Totally Different Charges
Condemned on Contradictory Charges
Annas and Caiphas Found Him Too Unworldly and
Too Divine
Pilate and Herod Found Him Too Human
2. Here the Responsibility for Jesus' Death Is Fixed on the
Entire Jewish Nation
3. Christ Raised the Mind of Man toward the Unseen
Becomes Insensible to the Barriers of Time and Space
4. Jesus Was the Breaker of the Law
He Was a False Prophet and Should Be Killed
The Blasphemer of the Name of God Should Die
He was a Deceiver and Seducer
A Young Nobody Posed as the Savior of the World
Scene 3. The Representative of the Priesthood of the Spirit
1. Led before the Representative of the Priesthood of the Flesh

40

The Question Was How to Snare a "Seducer"
  He Taught the People to Follow Himself
He Was Brought before Them Not for Trial
  In Their Minds He Was Already Condemned
  They Wanted Evidence to Force Pilate to Put Him to Death
  Sought Some Excuse for the Planned Injustice
    They Wanted to Know about His Secret Doctrines
      He Answered with Absolute Fearlessness Born of Innocence
        Only the People Who Had Believed Could Testify
          They Could Testify That There Was Nothing Secret about His Doctrine
          He Would Not Testify In His Own Behalf
            He Bade Them Summon Those Whom They Despised
        Affirmed That The Book of His Teaching Was Never Closed
          It was Open to All
            To Escape the Content of the Message
              The Form Is Criticized
                Violence Is Used when Capacity to Criticize Is Absent
                  They Did Not Rebuke but Tried to Make Him See His Fault
                    Appealed to the Principles of Justice
                    He Was to be Stricken for the Transgressions of Men
                      Bruised for Their Iniquities
                    In the Face of Insult His Patience Turned to Gentleness
                    There Were False Witnesses against Him
                      A Perversion of Words
                        The Jews Were to Be Destroyers, He the Restorer
                        They Claimed He Would Destroy the Temple
                          Instead They Would Destroy His Body

Divine Purpose Would Be
Attained, the Evil and Free
Actions of Men Would Be
Overruled by God
A Dangerous Disturber of the Na-
tion's Peace
They Question His Mission
To Claim to Be Messiah, That
Was Blasphemy
As a Messiah He Would Be a
Rebel against Them
The Charge of Sedition Was
Superseded by That of Blas-
phemy
Was He Clad with Divine Power
Has God Spoken to Us through
the Son
This is the Cry of All Man-
kind
He Could Not Convince
Unbelievers They Would
Soon See the Evidence of
His Divine Calling
God Would quickly Vin-
dicate Him
He Makes the Open
Avowal in His Enemies'
Camp
He Proclaimed His
Triumph, His Reign
He Would Judge the
World
The Triumph of Faith
over Experience, of
Ideal over Reality
He Was the Messiah Be-
cause He Had to Suffer
The Truth Must Always
Be Answered
He Yet Had to Die to
Achieve His Status as
Messiah

Answered by His Life
and Teachings as a
Whole
He Self-Condemned by the Pre-
vailing Law
He Has Attempted High-Trea-
son against the Theocracy
Must Pay the Penalty of Fail-
ure
The Charge of Blasphemy Could
Be Laid Before the Governor
Jesus Meant to Make Him-
self King
His Death Determined Be-
cause He Had Proclaimed His
Eternal Divinity
His Death Was Necessary to
Preserve the Spiritual Unity
between God and His Peo-
ple
His Conviction Was Made
on His Own Confession
Condemned for What He
Thought
For God to Become a
Man Degenerates Their
Idea of God
He Was Guilty of Con-
fusing The:
Supernatural and
Natural
Absoluteness and
Relativity
Earthly Affairs and
Religion
Their Standards of
Value Were Wrong

Scene 4
They Buffeted Him
1. The Veil Was on Their Hearts and Not on His Eyes
Their Pride and Hate Spoke Out
2. Their Slaps Convinced Them That He Was a Villain Rejected

43

by God and Man
The Worst in Man or the Disgrace of Man Is the Glory of God
The World Is Overturned and Everything Is Reversed in the Kingdom of God
The Power of Jesus over Souls Is Rooted in His Conformity to the Suffering of Men
All Condemned Man in the World Who Have Been Outraged or Crucified
Find in Jesus His Own Image and Idleness
The Victims Have Been Recreated a Second Time in the Image and Likeness of God
Even without Knowing or Willing It
He Reviled Not
When He Suffered, Threatened Not
Judgment Will Come
Jesus Hoped to the End
To Be No Fear of Death because of God
Evil Could Not Effect Its Designs

There Was a Mockery of His Office

Scene   5

He Was Set to Die not as a Martyr but as a Criminal
1. Jesus' Plan Was to Conquer by Suffering
Peter's Plan Was to Conquer by Resisting
Peter Doubted
2. The Ideal of the Kingdom of God
Was It the Fancy of a Dreamer?
Suppose Jesus Had Misunderstood the Nature of Man
His Greed, His Grossness and His Stupidity
Instead of Winning Men to Beauty Was to Succumb to Their Cruelty and Hate
The Potency of Fear Rises from the Mounting Aggregate of Doubt
Everything Seemed Finished
He Feared the Availability of an Ideal for the Company of Gross Men (Humanity)
He Doubts and Fears the Ideal as an Absolute Value
He Doubts and Fears the Practical Usefulness

44

among the Mass of Men
Before You Can See the Light You Must Deny
So That Pardon Can Be Created
A Refreshment of Memory and an Awakening of Love
Whenever Man Denies He Seeks to Show Himself
An Epitome of All Infidelities
The Compendium of All Denials
Shaken by an Agony of Contrition
A Disappointment of All His High Hopes
A Revelation of the Poor Stuff of His Own Character
Peter Cries
Filled with Repentance
He Knew He Would Be Forgiven
The Same Mercy Would Be Shown to All the World
Sinners and the Weak Were Never to Despair
The Poison Must Be Purged
The Dark Sea Drained
The Restoration Began When He Came within the Radiant Focus of a Face
Sickness Touched with a Healing Finger
Fear Is Purged by an Emotion of Love
Victory Came and Was Completed by Danger Defying Service

Scene 6. The Elders Had Trapped a Religious Faker
1. Jesus Was Not Godlike
2. He Had Done Enormous Damage to the Minds and Faith of the People
3. He Was Condemned as a Blasphemer
1. The Only Person Who Could Not Be Guilty of Such a Crime
Scene 7. If You Betray The Highest Ideals
1. No Sympathy from the World When You Want to Retreat
It Is Nothing to Them
He Had Served Their Purposes
Those Associated in the Crime
Attempted to Shake Off the Responsibility for the Common Ace
One of the Punishments in Concerted Sin is Mutual Recrimination
The Greater the Wrong, the More Reluctant One Is to

Admit It Had No Justification

    Evil Men in Order to Appear Innocent, Load Accusations of Guilt on Those Whom They Have Wronged

The Wrong-Doer Justifies His Sin

  Exaggerates the Alibi in Order to Cover Up His Perfidy and His Shame

 They Hated Their Miserable Tool

    Fellow Conspirators Discarded Judas as a Useless Tool

    They Thought Only of Not Contaminating Themselves

The Contrast between the Repentance of Judas and That of Peter

    Judas Was Repentant Unto Himself but Not Unto the Lord

    He Was Disgusted with the Effects of His Sin, but Not with the Sin

  He Could Not Accept Liability for His Own Sin

Everything Can Be Pardoned Except the Refusal to Seek Pardon

       His Remorse Was Only a Self-Hatred

       Self-Hatred Is Suicidal

It Is Salutary When Associated with the Love of God

Repenting to Oneself Is Not Enough

          Conscience Is a Leap Which Sometimes Goes Out in Darkness

          Death Should Be Dreaded

          Death Is One of the Penalties of Original Sin

          He Thought His Infamy Was Unforgiveable

          The Evil He Had Done Was Past Repairing

He Felt He Could Not Endure Life

  The Tremor in His Life

Toppled Every Drama and Ideal about Him in Chaotic Disorder

          The Black Cloud of Guilt and the Fear of Retribution

          Under the Goading Impulse of His Master, the Devil,

          To Whom He Had Become a Bond-Slave, Body and Soul

He Went out and Hanged Himself

He Was So Disgusted with Self That He Would Empty Himself of Self

The Body of Judas Landed on the Rocks and Moved No
More
   The Tree (Cross) and His Money Apron Followed Judas
         Judas Sold Jesus, but His Evil Collaborators
         Could Not Buy Him
            He Was Present Again on Easter
         Peter Knew He Had Sinned and Sought Redemption
         Judas Knew He Had Sinned and Sought Escape
      An Escapist from the Cross
Divine Pardon Presupposes but Never Destroys Human
Freedom
   Supernatural Remorse Leads to a Change of Heart
   The World's Remorse Leads to Death
   The Guilty Soul Is Separated from Infinite Love by Only
a Sigh
      If There Exists a Ray of Hope

ACT III The Outward Struggle (Con't.) (Trial before Pilate)
   Scene 1. The Trial of the King
      1. The Trial of the Prophet Was Over
      2. The Jews Were So Scrupulous In Not Soiling Themselves
         before The Paschal Meal (the Sacrifice of the Paschal
         Lamb)
         Yet They Come to Condemn the Very God the Paschal
         Meal Honors
         An Innocent Man They Condemn
      3. Pilate Was an Average Man
         Everything Almost, and Nothing Quite
         The Eternal Curse of All Average Men

   Scene 2. The Jews Asked Pilate to Legalize Their Verdict without a
         Trial
      1. The World Wants Their Decisions Accepted
         Although Each Would Be Responsible
      2. Pilate Believed That Society Rested Not on Worship and
         Humane Spirit but on Law and Discipline
         Rome's Worship of an Emperor-Deity Was Blasphemous
            Its Derogation of the Human Dignities to the Service
            and Aggrandizement of Empire Was Insufferable
            Its Dream of a World Dominion Pressed Forward by
            the Sword Was Abomination

No Compromise with That

If Death Was to Be the Issue of His Ministry, It Must Be Death on a Cross

The Cross Was the Answer of Empire to the Idea of the Beloved Community

The Exemplar of Love and the Agent of Redemption Confronted Pilate the Representative of Empire

Pilate Stands for an Ideology Which Thinks of a Derogation of God, Man, and Society to Human Ends

The Challenge of Empire to the Beloved Community

Jesus Was a Man of Passion, Intense Enthusiasm and Zeal for a Cause

He Portrayed All the Facets of Personality

Not Just a Sympathetic, Kind, Soft, Tender, Meek, and Humble Personality

He Was a Man of Action of the Highest Order

3. The Jews Substitute the Charge of High Treason for Blasphemy

From Blasphemy to a Political Charge

Blasphemy Is Equivalent to the Modern Term Heretic

The Charge Now Was Sedition

He Was Too Worldly, Too Political

He was Anti-Caesar, Anti-Rome

He Was a Deceiver, Inducing People to Follow Another Road Than That Dictated by Rome

The Second Charge Was a Perversion of the Facts

He Was Urging the People Not to Pay Taxes

Jesus Had Taught the Duty of Giving to Caesar His Due

The Third Charge Was That He Was Setting Up as a Rival King to Pilate

He Meant to Launch a Revolution to Make Himself King

Every Word Was a Lie

There Had Never Been Any Signs of Insurrection Connected with His Name

When the People Sought to Make Him King, He Had Refused

Scene 3. My Kingdom Is Not a Worldly One

1. His Kingdom Was of the Spirit

A Distinction between a Political and Religious Kingship

A Spiritual Kingdom to Be Established in Truth
>He Would Have Only Moral Subjects, Not Political Ones
>He Would Reign in Hearts, Not in Armies
2. He Would Establish a Kingdom without Fighting
>He Came into the World to Bear Witness to the Truth
3. That Is the Reason of My Being Born and Coming into the World

Acknowledged His Human Temporal Origin as the Son of Man

He Affirmed His Divinity

He Came to Die for the Truth
>It Was Not Merely an Intellectual Quest
>>What One Discovered Depended on One's Moral Behavior
>>>The Moral Condition of Discovering Truth
>>>Moral Conduct Has Something to Do with the Discovery of Truth
>>An Empire of Truth in Which He Was to Reign

Only He Who Is Open to the Truth Gives Ear To My Voice
>Whoever Belongs to the Truth, Listens to My Voice
>The Law That Truth Assimilates All That Is Congenial to Itself
>Evil Hates Light

The Man Whose Life Is True Comes to the Light

The Impulse Toward Truth Must Be in One

Pilate Wants to Accept the Truth but Cannot
>Jesus Was No Adversary of the World's Government of Pilate

The World Will Not Allow Him to
>Pilate Is the Poor Servant of His Duty

What Is Truth?
>Merely a Philosopher, After All

The Man of the World and the Prophet Are Torn Asunder
>Do Not See Eye to Eye

The World Turns Its Back On Truth and He Who Is Truth

When "What Is Truth?" Is Sneered At, It Is Followed by "What Is Justice?"
>Broadmindedness Eventually Ends in a Hatred of What Is Right
>Indifference to Right and Wrong

49

When Tolerant of Evil It Ends in Denying
Absolute Truth
Pilate and the World Would Crucify Truth
Skepticism and Doubt of What Is Truth
Pilate Believed That Each Man Determined for Himself
What Has to Be True
It Was Subjective, Not Objective
Scepticism Is Not an Intellectual Position but a Moral Position
Determined Not by Reason but by the Way One Acts
and Behaves
Pilate Resorted to Pragmatism and Utilitarianism
Unwillingness to Disturb the Status Quo
The Officials of the World Only Shrug Their Shoulders
Pilate and the World Asked the Question of the
Only Person in the World
Who Could Answer It in All Its Fullness
Jesus Could Not Answer as He Himself Was the Answer
No Human Works Could Measure Up to the Divine Act
He Is an Existing Truth
In the World the Strict Letter of the Law
Triumphs over Simple Justice

Scene 4. The World Condemns Men for Virtuous Qualities
1. The Whole World Roared for Death
He Was a Disturber of the World
He Turned the World Upside Down
He Was an Insurrectionist and Revolutionist
2. Pilate a Politician Plays Both Sides
Unwilling to Condemn an Innocent Man
Afraid He Could Not Save Him
A Mark of Deference to Herod
Would Kill Two Birds with One Stone
He Grasps at a Way of Escape from His Perplexities
He Saw an Escape from Judging Christ
A Chance to Placate an Enemy and Win a Friend
A Gesture of Friendship or Respect to Herod
Pilate's Supreme Interest
Scene 5. No Miracle to Release Himself
1. Herod Identified Religion and Magic
Herod Knew Religion but Kept His Vices
2. Jesus Would Not Convince Those Who Were Insincere
Truth Is Not to Be Given to Everyone

Only to Those Who Are "of the Truth"
Herod's Conscience Was Dead
He Wanted Miracles as Delights to His Curiosity
It Was Not His Soul He Offered for Salvation
But His Nerves for Titillation
He Spoke Not a Word to the Worldling
Jesus Gained the Moral Command of the Situation by Silence—
A Silence That Hurt
The Natural Man Cannot Find the Way of His Glorification in His Silence
Here We Have No Wise or Noble Man
No Man of Discernment after the Flesh
Authority, Fame, Recognition by the People Is What the Man of Wisdom (Worldly) Seeks
He Should Be Proudly Conscious of His Merits
Bask in His Own Admiration
The Greatest of All Chose Everyday Life as His Working-Place
His Humility Was Synonymous with Lack of Dignity
3. Pilate and Herod United Because of a Hatred of God
The Cross of Jesus Unites Both His Friends and Enemies
The Worldly Drop Their Lesser Hates in the Face of the Hatred of the Divine
1. They Wish to Sacrifice One Who May Be Their Rival in Popular Favor

Scene 6. A Clown Among Kings

Scene 7. A Gentile Woman Bore Witness to the Innocence of Jesus

Scene 8. The Jews Ask for the Release of a Real Murderer in Place of the Innocent
1. He Had Done the Very Things Which the Jews Were Trying to Persuade Pilate Jesus Was Likely to Do
2. Jesus Is Substituted for the Robber
The Devil Provides Two Deliverers and Two Christs
Barabbas Appealed to National Grievances
Jesus Appealed to Conscience
For Envy the Jews Had Delivered Up Christ for Trial

51

Pilate Gives Them a Choice between Two Charged with the Same Offense
Assumes That a Vote Means the Right to Choose between Innocence and Guilt
Goodness and Evil, Right and Wrong
Pilate Gives the Jews a Way out
A Tacit Admission of Their Conviction of Jesus to Be Superseded by Pardon
Pilate Indirectly Admits Jesus Merited Death
Puts the Name of the Condemned to Death Along with Jesus
He Relied on the Temple to Choose Justice
Pilate Pursued the Play-Acting of Democratic Action
The People Can Be Misled by False Leaders
A Democracy with a Conscience Became a Mobocracy with Power
The Priests Know the Fickle Humor of Their Own People
A Crowd Is Almost Blind
You Cannot Trust a Crowd-Psychology
Pilate Offered to Set Jesus at Liberty
Pilate Had Tried to Strike a Balance between Satisfying the Sanhedrin and His Own Conscience
Compromises in the Face of Justice

Scene 9. He Wore the Robe of Glory
1. He Put on the Masquerade of the Clown and the Fool
He Was to Wear the Clothes of Sinful Man
The Mask of the Compassion and Strength That Would Redeem the World
2. They Knew That He Was God and Yet They Tortured Him
They Defy God
He Was Wounded and Punished, Which Brought Us Peace
By His Bruises We Were Healed
All the While It Was for Our Sins
3. He was Dressed in a Fool's Crown and Seated on a Fool's Throne
They Bowed Down to Him in Mockery of His Royalty
In Derision Jesus Is Treated as a King

Scene 10. Pilate Knew the Prisoner Judged the Judge
1. Jesus Bore Himself as Though He Were Somehow beyond

the Reach of Man-Made Law
Safe from the Hurt of Its Penalties
It Was Not Courage but a Conviction in His Purposes That
Carried Him to the End

Scene 11. Pilate Does Not Avail Himself of the Truth before Him
  1. Man Treats as a Subject of Speculation
    When He Knows the Truth He Does Not Act Upon It
  2. Service is the Opposite of Ruling
    Given in the Lowliness and Weakness
    Not Mere Endurance or Quiet Acceptance
      The Humility of Action, That Actually Does Something
        A Humility of Power in Sacrifice and Service
     Still Stoops Undisturbed and Unwearying

      Pilate Offended at Seeming Disregard of His Authority
  1. Pilate Boasts of His Power to Kill or Release
  Pilate Only Had Power Because It is Given by Heaven
  Granted from Above
      Positions Reversed and Christ Was the Judge and
      Pilate The Prisoner
        Pilate Would Have No Power at All Because It
  Would Be Overruled
    The Judge is Judged
   Pilate Boasted of the Arbitrariness of His Power
      Jesus Referred to a Power That Is Delegated to Men
    Whether a Governor, King, or Ruler Knew It or Not
    All Earthly Authority Is Derived from on High

      Divinity and Suffering Are Both Repugnant to Unregenerated Men
  1. Divinity Because Man Secretly Wants to Be His Own God
  2. Suffering Because the Ego Cannot Understand Why a Seed
    Must Die Before It Springs Forth into New Life
    It Is Hard for the Intelligentsia to Believe That Greatness
    Can Be So Little
     The Scandal of Not Using His Power to Escape the
    Cross
      He Took upon Himself the Weakness and Guilt of
      Man
        When You Know That Your Power Comes from
      God

1. This Superior Knowledge Makes You More Guilty
   Pilate Sinned through Ignorance
   Caiphas and Judas Sinned against Knowledge

         The Pride of the Jews (World) Is the Pride That
         Apes Humility
1. Pilate Knows That the Spirit of Revolt Seethes beneath the
   Surface of the World
   It Is Ready at Any Moment to Burst Forth
   A Perpetual Uproar about a Few Ideas
   Feelings of Hatred and Distrust Were Universal
2. For the Jews Their God Was King
   They Spoke of Their City of God
         Government and Religion Was One

         Evil Reigns within and Does Not Lie Outside
1. To Be One Whom No One Can Injure in a World of Cheats
   and Confusions

Scene 12. Anyone Who Declares Himself A King (above Other People)
   Renounces Allegiance to the World
1. He Is a Rival and Speaks against the World
   The Jews Discovered How to Force Pilate's Hand
       They Threatened Pilate by Indirection, Accusing Pilate of
   Conspiracy against Rome
       The Jews Proclaimed They Had No King but Caesar
   (More Truth Than They Realized)
         They Made Themselves Vassals of the Empire
         They Rejected the Government of God in Order to Have
   a King
   God Gave Them in Anger
         As They Rejected the Kingship of Jesus Christ
         They Would Be Ground to Earth under the Kingship
   of Caesar
            They Had by Covenant Accepted Jehovah as King
            Now They Rejected Him in Person
         They Would Be Caesar's Subjects and Serfs All through
   the Centuries Since
         Pitiable Is the State or Nation Who In Heart and Spirit
   Will Have No King but Caesar
   Pilate Freed Himself from Further Pressure of the Jews

Without Reprisal, He Could Insult Them to His Heart's
Content
Pilate Declared Himself Innocent of Any Responsibility
for This Man's Death
Or Perversion of Justice
Pilate Declared Jesus Innocent
His Condemnation Was the Result of the Murderous
Hate of Unprincipled Men
They Accepted the Curse of His Blood
For Both Themselves and Their Children
He Would Lose His Governorship (His Position) and
His Head
It Was Now No Longer a Question of Saving Jesus
He Had to Save Himself
The Terrors of Tiberias Was More Important (Real)
Than Justice to Pilate
In the End Those Who Fear Men Rather Than God
Lose That Which They Hoped Men Would Preserve for
Them
Man Is Punished by the Instrument in Which They Con-
fided
Pilate Was in Servitude to His Past
Pilate Knew What Was Right but Lacked
the Moral Courage To Do It
He Was Afraid of Losing His Official Po-
sition
He Was Deterred through Cowardly Fear of His Accusing
Past,
When He Would Have Done Good
His Wrongs of the Past
He Foresaw a Tumult of the People If
He Persisted in The Defense of Christ
They Attached a Curse to Them-
selves
History Bears Testimony to Such Ful-
fillment
His Blood Would Destroy but Still
Redeem
The One Whom They Crucified Had Not Ratified Their
Sentence
In the End Some Will Repent
Jesus Hates to Suffer from His Own

People
And Not from Strangers
   He Hoped to the End It Would Be
The Strangers That Would Reject
Him

   The Majority Is Not Always Right in The Absolute
1. Voting Is Not Based on Conscience but on Propaganda
     Truth Does Not Win When Numbers Alone Become Decisive
     Numbers Cannot Decide Justice
       Right Is Still Right If Nobody Is Right
     Wrong Is Still Wrong If Everybody Is Wrong
  A Lamb Substituted for the People
      Went to Death in Atonement for Their Sins
        The Savior Should Suffer and the Sinners Go Free
        The Sinner Was to Be Redeemed with a Lamb
    The Savior Could Not Be Released, but the Sinner Could
Jesus Condemned Justly, for His Teaching Was Contrary to
    the Existing Order of Things
      In Order to Acquit
      One Must Believe That The Order of Things Is Better
Than the Existing Order of Things
      According to All Laws and Truths Excepting His
He Always Will Be Condemned
      The World Must Be Judged and Its Prince Cast Out

Scene 13. The Inscription (Titulus) Proclaim the Royalty of Jesus
        The Present Age Must Pass Away
   1. A New Order Comes

ACT IV The Triumph
  Scene 1. They Willed That He Should Die
      1. What He Was and What They Hated Could Never Die
        The Cross Was His Government or Law of Life
         When You Share the Ignominy of a Cross
           It Gives You a Feeling of Being Especially Good and
           Worthy

    Don't Mourn over Me for I Am Innocent
    Mourn over Your Own Destruction
       The Destruction of the World at the End of Time

The Final Condemnation of Man Because of His
Refusal to Accept the Invitation Offered Him
Fearlessness Leads To A Single End
The Tears of The World Would Not Prevent Him from
Doing His Work
   No Superficial Wailings Would Weaken His Prede-
   termined Purpose of Sacrifice
   No Dowry of Tears Could Make Them The Brides
   of His Heart
   A Priest Going To Sacrifice Not Just A Good Man
      Nothing Shall Prevent the Sacrifice
         Its Necessity
         Avail Yourself of Its Fruits
   He Purged Tears of Lamentation
   He Would Purge Death of Death by Rising from the
   Grave
   Sin Alone Was Worth Tears
      No Reason to Cry at All by Anything the World
      Does to You
         He Would Wipe Away All Tears
      Not to Have Misplaced Sorrow
         Look to Their Own Souls
            He Needed No Tears, They Did
               He Rejected Their Grief
                  His Purpose Would Be Accomplished
                     His Death Was Willed Freely by Him
                        A Necessity for Men
2. The "Green Tree" (Freedom and Truth)
   The Priceless Fruit of Life Eternal
      What the Powers of Evil Do
         How the World Treats the Innocent
            The Green (Innocent) Tree Was Himself
               He Was the Green Tree of Life Transplanted
               from Eden
         How the Sinful Shall Suffer
            The Dry Tree Is the Whole Human Race
            The Unconverted World
            They Treat Sinners?
               How Would the Guilty Be Punished for Their
               Own Iniquities?

               The Pinnacle of His Promise

1. The Chance to Die for Everyone

Scene 2. The Cross Was Done More Than All Else to Win the World
to Him
  1. Love That is Willing to Suffer to Achieve Its Object Is Powerful
    The Power of the Cross to Win the World
    He Identifies Himself with a Cause
      Consuming Devotion to a Cause
        Ready to Give up Everything Selfish for the People Whom He Loves
          In This Lies The Consummate Perfection of Character
          Consummates His Service to the World
  2. The Vertical Bar of God's Will is Negated by the Horizontal Bar of The Contradicting Human Will
    Christ Pays the Debt in Order That the Two Wills Will Be One
    Christ Says He Will Destroy Man
      Man Says We Will Crucify You
        In Every Possible Way We Will Make It Impossible For God to Live on Earth
        The Temple of His Body Was Destroyed Completely
          Christ Shows That Giving Up of Life Is the Only Way to Save Your Life
          He Paid the Price Man Alone Could Not Pay
            He Lays Down His Life for a Hostile and Alien World
              For a Humanity That Disgusted Him for Its Baseness and Spitefulness
      This in Order to Appease Men's Hatred
      Love Then Experienced Its Coronation
        That Is How He Won His Crown, His Supreme Authority and Power
      The Sacrifice Becomes the Fundamental Act of Establishing the New Covenant
      The Crown Was the Final Argument
      What More Can God Do?
        Up to Calvary Men Had Been Taught by Preaching
    To Follow the Spirit Is of Utmost Importance

It Is the Only Essential Thing
3. Jesus Did Not Live and Die So That Men Can Go on Sinning
   Must Pay Attention to the Welfare of People
   His Death Pointed to the Day When Men Could Sin No More
   All Nature Honored Him
     Sinners Alone Rejected Him
     It Took the Cross to Universalize the Mission of Christ
        The Lover That Overturns the World Is the Cross
          The Difficulty with the World Is That Death Is Overemphasized
            To Man Death Is Something to Fear and Be in Awe of
              What Is It but That the Body Is Returned to Dust?
              It Is Something That Is Not Desirable to Keep
                One Goes to Better Things
                  The Universal Spirit of God Draws Near
              Death on the Cross Is of No Moment after It Has Passed
                Life in the Body Is Transitory
                It Is the Soul That Counts

His Kingship Was Proclaimed in the Name of the Three Cities of the World
   1. Jerusalem, Rome, and Athens
        In The Language of the Good, the True, and the Beautiful
   2. Truth Was Made to Speak When Men Ridiculed
        The Cross Was His Pulpit
          Jesus Left His Thoughts on Dying
            What He Said Was Set Down for the Purpose of an Eternal Publication and an Undying Consolation
          Man Wants a Religion without a Cross
            They Ask (Taunt) God to Come Down from the Cross
              The Most Typical Demand of an Unregenerate World

When They See Self-Denial and Abnegation
Love Costs the Lover
The Cross Is Contradiction
   It Contradicts the World
   The Cross Is the Solution of the Contradiction
   of Life and Death
      By Showing That Death Is the Condition of
      a Higher Life
Mockery Is an Ingredient of the Cup of Sorrow
   Bear the Cup Patiently
      Man Draws Strength In His Trials from the
      Example of Christ
   The Cruelty of Lips Which Sneer Is Part of the
   Heritage of Sin
      As Much as the Cruelty of Hands That Nail
   They Poured Scorn onto the Pain
   The Kingdom of God Was Now Only Shame,
   Disgrace, Laughter, Blasphemy, and the Of-
   fense of the Cross
   Of Course He Could Not Save Himself
      The Rain Cannot Save Itself, If It Is to Bud
      the Greenery
      The Sun Cannot Save Itself, If It Is to Light
      a World
      The Soldier Cannot Save Himself, If He Is
      to Save His Country
      And Jesus Cannot Save Himself, If He Is to
      Save His Creatures!
   They Mock the Titles of King of Israel, Savior,
   And Son of God
      Must All the Kings of Earth Be Seated on
      Golden Thrones?
         He Had Decided to Rule from a Cross
            To Be King Not of Their Bodies through
            Power but of Their Hearts through
            Love
            He Would Come to Glory through Hu-
            miliation
They Thought He Was Lost When They Were
the Ones Lost
      The Really Damned Mock One Whom They
      Believed to be Damned

Hell Was Triumphing in the Human!
They Taunted Him with It
They Tried to Make Him Doubt His Divine Sonship
They Wanted to Anger the Dying Savior into the Use of His Superhuman Powers
To Achieve Such a Victory Was Satan's Desperate Purpose
Skeptics Want Miracles but Never the Greater Miracle of Forgiveness
No Descent from the Cross (Miracle) Would Have Won Man
It is Human to Come Down but Divine to Hang There
The Death on the Cross Is the Greatest Negation of the
External Miracles with Affirmation of the Internal Miracles
If He Had Come Down from the Cross Only an External
Miracle Would Have Been Performed
The Sign Is Shown That Death Has Been Conquered

True Success for Jesus Was to Complete One's Life

1. It Is to Attain to Eternal Life
   All Else Is Failure
2. People of the World Who Seem to Be Successful Are Failures
   Jesus Christ Was the Failure of Failures According to the Standards of Men
3. He Poured out the Prayer of Pardon and Forgiveness
   To His Enemies and Those Who Hated Him
   He Did Not Forget His Gospel with the Piercing of His Hands and Feet
   He Forgave Them Because They Know Not What They Do
   Their Crime Was Sentencing Life to Death
   A Perversion of Justice
   If They Knew What They Were Doing They Would Never Be Saved
   It Is Only the Ignorance of Their Great Sin That Saves

61

It Is Not Wisdom That Saves: It Is Ignorance
As Mediator between God and Man He Extended Pardon
As High Priest Who Offered Himself in Sacrifice, He Pleaded for Sinners
God in the Form of the Suffering Servant Fulfilled the Promise of Eden
God Had Promised Redemption through the "Seed of the Woman"
Who Would Crush the Serpent of Evil
Forgiveness Was Identified with His Sacrifice
He Interceded and Offered Himself for the Guilty
The New Abel's Blood Was Spilled to Lift the Wrath and to Plead for Pardon
Jesus Prayed Only for Those Who Would Repent
He Knew There Was No Forgiveness Except through Him
All Cannot Be Saved
Only Those Chosen through Repentance
Asks for Mercy
Commends Them to Mercy at the Hands of the Father
They Were Simply the Victims of Their Own Ignorance of Spiritual Truth
He Strove to Find Some Excuse for His Enemies
So Long as It Did Not Offend against the Truth
An Insult or Blow Was a Sign of Moral Need Flung Out from His Enemy's Heart
The Pitiable Need of Such Men of Ignorance
He Had Found Another Way of Proving His Superiority over His Enemy
Refuse to Serve Other Peoples' Selfish Actions
Reject All Forms of Selfishness
Such as Vanity, a Desire to Be Noticed and a Fear of Being Slighted
That Spirit Wrested the Offensive from Their Hands

Turned the Tragedy into a Triumph
Man Judges the Saving Power of God by Release from Trials
1. If It Cannot Give Relief from Trial, What Good Is It?
They Said Jesus' Teachings Were a Drug—an Opiate
Man Has No Soul
They Based Their Acceptance of the Christ on His Power to Take Himself Down from the Cross
A Man Would Have Had to Show his Powers to Sustain His Reputation
2. Jesus Bids Them Look to God at the Moment When the Courts Are
Inflicting Injustice
He Thinks of Souls When Men Are Dying
Talks About Paradise When Stomachs Are Empty and Bodies Racked with Pain
3. Men React in Different Ways
No Example Is Enough to Convert Unless the Heart Itself Is Changed
4. The World Has Room Only for the Ordinary
Never the Very Good or the Very Bad
The Good Are a Reproach to the Mediocre
The Evil Are a Disturbance
5. Jesus Is the Right Man in the Right Place
He Is between Two Thieves
Among the Worthless and Rejects
The Redeemer Is in the Midst of the Unredeemed
6. The Good Thief Asks for Deliverance from Sin
The Believer Asks No Proofs
His Confession of Guilt Led to Incipient Repentance Led to Faith in Jesus
He Had a Faith in the Ultimate Triumph of Good over Evil
He Expected a Supernatural Kingdom to Be Established
He Threw Himself upon Divine Mercy and Asked for Forgiveness
He Asked for External Life
It Was a Thief Not a Saint Who Was the Escort of the King of
Kings into Paradise

To Jesus the Words Are Like a Ray of Light
God Is Exhorting Him to Be Steadfast in the
Faith
Here Is a Word About His Kingdom
A Word from on High
He Believed When Others Disbelieved
He Ascribed to Jesus a Kingdom Which Was
Not of This World
Victim and Lord Were to the Good Thief Compatible Terms
The Promise of Paradise to the Thief
He Knocked Once, Sought Once, Asked Once,
Dared Everything
And Found Everything
The Moment This Criminal Looked to Jesus
He Received
Everlasting Life
Even on the Cross Here Was a Man Who
Saw the Truth
He Passed from Death unto Life
Jesus Gave a Thief the Assurance of Divine
Mercy
7. The Last Judgment Was Prefigured on Calvary
Anticipates His Final Role
The Two Divisions of Humanity on Each Side
The Saved and the Lost
The Sheep and the Goats
When He Came in Glory to Judge All Men
The Cross Would Be a Badge of Honor, Not Shame
He Took His Judgments to Heart
Condemning with Tears
He Condemned When He Kept Silence over
Men's Lack of a Sense
Of Truth
Be of Good Cheer Means You Can Be Saved
Jesus Wiped Away Past Errors and Mistakes
There Was No Cause to Be Worried by
a Sense of Guilt
He Was to Be the New Adam
1. Changing the Water of Sin into the Wine of Life
He Knew That the World Would Not Tolerate His Divinity

His Influence at an End, His Disciples Faith Had Vanished

1. His Message Had Fallen on Deaf Ears
   All Had Been in Vain
2. Women Had Responded to His Appeal for Loyal Devotion
   Feminine Love Rose in the Resurrection
   Masculine Love Was Hindered by His Death
3. All Men (Humanity) Were to Be Treated as Sons of Women
   Assigns a Spiritual Motherhood for Redeemed Humanity
   All Women Are Treated as Mothers
   To Love Men as He Loved Them
   He Beheld Love Triumphant and Eternal
   Raised It above the Personal to the Divine
   His Blood Poured Out as a Curse of Sin
1. Men Were Putting Out the Light Who Illumined Every Man Coming into This World
2. Jesus Denied Himself the Light and Consolation of His Divinity
   He Feels Faith and Hope Are Obscured
   The Craving to Escape Death Takes the Form of a Complaint
   The World Is a Lost World
   A Human Heart Is Breaking
   Suffering Passed from the Body into the Mind and Soul
   A Sense of Being Abandoned by God
   The Final Agony of Being Forsaken by the Father
   All His Ideals Were to End in Disaster
   The Father Withdraws the Support of His Immediate Presence
   Leaves to the savior of Men
   The Glory of Complete Victory over the Forces of Sin and Death
   Was Necessary for the Son to Know That Ultimate Horror
   Abandonment by the Father
   He Entered upon the Extreme Penalty of Sin Which Is Separation from God
   The Darkness of Deluded Humanity Hung over His Head
   He Saw All History Recapitulated in Himself
   When the Darkness of Sin Had Its Moment

of Triumph

Evil Cuts Off Every Thread Connecting Man with God

Only Sin Can Make the Darkness of Soul

The Mantle of Sin

Cost of Sin

Abandonment Felt When Standing in a Sinner's Place

The Soul That Despairs Never Cries to God

He Felt the Emptiness of Humanity through Sin

The Cross of Jesus Is the Greatest of Triumphs

He Certainly Could Not Be the Lord

1. Elias Had Not Yet Come

The Reception of Any Truth He Taught Depended Upon One's State of Will

They Do Not Want His Cross

The Uncrucified Christ Is the Worldlings' Desire

2. They Reproached Jesus for Hanging on the Cross

He Thirsted for Men's Salvation

1. He Fulfilled All Prophecies

2. He Did Not Attempt to Shed What Is Human

He Was Never Ashamed of Being a Man

3. His Triumph of Spirit over Matter

Jesus Knew That All Things Are Now Finished

He Desired the Speedy Return of His All-Conquering Spirit to Its Divine Source

4. Thirst Was the Symbol of the Unsatisfying Character of Sin

The Pleasures of the Flesh Purchased at the Cost of the Spirit Are Like Drinking Salt Water

He Had a Passion for Souls "Give Me to Drink" Meant "Give Me Your Hearts"

A Divine Love for Mankind

In Return Men Gave Him Vinegar and Gall

A Thirst for Mockery of What Is Most Sacred

1. He Could Not Save Himself

Why He Would Not Save Himself

So He Could Appear on Easter Morn

He Died That Others Might Live

He Gave His Life as a Ransom for Many

Not Weakness but Obedience to the Laws of Sacrifice

Men Can See Events Only in Succession
He Had Ordained All from the Beginning
From All Eternity God Willed to Make Men
in the Image of His Eternal Son
God Sent His Divine Son to This Earth
In Order That Fallen Man Might Know
The Beautiful Image
To Which He Was Destined to Conform
Not Just to Forgive Sin but to Satisfy Justice through Suffering
Now There Was an Obedient New Adam, A
Humble New Eve, and the Tree of the Cross
Supplants the Disobedient Man Adam, the
Proud Woman Eve, and the Tree of the
Garden

His Atoning Sacrifice Had Been Accepted by the Father
1. It Is Finished (Accomplished)
The Farewell to Time
The End of the Son Means the End of the World
His Work Was Finished
He Announced the Completion and Perfection of
His Mission
He Lived until All Things Were Accomplished as
Had Been Appointed
The Canceling Out the Material and Transmuting It
into the Divine, The Spiritual
His Life from Birth to Death Had Faithfully Achieved
2. He Showed That Inwardly He Could Prevail against All
Such Tribulation
His Own Purity Would Be the Power Which Should
Redeem Sinners
He Taught Others What Sin Really Means
We Make the Force of Circumstances Our Excuse
He Was to Overthrow All Hostile Forces
Now He Would Assuredly "Reign"
He Was Able to Live without Care in the Present Just
Because He Was So Sure of the Future
His Salesmanship Had Failed to Lead Judaism beyond
Itself
Judaism (the World) Had Lost the Opportunity of
Realizing All the Latent Possibilities and Capacities
Which It Possessed

3. What Was Achieved Was Redemption
    Since Redemption Was Completed the Life of the Spirit
    Could Now Begin the Work of Sanctification
A New David Had Arisen to Slay the Goliath of Evil

The Beginning of His Glory
    1. The Prodigal Son Was Returning Back Home
        He Had Left the Father's House and Gone Off into the
        Foreign Country of This World
            He Had Spent His Substance
                The Divine Riches of Power and Wisdom
                    He Had Wasted His Substance Among Sinners
                        There Was Nothing Left to Feed Upon Except
                        the Sneers and the Vinegar of Human Ingra-
                        titude
                    He Would Lay Down His Life of Himself
                        No One Would Take Away His Life from Him
        He Prepared to Take the Road Back Home to His
        Father's House
            His Eye on God
                For Him the Meaning of the Cross
                    Not One of Destruction and Death but of Dy-
                    namic, Ever-Resurgent Life
                    Death Was a Transition
                        Nothing but a Move to God
                He Would Die from an Act of Will
                    The Only Instance in History of a Dying One Who
        Was a Living One

His Spirit Went Up to Heaven
    1. Christ Entered into Heaven Itself
        To Appear in the Presence of God for Men
    2. Living Decides One's Future State
        The Peril of Living Is Greater Than the Peril of Dying
    3. His Earthly Mission Having Been Completed
        He Now Returned Again to His Heavenly Father
        Who Sent Him on the Work of Redemption
An Intervention of God in the Course of Nature Took Place
    1. God Did Not Allow These Great Events in the Spiritual
        World to Leave No Trace on the Material World
        God Is No One-Sided Idealist

External as Well as Internal Things Belong to Him
The Earth Gave Signs of Recognition When the
Lord Liberated Man from the Slavery of Sin
Though the Hearts of the People Could Not Be
Rent
The Rock Could

The Veil of the Temple Is Rent
1. Man Can Now Become Perfect (Holy)
By a New and Living Way
By the Blood of Jesus
2. Not Done by the Hand of Man
By the Miraculous Hand of God Himself
That Which of Old Was Sacred
Now Remained Opened and Manifest before Their
Eyes
The Treasures of God Were Revealed
3. A New Temple Would Be Raised Up in Three Days
What Was Holy Was Made Manifest
Christ Has Taken His Place as Our High Priest
Christ Came into the World to Be the Fulfillment
Judea Denied Him Welcome
A More Complete Tabernacle Would Arise
Which Human Hands Never Fashioned
It Does Not Belong to This Order of Creation at
All
As the Veil of the Temple Was Torn
The Priesthood Came into Its Own
The True Holy of Holies
The True Ark of the New Covenant
The True Bread of Life
The Son of the Living God
4. When He Died He Vanquished Death by Death
With Jesus' Death upon the Cross a New World-Era
Dawned
There Are Various Ways and Measures of Knowledge
1. A Stranger Understood Better Than One of His Own
He Did Not Hear Death; It Was Victory over Death
Jesus Was to Swallow up Death in Victory
He Manifested Humiliation and Power on the
Cross as He Did in His Public Life

A Soldier of Caesar Bowed in Adoration of the Divine
Sufferer

The Veil of His Flesh
    1. Two Veils Were Rent
        The Purple Veil of the Temple
        Did Away with the Old Law
        The Veil of His Flesh
            Opened the Holy of Holies of Divine Love
            Opened to the Guilty Access to God
            Sorrow for Sin Springs from a Vision of the Cross
                The Vileness of Sin Is Most Poignantly Revealed
                The Arrow of Sin That Wounds Brings the Balm
                of Forgiveness That Heals
                Those Who Looked at Him Were Healed of Sin
                    They Refused to Look on Him Whom They Had
                    Pierced
Scene 3.
Scene 4. If We Are Planted in the Likeness of His Death
    1. We Shall Rise with Him in the Glory of His Resurrection
Scene 5. Their Concern About His Burial Was a Token of Their Love
    for Him
    1. Not of Their Faith in Him as the Resurrection and Life
        Spiritually, They Knew Not Yet Who He Was
        Physically, They Were Mindful of Him
    The Women Become Heralds of His Resurrection

ACT V. The Proof of the Resurrection (Death Could Not Conquer Him)
    Scene 1. Hate Fell Back upon the Hearts of the Scribes
        1. The Immense Sadness of Their History Crushed down upon
           Them
            They Were Filled with Dissatisfaction and a Sense of
            Unfulfillment
                Jesus Took Away All Wherein We Find Pleasure
                Destroys All Whereon We Pride Ourselves
        2. The Pharisees Heave a Sigh of Relief
            Public Peace and Safety Have Been Restored
                The National Faith Has Gained a Complete Victory
                The Old Hope May Now Awake to New Life
                  They May Again Proclaim and Believe That They
                  Are the True Heirs
        3. Is Not the Voice of the People the Voice of God

They Knew Jesus Was Dead
> They Said He Would Not Rise Again, and Yet They Watched
>> Would He Still Win the War for Life and Truth and Love?

Scene 1–1. How Comes It That Jesus Does Not Remain Silent?
1. He Again Begins to Speak
2. It Was Futile of Men to Try to Get Rid of the Living God
> It Is of No Use to Brand Him an Enemy of the People
> It Was a Delusion of His Enemies to Think They Could Escape Sentence Which He Had Passed upon Them
>> By A Sentence Which They Passed on Him
>>> Jesus Is Given Up to Universal Contempt
>>> He Is Condemned, Executed, and Buried
>>> Yet We Are Not Done with Him
3. Conscience Knows Well That He Has Spoken the Truth
> Conscience Knows That It Was God Who Spoke to Him
> Whether We Accept or Resist Belief in Him, Our Self-Assurance Is at an End
>> Jesus Dead Proves to Be as Dangerous as Was the Living Jesus
>>> The Attempt to Get Rid of Him by Every Method within Human Power
>>>> Continues to Meet with No Success
>>> It Is Useless to Fight against God
>>>> Resistance Serves Only to Show Forth His Might and His Truth
>> Men Still Call Him a Deceiver in Spite of Their Conscience
>>> We See in Their Attitude the Unwilling Confession of the Vanquished Victors
>>>> We Are at the End of Our Resources
>> Men Try to Sit in Judgment upon God
>>> Discovery That God Has Sat in Judgment on Man
>>>> All That Is Left for Man to Decide
>>>>> Whether to Bow to God's Judgment or to Resist It
>>>>> Whether to Acknowledge God's Authority or Persist in Our Iniquity

Scene 1–2. The Enemies of Jesus Expected the Resurrection
1. His Friends Did Not

It Was the Believers Who Were the Sceptics

The Cross Is the Supreme Attempt to Turn Aside Judgment from Men

1. An Attempt to Win Back Human Freedom

   How Are We to Continue to Live by Selfishness and Self-Deception

   If Man Does Not Have the Last Word

Scene 2. Jesus' Death Tells All Human Pride, All Human Assurance, All Human Power That It Will Collapse under God's Judgment

1. The Last Remnants of Human Security Is Shattered

2. Are Reduced to Naught

   The Cross Is an Attempted Rebellion against God

   Was Bound to Fail

   He Is the Only Person in This Wicked World Whom No One Can Injure

3. Jesus Had Come to Tell Man That the Way to Everlasting Life Was Love

   Love—Each for the Other, Each for Him, and His Love for All

4. In Jesus' Dead Body His Soul Would Be Glorified

   He Was Pointing the Way to Man

   Jesus Was Not Dead

   The Dawn of the Glory That Was to Come

   His Resurrection from the Dead Vindicated All His Claims

   His Intercession with God Is Security for the Inheritance They Are to Receive

5. The Pleasures of the World Are Only Sham in Comparison with the Glory That Comes through Christ

   The Pleasures of This World Soon Turn to Ashes

   They Are Trinkets that Fascinate for Only a Season

   The Resurrection of the Dead Is the Bridge from the "Now" to the "Then"

   Easter Brings Us News of This Ungovernable Life Which Laughs at Death

   Can Be Checked by No Grave

   Easter Brings Us News of Life Eternal

   Henceforth He Will Not Die

   There Is a Personal Eternal Life of Perfection Free from All Earthly Toil and Travail

   A Life in Which There Will Be No Death, Sorrow, Crying, nor Pain

6. Man Speaks of God as Though He Knows Him

    We Act as Though We Were on the Best of Terms with Him When Dealing with God

        All Our Talking, Singing, Thinking, and Doing Become of Questionable Value

        In God Our Life Rests on a New Foundation

            Our Arrogance Is at an End

                Man Runs against and Resists God

                    He Cannot Bear That Another Should Be Lord

            To Be as God Does Man Seek the Fulfillment of Life

            To Do What We Want Is Sin

                Man Refuses to Recognize the Authority of God

                    God Places Man under the Dominion and the Law of Death

                Man Yearns for a Life That Vanquishes Death

                    Which Knows Not Sin but Behind Which There Is No God

                        Where There Is Forgiveness of Sin There Life and Happiness Are Found

                            The Agonizing Cry of God Must Be Silenced

            Jesus Had to Die Because the Sovereignty of God Is Revealed in Him

                Because Man Does Not Want the Sovereignty of God

                    Do Not Want God and Yet Man Cannot Live without Him

            The Cross Means That Man Pronounces His Own Death Sentence

                An Act of God Takes Place When Man Is at the End of His Resources

                    It Is the Living God Who Speaks the Last Word

                        There is a divine Possibility That Grace May Have the Last Word

                            It May Break Down Man's Resistance and Overcome His Death

            The Resurrection Tells of Death Which Has Been Vanquished

            Of a New Life and an Eternal Perfection "Together with Christ"

73

Scene 3. The Dead Man Who Lays in the Tomb Gives Us No Peace
1. It Is of Vital Interest to the Whole World That Jesus Should Be Dead
The Stone Must Stay before the Tomb So That We May Have Peace
He Must Leave Us in Peace
Man Will Gladly Mourn and Revere the Dead Man
Lament the Tragic Fact He Was Too Good and Too Great for Us to Bear Him
He Must Not Ask Us to Hear in His Words and Deeds, Sufferings, and Death
The Voice of the Living God Calling Us to a Sense of Our Responsibility
2. What Can Royal Soldiers Do before a Regal Spirit?

We Shall All Be Changed In A Moment
1. No Laws Are to Be Broken
Laws Will Be Accomplished and Completed by the Transformation of Mortal Being
2. The Resurrection Was Not a Mystery to Heaven
His Death Would Be
To Men His Resurrection Is a Mystery
3. His Cross Stands before the World
We Guilty and Condemned Sinners Must Decide Whether
We Confess Faith in Christ
Acknowledging the Supremacy of God's Truth and Desiring to Live by His Grace
His Empty Tomb Asks Man Whether He Is Really to Let God Have the Last Word
He Is Risen Is a Message of Joy
You Cannot Affirm or Deny Christ by Human or Practical Methods of Research
Christ Comes Only to Those Who Believe (Faith) in Him
He Ignored His Murderers and Would Not Show Himself to Them
4. He Took the Crucifixion to Multiply His Sonship into Other Sons of God
Before Man Could Be an Adopted Son of God
He Had to Be Redeemed from Enmity with God
Only by Grace and Adoption Were Men Sons of God

74

75

Men Are Slow and Foolish of Heart Even
When the Greatest Evidence is Available
Credulity toward Men and Incredulity to-
ward God Is the Mark of Dull Hearts
Readiness to Believe Speculatively and
Slowness to Believe Practically Is the Sign
of Sluggish Hearts
In Consequence of His Sufferings Men
Would Be Raised from a State of Sin to Fel-
lowship with God
Everything That Happened to Him Had
Been Foretold
It Was Not an Offence, a Scandal, a
Defeat, a Succumbing to the Inevitable
It Was Foreseen, Planned, and
Preannounced
Scene 8–1. Knowledge of Glory That Came through Defeat
Scene 9. The People Might Storm the House of Those Who Were
Unpopular
He Had Brought About Peace by the Blood of the Cross
1. He Came in His Own Person to Bestow It
Peace Is the Fruit of Justice
Only When the Injustice of Sin against God Has Been
Requited Can There Be an Affirmation of True Peace
Peace Implies Order
There Can Be No Peace to the Wicked
Because They Are at Enmity with Themselves,
Others, and God
Touching Him They Immediately Believed
1. It Was By His Wounds He Would Be Recognized
By Pain and Sorrow, Redemption Will Be Wrought
The Scars Remind Men That There Was a Sacrifice
There Were the Unmistakable Scars of Battle against
Sin and Evil
He Wore His Wounds to Prove That Love Was Stronger
Than Death
These Scars Would Be Points of Argument in In-
tercession before the Heavenly Father
Scars Would Be a Trophy of Honor He Would Bear
on the Last Day to Judge the Living and the Dead
Had He Risen with No Memorials of His Passion

Men Would Have Doubted Him with the Passing of Time

    They Would Have Obliterated from Their Minds the Remnants of His Shame and Agony on Earth

    He Bore the Memorials of His Redemption

He Bequeathed to Them His Share of the Cross and, After That, His Glory

    1. He Breathed on Them the Holy Spirit

      He Conferred the Power of the Holy Spirit

      It Was the Breath of the Spirit's Influence

      The Spirits' Power to Convert the World

      The Breath of the Risen Christ with All Its Regenerative Power

      He Was Already in His State of Glory for He Was Bestowing the Spirit

      He Was Not Associating the Apostles with the Life of His Resurrection

        At Pentecost He Would Associate Them with His Ascension

Scene 9–1. Thomas Refused to Believe without Evidence

    1. It Was Not Indifference or Hostility to Truth

      He Wanted Knowledge in Order to Have Faith

        It Was Unlike the Self-Wise Who Want Knowledge against Faith

    2. Thomas Frames for Us the World's Intermittent Cry of Bewilderment

      To Thomas Death Was No Victory, It Was Terrible Defeat

    3. His Attitude of Skepticism Commends Itself to the World

      Our Whole Modern Structure of Learning Rests on a Perverse and Mischievous Habit of Mind

      His Refusal to Be Influenced in His Opinions by What Other People Say

        Prefers to Be Allowed to Make up His Mind for Himself

        He Stands up with Obstinate Defiance for His Own Principles and Conditions

    4. Thomas Was Supposed to Believe in Spite of All the Facts and against All Reason

      He Knew That No Human Word Could Give Him Certainty and Strength

Faith in the Sense of Certainty and Strength Never Lies
with Human Power
> Faith Must Be Able to Say, "I Am Certain," Other-
> wise It Is Not Faith
>> Faith Languishes or Degenerates Because We Do
Not Dare to Go the Whole Way

Seize Your Doubting and Believe
1. Be Not Faithless
   His Gloom Was His Besetting Sin
2. Peace Rests upon His Death and Resurrection
   You Can Have No Peace Unless You Believe That
   No Peace in This Present World of Conflict
   Peace Comes Only When Death Is Known to Be
   Conquered
3. A Proof by the Senses Would Not Give Complete Peace
   Thomas Had to Believe
   One Can Now Face Life Joyously and Undismayed
   Can Refuse to Be Afraid of Anything
   The Skeptical Mind of Thomas Was Instantly Cleansed
   His Doubting Heart Was Purified
   A Conviction of the Glorious Truth That Christ Is
   Divine Flooded His Soul
   He Was No Longer Disobedient to the Heavenly
   Vision
   He Accepted the Light When It Came to Him
   The Light Blinded Them Spiritually
   He Was Disclosed Only to Witnesses
   Chosen by God
   A Healthy Man Is a Man of This World
   and Therefore Cannot See the Other
   World
   Here Was the First Indication of a New
   Existence
   The Doubts of a Depressed Humanity Are Healed
   by the Acknowledgement of Christ's Deity
   Now He Has a Certain and Living Faith Which
   Stays and Upholds Him
4. The Only Reason for the Resurrection Was Doubt That the
   Body Could Be Resurrected
   This to Prove That He Has Power over Death and Life
Unseeing Faith Has a Magical Quality That Overrules All Things

78

1. Faith Is Placed above Those Who Believe Only When They See

    They Need the Additional Testimony of the Senses

    There Are Others Who Will Not Believe Even When They See

2. The Faith of Future Believers Would Have to Be of the Highest Type

    They Would Not Be Able to Demand the Evidence of Sensible Proof

    It Is Not Possible to Believe without the Holy Spirit and Jesus' Word

    It is through Jesus' Word That the Spirit Works

    Only by Tribulation Do We Heed the Word

Scene 10. They Were Disappointed and Disheartened

1. They Needed Instruction from Jesus as to How to Catch Fish

    The Result Was So Surprising as to Appear Miraculous

    Now They Were Made Strong

2. The Highest Kind of Love Is a Supernatural Love

    Jesus Made Love the Condition of Service to Him

    He Proposed to Substitute Love for Fear

    The Confession of Love Must Precede the Bestowing of Authority

    Authority without Love Is Tyranny

    Peter No Longer Has Confidence in Himself

    He Relies on the Knowledge of Jesus

    Peter Was to Feed the Lambs

    The Man Who Had Fallen and Learned His Own Weakness Was the Best Qualified for Strengthening the Weak.

    Here Came the Victory for Love

    When Doubt and Fear Strove in Later Days for Dominance

    Peter Would Use the Formula Given

    Peter Went Step by Step Down the Ladder of Humiliation

    Peter Would Find Death by Crucifixion

    The Lord Followed Him with the Assurance of the Work for Which He Was Destined

    Peter Had Been Given the Keys and the Function of a Doorkeeper

    You Will Learn What It Really Means to Love

79

but Conquering Servant

His Cross Was to Be Remembered

The Death on the Cross Would Have Been Useless for the Removal of Human Guilt If He Had Not Risen from the Dead

It Behooved Him to Suffer Because He Had to Show the Evil of Sin

Evil Is Most Manifest in the Crucifixion of Goodness

The Worst Thing Evil Can Do Is to Kill Goodness

Having Been Defeated in That, It Could Never Be Victorious Again

It Might in the Future Win Some Battles, but It Would Never Win the War

Goodness in the Face of Evil Must Suffer

When Love Meets Sin, It Will Be Crucified

Goodness Used That Very Suffering as a Condition of Overcoming Evil

Goodness Took All the Anger, Wealth, and Hate, and Pleaded "Forgive"

No Healing Can Be Brought to Broken Wings by a Humanism Which Is Brotherhood without Tears

Must Have a Source of Knowledge Different from Any Other Teacher

Must Be Able to Burst the Fetters of Death

Prove That Truth Crushed to Earth May Rise Again

The Law He Gave Was That Life Is a Struggle

Unless There Is a Cross in Our Lives, There Will Never Be an Empty Tomb

Unless There Is the Crown of Thorns, There Will Never Be the Halo of Light

Unless There Is a Cross, There Will Never Be the Rising from Death

In Conquering the World Jesus

Did Not Mean His Followers
Would Be Immune from Woes,
Pain, Sorrow, And Crucifixion
He Gave No Peace Which
Promised a Banishment from
Strife
What the Resurrection Of-
fered Was Not Immunity
from Evil in the Physical
World, but Immunity from
Sin in the Soul
His Life Was a Model for His
Followers
They Were Encouraged to
Take the Worst This Life
Had to Offer with Courage
and Serenity
There Was to Be No Tal-
isman as Security from
Trials
As a Captain He Went into
Battle
In Order to Inspire Men to
Transfigure Lifes' Greatest
Pains into the Richest Gains
It Was the Cross of Christ
That Raised the Questions
of Life
It Was the Resurrection
That Answered Them
He Unfurls before an
Evil World the Pledge
of Victory
He Proclaimed the Fruits of His Cross Must Now Be Applied to All
Peoples and All Nations
1. Repentance Is Linked Up with the Application of the Re-
demption Won on Calvary
Repentance Was a Turning Away from Sin and a Turn-
ing to God
2. The Divine Order to Begin Preaching Redemption in Jeru-
salem Was a Mark of His Great Compassion
He Directed the Apostles to go to Those Who Had

Falsely Accused Him To Tell Them He Was Their Advocate and That He Would Plead Their Cause from on High

 Through His Scourgings and Stripes They Would Be Healed

 3. He Promised a Manifest Increase of the Spirit

  This Power Would Enable Them to Proclaim the Redemption

   They Were to Begin Their Mission to the World with the Descent of the Holy Spirit

  It Would Not Be Worldly Power

   Power over Living Souls to Channel into Them the Forgiveness and Grace Stored Up in the Reservoir of Calvary

   They Wanted an Earthly Kingdom; He Spoke of a Spiritual One

    They Wanted a Return of the Old Things

     He Told Them They Would Be "Witnesses" of a New Thing

      To Be a Witness Meant to Be a Martyr

    They Were Bound by the Idea of a Nation

    He Included the World in His Vision

   The New Power Would Be a Gift and Not Developed from Oneself

Scene 13. The Ascension Confirms That Death Had Been Conquered

 1. The Risen Christ Explains the Sudden Shift In the Feeling of the Disciples

   From Fear and Disillusionment They Will Now Go Forth Joyfully to Danger and Death

    Always Preaching as the One Absolute Dogma of the New Faith

     The Belief in the Resurrection, Pulls Down (Draws down) to Earth from Heaven Its Blessings on Men

     Pierced Hands Best Distribute Benediction

 2. The Ascension Was the Fruit of His Crucifixion

  It Was Fitting That He Suffer in Order to Enter into His Glory

 3. The Ascension Was a Departure of a Material Being

  His Resurrection Had Been an Actual Return of His Spirit to His Corporeal Body

  In the Ascension the Savior Did Not Lay Aside the Garment of Flesh with Which He Had Been Clothed

His Human Nature Would Be the Pattern of the Future Glory of Other Human Natures

The Incarnation or Assuming of a Human Nature Made It Possible for Him to Suffer and Redeem

The Coronation upon Earth, Instead of an Ascension into Heaven Would Have Confined Men's Minds and Hearts to the Earth

The Ascension Would Cause Men's Minds and Hearts to Ascend above the Earth

The Human Nature Which He Took as the Instrument for Teaching, Governing, and Sanctifying

Should Partake Of Glory As It Shared in Shame

The Ascension Put All Doubt Away by Introducing His Human Nature into Intimate and Eternal Communion with God

He Who Had Ascended Shall Return Descending from the Heavens in Human Form

4. By the Ascension His Triple Office of Teacher, King, and Priest Was Vindicated

No Longer Would He Be Mocked

The Vindication Would Be Complete When He Would Come in Justice as the Judge of Men

No One Could Complain That God Knows Not the Trials to Which Humans Are Subject

He Had Fought the Same Battles as Men and Endured the Same Temptations as Those Standing at His Bar of Justice

He Has Been through Every Trial, Fashioned As We Are, Only Sinless

The Cross and the Crown Combined Had Governed Every Detail of His Life

5. The Christ at the Right Hand of the Father Would Represent Humanity before the Father's Throne

He Would Be an Advocate of Men with the Father

He Would Send the Holy Spirit as Man's Advocate with Him

No Faith and Hope in Heaven, Only Love

For Love Endures Forever

INTRODUCTION

1. The Inward Struggle

Now Jesus begins the inward struggle. He had a struggle to make in order to restore the heritage of union with God. Here was a man who had the infinite intellect of God, which knows all things. He saw the past and future as present.

Jesus knew that He was to intercede with His Father and do this by submission and resignation. The divine had become human; He stooped to the dust of earth and became subject to the law of death; and all in order to set an example for mankind.

Death was not an easy task for one who was divine. It was hideous. But if He merely died as the Son of God the sacrifice would be negligible. No, He would have to die as a man but He would have to suffer much more than a mere man. This because in addition to having a human intelligence, He had a divine intelligence.

He did this only in order to obey His Father's will. He took upon Himself the iniquities of the world and became the sin-bearer. He felt the agony and torture of those who deny guilt, of those who sin with impunity and do no penance, of those on whom the burden of sin is as natural as that of the clothes they wear. They know no different nor do they care. He did this to cover all the past and future sins man had ever committed or would commit, every open act and every hidden thought.

The task which He had taken upon Himself was not easy. He had to endure the dreadful desertion that any sinner endures. He was to be treated in every respect as a sinner. He alone would pay His Father's justice. He pulled the whole guilt of the world upon Himself. And thus He shows and pledges the last, full payment of His loyalty, the absolute devotion of His *will* to His cause.

In addition to having a perfect intelligence, He had a perfect physical body. It naturally was more sensitive to pain than the ordinary human's. Do you remember how sensitive you were as a child? Human nature is calloused by crude emotions and evil experiences. It is conditioned by the past or what has happened. But physical pain was not predominant. He was extremely sensitive to the hate of His enemies, and to moral evil and sin. And all this sensitivity was far greater than that of a man who lives without God. For above all else the reason for such sensitivity was a deep, personal communion with God. He had a majesty of moral purity.

In such a state of moral purity, the Agony was hard to accept. It was hard to accept death because it was not natural, there was no reason or cause for it in such a perfect being. Here the contradiction is shown between God and the world, between the divine and the human. There were two wills struggling within Him. The human will resents the necessity of suffering and is unwilling to endure the suffering. The flesh is always weak. Yet He knew that this was the supreme contest with the powers of evil. He began to pray, for prayer is the soul's endeavor to open the way for God to do His divine will. Neither we nor Jesus could expect God to change His plans to suit our or His whim.

In prayer He overcame the temptation to reject the cross and to seek refuge in flight. He conquered the temptation to yield to doubt and despair. He had to conquer evil and sin from the inside and not the outside. He did not avoid or ignore sin, but associated Himself with the evil of the world. He had to make the choice between the World and God. He made it for all mankind. He had to suffer being rejected or cursed by the Father.

Under such circumstances, it is apparent that faith would threaten to give way under the weight of doubt. For how can one believe in God if iniquity triumphs? Doubt sees the prosperity of the wicked. Have we not all questioned it and fallen into bitterness and silent hatred? But in that way we let in death. We can never measure God's thoughts by our thoughts. We cannot make our faith depend upon God's doing what we wish.

Now Jesus was to endure every injustice and in enduring that injustice He gained the victory. The "cup" that He agreed to drink was the sense of failure and apprehension for His cause, for the justice of God cannot allow the sacrifice to be evaded. Jesus must taste death for every man. This allows men to gain eternal life through conflict and suffering. For every man there are two elements bound together—sin-bearing and sinless obedience.

Jesus was in a world outside which was alien and hostile. No one comprehended His purpose and His struggle. There was no one to share His spiritual experiences. He only came in contact with the handicaps of the world and the inadequacy of men. The calumny of men was the hostility with which His cause was greeted. The result was inescapable: the loneliness of His soul.

And yet salvation is forfeit if the injustice that weighs upon men gains the upper hand. The temptation cannot be allowed to work our ruin, but instead it must be the trial that will prove us right. We must

86

accept the will of the Father. To do so we need God's guidance. The way is clear, there must be no contempt toward men who cause the injustice. In this manner the power of the injustice is broken. For by this method we commit ourselves to Him Who judges righteously, and the bitterness which seeks to poison us is cut off. Only by a forgiving love which bears and endures all things can we hope for and attain all things. The forgiving love of Christ bestows the courage of faith, and injustice cannot have dominion over us. The anguish and desolation of the sinner must be alien and abhorrent.

Jesus longed for mankind to see God and life as they really are, so they could break away from rules and hopes of revenge and material prosperity as the highest good. Jesus tells us why we cannot have truth and peace, why men cannot enter upon their real spiritual inheritance of union with God in life. The only way, He says, is through service for the salvation of the world.

He points out that humans become so used to sin they do not realize its horror, that men never learn anything by experience in sinning. By such experience sinners become infected with sin. And actually the greatest evil is the exaltation of self-will against the loving will of God. Men scorn His wisdom as foolishness. In this way He sums up the whole history of the world in one cameo: the conflict between God's will and man's will. God so felt the opposition of human wills; there was another and separate principle working out its own ends, as if there were no God. And this full, unhindered growth of self-will was anti-Christ.

Jesus wanted man to be saved from committing the blackest deed of sin ever perpetrated by humans. And what was that but the killing of supreme goodness, truth and love.

Jesus had to endure this weakness of the flesh. The natural will had to be subdued by the higher will. He accepted the Father's will, the hard road of the Father. There was no other, easier route. An agony of suffering is laid when fear is piled upon fear. And blood must pour forth, for sin is in the blood.

Now Jesus vanquished the agony, for through prayer He had been refreshed. He had the need of inward fortification against the crushing circumstances of life but through prayer he regained strength and courage. He came away victorious. Christ emerged the victor.

BETRAYAL

Now Christ, the King of Heaven, was set up against Caesar, the king of earth. The only recourse now was for Him to be betrayed into the hands of sinners. The hour planned for by Himself had struck. He submitted Himself to death. Love fettered Himself to unfetter man.

Those bent on evil cannot recognize divinity. Even though the light shines in darkness, darkness does not comprehend it. Unbelieving minds are blinded by the fake god this world worshipped, blinded by all the false values they believed in.

Oh, yes, the people were awed and frightened, for calm and dignity were beyond the borders of their experience. They knew and felt His miraculous power, His glory flashed forth. Never is there humiliation without a hint of glory and power.

Next came the method of men and evil, the lips of treachery simulating love. When wickedness would destroy virtue it prefaces the evil deed by some mark of affection. In other words, you deny and compliment with the same lips. Always the answer that comes back to the betrayer, Judas and the world, is "friend." The only concern of Jesus and God is the pitiable failure of Judas's and the world's, and not the pitiable wrong done to Him. Blind anger and force are not the way to save the world, for he will restore any harm done to men. He stands not as a helpless prisoner but as a giver of bounty. Every act and word of the Gospel is but to point the way. The meaning of life is service to divine love. All they that take the sword shall perish with the sword. You cannot resist evil. Those who resort to arbitrary violence will feel that violence themselves. Revenge brings its own punishment.

In pointing this out to them He discussed the contrast between the cup and the sword. The sword wins by slaying, the cup by submission. Not the impatience of the violent but the patience of saints is the way to win souls. The cup has to be accepted voluntarily, you are not forced to undergo the passion. You do it out of love for God and then man.

Jesus was submitting voluntarily and according to plan, in accordance with foreseen and predicted developments. It was not an involuntary bowing to a fate but a voluntary surrender of some rights for the sake of others. Thus we see that those who seem weak may be divine. For Jesus has power at His command. He does not oppose those who seek to capture Him. He turns the other cheek and the blow falls on the heart of His persecutors. Thus He sets the example. He knew that one blow in return would destroy the cause. He refused their weapons and used His own. He willed His fate.

By Jesus' doing this, the power of darkness had its hour. True, evil could turn out the light of the world temporarily. Evil has its hour; God has His day. It would only be a momentary triumph in which the blind would think they had gained a victory. For darkness would soon lose its power at the resurrection. All was planned beforehand. Sin required atonement or reparation. He acted in man's name.

Now He advised His followers (disciples) that they were to save themselves (run) by any means while spreading the Kingdom of God. For the time being, until the resurrection would strengthen their faith, they were not to endure abuse or humiliation. Now He would tread the wine press alone. All other men were to be allowed to go free. He never wavered in His purpose and passion, for self-sacrifice seeks no vengeance. He had only one concern, and that was for His own sheep. They were not yet in a spiritual condition to die with Him. Later on they would suffer and die in His name. They could not suffer for Christ until Jesus had first suffered for them.

Now all His disciples forsook Him and fled in the darkness; they made no attempt to rescue Him. They betrayed Him, for they knew Jesus was determined to submit. For the moment they forgot the glory of the Messiah. But He had told them all this beforehand, that all was written. In this way they were already acquitted.

Jesus did not call Himself defeated. He was a success though apparently a failure. And sometimes those who appear successful are failures. You have to learn to be content in whatever state you are. The truly successful man is the one who can enjoy the life of God. If you allow suffering to affect you, you can do nothing. You must have zeal. God takes advantage over your despair, over your failure. Through the power of God you can rise up again.

He, the Pure One, fell; He was seized, bound, and delivered into the hands of sinners. Jesus stands against the world as redeemer and as judge. He was able to present Himself as such because there was not the slightest burden on His conscience. He was in no need of a redeemer. This is why He knew He was the deliverer. For He came to seek the lost world of men. He was immune from contamination. No one could change anything in Him. He was confident He could transform all men. Because He was secure He dared to set Himself up as judge of all mankind.

He won over insult and threat. He made no attempt or threat against them to escape pain. Love is an agony, passion is suffering, not wishing to escape suffering. In this way, and only in this way, it makes itself redemptive. And so the foremost value He proclaimed was that the unique quality of human life is the capacity to make the tragedy of life redemptive. He was put in chains for His testimony to the truth. They said He was not the Messiah because He used no power to destroy them. They insisted He was just another faker under arrest, time had caught up with Him. What chance had a Nazarene magician who was not a real prophet?

2. The Outward Struggle

A. TRIAL BEFORE THE SANHEDRIN

Now that the inward struggle was over, He would take up the outward struggle. Had He not come to the bailiwick of His enemies? He had been captured and put on trial before the Sanhedrin.

Both Divine and human natures were on trial, on totally different charges. He was to be condemned on contradictory charges. Whereas Annas and Caiphas found Him too unworldly and too divine, Pilate and Herod found Him too human. In addition He would be sentenced to the symbol of contradiction which is the cross. Here the responsibility for Jesus' death is fixed on the entire Jewish nation. Once and for all time, all mankind was to share the responsibility for the destruction of Truth.

Here Jesus raised the mind of man toward the unseen. He was to become insensible to the barriers of time and space.

Jesus was a breaker of the law. He was a false prophet and should be killed. The blasphemer of the name of God should die. He was a deceiver and seducer, a young nobody posing as the Savior of the world. Thus the representative of the priesthood of the Spirit was led before the representative of the priesthood of the flesh. The question was how to snare a "seducer." He had not taught the people to follow Himself, which was unpardonable to those in authority.

He was really not brought before them for trial, for in their minds He was already condemned. They merely wanted evidence to force Pilate to put Him to death. They sought some excuse for the planned injustice. So they begin to question Him about His secret doctrines. He answered with absolute fearlessness born of innocence, that only the people who had believed could testify. They were the only ones who could testify that there was nothing secret about His doctrine. He would not testify on His Own behalf, for they would not accept such testimony. He bade them summon those whom they despised. He affirmed that the book of His teaching had never been closed, that it was open to all. But they, in order to escape the content of the message, criticize the form. Violence is used when capacity to criticize is absent. Jesus did not rebuke but tried to make the soldier see his fault. He appealed to the principles of justice. He knew He was to be stricken for the transgressions of men and bruised for their iniquities. Therefore in the face of insult His patience turned to gentleness.

Now came the false witnesses against Him, a perversion of words. The Jews were to be destroyers, He the restorer. They claimed He would destroy the temple, instead they would destroy His body. But divine purposes would be attained, for the evil and free actions of men would be overruled by God.

Since He was a dangerous disturber of the nation's peace, they questioned His mission and what His object was. To claim to be Messiah, that was blasphemy; and as a Messiah He would be a rebel against Rome. Here the charge of sedition was superseded by that of blasphemy. What they wanted to know was: was He clad with divine power? "Has God spoken to us through the Son?" This is the cry of all mankind. He told them that He could not convince unbelievers, but they would soon see the evidence of His divine calling, for God would quickly vindicate Him. He made this open avowal in His enemies' camp. He proclaimed his Triumph, His reign. He was to judge the world. And this was the triumph of faith over experience. He was the Messiah because He had to suffer. The truth must always be answered. What He proposed was that He had yet to die to achieve His status as Messiah. But He told them that the question had been answered by His life and teachings as a whole.

And so it was that He was self-condemned by the prevailing law. He had attempted high treason against the theocracy and now must pay the penalty of failure. The charge of blasphemy could be laid before the governor, for Jesus meant to make Himself king. And thus it came about that His death was determined because He had proclaimed His eternal divinity. His death became necessary to preserve the spiritual unity between God and His people. His conviction was made on His own confession. He was condemned for what He thought. For God to become a man degenerates man's idea of God. He was guilty of confusing the supernatural and natural, absoluteness and relativity, earthly affairs and religion. Thus it was proven once and for all time that the standards of value of men were wrong.

Now there was nothing to stop them, so they buffeted Him. The veil was on their hearts and not on His eyes. Their pride and hate spoke out. Their slaps convinced them that He was a villain rejected by God and man. But this was what He came for, to show that the worst in man or the disgrace of man is the glory of God. For the world is to be overturned and everything in it reversed in the Kingdom of God. The power of Jesus over souls is rooted in His conformity to the suffering of men. He serves as the example of all condemned men in the world who have been outraged or crucified. Each and all such can find in Jesus his own image and likeness. The victims have been recreated a second time in the image and likeness of God, even without knowing or willing it.

He did not revile, but when He suffered, threatened not. For judgment will come. Jesus hoped to the end that it would not. There was to be no fear of death, for evil could not effect its designs because of God.

Now there was also mockery of His office.

B. PETER: DOUBT

Jesus was not to die as a martyr but as a criminal. Jesus' plan was to conquer by suffering; Peter's plan was to conquer by resisting. Peter now began to doubt. The ideal of the Kingdom of God, was it the fancy of a dreamer? Suppose Jesus had misunderstood the nature of man, his greed, his grossness, and his stupidity? Instead of winning men to beauty, was He to succumb to their cruelty and hate? The potency of fear rises from the mounting aggregate of doubt. Everything seemed finished. Peter feared the availability of an ideal for the company of gross men (humanity). He doubted and feared the ideal as an absolute value or its practical usefulness among the mass of men.

But Peter did not then realize that before you can see the light you must deny. This is so that pardon can be granted. Then there would be a refreshment of memory and an awakening of love. Whenever man denies he shows himself as the epitome of all infidelities and the compendium of all denials.

Now Peter began to be shaken by an agony of contrition. There was surely a disappointment of all his high hopes. But then came the revelation of the poor stuff of his own character. Peter cried out. He was filled with repentance. He knew he would be forgiven. And then He realized that the same mercy would be shown to all the world. Sinners and the weak were never to despair. The poison must be purged—the dark sea drained. The restoration began when he came within the radiant focus of a face. His sickness was touched with a healing finger. Fear is purged by an emotion of love. Victory came and was completed by danger defying service.

The Elders now decided that they had trapped a religious faker. Jesus was not Godlike. He had done enormous damage to the minds and faith of the people. He was condemned as a blasphemer, the only person who could not be guilty of such a crime.

C. JUDAS: REMORSE

Now Judas learned that if you betray the highest ideals you will get no sympathy from the world when you want to retract. It is nothing to them. He had served their purposes. So those associated in the common crime always attempt to shake off the responsibility for the common act. One of the punishments in concerted sin is mutual recrimination. The greater the wrong, the more reluctant one is to admit it had no justification. Evil men, in order to appear innocent, load accusations of guilt on those whom they have wronged. The wrongdoer justifies his sin. He always exaggerates the alibi in order to cover up his perfidy and his shame. Thus, then they began to hate their miserable tool. Fellow conspirators discarded Judas as a useless tool. They thought only of not contaminating themselves.

There was a contrast between the repentance of Judas and that of Peter. Judas was repentant unto himself but not unto the Lord. He was disgusted with the effects of his sin, but not with the sin. He could not accept liability for his own sin. And what this teaches is that everything can be pardoned except the refusal to seek pardon. His remorse was only a self-hatred, which is suicidal. It is salutary only when associated with the love of God. Repenting to oneself is not enough. Conscience is a lamp which sometimes goes out in darkness. Death must be dreaded for death is one of the penalties of original sin. Judas thought his infamy was unforgiveable, that the evil he had done was past repairing. He felt he could not endure life. The tremor in his life toppled every dream and ideal about him in chaotic disorder. And the black cloud of guilt and the fear of retribution came over him.

So, under the goading impulse of His master, the devil, to whom he had become a bond-slave, body and soul, he went out and hanged himself. He was so disgusted with self that he would empty himself of self. The body of Judas landed on the rocks and moved no more. The tree (cross) and his money apron followed Judas. Judas had sold Jesus, but his evil collaborators could not buy him. He was present again on Easter.

Peter knew he had sinned and sought redemption. Judas knew he had sinned and sought escape. He was an escapist from the Cross. Divine pardon presupposes but never destroys human freedom. Supernatural remorse leads to a change of heart. And that is the difference. The world's remorse leads to death. Infinite love is available if there is a ray of hope.

D. TRIAL BEFORE PILATE

Next in the outward struggle was the trial before Pilate. The trial of the King was about to begin as the trial of the prophet was over. The Jews were so scrupulous in not soiling themselves before the paschal meal celebrating the sacrifice of the paschal lamb, yet they came to condemn the very God the paschal meal honors. An innocent man they condemned.

Pilate was an average man. He was everything, almost, and nothing quite, which is the eternal curse of all average men.

Now the Jews asked Pilate to legalize their verdict without a trial although each would be responsible. The world always wants their decisions accepted. Pilate believed that society rested not on worship and humane spirit but on law and discipline. Rome's worship of an emperor-deity was blasphemous to the Jews. Its derogation of human dignity to the service and aggrandizement of Empire was insufferable. Its dream of a world dominion pressed forward by the sword was abomination. There could be no compromise with that.

For Jesus, if death was to be the issue of His ministry, it must be death on a cross. For the cross was the answer of Empire to the idea of the beloved community. Or *vice versa*, the cross was the answer of the beloved community to that of Empire. Here the exemplar of love and the agent of redemption confronted Pilate, the representative of Empire. Pilate stands for an ideology that believes in subjugation of God, man, and society to human ends. It was the challenge of the empire to the beloved community. Jesus was a man of passion, intense enthusiasm, and zeal for a cause. He was an extremist of the highest order. He contained all the facets of personality, not just a sympathetic, kind, soft, tender, meek, and humble personality; he was also a man of action of the highest order.

The Jews now substituted the charge of high treason for blasphemy. They changed their indictment from blasphemy to a political charge because they knew that Pilate would not consider the accusation of "heretic." The charge now was sedition, that Jesus was too worldly, too political. He was anti-Caesar, anti-Rome. He was a deceiver inducing people to follow another road than that dictated by Rome.

The second charge was a perversion of the facts; they said He was urging the people not to pay taxes. Instead Jesus had taught the duty of giving to Caesar his due. The third charge was that He was setting himself up as a rival king to Pilate. He meant to launch a revolution to make Himself King. Every word was a lie. There had never been any signs of insurrection connected with His name. When the people sought to make Him King, He had refused.

1. THE TRUTH When Pilate asked Him about His kingdom, He told him that His kingdom was not a worldly one, but was of the spirit. He made the distinction between a political and a religious kingship. It was to be a spiritual kingdom established in truth. He would have only moral subjects, not political ones. He would reign in hearts, not in armies. He would establish a kingdom without fighting.

He came into the world to bear witness to the truth. He acknowledged His human, temporal origin as the Son of man. He affirmed His divinity. He came to die for the truth. It was not merely an intellectual quest. What one discovered depended on one's moral behavior. There was a moral condition of discovering truth. In other words, moral conduct has something to do with the discovery of truth. There was to be an empire of truth in which He was to reign.

He told Pilate, "only he who is open to the truth gives ear to My voice." And that "whoever belongs to the truth, listens to My voice." Here He proclaims the law that truth assimilates all that is congenial to itself. For evil hates the light, and the man whose life is true comes to the light. The impulse toward truth must be in one or he will never find the truth.

Pilate wanted to accept the truth but could not. He knew that Jesus was no adversary of the world's government of Pilate. The world would not allow Pilate to accept. Pilate was merely the poor servant of his duty. So he asked, "what is truth?" He presumed Jesus was merely a philosopher, after all. The man of the world and the prophet as always were here asunder, they did not see eye to eye. The world turns its back on truth and He who is truth. When "what is truth?" is sneered at it is followed by "what is justice?" Broadmindedness always eventually ends in a hatred of what is right, and there always shows up an indifference to right and wrong. When man is tolerant of evil he ends in denying absolute truth. Pilate and the world would crucify truth. They always have a skepticism and doubt about what is truth. Pilate believed as men today, that each man determines for himself what was to be true. It was subjective, not objective. Always the belief that it is man's decision that counts. But they forget the skepticism is not an intellectual position but a moral position—that it is determined not by reason but by the way one behaves.

And so Pilate, as men of today, resorted to pragmatism and utilitarinism. They are always unwilling to disturb the status quo. The officials of the world only shrug their shoulders. Pilate and the world asked the question of the only person in the world who knew the answer in all its fullness. Jesus could not answer as He Himself was the answer. No human works could measure up to the divine act. He is an existing truth.

But the world is always skeptical and condemns men for virtuous qualities. It was no different then than now. The whole world roared for death. They said He was a disturber of the world. He turned the world upside down, He was an insurrectionist and revolutionist.

Pilate was a politician and he intended to play both sides. He was unwilling to condemn an innocent man but he was afraid he could not save Him. Now an unexpected recourse came to Pilate: he would show a mark of deference to Herod by sending Jesus to Herod for a decision. He would kill two birds with one stone. He grasped at a way of escape from his perplexities. Pilate not only saw an escape from judging Christ but it was a chance to placate an enemy and win a friend. This was a gesture of friendship or respect to Herod.

Herod demanded miracles. He identified religion and magic. Herod knew religion but kept his vices. He was no different from men of today. But Jesus would perform no miracle to release Himself. He would not convince those who were insincere. Truth is not to be given to everyone but only to those "of the Truth." Herod's conscience was dead, he wanted miracles as delights to his curiosity. It was not his soul he offered for salvation but his nerves for titillation.

Jesus spoke not a word to the worldling. Jesus gained the moral command of the situation by silence—a silence that hurt. No natural man can find the way of Jesus' glorification in His silence. But what is forgotten is that here we have no wise or noble man, no man of discernment after the flesh. For what does the man of wisdom (worldly) seek but authority, fame, and recognition by the people. Such a man of the world wants to be proudly conscious of his merits—he wants to bask in his own admiration. But the greatest of all chose everyday life as His working place; but for the world His humility was synonymous with lack of dignity.

Here Pilate and Herod united because of a hatred of God, just as men do today. The cross of Jesus always unites both His friends and enemies. The worldly drop their lesser hates in the face of the hatred of the divine.

Now Herod could find nothing wrong in Jesus but had Him scourged and treated Him as a clown among kings. The Jews' only wish was to sacrifice One who might be their rival in popular favor. There was one, though, who stood up for Jesus. It was Procula, the wife of Pilate. A gentile woman bore witness to the innocence of Jesus.

2. SUBSTITUTION—EVIL IS CHOSEN OVER GOODNESS AND TRUTH Now it was the custom that on this day, at the Passover, the people could ask for the release of one prisoner. The Jews asked for the release of a real murderer in place of the innocent. All that happens serves but to prove the perverted mind of man. The act which happened then is but a sample of all the acts that happen today. No, the world is not getting better and neither does the mind of man change.

The Jews asked for the release of a man who had done the very things they were trying to persuade Pilate Jesus was likely to do. Jesus was substituted for the robber. The Devil provides two deliverers and two Christs. Barabbas appealed to national grievances while Jesus appealed to conscience. Pilate knew that it was from envy the Jews had delivered up Christ for trial. Now he gave them a way out, a choice between two charged with the same offense—one innocent and one guilty. He assumed, as the world assumes today, that a vote means the right to choose between innocence and guilt, between goodness and evil, right and wrong. The way out was that he would tacitly admit their conviction of Jesus, but such conviction was to be superseded by pardon. Thus he indirectly admitted Jesus merited death by putting the name of one condemned to death along with Jesus.

Pilate relied on the people to choose justice just as democracy today relies on the people to choose for the best. Pilate pursued the playacting of democratic action. But the Jews would have nothing to do with it, they were unable to choose justice. Their minds were conditioned as the minds of men are conditioned today. Also he forgot that the people can be misled by false leaders. Then as always a democracy with a conscience became a mobocracy with power. The priests know the fickle humor of their own people, that a crowd is almost blind and that you cannot trust a crowd psychologically.

Pilate offered to set Jesus at liberty. Pilate still played both sides. He tried to strike a balance between satisfying the Sanhedrin and his own conscience. He compromised in the face of justice. There was no difference from what men do today—they say justice depends, it changes, it needs interpretation, and ask, "what is absolute justice?"

3. THE TRUE JUDGE It is paradoxical that when Jesus put on the masquerade of the clown and the fool, He wore the robe of glory. For what was foolish in the mind of man was the strength of His cause—it was the symbol of sacrifice. He was to wear the clothes of sinful man. This masquerade of the clown was the compassion and strength that would redeem the world. The Jews knew that He was God and yet they tortured Him. And by this act they defied God. So through His wounds and punishments man was brought peace. By His bruises we were healed. All this was not for anything He had done but all the while it was for men's sins, men's denial. This was to be a means of escape, a way out, for men.

97

But the Jews did not understand, just as men do not understand today. Jesus was dressed in a fool's crown and seated on a fool's throne. And the Roman soldiers bowed down to Him in mockery of His royalty; in derision Jesus was treated as a king.

Pilate knew the prisoner judged the judge. Jesus knew that the role of man, his thoughts and acts, was unimportant in the light of man's potentiality or the blueprint of man God had made. So Jesus bore Himself as though He were somehow beyond the reach of man-made law. He knew He was safe from the hurt of its penalties. It was not courage but a conviction in His purpose that carried Him to the end. This knowledge of the Spirit over flesh, of truth over error, rises above anything that the world possesses. He suffers all that man may conquer all. He sees beyond the tawdry benefits and logic of today. What greater vision of what man can be is there than what Jesus delineates? You can deny until doomsday and yet the fact exists that no greater or more ecstatic picture is possible for man than what Jesus gives.

But Pilate did not avail himself of the truth before him. For man, then as today, always treats the truth as a subject of speculation. When he knows the truth he does not act upon it. For service is despicable, it is the opposite of ruling and therefore is lowly and weak. But for Jesus, the service of which He speaks is not mere endurance or quiet acceptance, it is the humility of action, that actually does something. There is a humility of power in sacrifice and service that stoops undisturbed and unwearying.

Pilate became offended at the seeming disregard of his authority and began to boast of his power to kill or release. But Jesus pointed out to him that he, Pilate, only had power because it was given him by Heaven—that it was granted from above. And so their positions were actually reversed and Christ was the judge and Pilate the prisoner. He showed that actually all the judges in the world were now being judged.

Jesus here referred to a power that is delegated to men. Whether a governor, king, or ruler knows it or not, all earthly authority is derived from on high.

It is always so, divinity and suffering are both repugnant to unregenerated men. Divinity because man secretly wants to be his own god. Suffering because the ego cannot understand why a seed must die before it springs forth into new life. It is hard for the intelligentsia to believe that greatness can be so little. For men it was a scandal when Jesus did not use His power to escape the cross. But Jesus wanted to take upon Himself the weakness and guilt of man, He wanted to picture to men just how they really looked.

He pointed out to Pilate that the Jews knew their power came from

God and this superior knowledge made them the more guilty. Whereas Pilate sinned through ignorance, Caiphas and Judas sinned against knowledge.

Pilate knew that the spirit of revolt seethes beneath the surface of the world. It is ready at any moment to burst forth. There is a perpetual uproar about a few ideas. Feelings of hatred and distrust are universal. Always the pride of those who rule apes humility. For the Jews their God was King, they spoke of their city of God. Government and religion were one.

Jesus points out that evil reigns within and does not lie outside. He wanted them to realize that He was one whom no one could injure in a world of cheats and confusions. And they could be the same. And that anyone who declares himself a king and above other people renounces allegiance to Caesar or the world. He was doing it; they could do it.

4. *THE ART OF SUBTERFUGE (COMPROMISE)* But the Jews pointed out to Pilate that Jesus was a rival and spoke against the world. They had discovered how to force Pilate's hand. They threatened Pilate indirectly, accusing Pilate of conspiracy against Rome. He would lose his governorship and position and probably his head. Pilate realized that it was now no longer a question of saving Jesus, he had to save himself. The terrors of Tiberius were more important and real than justice to Pilate. In the end those who fear men rather than God lose that which they hoped men would preserve for them. Man is punished by the instrument in which he confided.

Pilate was in servitude to his past. He knew what was right but lacked the moral courage to do it. He was afraid of losing his official position. He was deterred through cowardly fear of his accusing past, when he would have done good. It is always the same, the compromises of men are incurred because of the wrongs of their past.

Now Pilate began to foresee a tumult of the people if he persisted in the defense of Christ.

The Jews began to proclaim they had no king but Caesar. There was more truth in this than they realized. They voluntarily made themselves vassals of the empire in order to achieve their will and wishes. They rejected the government of God in order to have a king God gave them in anger. And this has ever been so and continues to be—man rejects God. And as they reject the kingship of Jesus Christ, they will always be ground to earth under the kingship of Caesar. Oh, yes, they had by covenant accepted Jehovah as King but now in perfidy they rejected

Him in person. They would be Caesar's subjects and serfs all through the centuries since. Pitiable is the state or nation who in heart and spirit will have no king but Caesar.

Now Pilate freed himself from further pressure by the Jews by acquiescing to their demands. He accepted the conviction of Jesus. Without fear of reprisal, he could insult them to his heart's content. But he retained the edge by declaring himself innocent of any responsibility for this man's death or perversion of justice. He will convict Him but he declares Jesus innocent. And so Jesus' condemnation was the result of the murderous hate of unprincipled men. And this merely describes the condition of man and the world. But they willingly accepted the curse of His blood for both themselves and their children. This in order to achieve their ends. And there has been no change since; man willingly continues to accept the curse of his hate, the curse of his perverted ends and purposes.

They attached a curse to themselves and history bears testimony to such fulfillment. His blood would destroy but still was possible of redeeming, for the one whom they crucified had not ratified their sentence. In the end some will repent.

Jesus would much rather have suffered from strangers than from His own people. He hoped to the end that it would be the strangers that would reject Him.

5. THE MAJORITY DENY THE TRUTH (A BETTER ORDER OF THINGS) It is apparent that the majority is never right when the absolute is involved, for voting is not based on conscience but on propaganda. Truth does not win when numbers alone become decisive. Numbers cannot decide justice. Right is still right even if nobody is right. Wrong is still wrong if everybody is wrong.

Now Jesus was innocent and therefore the metaphor of a lamb was used to describe his act. And He the lamb was substituted for the people. He went to death to atone for their sins, in fact for their very act of denying Him. For in denying Him, they denied all acts and thoughts of good, in fact they denied truth itself. They denied their heritage, their potentiality of perfection and freedom. In fact, whenever men deny God, they do not so much deny God as they deny themselves. They see only the perverted image of themselves, their own wrongs bog them down into the mire.

The Savior was to suffer and the sinners go free. The sinner was to be redeemed with a lamb. The Savior could not be released, but the sinner could.

Now it is true that Jesus was condemned justly, for His teaching was contrary to the existing order of things. And since He was to take the place of all sinful men, He must be guilty in the sight of the world or sinful men. In order to acquit Him, one must believe that the true order of things is better than the existing order of things. And man in his unregenerated state cannot believe that. According to all laws and truths excepting His, He will always be condemned. Not until you reject the world can you see the truth. Consequently the world must be judged as wanting and its Prince cast out.

And at the end the inscription (titulus) over the cross proclaimed the royalty of Jesus. But before this can appear, the present age must pass away and a new order come.

3. The Way to the Cross

And here on the Cross the greatest triumph takes place. They willed that He should die. But what He was and what they hated could never die. The Cross was His government or law of life. He was telling them that when you share the ignominy of a cross, you share the new message in your heart. It gives you a feeling of being especially good and worthy.

A. THERE WAS NO REASON FOR TEARS

On the way to the Cross, He told the women not to mourn Him for He was innocent. Instead He told them to mourn over their own destruction, the destruction of the world at the end of time. It will be the final condemnation of man because of his refusal to accept the invitation offered him.

He pointed out that fearlessness leads to a single end, that the tears of the world would not prevent Him from doing His work. That no superficial wailings would weaken His predetermined purpose of sacrifice. No dowry of tears could make them the brides of His heart. He was a priest going to the sacrifice and not just a good man. Nothing would prevent the sacrifice. There was a necessity for the sacrifice and they should avail themselves of its fruits.

He purged tears of lamentation. He would purge death of death by rising from the grave. Only sin alone was worth tears. There was no reason to cry at all for anything the world does to you. He would wipe away all such tears. He advised them not to have misplaced sorrow but to look to their own souls. He needed no tears, they did. He rejected their grief. His purpose would be accomplished. His death was willed freely by Him.

He told them that He was the "green tree" of freedom and truth, and that He held forth the priceless fruit of life eternal. He pointed out what the powers of evil do, how the world treats the innocent. But He was the green and innocent Tree transplanted from Eden.

He told them how the sinful shall suffer; that the dry tree is the whole human race, the unconverted world. That if the Romans so treated Him who was innocent, how would they treat sinners? How would the guilty be punished for their own iniquities?

And this triumph was the pinnacle of His promise, the chance to die for everyone.

4. The Cross (The Triumph)

The Cross has done more than all else to win the world to Him. Love that is willing to suffer to achieve its object is powerful. This is what is meant by the power of the Cross to win the world. Jesus identifies Himself with a cause, has a consuming devotion to a cause. He was ready to give up everything selfish for the people He loves. In this lies the consummate perfection of character. The Cross merely consummated His service to the world.

A. THE HUMAN WILL IS CONTRADICTED (HOW HE WON HIS CROWN)

Here the Cross itself is important. (He died on a cross and not a tree as some proclaim), because the vertical bar of God's will is negated by the horizontal bar of the contradicting human will. Christ pays the debt in order that the two wills will be one. Christ says He will destroy man, man says we will crucify you. They proclaimed by the cross that they would make it impossible for God to live on earth. And in every thought and act, man continues to proclaim his sentence. The temple of Jesus' body was destroyed completely.

Christ is here proclaiming that the giving up of life is the only way to save your life. He paid the price man alone could not pay. He lays down His life for a hostile and alien world, for a humanity that disgusted Him with its pettiness and vulgarity, its baseness and spitefulness. This was in order to appease men's hatred. Here love experienced its coronation. It is how He won His crown, His supreme authority and power. The sacrifice becomes the fundamental act of establishing the new covenant between God and man in order to raise up and establish the New Order. The Cross was the final argument. What more can God do? Up to Calvary men had been taught by preaching. It took the cross to universalize the mission of Christ. The lever that overturns the world is the Cross.

The difficulty with the world is that death is overemphasized. To man, death is something to fear and be in awe of. But what is it but that the body is returned to dust? And the body is just something that it is not desirable to keep. And when this happens, one goes on to better things. When one begins to realize this or when this happens, the universal Spirit of God draws near.

And so as when any other hardship is encountered and passes, likewise death on the cross is of no moment after it has passed. For life in the body is but transitory. It is only the soul that counts—the character which you have built up as an asset. As you can see, to follow the Spirit is of the utmost importance—it is the only essential thing.

Jesus did not live and die so that men can go on sinning. Man must pay attention to the welfare of people. His death pointed to the day when men could sin no more. And then occurred the blackness, the covering of the sun, and later on earthquakes when all nature honored Him—sinners alone rejected Him.

B. MOCKERY (DEATH—THE CONDITION OF A HIGHER LIFE)

His kingship was proclaimed in the language of the good, the true and the beautiful. Truth was made to speak when men ridiculed. The Cross now became His pulpit. He left His thoughts on dying. What He said was set down for the purpose of an eternal publication and an undying consolation. For, you see, man wants a religion without a cross. So they ask and taunt God to come down from the cross. This is a most typical demand of an unregenerate world when they see self-denial and abnegation. But love costs the lover and so He refuses to come down from the cross.

The cross is contradiction; it not only contradicts the world but also acts as the solution to the contradiction of life and death. This it does by showing that death is the condition of a higher life.

Mockery is always an ingredient of the cup of sorrow. One must bear the cup patiently, and to do this man draws strength in his trials from the example of Christ. The cruelty of sneering lips is part of the heritage of sin, as much as the cruelty of hands that nail. They poured scorn onto the pain. The Kingdom of God was now only shame, disgrace,

103

laughter, blasphemy and the offense of the cross.

Of course He could not save Himself. The rain cannot save itself, if it is to bud the greenery. The sun cannot save itself, if it is to light a world. The soldier cannot save Himself, if he is to save his country. And Jesus cannot save Himself, if He is to save His creatures!

They mocked the titles of King of Israel, Savior, and Son of God. They assumed that all the kings of earth must be seated on golden thrones. But He was different, He had decided to rule from a cross—to be a king not of their bodies through force but of their hearts through love. He insisted on coming to glory through humiliation. Of course it was the only way for it was a law of the universe.

They thought He was lost when they were the ones lost. The really damned mocked One whom they believed to be damned. Hell was triumphing in the human! They taunted Him with "if." They tried to make Him doubt His divine sonship. They wanted to anger the dying Savior into the use of His superhuman powers. To achieve such a victory was Satan's desperate purpose. Skeptics want miracles but never the greater miracle of forgiveness. Jesus knew that no descent from the cross (a miracle) would have won man. It was human to come down but divine to hang there. The death on the cross is the greatest negation of the external miracles and affirmation of the internal miracles. If He had come down from the cross only an external miracle would have been performed. The sign is here shown that death has been conquered. He refused to come down because Jesus knew He would rise from the dead. Unless we all have faith in exactly that, death will control us. We will refuse to accept the necessary sacrifice.

For Jesus, true success was to complete one's life by the necessary sacrifice. And in doing this to attain to eternal life. For all else is failure. The people of the world who seem to be successful are failures. Jesus Christ was the failure of failures according to the standards of men.

C. PARDON AND FORGIVENESS

Jesus now poured out the prayer of pardon and forgiveness to His enemies and those who hated Him. He did not forget His gospel with the piercing of His hands and feet. And why did He forgive them? "Because they know not what they do." Their crime was sentencing life to death. Was not this a perversion of justice? If they knew what they were doing they would never be saved. It is only the ignorance of their great sin that saves. It is not wisdom that saves: it is ignorance.

He extended pardon because He was mediator between God and man. As the High Priest who offered Himself in sacrifice, He pleaded for sinners. God in the form of the suffering servant fulfilled the promise of Eden. For even back then, God had promised redemption through the "seed of the Woman," He who would crush the serpent of evil. Forgiveness was to be identified with His sacrifice. He was interceding and offering Himself for the guilty. The New Abel's blood was spilled to lift the wrath and to plead for pardon.

Now Jesus prayed only for those who would repent. He knew there was no forgiveness except through Him. All cannot be saved but only those chosen through repentance. So He asked and commended them to mercy at the hands of the Father. And the excuse He gave was that they were simply the victims of their own ignorance of spiritual truth. Thus did He strive to find an excuse for His enemies so long as it was not an offense against the truth. He was saying that the insults or blows were but a sign of moral need flung out from the hearts of His enemies. There was such a pitiable need of such men of ignorance. This was the way He had found of proving His superiority over His enemy. He refused to serve other people's selfish actions. Instead He rejected all forms of selfishness, such as vanity, a desire to be noticed or a fear of being slighted.

With this spirit He wrested the offensive from their hands, turning the tragedy into a triumph. Man instead judges the saving power of God by release from trials. If it cannot give relief from trial, what good is it? They said Jesus' teachings were a drug—an opiate, that man has no soul. They needed proof of His power. Any man has to show his powers to sustain His reputation. Then we can only accept the Christ if He has power to take Himself down from the cross.

D. TO PASS FROM DEATH UNTO LIFE (BELIEF AND REPENTANCE)

Jesus bade them to look to God at the very moment when the courts were inflicting injustice. He thinks only of souls when men are dying. He talks about paradise when stomachs are empty and bodies racked with pain. But men react in different ways. Consequently, no example that Jesus could give is enough to convert unless the heart itself is changed. The world has room only for the ordinary, never the very good or the very bad. The good are a reproach to the mediocre. The evil are a disturbance.

Jesus found Himself the right man in the right place. He was between two thieves. He was among the worthless and rejects. The Redeemer was in the midst of the unredeemed. The good thief asked for deliverance from sin. It is always the believer who asks no proofs. His confession of guilt led to incipient repentance, led to faith in Jesus. He had a faith in the ultimate triumph of good over evil. Consequently he expected a supernatural kingdom to be established. He threw himself upon divine mercy and asked for forgiveness. He asked for eternal life. It was a thief, not a saint, who was the escort of the King of Kings into paradise.

To Jesus the words were like a ray of light. God was thereby exhorting Him to be steadfast in the faith. Here was a word about His Kingdom, a word from on high. This thief believed when others disbelieved. Even the disciples were doubting. And then this thief ascribed to Jesus a Kingdom which was not of this world. Victim and Lord were to the good thief compatible terms.

Then came the promise of paradise to the thief. He knocked once, sought once, asked once, dared everything, and found everything. The moment this criminal looked to Jesus he received everlasting life. This is what Jesus had come to teach and here he teaches it clearly and concisely in simple terms. Even on the cross here was a man who saw the truth. And when he saw, he passed from death unto life. Jesus had given the thief the assurance of divine mercy.

In this assurance the last judgment was prefigured here on Calvary. Jesus anticipated His final role. Here He was in the midst, the two divisions of humanity on each side—the saved and the lost—the sheep and the goats. When He came in glory to judge all men, the cross would be a bade of honor, not shame. Jesus took His judgments to heart, he always condemned with tears. He condemned when He kept silence over men's lack of a sense of truth. When He said, "Be of good cheer," it meant you can be saved. Jesus wiped away past errors and mistakes. He always assured them there was no cause to be worried by a sense of guilt. He was to be the New Adam (a prototype), changing the water of sin into the wine of life. He knew that the world would not tolerate His divinity.

E. LOVE TRIUMPHANT AND ETERNAL

Now that His influence was at an end, His disciples' faith had vanished. He realized His message had fallen on deaf ears—all had been in vain. But women now responded to His appeal for loyal devotion. Whereas masculine love was hindered by His death, feminine love would rise to new heights after the resurrection. He now told His human mother that all men (humanity) were to be treated as sons of women. By doing so He assigned a spiritual motherhood for redeemed humanity.

All women are to be treated as mothers. In other words, men are to be loved as He loved them. He beheld love triumphant and eternal. He raised it above the personal to the divine.

F. ABANDONMENT

Here on the cross His blood poured out as a curse of sin. Men were slowly putting out the light who illumined every man coming into this world. Jesus was now alone; He even denied Himself the light and consolation of His divinity. He felt faith and hope were obscured. The craving to escape death took the form of a complaint. The world was a lost world. A human heart was breaking. Suffering now passed from the body into the mind and soul. All these things which happened to Jesus there on the Cross, or throughout His life, are the same experiences that men must go through when they take up their own cross.

Jesus now had a sense of being abandoned by God. It was the final agony of being forsaken by the Father. All His ideals were to end in disaster. The Father withdrew the support of His immediate presence, for it was essential for Jesus alone to experience the glory of complete victory over the forces of sin and death. It was necessary for the Son to know that ultimate horror of abandonment by the Father. Jesus entered upon the extreme penalty of sin which is separation from God. The darkness of deluded humanity hung over His head. Jesus saw all history recapitulated in Himself. It is always so, that when the darkness of sin has its moment of triumph, evil cuts off every thread connecting man with God. Only sin can make the darkness of soul. Man wears the mantle of sin, which shows the cost of sin. And so Jesus felt this abandonment when standing in a sinner's place. The soul that despairs never cries to God. He felt the emptiness of humanity through sin.

And now they said He certainly could not be the Lord, for Elias had not yet come. It is always apparent that the reception of any truth Jesus taught depended upon one's state of will. They did not want His cross, the uncrucified Christ was the worldlings' desire. They reproached Jesus for hanging on the cross.

G. THE THIRST FOR MAN'S SALVATION (THE TRIUMPH OF SPIRIT OVER MATTER)

But Jesus thirsted for men's salvation. He had now fulfilled all prophecies. He did not attempt to shed what is human. He was never

107

ashamed of being a man. But His triumph was not in accepting death on the cross so much as it was the triumph of spirit over matter. He knew that all things were now finished. And He desired the speedy return of His all-conquering spirit to its divine source.

He thirsted because thirst was the symbol of the unsatisfying character of sin. For the pleasures of the flesh purchased at the cost of the Spirit are like drinking salt water. He had a passion for souls. "Give me to drink" meant "Give me your hearts." He had a divine love for mankind. And in return what did men give Him—nothing less than vinegar and gall.

H. ALL PLANNED THE BEAUTIFUL IMAGE TO WHICH MAN WAS DESTINED TO CONFORM
THE OBEDIENT NEW ADAM SUPPLANTS THE DISOBEDIENT MAN ADAM
THE LAWS OF SACRIFICE

But the Jews had a thirst for mockery of what is most sacred. They pointed out that He could not save Himself, but they did not realize why He would not save Himself. Otherwise He could not appear on Eastern morn. Otherwise others would not live. He gave His life as a ransom for many. It was not weakness at all but obedience to the laws of sacrifice. Men can see events only in succession. But He had ordained all from the beginning. From all eternity God willed to make men in the image of His eternal Son. God sent His divine Son to this earth in order that fallen man might know the beautiful image to which he was destined to conform. It was not just to forgive sin but to satisfy justice through suffering. Now there was an obedient New Adam, a humble New Eve and the Tree of the Cross. This tree supplants the disobedient man Adam, the proud woman Eve and the tree of the Garden.

I. MISSION ACCOMPLISHED: FAREWELL TO TIME
SURE OF THE FUTURE
THE MATERIAL WORLD CANCELED OUT

Now that all was finished, He knew that His atoning sacrifice had been accepted by the Father. He now said farewell to time. The end of the Son meant the end of the world. He knew that His work was finished, so He announced the completion and perfection of His mission. He had lived until all things were accomplished as had been appointed. He had canceled out the material world and transmuted it into the divine, the spiritual. His life from birth to death had faithfully achieved his goal.

He had shown that inwardly He could prevail against all tribulations. His own purity would be the power which should redeem sinners. He had taught others what sin really means. Men make the force of circumstances their excuse. But He had and would overthrow all hostile forces, now He would assuredly "reign." His great achievement was the ability to live without care in the present just because He was so sure of the future.

It is true that His salesmanship had failed to lead Judaism beyond itself. Now Judaism and the world had lost the opportunity of realizing all the latent possibilities and capacities it possessed. Instead what He had achieved was redemption. Since redemption was completed, the life of the Spirit could not begin the work of sanctification. A new David had arisen to slay the Goliath of evil.

J. THE RETURN HOME: DEATH A TRANSITION TO ACHIEVE
LIFE
LIVING ALWAYS DECIDES ONE'S
FUTURE STATE

Now the beginning of His glory was to take place. The prodigal Son was returning back home. He had left the Father's house and gone off into the foreign country of this world. He had spent His substance, the divine riches of power and wisdom. He had wasted His substance among sinners. There was nothing left to feed upon except the sneers and the vinegar of human ingratitude. He had laid down His life of Himself, for no one would take away His life from Him. He prepared to take the road back home to His Father's house. His eye had ever been on God. For Him the meaning of the cross was not one of destruction and death but of dynamic, ever-resurgent life. Death was but a transition to achieve that life. It was nothing but a move to God. And so He was the only instance in history of a dying one who was a living one. He died from an act of will.

His spirit went up to heaven. Christ entered into heaven itself to appear in the presence of God for men. For living always decides one's future state. So that makes the peril of living greater than the peril of dying. His earthly mission having been completed, He now returned again to His heavenly Father, who sent Him on the work of redemption.

K. MAN CAN NOW BECOME PERFECT (TREASURES OF GOD REVEALED)

Now an intervention of God in the course of nature took place, for God did not allow these great events in the spiritual world to leave no trace on the material world. God is no one-sided idealist—external as well as internal things belong to Him. The earth gave signs of recognition when the Lord liberated man from the slavery of sin. Though the hearts of the people could not be rent, the rock could.

The veil of the Temple was also rent. This so man could become perfect and Holy. And this by a new and living way—by the blood of Jesus. This rending was not done by the hand of man but by the miraculous hand of God Himself. That which of old was sacred now remained opened and manifest before their eyes. The treasures of God were revealed.

But even so, a new Temple would be raised up in three days. What was holy would be made manifest, and Christ with a new body (temple) would take His place as our High Priest. Christ had come into the world to be the fulfillment, but Judea had denied Him welcome. Now a more complete tabernacle would arise and one which human hands had never fashioned. It does not belong to this order of creation at all. As the veil of the old Temple was torn the priesthood came into its own. The true Holy of Holies, the true ark of the New Covenant, the true bread of life, the Son of the living God.

L. DEATH VANQUISHED BY DEATH (DEATH SWALLOWED UP IN VICTORY)

When He died He vanquished death by death. By Jesus' death upon the cross a new world era dawned.

There are various ways and measures of knowledge. A stranger, none other than a Roman soldier, understood better than one of His own. This stranger did not hear or see death, he saw and heard only victory over death. Jesus had swallowed up death in victory. He had manifested humiliation and power on the cross as He did in His public life. A soldier of Caesar bowed in adoration of the divine sufferer.

M. DIVINE LOVE OPENED TO THE GUILTY: ACCESS TO GOD

Two veils had been rent, the veil of His flesh and the purple veil of the Temple. The latter did away with the old law. The veil of His

110

flesh opened the Holy of Holies of divine love—opened to the guilty, giving access to God.

And what does the cross bring to us? Sorrow for sin springs from a vision of the cross. The vileness of sin is most poignantly revealed. But we cannot forget that the arrow of sin that wounds brings the balm of forgiveness that heals. Those who looked at Him were healed of sin. But lo, they refused to look on Him whom they had pierced.

And lest we forget, remember if we are planted in the likeness of His death we shall rise with Him in the glory of His resurrection.

The concern of His secret followers and some of the women about His burial was a token of their love for Him and not of their faith in Him as the resurrection and life. Spiritually, they knew not yet who He was but physically, they were mindful of Him.

5. The Proof of the Resurrection (Death Could Not Conquer)

The women now became heralds of His resurrection. He would now submit proof that death could not conquer Him.

A. HATE (MAN DEMANDS THE LAST WORD)

First let us consider the hate that fell back upon the hearts of the scribes. The immense sadness of their history crushed down upon them. They were filled with dissatisfaction and a sense of unfulfillment. Had not Jesus taken away all wherein we found pleasure, destroyed all whereon we prided ourselves? But now the Pharisees heaved a sigh of relief. Public peace and safety have been restored. The national faith has gained a complete victory. The old hope could now awake to new life. They might now again proclaim and believe that they were the true heirs. Is not the voice of the people the voice of God? They now knew that Jesus was dead. They said He would not rise again, and yet they watched. Would He still win the war for life and truth and love?

How comes it that Jesus does not remain silent? He now again begins to speak. It was futile for men to try to get rid of the living God. It had been of no use to brand Him an enemy of the people. It was a delusion of His enemies to think they could escape the sentence He had passed upon them, by a sentence they passed on Him. Jesus was given up to universal contempt; He was condemned, executed, and buried. Yet we are not done with Him.

Conscience knows well that He has spoken the truth. Conscience knows that it was God Who spoke to him. Whether we accept or resist belief in Him, our self-assurance is at an end. Jesus dead proves to be as dangerous as was the living Jesus. The attempt to get rid of Him by every method within human power continues to meet with no success. It is useless to fight against God. Resistance serves only to show forth His might and His truth. Men still call Him a deceiver in spite of their conscience. We see in their attitude the unwilling confession of the vanquished victors. We are at the end of our resources.

Men try to sit in judgment upon God but the discovery is made that God has sat in judgment on man. All that is left for man to decide is whether to bow to God's judgment or to resist it, whether to acknowledge God's authority or persist in our iniquity.

The enemies of Jesus expected the resurrection, His friends did not. It was the believers who were the skeptics.

The cross was the supreme attempt to turn aside judgment from men. It was an attempt to win back human freedom. But how are we to continue to live by selfishness and self-deception if man does not have the last word? Jesus' death tells all human pride, all human assurance, all human power that it will collapse under God's judgment. Thus the last remnants of human security are shattered, reduced to nought. The cross is an attempted rebellion against God which was bound to fail. He is the only person in this wicked world whom no one can injure. Jesus had come to tell man that the way to everlasting life was love. Love—each for the other, each for Him, and His love for all.

B. THE RESURRECTION WOULD VINDICATE ALL CLAIMS
(LIFE WHICH LAUGHS AT DEATH)
(ETERNAL LIFE)

In Jesus' dead body His soul would be glorified. He was pointing the way to man. Jesus was not dead. The dawn of the glory that was to come and His resurrection from the dead would vindicate all His claims. His intercession with God is security for the inheritance they are to receive. The pleasures of this world are only sham in comparison with the glory that comes through Christ. The pleasures of this world soon turn to ashes, they are trinkets that fascinate for only a season. The resurrection of the dead is the bridge from the "Now" to the "Then." Easter brings us news of this ungovernable life that laughs at death. It can be checked by no grave. Easter brings us news of life eternal. Henceforth He will not die. He is proof alone that there is a personal, eternal life of perfection, free from all earthly toil and travail, a life in which

112

there will be no death, sorrow, crying, nor pain.

Man speaks of God as though He knows Him. We act as though we were on the best of terms with Him. When dealing with God all our talking, singing, thinking, and doing become of questionable value. In God our life rests on a new foundation—our arrogance is at an end. Man runs against and resists God, he cannot bear that another should be Lord. When man seeks to be like God he seeks the fulfillment of life—to do what we want is sin. Man always refuses to recognize the authority of God. Then it is that God places man under the dominion and the law of death. Man yearns for a life that vanquishes death, which knows not sin but behind which there is no God. Only where there is forgiveness of sin are life and happiness found. For man the agonizing cry of God must be silenced.

Jesus had to die because the sovereignty of God is revealed in Him. And this because man does not want the sovereignty of God. He does not want God and yet man cannot live without Him. The cross means that man pronounces his own death sentence. And yet over and above all this, an act of God takes place when man is at the end of his resources. It is the living God Who speaks the last word. There is a divine possibility that grace may have the last word. It may break down man's resistance and overcome his death.

Now the resurrection comes which tells of death that has been vanquished. It teaches us of a new life and an eternal perfection "together with Christ."

1. MAN WANTS PEACE, NOT RESPONSIBILITY The dead man who lies in the tomb gives us no peace. It is of vital interest to the whole world that Jesus should be dead. The stone must stay before the tomb so that we may have peace. He must leave us in peace. Man will gladly mourn and revere the dead man. He can lament the tragic fact He was too good and too great for us to bear Him. But He must not ask us to hear in His words and deeds, sufferings and death, the voice of the living God calling us to a sense of our responsibility. What else can royal soldiers do before a regal Spirit?

2. THE RESURRECTION IS NOT A MYSTERY Now we know we shall all be changed in a moment. No laws are to be broken. Love will just be accomplished and completed by the transformation of mortal being. The resurrection was never a mystery to Heaven but His death would be. Contrariwise to men His resurrection is a mystery.

3. A MESSAGE OF JOY TO THOSE WITH FAITH His cross stands before the world. It asks a question. We guilty and condemned sinners must decide whether we confess faith in Christ, whether we acknowledge the supremacy of God's truth and desire to live by His grace. His empty tomb asks man whether he is really to let God have the last word. "He is risen" is a message of joy. You cannot affirm or deny Christ by human or practical methods of research. Christ comes only to those who believe or have faith in Him. He ignored His murderers and would not show Himself to them.

Jesus took the crucifixion to multiply His Sonship into other sons of God. Before man could be an adopted son of God he had to be redeemed from enmity with God. Only by grace and adoption were men sons of God.

(Success the Only Standard) (Men Resolved to Be Miserable) (Disappointment Due to the Inviality of Human Hopes)

4. A LIE WAS BOUGHT TO ESCAPE THE FACT But the Jews wanted nothing to do with life eternal. They bought a lie in order to deny the resurrection. Anything was expedient in order to escape the fact of the resurrection. Naturally there was incredulity in the face of the extraordinary for there was neither precedent nor analogy that a dead person could return to life. The resurrection was some mysterious and remote event, not a present possibility. Modern skepticism is without hope. The skepticism of the disciples started with a hope; they were permitted to doubt so that the faithful in centuries to come might never be in doubt.

What blinded their eyes was their unbelief. All men have walked on the road where all seems lost. And why is this? Because the world, the philosophers and sages, our passions take Christ from man. When the resurrection is doubted the joy and knowledge of his presence is concealed. It is always so; what men see of Him depends on the disposition of their own hearts. If they would but show and admit their wounds He would pour in the oil of His healing.

The cure for sorrow is to see things that disturb in their right relations. Disappointment is always due to the triviality of human hopes. The original drawings of humans always have to be torn up because they are too little in the eyes of God. Their plans are too small, their policies are too limited. And so it is, that the hand that breaks the cup of petty desires always offers a richer chalice.

But the Jews were lost. They could not fit catastrophe into the idea of a Master. Their only standard was, as man's only standard is today, that He must always be successful by worldly standards. Men cannot believe in the foolishness of the cross.

Instead men are resolved to be miserable. They resist the evidence of those who verify. Men are slow and foolish of heart even when the greatest evidence is available. But it is as certain as that the day follows the night that credulity toward men and incredulity toward God is the mark of dull hearts. A readiness to believe speculatively and a slowness to believe practically is the sign of sluggish hearts.

5. GLORY COMES THROUGH DEFEAT (PEACE) And what is the consequence of Jesus' sufferings? Men would be raised from a state of sin to fellowship with God. Now it is to be seen that everything that happened to him had been foretold. It was not an offense, a scandal, a defeat, a succumbing to the inevitable; it was forseen, planned and preannounced. What closed the case? What consummated the plan? It was the knowledge of glory that came through defeat.

And as His friends waited they locked themselves in the upper room for fear that the people might storm the house of those who were unpopular.

By the blood of the cross He had brought about peace. Now He came in His own person to bestow it. Peace is the fruit of justice. He had performed the duties of justice on the tree, now He harvested the fruits of that tree. Only when the injustice of sin against God has been rectified can there be an affirmation of true peace. Peace implies order, consequently there can be no peace to the wicked. And that because they are at odds with themselves, others and God.

6. SCARS REMIND THERE WAS A SACRIFICE (SCARS OF BATTLE AGAINST SIN AND EVIL) In touching Him they immediately believed. It was by His wounds He would be recognized. It was only by pain and sorrow that redemption would be wrought. The scars continually remind men that there was a sacrifice. These were the unmistakable scars of battle against sin and evil. He wore His wounds to prove that love was stronger than death. These scars would be points of argument in intercession before the Heavenly Father. Scars would be a trophy of honor He would bear on the last day to judge the living and the dead. Had He risen with no memorials of His passion, men would have doubted Him with the passing of time. They would have obliterated from their minds the remnants of His shame and agony on earth. He bore the mementoes of His redemption.

7. THE SPIRIT'S POWER TO CONVERT THE WORLD He bequeathed to them His share of the cross, his rewards, and, after that, His glory. He breathed on them the Holy Spirit. Thus He confers the power of the Holy Spirit. It was the breath of the Spirit's influence which was the

Spirit's power to convert the world. It was the breath of the risen Christ with all its regenerative power. He was already in His state of glory for He was bestowing the Spirit. He was now associating the apostles with the life of His resurrection. At Pentecost He would associate them with His Ascension.

8. CEASE YOUR DOUBTING AND BELIEVE The doubtful Thomas refused to believe without evidence. It was not indifference or hostility to truth. He merely wanted knowledge in order to have faith. It was unlike the self-wise who want knowledge to use against faith. Thomas frames for us the world's intermittent cry of bewilderment. To Thomas death was no victory, it was terrible defeat. His attitude of skepticism commends itself to the world. Our whole modern structure of learning rests on a perverse and mischievous habit of mind. He refused to be influenced in his opinions by what other people said, preferring to be allowed to make up his mind for himself. He stood up with obstinate defiance for his own principles and conditions. Thomas is merely a representative of the modern mind.

Thomas was supposed to believe in spite of all the facts and against all reason. He knew that no human word could give him certainty and strength. Faith in the sense of certainty and strength never lies with human power. Faith must be able to say, "I am certain," otherwise it is not faith. Faith languishes or degenerates because we do not dare to go the whole way.

But Jesus goes right to the point. "Cease your doubting and believe. Be not faithless." He knew Thomas's gloom was His besetting sin. Peace rests upon His death and resurrection. You cannot have peace unless you believe that. There is no peace in this present world of conflict for peace comes only when death is known to be conquered. Jesus points out here that a proof by the senses would not give complete peace, that Thomas had to believe. When that takes place, one can now face life joyously and undismayed. One can refuse to be afraid of anything. The skeptical mind of Thomas was instantly cleansed, his doubting heart was purified. A conviction of the glorious truth that Christ is divine flooded his soul. He was no longer disobedient to the heavenly vision. He accepted the light when it came to him.

The light blinded them spiritually. Jesus was disclosed only to witnesses chosen by God. A healthy man is a man of this world and therefore cannot see the other world. Here was the first indication of a new existence.

The doubts of a depressed humanity are healed by the acknowledgement of Christ's deity. Now Thomas had a certain and living faith which stayed and upheld him.

116

The only reason for the resurrection was doubt that the body could be resurrected. It was to prove that He has power over death and life.

This teaches the lesson that unseeing faith has a magical quality that overrules all things. Faith is thus placed above those who believe only when they see, of those who need the additional testimony of the senses. And then there are others who will not believe even when they see. Christ was telling them that the faith of future believers would have to be of the highest type. They would not be able to demand the evidence of sensible proof. The only way they would be able to believe would be with the Holy Spirit and Jesus' word. It is through Jesus' word that the Spirit works and only through tribulation do we heed the word.

9. LOVE—THE CONDITION OF SERVICE TO HIM: SUBSTITUTE LOVE FOR FEAR

LOVE PRECEDES AUTHORITY Now the disciples were disappointed and disheartened. They needed instruction from Jesus as to how to catch fish. How to convert. The result of His instruction was so surprising as to appear miraculous. They caught many fish. Now they were made strong.

In addition He taught them about love. Jesus made love the condition of service to Him. He proposed to substitute love for fear. And their confession of love must precede the bestowing of authority. For authority without love is tyranny. Peter began to realize that he no longer had confidence in himself. He relied on the knowledge of Jesus. Peter was to feed the lambs. The man (any man) who had fallen and learned his own weakness was the best qualified for strengthening the weak. Here came the victory for love. When doubt and fear strove in later days for dominance, Peter would use the formula given.

Peter went step by step down the ladder of humiliation. Eventually Peter would find death by crucifixion. The Lord followed him with the assurance of the work for which he was destined. Peter had been given the keys and the function of a doorkeeper. Jesus was telling Peter that he would learn what it really means to love. He pointed out that His love is a vestibule to death. For is it not so that the man of perdition will always be after you? There is one who opposes and exalts himself above all that is called God. He is the one who is called the opposite of Christ.

10. ALL POWER WAS MERITED BY PASSION AND DEATH Now in another place He assured them that all power had been given to Him in heaven and earth. He affirmed His absolute Godship and that He has everlasting dominion and glory. It was a power that He had merited by His passion and His death. This authority was to extend to both earth and heaven. The resurrection gave Him power upon earth where He

117

had conquered both its sins and its death. The ascension gave Him power in heaven to act as mediator between God and man. His authority was supreme.

11. SALVATION BY REPENTANCE (SURRENDER OF HEART AND WILL TO THE MASTER) Now He instructed them to go and teach all nations. Tell them about the salvation through faith in Jesus the Christ which must be followed by their repentance and baptism. Tell them that it is freely offered to all. But know this, that the rejection of the offer thenceforth would bring condemnation. And be assured that signs and miracles will follow them that believe. He confirmed their faith in the power divine.

They were not merely to teach for He who gave the commission was not merely a teacher. Their aim was to make disciples. Those converted to disciples would have to surrender heart and will to the Divine Master. Men were to turn over their human natures to Him in order that they might enter into glory. Being born of the spirit would make man a participant of Jesus' divine nature.

12. AN INTERIOR ILLUMINATION He now assured them that He would be with them always to the end of the world. And then He would come back to them as a spiritual presence. But in the meantime, His living presence would be with us; in our hearts, in guidance, sympathy, companionship and counsel.

He pointed out to them that it takes an interior illumination to read the prophets. It is inseparable from good will and love.

13. THE WORLD IS EVIL AND A STRUGGLE, AND YET CHRIST PROMISES VICTORY. THE KEY IS GOODNESS. His own autobiography always referred to the atonement He would make between God and man. The Old Testament referred to Him as the suffering but conquering servant. The death on the cross was to be remembered. But the death on the cross would have been useless for the removal of human guilt if He had not risen from the dead. It behooved Him to suffer because He had to show the evil of sin. Evil is most manifest in the crucifixion of goodness. The worst thing evil can do is to kill goodness. Having been defeated in that, it could never be victorious again. It might in the future win some battles, but it would never win the war. Goodness in the face of evil must suffer. When love meets sin, it will be crucified. Goodness was to use that very suffering as a condition of overcoming evil. Goodness took all the anger and hate and pleaded, "Forgive." No healing can be brought to broken wings by a humanism which is brotherhood without tears.

118

One must have a source of knowledge different from any other teacher. One must be able to burst the fetters of death in order to prove that truth crushed to earth may rise again. The law He gave was that life is a struggle. That unless there is a cross in our lives, there will never be an empty tomb. Unless there is the crown of thorns, there will never be the halo of light. Unless there is a cross there will never be the rising from death. In conquering the world Jesus did not mean His followers would be immune from woes, pain, sorrow, and crucifixion. He gave no peace which promised a banishment from strife. What the resurrection offered was not immunity from evil in the physical world, but immunity from sin in the soul.

His life had been a model for His followers. They were encouraged to take the worst this life had to offer with courage and serenity. There was to be no talisman as security from trials. As a Captain He went into battle in order to inspire men to transfigure life's greatest pains into the richest gains. It was the cross of Christ that raised the questions for life. It was the resurrection that answered them. He unfurls before an evil world the pledge of victory.

14. PROCLAIM THE REDEMPTION He proclaimed the fruits of His cross must now be applied to all peoples and all nations. Repentance is linked up with the application of the redemption won on Cavalry. Repentance was a turning away from sin and a turning to God. The divine order to begin preaching redemption in Jerusalem was a mark of His great compassion. He directed the apostles to go to those who had falsely accused Him, to tell them He was their advocate and that He would plead their cause from on high. That because of His scourgings and stripes they would be healed.

Now He promised them a manifest increase of the spirit. This power would enable them to proclaim the redemption. They were to begin their mission to the world with the descent of the Holy Spirit. It would not be worldly power. It would be a power over living souls to channel into them the forgiveness and grace stored up in the reservoir of Calvary. They wanted an earthly kingdom, He spoke of a spiritual one. They wanted a return of the old things, He told them they would be "witnesses" of a new thing. But He admonished them that to be a witness meant to be a martyr. They were bound by the idea of a nation, He included the world in His vision. The new power would be a gift and not developed from oneself.

6. The Ascension: Human Nature Installed as the Epitome of Perfection
Men's Minds and Hearts are not Confined to the Earth
Christ Would Represent Humanity before the Father's Throne

Now came the ascension, which confirmed that death had been conquered. The risen Christ explains the sudden shift in the feeling of the disciples. From fear and disillusionment they would now go forth joyfully to danger and death, always preaching as the one absolute dogma of the new faith the belief in the resurrection. That it pulls or draws down to earth from heaven its blessings on men. Pierced hands best distribute benediction.

The ascension was the fruit of His crucifixion. It was fitting that He suffered in order to enter into His glory. The ascension was a departure of a material being, this because His resurrection had been an actual return of His spirit to his corporeal body. In the ascension the Savior did not lay aside the garment of flesh with which He had been clothed. He had come to save human nature. His human nature would be the pattern of the future glory of other human natures. And only the incarnation or assuming of a human nature made it possible for Him to suffer and redeem. A coronation upon earth, instead of an ascension into heaven, would have confined men's minds and hearts to the earth. And that was the very thing He did not wish, which He was working against. The ascension would cause men's minds and hearts to ascend above the earth. Human nature was to be installed as the epitome of perfection, as the very Truth itself. Therefore the human nature which He took as the instrument for teaching, governing, and sanctifying should partake of glory as it shared in shame. The ascension put all doubts away by introducing His human nature into intimate and eternal communion with God. He Who had ascended shall return descending from the heavens in human form.

By the ascension His triple office of Teacher, King, and Priest was vindicated. No longer would He be mocked. The vindication would be complete when He would come in justice as the Judge of men. No one then could complain that God knows not the trials to which humans are subject. He had fought the same battles as men and endured the same temptations as those standing at His bar of justice. He has been through every trial, fashioned as we are, only sinless. The cross and the crown combined had governed every detail of His life.

Now is was only proper that the Christ at the right hand of the

Father would represent humanity before the Father's throne. He would be an advocate of men with the Father. He would send the Holy Spirit as man's advocate with Him. No faith and hope exists in heaven, only love. For love endures forever.

PLAY V: THE TRIUMPH

Contents

CHARACTERS
(IN ORDER OF APPEARANCE)

Second Voice
Jesus
First Voice
Disciples
Angel
Judas
Raiders (A Band of Men)
Priests
Roman Soldiers
Crowd
Peter
The Captain (The chiliarch)
Malchus
Temple Authorities

Mark
Sadducees and Pharisees
Guards
Caiphas
Annas
Sanhedrin (Council)
The Nasi
Witnesses
A Soldier
John
A Maid Servant
Servants
A Maid
All
A Cock
A Man
The Chief Priests
A Messenger
Pilate
A Servant of Pilate
Romans and Syrians (Gentiles)
The Jews
Herod
An Aide of Herod
The Soldiers of Herod
Claudia
A Slave Girl
Barabbas
The Lictor (Lictors)
The Tribune
The Centurion (Abenadar)
The Procession
Simon
The Onlookers
Women
The Executioners
The People (Crowd)
The Thieves (The Condemned):
    Cestas
    Dysmas
The Patient Ones (Women and John)
    Mary, mother of Jesus

John
A Woman and the woman's husband
A Man
An Earthquake
Mary Magdalene
Pilate's Guards (Soldiers)
Joseph of Arimathea
Joseph and Nicodemus
The Group (The three men with a few women)
The Group (Disciples and women)
The Sergeant
Two Angels
Cleopas and Nathaniel (Two disciples)
Thomas
The Brethren (Many followers)

SCENES

The Triumph

127

ACT I

THE INWARD STRUGGLE
(HE HAD A STRUGGLE TO MAKE)

Scene 1

THE GARDEN OF GETHSEMANE

SECOND VOICE: The Bible begins with a beautiful garden story; the Gospels end with a more wonderful one. As Adam lost the heritage of union with God in a garden, so now Jesus ushered in its restoration in a garden. Eden and Gethsemane were the two gardens around which revolved the fate of humanity. In Eden, Adam sinned; in Gethsemane, Jesus interceded with His Father. In Eden, God sought out Adam in his sin of rebellion; in Gethsemane, the New Adam sought out the Father and His submission and resignation. In Eden, a sword was drawn to prevent entrance into the garden and thus the immortalizing of evil; in Gethsemane, the sword would be sheathed.

Caiphas was an intelligent man and he knew that if Judas would live with one who proclaimed himself the Christ and then betray Him for a pittance, then Judas, if given the opportunity, would betray the high priest for an even smaller sum.

Caiphas tried to think of all the possibilities. He ordered the disciple to lead the arresting party and to make sure that he pointed out the right man to the Roman soldiers. He envisioned a general melee when the

131

raid was in progress, and he did not want Jesus to escape. Judas was to identify Jesus by walking up to Him and kissing him. By this they would know the man.

Furthermore, the high priest did not want to arrest the Disciples on this night. They were sheep. They would disperse at the first sign of attack on the shepherd.

It was decided to send a raiding party to the house, and if Jesus and His followers had left the upstairs room, then they would go to Gethsemane at the foot of the Mount of Olives, because when Jesus was in Jerusalem, He often slept there with His men. Should they not be there, the soldiers should go to Bethany to the home of Martha and Mary, because that was the only other place Jesus would repose.

No doubt Caiphas thought it would, of course, simplify everything if Jesus could be caught in the cenacle, resist arrest, and receive a Roman spear wound as a consequence. Then the thousands of followers of Jesus in and around the city could expend their venom on the Romans, an ideal situation for Caiphas.

What Caiphas most wanted was to take the onus for Jesus' death off the temple—off himself and off the judges of the Sanhedrin, the Jewish supreme court which would have to try Jesus.

If the Savior was to be arrested and tried, it would have to be under the law, as a false prophet. Also each sentence of death was passed on, before execution, by the Roman procurator. He usually affirmed it without question. If he confirmed it, the governor often forced the prisoner to undergo the Roman form of execution—crucifixion.

Now the city was still under the high moon, and only in the northeast could sounds be heard. There, leaving the double archway of Antonia, was a detachment of Roman soldiers.

Caiphas, in his pleas for assistance from the Romans, had overstated his case and the detachment, instead of being led by a centurion, was led by the Tribune himself—the ranking military man in the city.

The Tribune understood the legalities of the situation. He was not to meddle in the arrest because blasphemy against Yahweh was not a crime against Rome, and there was no statute under the rule of the empire on which Jesus could be tried. This was a Jewish problem; they were dealing with a provincial troublemaker who, somehow or other, had hurt the prestige and practices of the great temple.

All the Tribune had to do was to assist the temple guards in executing the orders of the high priest. If there was any resistance, the Romans would be fully authorized to beat many Jews to death.

Lanterns were carried before and behind the column of soldiers. The man kept a smart pace, the swinging lanterns causing their bare legs to dance in black on the pavement. Their orders were to report to the high priest. He would lead them to the culprit.

When Jesus and those with him had crossed the Kidron they went to an olive orchard on the western slope of the Mount of Olives. It is called Gethsemane, referred to as "The Garden of Gethsemane." The name Gethsemane means "oil vat" or "oil press." It was given to the place because of the presence there of an important or large oil press. Gethsemane then was an olive orchard with a wall around it. It was a place to which Jesus had often resorted with His Disciples. It was possible to find quiet and seclusion there, especially at night. Thither Jesus and His Disciples now retired. But Judas too—the traitor—knew the place, for often Jesus visited there with his disciples.

Jesus wanted to go there that night to be alone with His Disciples, a thing difficult to arrange in Jerusalem, or even in Bethany.

In Jesus there was a change. There was an increasingly urgent sense that danger was pressing. On this last day of His life, Jesus looked for a hiding place. In the dead of night, they squeezed through the quickset hedge surrounding one of the olive orchards watered by the Brook Cedron on the western slope of the hill.

It was empty in the streets, and a dead silence reigned over all.

Now, at 1:00 A.M., it was a time for waiting. The work was finished. There was an end to the preaching, an end to the miracles, an end to the instruction of the apostles, an end to prophecy. The time for waiting had come. There were about ninety minutes left of freedom, and there was nothing of consequence to do with them. Jesus had publicly audited His accounts to the Father in the presence of the chosen ones, and in these prayers He had prayed for Himself first—as all good priests should do—and then He had prayed for the men who would carry His story of love to the people.

And, as He knew when He had told the Father that He would consent to be born and to live as a man, and to die *as a man*, the moment of trial would be slow and terrifying and His Godside would not be able to save him a bit of pain, a shred of shame, or even shield Him from the horror of anticipating the awful things that were to come.

JESUS: [*Comes into the garden.*] Sit you here while I go and pray yonder. Pray that you enter not into temptation. [*Draws apart with the three whom he loves best, and leaving the others at rest beneath the trees, he goes on a little way through the gloom.*]

SECOND VOICE: He is loath to unveil the confusion of His thoughts and feelings to the whole company of his followers.

JESUS: [Trembling, afraid to be alone, he doubles his hands into fists and holds them against his breast. He speaks entreatingly to James, Peter, and John.] My soul is exceeding sorrowful to death. (My soul is crushed with anguish to the point of death), tarry you here, and watch (tarry you here, and watch with me—wait here and watch)! Sit here while I pray. (I am plunged in sorrow, enough to break my heart! Stay here and keep awake. My heart is almost breaking! You must stay here and keep watch.—My soul is ready to die with sorrow; do you abide here and watch with Me. Sit you here, while I go and pray *yonder*.) [*He points with His hand to the place where He would go.*]

SECOND VOICE: He began to be downcast and low-spirited, so low-spirited that He longs for death.

Jesus' intercourse with the disciples was that of a friend who *needed* friends. Jesus with grim austerity and self-control marched ahead, without them, to meet His destiny. There was something in the breathless air of the night, in the strained and restless silences of their vigil that gave edge to their nerves, and stirred their minds with portents of evil. This tenseness explains the unresponsiveness of these men to the critical anxiety of their beloved friend. It is not conceivable that they had changed their minds. It is rather that the anodyne of anxiety finally broke down their proud and incursive spirits, and left them powerless to aid him.

"Be vigilant," He meant, for such mischief as the shadows concealed might any moment break out. He had a struggle to make, one that was to engage all His faculties, and He wanted to depend on the eyes and ears of His friends to sound a warning when danger threatened. He wanted to be alone with the Father but, for the first time in His life, wanted to be not quite alone with Him.

Peter and James and John tried to help; they wished to console. But the Messiah merely shook his head. He was beyond any help of man, precisely because He was now more man than god. *As a man* He was able to sustain the fullness of suffering. And, as man, Jesus had not only the nervous structure of all other humans, plus the emotional capacity for great joy in addition to a great sensitivity, but as the Son of God He had a knowledge of what was to come.

FIRST VOICE: To think that the situation had come to this point, that men created by God would take such action. He began to show the full measure of distress that had come over Him. The presentiments and apprehensions that had haunted Him all through the supper now swept over Him with redoubled force and almost overwhelmed Him. He was no stoic; He tasted the depth of human experience of the dread and pain of death. He must be alone with this fearful experience, and yet He wanted his three companions close at hand. He was now taking them into the darkness of hell to show them another aspect of His face.

[**DISCIPLES** *nod in silence and watch Him make His way through the low-branched trees for a short distance.*]

[**JESUS** goes forward a little—"a stone's cast"—and falls on the ground, on his face. There He pauses beside a big, flat rock. He kneels for a few moments.]

FIRST VOICE: Here as nowhere, the Divine became human, stooped to the dust of the earth. The old Adam was broken in the new. He made two depressions in the hard stone, "as in wax," made by the knees of the Lord. The Divine had become human and grew heavy, as if He also had become subject to the law of gravitation, to mechanics, to death.

SECOND VOICE: He was soon enveloped by deep sorrow, which appears to have been, in a measure, surprising to Himself, for we read that He "began to be sore amazed, and to be very heavy."

Now death, whose shape He has hitherto contemplated only through a mist of obscuring phraseology, now confronted Him in hideous of the olives, the sheen of the stars, exercise their due effect on His emotions. The foretellings of scripture are (almost) forgotten, or seem ambiguous. As a natural result of these mingled influences, He is assailed with a burning desire for life. He will beseech the Father to let Him live!

JESUS [Going forward a little, *but not so far but that the three could hear what He says*, He falls on His face. A few paces farther, He throws himself on the ground. *Abandoning Himself to overwhelming mortal fear, He throws Himself full length on the rock, face down. With forehead and hair bedewed by the herbage, He prays in a loud voice.*] Father, all things are possible to you! Take away this cup from me!
(Father, if You will, turn aside this cup from me!)
[An interval elapses.] Nevertheless, not what I will, but what You will!
(Yet not my will but thine be done.—Yet not what I please but you do!—Not as I will, but as You will.—Nevertheless not my will, but thine, be done.—Nevertheless not as I will, but as You will.) (My Father, if it is possible, let this chalice pass Me by; only as Your will is, not as Mine

135

is.—O my Father, if this cup may not pass away from me, except I drink it, Your will be done.—Father, if You be willing, remove this cup from me; nevertheless, not my will but Yours be done.)

FIRST VOICE: He prays for life. Yet, as a dutiful son, even while doing so He leaves the final decision to His Father. He prayed that if it was possible he might be spared the hour of trial. No one knew better than Jesus that if He died as the Son of God the gesture would be small, the sacrifice negligible.

From this moment until the hour when He expired, He knew that He would have to suffer much more than anyone else who might travel the same path and endure the same things; the mere waiting was almost beyond Him. Every minute of every hour must now be borne as a man with extraordinary courage in order to achieve the victory of God, the one God.

The Father can make the cup pass the Son—can, but does not wish to. That is what "troubles" the Son, that is what He finds "awful," that is what is "horror-amazement" in all His life and death, for Himself an "offense" and the "madness" of the Cross. He could not have said this if He had not known that the will of the Son was not *yet* the will of the Father. "I and my Father are one in eternity," but in earth time they are still two. A contradiction here is shown between God and the world, between even the Father and the Son or rather the Divine and the human.

By the "death struggle," the agony, His will is torn asunder. He wants and yet does not want to drink the cup, thirsts for it and yet "turns away," the passion to suffer and the dread of suffering. The justice of the Father could not hear the prayer of the Son, just as today it cannot hear some of our prayers.

Isaias had foretold that there would be laid upon Him the iniquity of us all. In fulfillment of that prophecy He tasted death for every man, bearing guilt as if it were His own. Two elements were inseparably bound together—sin-bearing, and sinless obedience.

His two natures, the divine and the human, were both involved in this prayer. He and the Father were One. Unbroken was the consciousness of His Father's love. But on the other hand, His human nature recoiled from death as a penalty for sin. The natural shrinking of the human soul from the punishment which sin deserves was overborne by divine submission to the Father's will. The no to the cup of the Passion was human; the yes to the divine will was the overcoming of human reluctance to suffering for the sake of redemption. To take the bitter cup of human suffering that atones for sin and to sweeten it with little drops of "God wills it" is the sign of One who suffered in man's name, and yet One whose suffering had infinite value because He was God as well as man.

One can dimly guess the psychological horror of the progressive stages of fear, anxiety, and sorrow which prostrated Him before even a single blow had been struck. It has been said that soldiers fear death much more before the zero hour of attack than in the heat of battle. His mental sufferings were quite different from the sufferings of a mere man, because in addition to having human intelligence, He also had a divine intelligence. Furthermore, He had a physical organism which was as perfect as any human organism could be; therefore it was much more sensitive to pain than our human nature, which has been calloused by crude emotions and evil experiences. The mind of man loads itself with what has happened and what will happen.

Could the Lord have so prayed if He had not felt two wills struggling within Him and it was as yet unknown which of them would conquer? Jesus thought perhaps the Father could do something where He had failed. Surely the Master never wanted to beg God to change His lot more than in this terrible hour. Yet not his prayer's conclusion: "Not what I will but what You will." Prayer is not primarily asking God to do special things for us; prayer is never expecting God to alter His plans to suit our whim; prayer at its deepest must always be the soul's endeavor to open the way for God to do His divine will. We do not try by prayer to "move the arm that moves the world," but rather so to enter into spiritual fellowship with God's purpose, that the arm that moves the world can move us.

He died for the first time beneath the olive trees of Gethsemane, without any opiate. In this hour especially, prayer meant for Him sacrifice. In prayer He sacrificed His own will.

In Gethsemane He was tempted to imperiously require God to exempt Him from the cross. Why must He, the well-beloved Son of God, endure that shame? The agony of that final dealing with His old temptation brings blood to His brow, that caused Him to suffer such torture as to produce an extrusion of blood from every pore, before He conquered it at last.

When we consider the way we resent the necessity of suffering, even when it comes as the consequence of our own sin, or as part of the ordinary course of human life, when we think further of our unwillingness to endure the suffering that comes from avoidable sacrifice for others, we can understand a little the Master's struggle. But before His victory over it, before His full acceptance of His work of saviorhood with all its consequences, we must stand in inexpressible wonder.

In that hour of anguish Christ met and overcame all the horrors that Satan, "the prince of this world," could inflict. The frightful struggle incident to the temptations immediately following the Lord's baptism was surpassed and overshadowed by this supreme contest with the powers of evil. In some manner, actual and terribly real, though to man incomprehensible, the Savior took upon Himself the burden of the sins of mankind from Adam to the end of the world.

SECOND VOICE: He continued to pray for a long time. He was afraid; yes, He must also know fear. The smell of blood made Him shudder; He felt his body shrink from the physical torture that lay before him. One part of His being shrank from his terrible destiny.

DISCIPLES: [*Are hearing His broken ejaculations.*]

JESUS: <u>Father! (he pleaded) Anything is possible for you! Take this cup away from me!</u> (My Father, if it is possible, let this cup be spared me!—If you be willing, remove.)
<u>The spirit truly is ready, but the flesh is weak.</u>

FIRST VOICE: He said this not only about our flesh, but about His own as well. He had become human. He lived and was not a ghost so He was afraid of suffering and death. He took upon Himself the disgrace common to all humanity—death. Like any other "trembling creature," He, the Uncreated, suffered. Otherwise the cross has no meaning.

The disciples knew what they were doing when in announcing the glory of the resurrection, they also announced the "disgrace" of the agony. Much would the prince of earth give to take away the crown of the Lord. In the agony Jesus was brought face to face with all the powers of hell, with the horror of eternal death, with eternal annihilation *for Himself.* Otherwise His sacrifice for us would not have been complete.

Even in the garden of Gethsemane, it was not too late for Him to have saved His life. He could have said to Himself, *I have delivered my message faithfully, and it is no use.* But He did not; He believed so much in His own teachings that it was completely impossible for Him to do anything else but what He did.

He could have escaped and given up preaching. The rulers in Jerusalem would have been glad to be rid of Him on such terms. This was the last great temptation and decisively He dismissed it.

At the beginning of His ministry He had met the temptations peculiar to manhood and to one consecrated to a great mission. At the transfiguration He decided to brave the dangers that lurked in Jerusalem and to give Himself, if need be, for His cause. Now at this third supreme crisis of His life He was face to face with death, clothed in the hideous garb of treachery, hate, greed, injustice, and entrenched graft. In the darkness, lighted only by the stars, without the consoling friendship of His Disciples, who had fallen asleep, overcome by the wearying anxiety of the strenuous days and the night vigils that had preceded, Jesus resisted the natural temptation to seek refuge in flight. He also conquered the deadlier temptation to yield to doubt and despair.

All the sin, all the evil, all the damnation of this world He had to receive it *into Himself* in order to conquer it from the inside and not from the outside, as if to associate Himself in the evil of the world.

The Son had to make His choice between the world and His Father—*as if to cease loving His Father*—and it was this that He feared most, not physical torments, not death, but this. He alone, infinitely loving His Father, the only begotten Son, was to suffer infinitely, forsaken by His Father, "rejected" as it were, "cursed." That is what was meant by descent into hell.

JESUS: [*Cries aloud.*] <u>My God, my God, why have You forsaken me?</u>

FIRST VOICE: Jesus in his suffering death endured every injustice. It is an affliction, a deep and unconquerable affliction, when justice is destroyed, when injustice gains the victory and God is silent.

Jesus was wondering why God had cast Him off and allowed Him to mourn because of the oppression of the enemy? This imperceptibly becomes an accusation, and is the reason for this *why?* One's faith, trust in God, threatens to give way under the weight of doubt. For how is one to believe in God, how can one fear, love, and trust God above all things, if in the world iniquity triumphs and the will of God's enemies prove itself the stronger? This affliction was also part of Christ's sufferings. Injustice carries the day and is victorious. Why? Where is the justice of God? One becomes envious when he sees the prosperity of the wicked.

It is so very easy to grow bitter when our *why* remains unanswered by God and to seek solace elsewhere. It is bad when things come to that pass, for that is death. And the real, the great, temptation is when one is powerless to resist and may fall into bitterness and silent hatred, and thus let in death.

We dare not persist in asking "why?" and keep on obstinately demanding the rights that have been taken from us. If we do so, we shall suddenly find that we are measuring God's thought by our thoughts and making our faith depend upon God's doing what we wish.

For our salvation does not depend upon whether we have been given our rights nor upon the doing of our will; but it is lost and forfeit if the injustice which weighs upon us gains the upper hand and determines our thoughts and actions.

God's guidance! That is what we need if the tribulation through which we must pass is to become the temptation which will work our ruin, but the trial which will prove that we are right.

Jesus prayed until He could put aside the thought of injustice and accept the will of His Father. Here is the guidance we need. There we find no bitterness toward and no contempt of the ungodly nation, the "deceitful and unjust men" who cause the injustice. Its power is broken for He commits Himself to He that judges righteously. And even the evildoers are encompassed by a forgiving love which "beareth all things and endureth all things and which therefore hopeth all things and attaineth all things."

Our accusing *why?* is silenced: because we recognize we have no right to ask for anything, but that we are ourselves dependent upon grace and forgiveness. Then the roots of the bitterness which seeks to poison us are cut off as it must wither and die. The forgiving love of Jesus Christ bestows the courage of faith. Where faith wakens and comes to life the injustice which is done us loses its power to tempt us and cannot have dominion over us.

Other martyrs could endure torture and death with serenity, why then did Christ act otherwise? If it is true that the wages of sin is death, then death—at least the death that is our lot—must be as unnatural to mankind as sin. In death we see the breath of God's anger, the judgment of the Holy God who turns His face from the sinner. And so the pure and sinless One suffered as only the sinner suffers, because the sin of mankind was laid upon Him, because God did not intervene to shield His Son. His death was to be transformed into the atonement for the sins of the world. Jesus' trembling and dread can only be explained by the unique peculiarity of His person, to whom the anguish and desolation which the sinner rightly suffers was fundamentally alien and abhorrent.

And so, when in death He felt Himself deserted by God, His trembling was far greater than that of the man who lives without God. From the trembling in Gethsemane and the fear on the cross there shines a majesty of moral purity and deepest personal communion with God such as no man has ever possessed.

Other men and martyrs, in the hour of death, have felt the presence of God in a way they had never hitherto experienced. Jesus, on the contrary, tasted to the full the bitterness of being forsaken by God. His death was not made easy; it was part of His mission to drain the cup to the dregs.

A peculiar note of hesitancy appears in the thought of the Passion. At one time death seems an absolute necessity; then again—for example, in Gethsemane—Jesus recognizes once more the possibility that the Passion may still be spared him. The idea of the Passion subsisted without respect to earthly success or failure. The hesitancy had its ground in the divine will itself. By a messianic program established once and for all the divine omnipotence behind it is in no wise bound! It knows no determination at all.

The Affliction also of the last times had its place indeed in the divinely ordained course of the messianic drama. But yet it lay in God's unrestricted omnipotence that he might eliminate it and permit the Kingdom to dawn without this season of trial. We perceive from the Lord's Prayer that there is no absolute necessity for this Affliction, but that it is only relatively determined in God's mighty will. Through conflict and suffering men are able to wrest themselves free from this power to become instruments of the divine will in the Kingdom of God.

Why did Jesus pray in this way? It was not because He was not brave, but because He was so human. Now in this greater crisis, with the cross so near, he instinctively sought relief and strength in prayer.

His humanity was so real that He loved life, and now that He was weary with days of strife and discussion with adversaries, and had far into the night undergone the strain of uttering parting and loving words to His Disciples, the fate before Him seemed to Him in His weariness to be harder than he could bear. He was to be cut off in His prime with his work undone.

Perhaps even He was tempted to think that He was a failure—that He had lived in vain. How He loved his Jewish brethren! How He longed to open their eyes so that they might see God and life as they really are—might break away from traditional rules and hopes of revenge and material empire as the highest good God had for men, and enter upon their real spiritual inheritance of union with God in life and of service for the salvation of the world! He had tried to do this, but, instead of letting Him lead them, their hearts were filled with hatred of Him and at that very moment they were plotting His death. How He longed to help all men to live the satisfying life with God that He had lived! But between Him and the world stood His Jewish brethren.

His tender love was baffled; His heart, sensitive to hate beyond our comprehension, was tortured by the malignity of His enemies.

Jesus, prostrate on the ground in Gethsemane, sought strength to go forward and endure. What was predominant in His mind was not physical pain, but moral evil or sin. There was indeed that natural fear of death which He would have had because of His human nature, but it was no such vulgar fear that dominated His agony. It was something far more deadly than death. It was the burden of the mystery of the world's sin which lay on His heart. He had the infinite intellect of God which knows all things and sees the past and the future as present.

Poor humans become so used to sin that they do not realize its horror. The innocent understand the horror of sin much better than the sinful. The one thing from which man never learns anything by experience is sinning. A sinner becomes infected with sin. It becomes so much a part of him that he may even think himself virtuous, as the feverish think themselves well. It is only the virtuous, who stand outside the current of sin, who can look upon evil as a doctor looks upon disease, who understand the full horror of evil.

What Jesus contemplated in this agony was the fact that the world was about to spurn His father by rejecting Him, his Divine Son. What is evil but the exaltation of self-will against the loving will of God, the desire to be god unto oneself, to accuse His wisdom as foolishness and His love as want of tenderness?

He shrank not from the hard bed of the cross, but from the world's share in making it. He wanted the world to be saved from committing the blackest deed of sin ever perpetrated by the sons of men—the killing of Supreme Goodness, Truth, and Love. Around His head seemed to beat the very storms of iniquity. Here was the whole history of the world summed up in one cameo: the conflict of God's will and man's will.

It is beyond human power to realize how God felt the opposition of human wills. What is sin for the soul but a separate principle of wisdom and source of happiness working out its own ends, as if there were no God? Antichrist is nothing else but the full, unhindered growth of self-will.

This was the moment when Jesus, in obedience to His Father's will, took upon Himself the iniquities of all the world and became the sin-bearer. He felt all the agony and torture of those who deny guilt, or sin with impunity and do no penance. It was the prelude of the dreadful desertion which He had to endure and would pay to His Father's justice, the debt which was due from us: to be treated as a sinner. He was smitten as a sinner while there was no sin in Him—it was this which caused the agony, the greatest the world has even known.

As sufferers look to the past and the future, so the Redeemer looked to the past and to all the sins that had ever been committed; He looked also to the future, to every sin that would be committed until the crack of doom. It was every open act of evil and every hidden thought of shame. The sin of Adam was there, when as the head of humanity He lost for all men the heritage of God's grace. All sins were there: Sin! Sin! Sin!

Evil desires lay upon His heart, as if He himself had given them birth. Lies and schisms rested on His mind, as if He Himself had conceived them. Blasphemies seemed to be on His lips, as if He had spoken them. From the north, south, east, and west, the foul miasma of the world's sins rushed upon Him like a flood; Samsonlike, He reached up and pulled the whole guilt of the world upon Himself as if He were guilty, paying for the debt in our name, so that we might once more have access to the Father. He was, so to speak, mentally preparing Himself for the great sacrifice, laying upon His sinless soul the sins of a guilty world. To most men, the burden of sin is as natural as the clothes they wear, but to Him the touch of that which men take so easily was the veriest agony.

In Gethsemane, He pledged the last full payment of his loyalty. Here was the perception of the absolute devotion of his *will* to his cause. Underlying the entire composition of his life was this master theme of loyalty. He is always calling His disciples to a dangerous campaign. He represents a cause to which he is utterly loyal, and his note is that of a great leader. The "cup" was rather the sense of failure and apprehension for his cause.

JESUS: [Returns and finds the Disciples sleeping. He speaks to PETER.] He prayed so long that the Disciples, watchful at first, fell asleep. Simon, are you asleep? Had you not strength to watch one hour? Watch and pray, lest you enter into temptation. (What, could you not watch with me one hour? Watch and pray, that you enter not into temptation.—Could not you watch one hour?—Could you not then watch one hour with me?—Could you not watch with me one brief hour?—How can you be sleeping?) The spirit indeed is eager, but the flesh is weak. (Simon, are you asleep? Weren't you able to watch for one hour? You must all watch, and pray that you may not be subjected to trial! One's spirit is eager, but human nature is weak.)

SECOND VOICE: As he prayed, His anguish deepened and became unbearable. He stood. He was close to a stupor of fright at the visions He had seen and He came back to the three, perhaps to seek human solace. His agitation was pronounced. He had a sense of being tracked down, like one who hears the voices of pursuers; He felt like a hunted beast when the hounds are close at hand. Weak and helpless, a poor mortal in sore distress, He turned back to His dear companions for solace. Will not they open their arms to receive Him? Will not His friends help Him in His affliction?

The disappointments of a lifetime are summed up in these few words. The men who lie there are the most devoted among His followers, the ones to whom He has poured out His whole heart for a year and more. Now, the first time their friend and master craves aid from His fellow men and does not lean for support on God alone, when Jesus has been turning over in His mind the enigma of His relation to God—this is the moment when their senses are dulled by wine and by the darkness. They lie there asleep!

It is possible that fresh doubts assail the Prophet, perhaps He has chosen the wrong path. Not one of them knew that their friend was yearning for their help. They left Him to suffer anguish and terror alone. Perhaps from first to last it had been an illusion? Was He really the Messiah, the Son of God? If that and nothing more were the fruit of His gospel, was such a mission worth dying for?

In between the sins of the past which He pulled upon His soul as if they were His own, and the sins of the future which made Him wonder about the usefulness of His death was the horror of the present. Thus in the little grove was the incongruous sound of the Son of Man beseeching mercy and, mingled with it, the sleep-borne noises of healthy men whose faculties had been short-circuited by fatigue.

JESUS: <u>After a while Jesus arose, went to them, aroused them, gently chided them for their inability to watch with Him for an hour, and then went back to His prayer. He was very gentle with them. Jesus' word was one of pity, not of condemnation.</u>

He went to warn and remind them that in this dreadful night they should keep their minds clear by prayer.

[**DISCIPLES:** *Arise, sigh a little, fall back.*]

SECOND VOICE: There the Disciples, in the affair of the garden, were not witnesses of the glory of their friend in a blinding and transfiguring light as in the transfiguration. They were silent and stunned observers—if they saw anything at all—of the desperation of their friend in the half-light of shadows cast by the thick foliage of olive trees under the paschal moon.

[<u>JESUS goes back and prays.</u>]

FIRST VOICE: The spirit indeed is eager, but the flesh is weak.

144

Here He had to overcome the weakness of the flesh—the natural will had to be subdued by His higher will.

Consider then the altitude and solitude of the Master's spirit. The situation in Gethsemane is typical of His whole life; the world, outside, alien and hostile; a few of His Disciples at the garden gate, sympathetic but dull of understanding; Peter, James, and John closer to the Master and comprehending more His purpose and His struggle; but far beyond them all, under the trees, Jesus himself fights out His battle alone with God! He longed for the sympathetic companionship of some human friend who really could enter into His proudest purposes and share His spiritual experiences.

Review in your thoughts now the burdens of the Master: the discouraging handicaps of the Jewish field in which He worked, the inadequacy of the men who were His instruments, the calumny and hostility with which his saviorhood was greeted, the imminent certainty of His own crucifixion and the persecution of His friends, and finally the loneliness of His own soul.

JESUS: [Prays "with strong crying." This time He kneels, and His forehead touches the rock and, as He prays, He rocks back and forth as though in deep physical pain.] O my Father, if this cup may not pass away from me, except I drink it, your will be done.

SECOND VOICE: Aroused from slumber the three apostles saw Jesus again retire, and heard Him pleading in agony. Jesus went back to pray, now even further into the realm of agony than before.

FIRST VOICE: This, He knew, was the hard road to His Father. There was no other, easier route.

[**JESUS** returns again and finds them sleeping, for their eyes were very heavy.]

SECOND VOICE: Again, He was thrown back upon His friends—for insensible as they were, they were there, He could shake them, touch their hair. Thus, the Son of Man became a pendulum swinging between man's torpor and God's absence—from the absent Father to the sleeping friend.

[**DISCIPLES** *are embarrassed or ashamed and do not know how to answer Him.*]

145

SECOND VOICE: The three had fallen asleep again almost before he had returned to the rock. They simply could not keep their eyes open.

JESUS: [Returns again to pray.] <u>O Father, if this cup may not pass away from me, except I drink it, Your will be done.</u>

SECOND VOICE: A third time He went to His lonely vigil and individual struggle. [*An* ANGEL *appears to Him from heaven, strengthening Him.*]

SECOND VOICE: Not even the presence of this super-earthly visitor could dispel the awful anguish of His soul.

[<u>JESUS is sweating as if great drops of blood were falling down to the ground. He withdraws a damp hand from His forehead.</u>]

SECOND VOICE: And being in an agony He prayed more earnestly: and His sweat was as great drops of blood falling down to the ground. He could find no rest anywhere. "Like running blood was His sweat." The salt sweat, gleaming on his face and forehead, began to change color. It reddened and deepened in hue until, in His agony, He knew that it was blood. It occurs when fear is piled upon fear, when an agony of suffering is laid upon a older suffering until the highly sensitized person can no longer sustain the pain. The little capillaries burst when they come in contact with the sweat glands. The blood is exuded with the perspiration.

For at this moment His own will was to escape from the horror before Him.

Whence came this blood? The supplication stopped on His lips; He listened. At certain hours of life, in the silence of the night, every man has experienced the indifference of matter which is blind and deaf. This matter crushed Christ; in His flesh He felt the horror of an infinite absence. The Creator had withdrawn, and creation was but the bottom of an empty sea; the dead stars were scattered in space.

No wonder, then, with the accumulated guilt of all the ages clinging to Him as a pestilence, His bodily nature gave way. As a father in agony will pay the debt of a wayward son, He now sensed guilt to such an extent that it forced blood from His body, blood which fell like crimson beads upon the olive roots of Gethsemane. It was not bodily pain that was causing a soul's agony, but full sorrow for rebellion against God that was creating bodily pain. Without a lance, but through the sheer voluntariness of Jesus' suffering, the blood flowed freely.

Sin is in the blood. Since sin is in the blood, it must be poured out. He willed that sinful men should never again shed any blood in war or hate, but would invoke only His precious blood now poured out in redemption. Since all sin needs expiation, modern man, instead of calling on the blood of Christ in pardon, sheds his own brother's blood in the dirty business of war. All this crimsoning of the earth will not be stopped until man in the full consciousness of sin begins to invoke upon himself in peace and pardon the redemptive blood of Christ, the Son of the Living God.

From the terrible conflict in Gethsemane, Christ emerged a victory. The further tragedy of the night, and the cruel inflictions that awaited Him on the morrow, to culminate in the frightful tortures of the cross, could not exceed the bitter anguish through which He had successfully passed.

JESUS: If it be not your will that this cup pass from me, then, Father, your will be done.

SECOND VOICE: It was the victory chant after the battle. With the calm peace of the conqueror He could make ready for the end. There were times when the Master needed comfort, times when He had done His best and must face the inevitable. The need of comfort is the need of inward fortification against the crushing circumstances of life. The Master was fortified; even from Gethsemane He came victorious.

We know that Jesus vanquished the "Agony" and when it was done.

[**JESUS** returns again the third time.]

SECOND VOICE: He found the Apostles asleep three times. Men who were worried about the struggle against the powers of darkness could not sleep—but these men slept.

By this time communion with God had accomplished its work. Through prayer He had been refreshed; He had regained strength and courage. This time He did not disturb them. The high tide of His revolt had subsided; the courage which had never deserted Him throughout the three years cleared His soul, steadied His muscles. The fatigued followers were allowed to sleep on until the last moment. Their sympathy was needed no longer; while His friends slept, His enemies plotted.

147

JESUS: <u>Sleep on now and [take your] rest! It is enough.</u> (Are you still sleeping and taking your rest? Enough of this! Sleep and take your rest hereafter.)

SECOND VOICE: He made excuses for his Disciples even when they would not watch with Him.

Scene 2

THE PALACE OF THE HIGH PRIEST

SECOND VOICE: We must now go back in thought to the palace of the high priest. When Judas withdrew from the house of John Mark, after having partaken of the Passover, he went apparently to a place appointed; it was either the temple or the high priest's palace. There he was detained until midnight or later.

The priests had laid their plans cleverly to take advantage of the offer of Judas. They accomplished the death of Jesus by legal means. Their sin was not that they went beyond the law, but that they failed to appreciate and reverence the greatest, purest, and best person ever born, and allowed their devotion to their ecclesiastical organization and its traditions to goad them on to a judicial murder.

Under the Roman government the Sanhedrin, or Jewish council, had jurisdiction over the temple and all religious matters throughout Judea and Galilee. For the purpose of keeping order in the temple, they had a temple guard composed of Levites. They were a kind of temple police, and they were under the control and direction of the Sanhedrin. This police force was under the command of officers called "captains." It was this temple police who were employed to arrest Christ. While the Sanhedrin, with the high priest at its head, had the right to make an arrest by means of this police, they had no right to capital punishment. That power the Romans had taken away from them. If then, they would have Jesus legally put to death, they must arrest Him and find against Him some charge that the Roman governor could regard as a capital offense and convince the governor of its truth. They now proceeded to arrest Jesus.

In order to carry out their plans the priests waited until after midnight, and then, at a time when all the populace and the pilgrims with whom Jesus was so popular were sleeping, scattered in many homes and camps, they sent a detachment of this temple police force, commanded by a captain and accompanied by one or more priests, to arrest Jesus. The force probably was not very large, though a few stragglers

148

from the streets may have followed. It seemed like a "multitude" or a crowd.

The Jewish rulers assembled a body of temple guardsmen or police and obtained a band of Roman soldiers under command of a tribune. This company of men and officers, representing a combination of ecclesiastical and military authority, set forth in the night with Judas at their head, intent on the arrest of Jesus. They were equipped with lanterns, torches, and weapons.

These Roman "legions" or "cohorts" were necessary to set up Christ, the King of Heaven, against Caesar, the King of earth.

This was a strange party to be leaving the city. No one had ever seen Pharisees marching with Roman legionnaires. And it is beyond dispute that the legionnaires had never marched with Sadducean elders. Each of these three groups had reason to distrust the other two. And all three were being led by Judas Iscariot, one of the chosen Disciples of the blasphemer.

JUDAS: The one I kiss, that is He. Arrest Him and lead Him away, carefully.

[**RAIDERS' LEADERS** *nod.*]

SECOND VOICE: It was a good idea and it simplified matters. They need not be troubled with running apostles. All they had to do was let Judas lead everyone to the man whom he would kiss.

Scene 3

THE GARDEN (RETURN)

SECOND VOICE: And while He yet spoke, lo, Judas, one of the twelve, came, and with him a great multitude with swords and staves, from the chief priests and elders of the people.

Jesus' lone vigil had not continued long before the torches of the rabble could be seen across the Kidron Valley and the sound of their footsteps could be heard in the still night. From His vantage point on the side of the hill He could mark the progress of their torches across the brook and up the path. Through the foliage, He could see the many torches and lanterns. The clang of their arms rang jarringly through the trees; rough exclamations smote the evening air like profanity in a temple. He could hear the clank of metal shields and the murmur of many voices. There was no use of further watching.

149

Now He needed no one but Himself. He remained motionless, His face no longer against the earth, nor bent over these sleeping men. He heard their sighs, their snoring, and beyond, the confused sound of steps, of voices . . . and finally:

JESUS: [In the garden, JESUS gets to His feet. His face is again severe in dignity. He walks back to the three apostles and at once they sit up. To the three:] The hour has come; behold, the Son of man is betrayed into the hands of sinners. (The time is up! See, the Son of Man is betrayed into the hands of wicked men.—as I speak, the time draws near when the Son of Man is to be betrayed into the hands of sinners.—The hour has struck, look, the Son of Man is being betrayed into the hands of sinful men.)

[DISCIPLES *look up at him dumbfounded.*]

JESUS: Arise, let us be going. Behold, the betrayer is near.

[DISCIPLES *rub their eyes like bewildered children roused suddenly in the deep of the night.*]

SECOND VOICE: While Jesus was still talking in Gethsemane with His Disciples, torches and lights appeared. In their gleam could be seen weapons and armed men. They formed a detachment from the Second Italian Cohort, which Pilate as usual had brought up from Caesarea to garrison Jerusalem during the Passover, and were accompanied by the regular temple police.

[JESUS returns to where the eight DISCIPLES were left.]

SECOND VOICE: Hastening, they rejoined the other Disciples and awakened them. The other men were so intent on what they were hearing (talk of their fellow Disciples) that Jesus and the three were almost in their midst before they saw Him.

[JESUS *walks with a firm and vigorous step. The dancing light of a lantern leaps back and forth amid the trees, stopping every now and then like a discarnate spirit searching the darkness. As it leaps again, the noise of many voices hums about it.*]

[DISCIPLES *look at each other anxiously in the darkness.*]

JESUS: Let us be going, the hand of him that betrays me is near.

150

(Rise! Let us go. Look, my betrayer is close at hand.—Rise, let us be going: he is at hand that does betray me.—Get up, let us be going! Look, here comes my betrayer!—Rise up, let us go on our way; already, he that is to betray me is close at hand.)

[Now comes a clamor, and the clash of weapons. The hiding place has been discovered. A **BAND OF MEN,** *carrying lanterns and torches, presses into the garden.*]

SECOND VOICE: Their leader was the captain of the temple guard. Not being able, at this season of festival, to withdraw many of his own company from the temple, he had sharked up a posse consisting mainly of the high priest's servitors, and had armed them with chance-found swords and staves and cudgels.

[**JESUS,** standing with the Eleven, calmly awaits the traitor's coming.]

SECOND VOICE: Then all pressed about Him and He was lost in their midst, for the tribune who came out this night with the attendants of the high priest and some soldiers of the cohort, carrying torches, saw in the light of the flames naught but a quiet little group of Jews, and among them there was none who seemed to stand out or to dominate. The Author of life was one of these bearded Nazarenes, undistinguishable from the others, since it was necessary for Judas to point Him out.

We must not hastily blame the Jewish people for what ensued; a great many of them were really on His side, if they could have been fairly counted. It was the dominant crowd, the Rome-appointed high priest and his agents who controlled Jerusalem, who now went into action.

And immediately, while he yet spoke, comes Judas, *one of the twelve* . . . and with him a great multitude with swords and staves, from the chief priests and the scribes and the elders.

The hour He had ardently yearned for was now at hand. In the distance was the regular tramp of Roman soldiers, the uneven and hurried treading of the mob and the temple authorities with a traitor in the front.

He who had freed Lazarus from the bonds of death now submitted Himself to death.

[**JESUS** begins walking steadily toward the interlopers, as if to acknowledge the drunken curtseyings of the lantern. For ten paces He walks alone.]

151

[*The* **DISCIPLES** *stand drawn close together by the sense of sudden peril.*]

SECOND VOICE: Jesus, therefore knowing all things that should come upon Him, went forth to meet them. So Jesus, knowing well what was to befall Him, went forth to meet them. So Jesus, knowing well what was to befall Him, went out to meet them. In order to save the only people in the world who could carry on His work, He acted in such a way that the Disciples should not be seized together with Him.

JESUS: [*Steps forward to meet them. With overpowering majesty He demands slowly and distinctly. The white-robed* JESUS *stands there in a little clearing, His face tired and strained, as the torchlights fall on Him.*] Whom seek you?

FIRST VOICE: Adam hid from God in the Garden of Eden; God now searched out the sons of Adam in the Garden of Gethsemane. In the full consciousness of all the Old Testament prophecies concerning Himself as the Lamb of God and of His self-willed offering for sin, He went forth in self-surrender.
Addressing with overpowering majesty the multitude which had gathered armed with swords and stones, He challenged them to name the One they sought.

PRIESTS: [*Startled, awed, they can only mumble His name.*] Jesus of Nazareth.

[**ROMAN SOLDIERS** *now join in the shouted reply.*]

JESUS: [With calm face, says the quiet words.] I am he.

SECOND VOICE: Judas—the traitor—was standing by them, for he had carried out his wicked promise and was acting as guide.

FIRST VOICE: It was evident that even under the full moon they did not recognize Him. Strangely enough, those who are bent on evil cannot recognize Divinity even when it stands before them. The Light can shine in darkness, but the darkness does not comprehend it. It takes more than lanterns and a full moon to perceive the Light of the World. Unbelieving minds have been blinded by the god this world worships.

[**PRIESTS** *and crowd fall backward.*]

SECOND VOICE: A paralyzing awe came over all of them, and they fell backward on the ground. The armed band hesitated. Instead of advancing to take Him, the crowd pressed backward, and many of them fell to the ground in fright. The simple dignity and gentle yet compelling force of Christ's presence proved more potent than strong arms and weapons of violence.

There was confusion again and it was obvious that the guards from the temple had heard stories of His miracles and they were afraid.

His coming forward perfectly calmly and trustingly to meet them caused them great fear. He was like Daniel in the lion's den. Fear He showed not. *Now what tricks is he up to?* they probably thought.

Judas had given them instructions how Jesus should be "taken" after the signal of the kiss: "Take him and lead him away safely." This means "beware of Him, for even unarmed, taken prisoner and bound, He is to be feared." He was believed to be a mighty and terrible sorcerer, and was to be convicted as a sorcerer, a magician. It seems as if all those who approached Him felt to a greater or lesser extent the miraculous power that issued from Him. The people did not really know whether this "power" was good or evil, from God or from the devil. And naturally this increased the awe.

Judas better than anybody knew the miraculous power possessed by his Master, and must have been frightened of it this night as never before.

The men fell back; the superstitious soldiers had heard that Jesus was a wonder worker; they feared that His arrest might turn out to be dangerous business. They had expected angry denunciation, perhaps resistance; these they understood and could cope with. But such calm, such dignity were beyond the boundaries of their experience. Involuntarily they gave way and, rough veterans as they were, some of them "fell to the ground." It was a tribute, silent but magnificent.

FIRST VOICE: So now the Godhead, dwelling within that human body, was about to be put to death, flashed forth to throw the soldiers and the rabble into a huddled mass. Never is there any humiliation without a hint of glory. He could have walked away free, with the soldiers and His enemies prone upon the ground, but it was the "hour" when Love fettered Himself to unfetter man.

JUDAS: [*Comes to* JESUS—*comes stealthily—goes straightway to Him. Walks into the little open space and looks at* JESUS. *His eyes open with happy surprise and his mouth forms a smile. He opens his arms and hurries to the Messiah. The treasurer throws both arms around* JESUS *and lifts his lips up to the Master's cheek. He does so affectionately.*] Hail, Master. (Master.) [And kisses Him.]

153

[Thereupon, the captain's men hold up their lanterns, to make sure of their prey, and to see what He is like.]

[JESUS looks at JUDAS with compassion—looks the Disciple in the face.]

SECOND VOICE: This idea of the traitor must have come from some supernatural and devilish source. This betrayal by a kiss bewildered even He who expected all. This mouth on His cheek! Until the end this creature astonished Him. He thought He had touched the depths of human baseness, but this kiss. . . .

He had won a victory over His own spirit; the strain of anxiety and fear had won a victory over theirs; and as He finally shook them awake, the betrayer pushed his way toward Him, through the darkness, and kissed Him. In default of the alert devotion of true friends, the lips of treachery simulated love, and gave Him over to His enemies.

As a preconcerted sign of identification the recreant Iscariot, with treacherous duplicity, came up with a hypocritical show of affection. He profaned the Lord's sacred face with a kiss.

When wickedness would destroy virtue and when man would destroy and crucify the Son of God, there is felt a necessity to preface the evil deed by some mark of affection. He profaned the Lord's sacred face with a kiss.

When wickedness would destroy virtue and when man would destroy, Judas would compliment and deny Divinity with the same lips.

JESUS: [Looks at JUDAS with compassion—looks the Disciple in the face.] Friend, wherefore are you come?

[The SOLDIERS surround Him.]

JESUS: Judas, betray you the Son of Man with a kiss?

SECOND VOICE: Only one word came back in answer to the kiss: "Friend." When Judas betrayed Him, He was concerned with Judas's pitiable failure—turned into an apostate when he might have been an apostle—rather than with the bitter wrong done to him.

[Then comes that posse and lays hands on JESUS, and takes him.]

SECOND VOICE: And he that betrayed Him having given them a token, saying, "Whoever I shall kiss, that same is He; take Him, and lead Him away safely."

154

DISCIPLES: Lord, shall we smite with the sword?

SECOND VOICE: The apostles were ready to fight and die for their beloved Master. Peter did not wait for a reply.
[*One of the apostles in the rear passes one of the old swords up to* PETER. *He unsheathes it and, without a word, steps in front of* JESUS *and swings it diagonally upward and strikes a servant of the* HIGH PRIEST, *and smites off his ear. He aims for the neck of the* SERVANT *of the* HIGH PRIEST, *who sees the blow coming and inclines his head away from it. An ear is sheared off and the* CHILARCH, *expecting a melee, orders his men to draw their swords.* PETER steps out of the circle and follows JESUS.]

THE CAPTAIN: Draw your swords. [*At first there is a tumult.*]

SECOND VOICE: Pitifully inadequate as two swords would appear to resist the Roman legionnaires, the Disciples had no doubt they would possess miraculous powers. Convinced that the miracle would yet take place, Peter drew his sword and cut off the right ear of a slave of the high priest—the name of that slave was Malchus.
Peter's mind was like a vortex of spinning devils. He was choking with terror. In half a dozen stumbling strides he accosted the man carrying the lantern. The fear that palsied Peter's mind gave the strength of desperation to his arm. Blindly he struck out. In his fist was gripped the hilt of a broad sword. The man with the lantern staggered as a heavy blow split his ear.
On entering the garden, the Savior had told Peter, James, and John "to watch and pray." Peter now decided to substitute action for prayer. Peter's zeal was mistaken in the choice of means.

[**MALCHUS** *staggers as a heavy blow splits his ear. The servant now feels the side of his face and screams.*]

JESUS: [*Asks liberty of His captors by the simple request. Addresses the* DISCIPLES.] Suffer you thus far.

SECOND VOICE: This means "Hold now; thus far you have gone in resistance, but let it be no further; no more of this."

[**JESUS** is shocked. He first touches the ear of the wounded man and restores it. He steps forward and heals the injured man by a touch. JESUS grabs him tightly with one hand and touches the side of his face with the other, picks up the severed ear and restores it.]

155

SECOND VOICE: The man, Malchus, was healed at once, but the healing went unnoticed in any public sense.

FIRST VOICE: When the battle closed in between Jesus and the Jewish and Roman authorities, He was not passive. He was entirely active and assumed moral command in every situation. He not only healed Malchus but He pronounced the doom of those who came to arrest Him with swords. They came to arrest Him and get sentence against Him, and the first thing they confronted was the fact that they heard the sentence of doom passed upon themselves. He then assumed further moral command by stooping down, picking up the severed ear of his enemy and restoring it. In the moment of passing under their power He arises in sublimity, assumes moral command and stands, not as a helpless prisoner, but as a giver of bounty.

His power was so great that there lay in it a boundless temptation to forget that the meaning of life is service. But all Jesus' power, always and without exception, was put at the service of divine love, and even on the last night He would not allow that a man should be injured because of Him.

JESUS: [Speaks sternly.] Put up again your sword into its place, for all they that take the sword shall perish with the sword. The cup which my Father has given me, shall I not drink it?

FIRST VOICE: This is a reminiscence of the Sermon on the Mount: "resist not evil." To Peter's surprise and despair, Jesus reprimanded him.

At the instant when the torches first threw their red light on the rugged faces of those who bore them, when swords and helmets reflected the gleam, when the power of the State confronted Him in the persons of its armed instruments, the anguished and hunted man recovered His equanimity; He regained the poise befitting Him in face of worldly authority; and the conviction of being the Chosen One of God, reviving, restored to Him the serenity which had been absent during these night hours in the garden of Gethsemane. Over and done with, at last, was the torment of waiting. The blow had fallen. In this solemn moment, His first thought was to be faithful to His own teaching.

Furthermore, those who arbitrarily and presumptuously resorted to violence, Jesus told Peter, would feel that violence itself. Revenge brings its own punishment. Bodies can be conquered with unsheathed swords but those same swords often turn against those who wield them.

That was only a human lesson verified by history.

Here in contrast were set the sword and the cup; the sword wins

156

by slaying, the cup by submission. Not the impatience of the violent, but the patience of saints was to be His way of winning souls. He spoke of the cup not as coming from Judas, nor from the Sanhedrin, nor from the Jews, nor from Pilate or Herod, but from His own Heavenly Father. It was a cup which contained the Father's will that, in love for man, He should offer his life that they might be restored again to Divine sonship. Nor did He say that a sentence was laid upon Him to undergo His passion, but rather that He Himself out of love could not do otherwise.

[**PETER** *does as he is told.*]

SECOND VOICE: Peter threw away the sword in the scabbard, sticky with the blood of Malchus, into the shadow of the bushes in the darkness.

JESUS: [<u>Turning to the circle, He speaks to his foes rather than to His friends, and raises his voice to deliver an essentially combative message.</u>] <u>Think you that I cannot now pray to my Father, and He shall presently give me more than twelve legions of angels? But how then shall the Scriptures be fulfilled, that this is the way it must be.</u>

SECOND VOICE: He pointed out the needlessness of armed resistance, and emphasized the fact that He was submitting voluntarily and in accordance with foreseen and predicted developments. Peter had yet to learn that He who seemed so weak was truly Divine; that if He wished, He could summon to His aid an army greater than any of the earth.

If there was to be an appeal to force, Peter's little sword would shrink into insignificance compared to the heavenly hosts under the great Commander.

FIRST VOICE: But His refusal to summon the angels was not an involuntary bowing to a fate. It was rather a quiet surrender of some of His own rights; a voluntary abstinence from the use of superior force for the sake of others, a standing unchained with perfect power to go away, and yet submitting for love of mankind—such is sacrifice at white heat.

While speaking of the power at His command, Jesus never lifted a finger to oppose those who had been sent to capture Him.

He turned the other cheek, and where did the blow fall—on the other cheek? No, no—on your heart and mine. Had He struck one blow in return, it would have been the death blow to His own gospel. For

Christ conquers not by the quantity of His muscle, but by the quality of His spirit. But, thank God, He refused their weapons and used His own. And we are at His feet. Thus, through prophecy, the death of Jesus is exalted into something over which man is not only to mourn and tremble, but which he must above all comprehend.

He knew His fate, yet He offered no resistance; and therefore He must have willed it so.

JESUS: [Speaks to the multitudes with a little edge of scorn in the tone.] Are you come out as against a thief with swords and staves to take me? I sat daily with you teaching in the temple, and you laid no hold on me.

SECOND VOICE: But, though surrendering Himself unresistingly, Jesus was not unmindful of His rights; and to the priestly officials, chief priests, captain of the temple guard, and elders of the people who were present, He voiced this interrogative protest against the illegal night seizure.

[**TEMPLE AUTHORITIES** *say nothing. Some look away.*]

JESUS: [Adds, perhaps partly to Himself.] But this is your hour, and the power of darkness.

SECOND VOICE: The words beat on deaf ears. Not a soul understands Him.

FIRST VOICE: Many times He told His enemies and Herod that they could do nothing to Him until His "hour" had come. Now He announced it; it was the hour when evil could turn out the Light of the World. Evil has its hour; God has His day. He submitted to arrest because the hour had come.

In this hour, God gave to evil the power to affect a momentary triumph in which the spiritually blind would think they had gained a victory. So too, in this hour, darkness would have a power that would be powerless at the Resurrection.

JESUS: But let the Scriptures be fulfilled! All this was so ordained, to fulfil what was written by the prophets.

FIRST VOICE: He was alluding to the words in Isaiah about the suffering servant of Jehovah with whom He identified Himself: "When he was oppressed, he humbled himself, and opened not his mouth; like a sheep that is led to the slaughter, . . . He opened not his mouth." Also "Such is His due, that gave Himself up to death, and would be counted among the wrongdoers; bore those many sins, and made intercession for the guilty."

Looking beyond all secondary causes, such as Pilate and Annas, the Romans and the Jews, Jesus saw not enemies to be defeated by a sword, but a cup offered by His Father.

Sin required atonement or reparation. Being man, He could act in man's name; being God, His Redemption for sin would have infinite value.

JESUS: Whom are you seeking?

CROWD: Jesus the Nazarene.

JESUS: [He insists. He brushes aside the APOSTLES and, like a mother, comes forward, swelling Himself up to cover his brood.]
I told you that I am He, if therefore you are seeking me [points behind to the APOSTLES], allow these others to depart.
(It is I! Let them go! If therefore you seek me let these others go their way. If I am the man you are looking for, let these others go free. Therefore, since you are looking for me, let these men go unmolested.) [*Whispers to himself.*] Father, of them which You gave me have I lost none.

FIRST VOICE: Let them go, let them run and save themselves and spread the seed of the Kingdom of God. Here was His innermost wish.

It is possible that had any of the eleven been apprehended with Jesus and made to share the cruel abuse and torturing humiliation of the next few hours, their faith might have failed them. Doubtless, even a greater burden on the Master's heart than His own suffering was the fact that He and His cause were sure to involve his followers in suffering. Jesus had no illusions about the sacrifice His movement was going to cost His friends.

This was His hour, but not the hour of the Apostles. Later on, they would suffer and die in His name, but presently they could not understand Redemption until the Spirit had enlightened them. He would tread the wine press alone. They were not yet in a spiritual condition to die with Him; in a few moments they would all desert Him. Furthermore, they could not suffer for Christ until Jesus had first suffered for them. The whole purpose of His redemptive death, in a certain sense, was to say to all men, "Let these others go free."

In the last year of His public work the forces of opposition took on a form and coherency whose significance was perfectly clear. If He refused to retreat or to compromise, there could be but one end to His career. At every sunset he was conscious that He had walked just one day nearer to His own ordeal.

He knew men, He knew their greed, envy, and hatred and yet He would not waver. He would have courage to go on, never wavering in His purpose and passion. He had come this far—He could not disappoint His Father or the needy, whose spirit is of God.

Self-sacrifice seeks no vengeance. Giving His enemies power to stand, He, as the Good Shepherd, had only one concern, that of His own sheep.

[**The RAIDERS** *begin to take courage. They step forward and, as they crowd around, not yet daring to touch him,* JUDAS *moves away and becomes lost in the crowd.* JESUS *makes no attempt to resist.*]

[*Then all the* **DISCIPLES** *forsake Him and flee.* Then they all left him alone and fled.—*The only sound is of heavy feet running through the olive trees.* The disciples fled in terror. From among the olive-trees comes the crackling of twigs and the rustling of garments, as they flee away in the darkness. *In the light of the torches, the pack throws itself upon the willing prey.*]

SECOND VOICE: As Malchus fell forward, the light went out, and the wild confusion was muffled by the darkness. The only sound was of heavy feet running through the olive trees. The disciples are terrified, and make no attempt to rescue their Master. All of them betray Him.

In the confusion that followed, the disciples made their escape, though Peter put in an appearance in the courtyard of the high priest's house later in the night. John also crept on safely behind the mob, to appear later in the house of the high priest.

The Apostles, hearing the clinking of chains and seeing the glistening swords, forgot all the glory of the Messias, deserted Him, and fled. The eleven Apostles, seeing that resistance was useless, not only on account of disparity of numbers and supply of weapons but chiefly because of Christ's determination to submit, turned and fled.

When the disciples saw that their master was a prisoner and that they could not help Him, they all ran away and hid themselves. They feared, especially after Peter's attack upon one of the guards, that they too might be arrested; so they fled.

He had no need to think of the disciples's safety. Already they had made their swift escape—the last of the deserters—

—first his hometown

—his friend and forerunner

—then his relatives

—then the crowd

—finally the eleven

All who had stood at his side had gone and left him to face his fate alone. He had apologized and acquitted them beforehand, because what was "written," "prophesied," was inevitable. He had said, "The sheep shall be scattered."

FIRST VOICE: The high priest must offer the sacrifice alone.

Jesus Christ was crucified as a failure, and His disciples all ran away from Him. Nevertheless, Jesus Christ did not call Himself defeated. Jesus was a success, though apparently a failure.

He had learned in whatever state He was, to be content therewith. The truly successful man is the one who can enjoy the life of God. So long as you suffer because of crucifixions, destitutions, or persecutions, you can do nothing. You must have zeal. God takes advantage of your despair over failure. If through the power of Jesus you can rise up again, the success will compensate your failure billions of times over.

SECOND VOICE: And there followed Him a certain young man, having a linen cloth cast about his naked body.

[**MARK:** *wears a linen cloth, having come there without even taking time to clothe himself, and follows* JESUS *as He was being led a prisoner toward Jerusalem. The* YOUNG MAN *lay hold of him. The linen cloth comes off and he flees from them naked. The* GUARD *catches hold of the linen garment, and* MARK, *slipping out of this, flees and escapes. He saves himself by slipping out of the hands clutching him and leaving them the cloth, and then running away.*]

SECOND VOICE: The high priest's crew tried to hold everybody they could lay their hands on. They were picking up everybody found near Jesus. Mark was detected by the alert guard. The soldiers spied him trailing along behind the bound Jesus.

Young Mark's interest in the arrest of Jesus and his close approach caused some of the guardsmen or soldiers to seize him, but he broke loose and escaped, leaving the sheet in their hands. He left behind his wrap and escaped from them.

[**The BAND and the CAPTAIN and OFFICERS** of the Jews take JESUS, and bind him. The proper manner taught by the academy of soldiery in Rome was to take the victim by the right wrist, twist his arm behind him so that his knuckles touched between his shoulder blade and, at the same time, jam the heel down on his right instep.

Some of the **TEMPLE GUARDS,** *not wishing to be shamed in the presence of the Gentiles, grab the other arm and put it behind his back and bring out rope and tie his hands. A long noose is placed about his neck. Two* SOLDIERS *grab His arms, twisting them behind Him. Then they tie His hands, loop the rope several times around His body and knot it, leaving a length of rope to lead Him away.*

He was patient with his captors. Now that JESUS *is fettered and so one has been struck dead, the Levites begin to take courage and issue orders.*]

SECOND VOICE: The Romans decided that this emotional scene had gone far enough. They came forward and arrested Jesus. They led him away to Annas first, for he was father-in-law to Caiphas, who was the high priest that same year.

Now Caiphas was he who gave counsel to the Jews that it was expedient that one man should die for the people.

FIRST VOICE: When at last He was delivered into their hands, it was for Him a painful thing that such an experience should mean falling "into the hands of sinners." For He, the pure one, never belonged in such hands. Was He not the green wood, in contrast to all the dry?

Jesus stands over against the world as Redeemer and as Judge. How could He have presented Himself as such to us if there were the slightest burden on His conscience. Only because He knew that He Himself was in no need of a redeemer could He know that He was the Deliverer, come to seek the lost world of men. And as such He saw Himself to be so immune from contamination that in a wonderful way He did not fear even the most degenerate.

No one could change anything in Him, but He was confident that He could transform all men. Jesus was always conscious of His security, and thus He dared to set Himself up as the Judge of all mankind.

Only the solace of a garden could quiet His racing heart. But He did win; and when He was finally in possession of Himself, He could speak with gentleness when His friends faltered, walk with dignity when His enemies menaced, and maintain a silence, majestic and accusing, when insulted.

Jesus was dragged away in the midnight darkness to the palace of His relentless persecutor. Jesus was left alone with his captors, who took

Him down across the Kidron into the sleeping city, to the house of Caiphas, the high priest.

FIRST VOICE: As Isaias foretold, He would be *led* like a lamb to the slaughter. As the new Jeremias, the Man of Sorrows, He was put in chains for His testimony to the truth.

THE CHILIARCH: Shall the prisoner be taken to the temple for trial?

[*Conflicting shouts from the crowd echo through the grove.*]

[**SADDUCEES AND PHARISEES** *consult.*]

SADDUCEES AND PHARISEES: No. Take the prisoner to the home of the high priest.

SECOND VOICE: The priests were pleased that the whole matter had been accomplished with such quiet dispatch. Jesus had muttered no incantation, had conjured no balls of blue fire or brimstone to destroy all of them. This, of course, proved that He was no more a Messiah than they. If He were the Messiah, then He had the power to destroy them. If He did not use the power then He did not have it, and if He did not have it then He was just another faker under arrest.

Time had caught up with Him, they thought. If He had only remained in Galilee with his preachments of love, He could hae been rich someday. But no. He had to storm Jerusalem, and Jerusalem was known to kill real prophets. What chance had a Nazarene magician?

ACT II

THE OUTWARD STRUGGLE
(TRIALS BEFORE THE SANHEDRIN)

Scene 1

ON THE STEPS OF CAIPHAS'S RESIDENCE

[The bound and captive CHRIST is haled before the Jewish rulers.]

[**CAIPHAS** *comes down the steps slowly.*]

SECOND VOICE: Now, with the end in sight, Caiphas had patience. His first interest was not in confronting Jesus, but in getting the reports of his men on how the arrest had been accomplished, what the attitude of the Romans might be, where the disciples of Jesus were, and whether there had been any popular uprising against the will of the Sanhedrin.

The high priest heard the reports. They were all good. The matter had been handled discreetly and the city was not even aware of what had happened. Caiphas was elated. He had struck a good blow for God and for the temple. A sore had festered on the body of Judea and he, Caiphas, had cauterized it.

CAIPHAS: Take him to Annas (Hanan).

SECOND VOICE: This was a diplomatic move. Caiphas could wait. It was proper to permit Annas a first look at the face of the prisoner and to conduct the first examination. Besides, Caiphas knew what his father-in-law would do: he would order the prisoner returned at once to the

164

high priest and the Great Sanhedrin for trial.

SADDUCEES AND PHARISEES *are busy congratulating each other on a good night's work.*]

SECOND VOICE: Caiphas was more deeply interested in the fact that the Sadducees and the Pharisees who had been part of the apprehending party were now friendly, and were busy congratulating each other on a good night's work. Caiphas felt proud that the dissident forces were united. He, Caiphas, had arranged this by nominating the committee which was to accompany the guards to endure that everything was done lawfully.

And who but Caiphas had engineered the trap for the Romans? Who went to Pontius Pilate, almost groveling for assistance in an internal matter which was of no concern to the barbarous Gentiles? Caiphas. And now, when sentence of death was passed upon Jesus, how could Pilate admit that the soldiers of Tiberius Caesar had assisted in the arrest while denying affirmation of the sentence? If he refused to confirm the execution he would tacitly be conceding that he had sent a maniple—two companies—to arrest one innocent man. This would make a juicy subject for one of Herod's secret notes to the emperor.

No, Pilate was trapped and well trapped. However, this was not the immediate matter to occupy Caiphas's attention. At the moment he was most concerned with the need to send out more servants to demand the attendance at once of all members of the Great Sanhedrin at a special convocation; the need to get witnesses from among the Levites in the temple to come to the hearing and to swear that they had heard Jesus, preaching in the Court of the Gentiles, pronounce Himself the Son of man; and the need to arrange for demonstrators at the temple after daylight, so that when Jesus was led to Pilate for confirmation of sentence, all the citizens around him would be unfavorable to his cause.

Scene 2

THE COUNTRY HOUSE OF ANNAS

FIRST VOICE: Jesus had two natures: divine and human. Both were on trial and on totally different charges. Thus was fulfilled the prophecy of Simeon that He was a "sign to be contradicted."

The judges could not agree as to why He should die; they could only agree that He must. The religious judges, Annas and Caiphas, found Him guilty of being too human. Before the one, He was too unworldly; before the other, He was too worldly; before the one, He was too heavenly; before the other, too earthly. Condemned on contradictory charges, He was sentenced to the symbol of contradiction, which is the cross.

The first trial was on the grounds of religion. A formal trial demanded the presence of the Sanhedrin. The aim of these trials was to fix the responsibility for Jesus' death on the entire Jewish nation.

The chief aim of Annas and his fellow conspirators was to relieve themselves, as well as their nation, of public responsibility for Jesus' death, and this aim they nominally realized. Annas appears to have still been the ruling spirit in the Jewish hierarchy and was the one who, inspired by personal spite, planned and carried through the conspiracy which resulted in Jesus' death.

The complaint of the chief priests against the Master was no charge to make against a dreamer: "He stirreth up the people." Napoleon thought of him as a great leader who had a cause, and in the face of overwhelming handicaps made a success of it. He says, "Christ alone has succeeded in so raising the mind of man toward the unseen that it becomes insensible to the barriers of time and space."

SECOND VOICE: When Jesus was led away from Gethsemane he was taken to the house of Annas, which was situated on the eastern slope of the western hill. He continued to be even more influential than the actual high priest. He exerted a potent influence in all the affairs of the hierarchy. In those days it was a much better position to have been in than to be high priest. He enjoyed all the dignity of the office, and all its influence also, since he was able to promote to it those most closely connected with him. And while they acted publicly, he really directed affairs, without either the responsibility or the restraints which the office imposed. He was actually the prominent figure of the day, even though Caiphas was the presiding officer of the Sanhedrin at the moment. He still retained the title by courtesy and he was still the power behind the throne.

Annas was the recognized "boss" of the city and to him Jesus was brought for an informal and highly irregular preliminary examination.

His influence with the Romans he owed to the religious views he professed, to his open partisanship of the foreigner, and to his enormous wealth.

He and his sons controlled the temple market which Jesus four days before had driven from the temple courts. This market was a source of revenue that helped to make Annas and his house rich. Caiphas, who was high priest in this year 30, was a son-in-law of Annas. Annas was a crafty Sadducee, for many years a sort of boss exercising perhaps more real power than when he held the office of supreme priest. We can understand how antithetic in every respect a Messiah, and such a Messiah as Jesus, must have been to Annas.

Perhaps the guards who had arrested Jesus stopped to let Annas know that the reformer was now actually within his power. A thrill of pleasure passed through the heart of Annas on this Gethsemane night. He knew, the wise Hanan, that something new was to happen this night contrary to the prophets and that it was he, Hanna, who had done it.

No, somebody everyday would know what had saved Israel, who and why, and they would all bow down to him and say, "Glory to Hanan, the high priest of God, the greatest of the sons of man! He fulfilled the Law which says that "the blasphemer of the name of God should die; should be stoned by the people."

Did not the scriptures warn of false prophets and that they should be killed? This Hanan would do, he would kill the breaker of the Law, the deceiver, the seducer, rabbi Jeshua. Blessed art thou, Israel! Who is like unto thee, the people protected by God! And who is the most blessed in all Israel? Hanan the wise. Some were afraid because the people might stone them.

They wanted to "kill Him secretly, stab or strangle Him in the dark." But Hanan the wise knew the game he was going to play and he was not afraid. No, he would not stab or strangle or stone the Law Breaker in the dark, but would raise Him up high on the accursed tree, hang Him so that all the people should see the vengeance of the Law. He would hew to the Law in every point and line. But it was not wise yet to let the world know who was responsible. Hanan's name must be kept clear of it all. Pilate would be his cat's-paw. The Gentile dog would be held responsible for crucifying Jesus.

All was ready. Hanan had only to clap his hands for the game to begin, such a game as that in the Roman puppet show, and he, hidden behind the scenes, would pull the strings, whereupon all the puppets from Pilate to Caiphas would begin to dance, and none would know who pulled the strings. To be all knowing, all powerful, and yet unseen was Hanan's delight.

And now He was there.

[Bound and shackled, **JESUS** is conducted inside the residence of Annas.]

[The old man **ANNAS** *waits and studies the young man*]

167

SECOND VOICE: He sat and he looked and wondered, idly, what motivated a young nobody into posing as the Saviour of the world. This man did not appear to be a lunatic. The reports that had been coming in for over a year tended to show the opposite. Jesus of Nazareth was intelligent; he was well versed in the law although no one knew what rabbinical school he had followed; he was tall and as well muscled as a farmer; he was not given to extravagance or indulgence in the grape; he was not betrothed and no scandal adhered to so much as the hem of his garments.

Then why? Why did he have to be a Messiah? For two years or more, this man had increased the tension in Palestine—first in his native Galilee, then in Jerusalem and even in Jericho. His basic tenet had been love, which, in the eyes of the old priest, was not dangerous. But the people had begun to fall away from the temple, first in little groups, then in larger ones.

He would not try this man. Let Caiphas do it.

The law said that not fewer than twenty-three members of the Great Sanhedrin could try a capital case, and the old man was certain that, by this time, his son-in-law had awakened and summoned the judges. Still, it was interesting to inquire why a man would want to pose as the Messiah, since he must have known that sooner or later he would be challenged by the temple. At that, he might have escaped challenge and the charge of blasphemy if he had not kicked the tables of Annas's money-changers and condemned Annas's animal market.

ANNAS: Why do you teach heresy?

[JESUS gave no answer.]

ANNAS: [*To the* GUARDS] Bind him more securely. [*The* GUARDS *tighten the bonds.*] Take him to Caiphas.

[JESUS was led out by the guards.]

SECOND VOICE: And they that had laid hold on Jesus led Him away to Caiphas the high priest, where the scribes and the elders were assembled.

Scene 3

AT THE RESIDENCE (PALACE) OF CAIPHAS

SECOND VOICE: The trial that was now to take place was before the Sanhedrin composed of seventy-one members, including its chief

168

member, who was always the high priest. The Sanhedrin had its own laws, and the most important of these was, as far as Jesus was concerned: "A tribe, a false prophet and a high priest and not judged save by a court of seventy-one." If the Saviour was to be arrested and tried, it would have to be under this law, as a false prophet.

The usual sentence in a criminal case was death. Each sentence of death was passed on, before execution, by the Roman procurator. He usually affirmed it without question. But if he felt so disposed he could hear the case before his own judicial chair. If he confirmed it, the governor often forced the prisoner to undergo the Roman form of execution—crucifixion.

FIRST VOICE: The "old law" ordained that each animal sacrificed for the sins of the people be led before the priest. So Jesus, the representative of the priesthood of the Spirit, was led before Caiphas, the representative of the priesthood of the flesh.

SECOND VOICE: It was thus evident that he and the Sanhedrin had resolved upon the death of Jesus before the trial took place. A night trial of the Sanhedrin was illegal, but in mad desire to do away with Jesus, it was held nevertheless. Though it had no right to proceed to a capital execution, it did retain, however, the power to institute trials.

According to the Talmud the matter here under discussion was how to snare a "Seducer," who should teach the people to follow "other gods" (as understood by the upholders of the Law, in the teaching of the rabbi Jeshua "another god" was He Himself).

They plotted how he should be artfully enticed into a house where two witnesses would be already hidden to see and to hear everything that He would say, how He was to be seated in the middle of the room with the lights of the lamps and candles falling upon His face, in order that the hidden witnesses should be in a position to notice every slight change of expression, and then to induce him to "blaspheme."

In a meeting of the **Sanhedrin** at the palace of Caiphas, the chief priests, scribes, and elders of the people were assembled all eagerly awaiting the result of the expedition led by Judas. It was in the small hours after midnight.

Caiphas was not stupid, but his chief wisdom consisted in obeying Hanan in everything, as Hanan was the wily old fox. He obeyed Him in this matter of Jesus, fully believing in Hanan's wise calculation as to the stunning effects of a sudden blow—believed Him and was not mistaken. (A greater deed was never done in a shorter space of time. Nine hours proved sufficient.) The people had no time to complain before it was all over.

The two sittings of the court were separated from each other by a few hours only instead of by twenty-four, as the Law required. Hanan found a way to get 'round the Law and decided that "he could." They all bowed to the wisdom of Hanan. The first sitting was fixed for three o'clock at night and the second for dawn.

Since the matter was urgent, it would be enough to account this night-sitting as the first day, and morning (when it dawns) as the second, it was decided. For a death sentence was in view. The Sadducees who held sway in the high priestly house and in the Sanhedrin were not content, like the Pharisees, to discuss forever, to talk without acting. One who thinks that, knows them little! They had handed down the reins of power from one generation to another; and their wealth, too, passed on by inheritance. They were monopolists.

If, in general, they were prone to look on indifferently, to remain inert, when the Pharisees were already boiling over with wrath, they made up for this by acting promptly and effectively at critical moments, and thus nipping danger in the bud. Such a moment had now come. Witnesses were without.

[JESUS is brought in bound and shackled. Here is the accused, still unbound. They lead him into their council.

On the walls of this house, near the ceiling, there is a scroll in reddish gold of the ancient script in which the Lord had written on the tablets of Moses in the old time these words: "Listen, Israel, I am thy only God."

The prisoner is brought in and placed on a dais *in the middle of the semicircle between two tall, wax candles in silver sconces level with His face. The tightly knotted ropes around His wrists are untied and leave deep, dark-red marks on the dusky skin. Straight down hang the hands and straight down the folds of the gown.*

His quiet face is calm and simple, exactly as it had been when sitting among them every day He taught the people in the temple. *The eyelids drop and the lips are set tightly.*

SECOND VOICE: In the palace of the high priest, Jesus had been led through gateways and corridors, up broad staircases, and at length into a large room made airless and soundproof by thick hangings. Squatting with their feet under them on the carpets or the low couches in a semicircle "so that they could see each other's faces and judge impartially," the seventy members of the Sanhedrin awaited the prisoner knowing that He had been already taken.

170

[*By the light of the smoking tapers,* **JESUS** sees a semicircle of faces, *the expectant faces of silent men, squatting on cushions. Then, from the middle of these, His gaze singles out one who has been sheltered and propped up by pillows and coverlets, a man of advanced age, with a fleshless and wrinkled countenance, yellow in color and parchmenty in texture like the ancient rolls of the Law He has seen in the temple. From this deathlike mask proceed piping and gurgling sounds, which gradually form themselves into words.* This is ANNAS.]

[*They scrutinize Him.* **Members of the Sanhedrin** are still hurrying inside to the private apartments of the **HIGH PRIEST** *after the prisoner has been led in.*]

SECOND VOICE: The latecomers knew the identity of the prisoner and what the charge was because, of late, the Galilean Messiah had been discussed gravely at the meeting of the supreme council and plans had been advanced concerning the best way of trapping Him. So that, no matter how late their arrival, the members could take their places in the three-tiered semicircle and listen to the proceedings with comprehension.

Even though the deed was abominable, none dared go against Hanan, knowing too well that even one word uttered in the defense of Jesus in the High Court might lead to exclusion from the synagogue.

[*When the Gaililean is brought before them, these priests for whom priestcraft is in large measure a political affair, men of ripe age and wide experience, scrutinize Him more closely than He troubles to scrutinize them. They compare His aspect and demeanor with those of other lawbreakers, but He knows that His case has been prejudiced. Therefore, both parties are aware what the upshot will be, the accusers who are sure of their ground show more emotion than the doomed man.*

The miracle worker, the enemy of the high priest—was this He, this poor wretch?

He is immediately put upon trial. He has been led before the high priests, not for trial, for in their minds he is already condemned, but that they might gain evidence to aid them in forcing Pilate to put Him to death.]

SECOND VOICE: But Peter followed him afar off unto the high priest's palace, and went in, and sat with the servants, to see the end. And Simon Peter followed Jesus, and so did another disciple: that disciple was known to the high priest, and went in with Jesus into the palace of the high priest.

Peter, who had slunk along at a safe distance, had the nerve to work his way into the open courtyard around which the high priest's residence was built. In the chill of early morning, the waiting guards had made a fire out there to keep themselves warm, and Peter edged up to it and warmed himself.

[**CAIPHAS** *claps his hands.*]

SECOND VOICE: Then the owner of the puppet show clapped his hands and the show began. [**JESUS** *stands throughout, roped and hobbled of foot, with guards standing behind him.*]

CAIPHAS: Omit the roll call. Read the charge. [*Motions to the* NASI.]

NASI: [*Stands and publishes it.*] Jesus of Nazareth did on diverse occasions proclaim Himself to be the Messiah, the true Son of God, and in so doing has blasphemed against God and has profaned the temple.

SECOND VOICE: The proper way to have opened the session would have been to take the roll call. This would be followed by a recitation of the charge by the Nasi, who would stand to publish it.

CAIPHAS: How do you plead?
[*Waits for an answer.*]

JESUS: [No reply.]

CAIPHAS: How do you plead?

JESUS: [No reply.]

CAIPHAS: How do you plead?
[*No reply—The steady eyes of the prisoner move from face to face, from row to row, until He has seen them all. In the group, He sees at least two disciples.*
The Sanhedrin sits, with averted eyes, and listens to the proceedings.]

SECOND VOICE: In the group, Jesus saw at least two disciples. Like so many of his highly placed followers, their adherence to his teachings was secret. This was not the hour for them to reveal themselves, just as it was not the hour for Peter and the others.

172

CAIPHAS: [*With a tone of prudent benignity.*] Who are your disciples and how many do you have? Which of them loves you more, Rabbi Jeshua, friend Judas, or friend John? Is it true, Rabbi Jeshua, that you said the Son of man shall be killed and in three days shall rise again? [*Waits for an answer.*]

SECOND VOICE: The judge was not so much concerned with the names of Jesus' followers as with their number; the purpose of this inquiry was to draw from Him an answer suited to their condemnation.

CAIPHAS: What is your doctrine? What do you teach?

SECOND VOICE: Such a preliminary inquiry was utterly unlawful, for the Hebrews' code provided that the accusing witnesses in any cause before the court should define their charge against the accused, and that the latter should be protected from any effort to make him testify against himself.

Since Caiphas had already determined that Jesus should die. he had no intention of learning anything; rather he sought to find some excuse for the planned injustice. The first questions were about Jesus' organization and followers, whom the Sanhedrin feared as a threat to themselves; for earlier the Pharisees had reported: "Look, the whole world has turned aside to follow him."

[*Several* **witnesses** *are called and testify to this, that, and the other.*]

SECOND VOICE: Old Annas, it would seem, though he was accuser and judge rolled into one, wanted to give an impression of impartiality. In the end, however, he lost patience because the accused made no answer to any of the charges, and he himself directly questioned Jesus.

ANNAS: What is your doctrine?

SECOND VOICE: The query about His doctrine was to discover if He was the head of a secret society or if He was preaching some novelty or heresy.

The Prophet stood there amid His enemies. Was He to disclose His innermost being to such as these?

JESUS: [Answers coldly, looking steadily at the man. He raises His voice a little. Despite Himself, he still speaks as master.]

I spoke openly to the world; I have always taught in the synagogues and in the temple, where the Jews always resort, and I have hidden nothing. (I spoke openly to the world; always have I taught in synagogue or in the Temple, where all the Jews gathered, and in secret have I spoken nothing (and in secret, I said nothing).—I have spoken openly before the world; My teaching has been given in the synagogue and in the temple, where all the Jews foregather; nothing that I have said was said in secret.)
Why ask you me? Ask those who heard me, what I said to them. Behold, they know what I said.
(Why do you ask *me*? Ask those who heard what I spoke to them; See, these know what I said.—Why do you question Me? Ask those who listened to Me what My words were; they know well enough what I said.)

SECOND VOICE: His open teaching must have been well known, what He was asked about was His secret teaching. Jesus had "charged" His disciples not to tell any man that He was the Messiah-Christ, nor of what happened on the Mount of Transfiguration, nor that the Son of man must suffer, be killed, and on the third day rise again—all these were secrets.

Jesus saw the trickery behind the questions and, with absolute fearlessness born of innocence, answered that His doctrine was known to the people and those who heard Him could give testimony thereof. He had no underground, no Fifth Column, no doctrine that was for the few. There was nothing secret about His doctrine; everyone heard it, for He preached in public.

The Nazarene looked steadily at the man who must soon face the Father and be accountable for his acts.

Under the rules of trial procedure, Jesus knew—and so did Annas—that it was against the law to solicit the testimony of any except witnesses and corroborators. Jesus' reply should have been a sufficient protest to the high priest against further illegal procedure. The reply was a lawful objection against denying to a prisoner on trial his right to be confronted by his accuser.

FIRST VOICE: Jesus spoke to the *world,* as well as to the Jews. He would not testify in His own behalf; everyone knew what He taught. Caiphas was only pretending to be ignorant of that which was common knowledge. Had not the Sanhedrin already excommunicated anyone who believed in Jesus? The temple authorities had long been turning their backs upon the people; now He bade them summon those whom

174

they despised. Against this aristocratic isolation between office and people, Jesus placed His doctrine and His followers. He answered by affirming that the book of His teaching was never closed; it was open to all.

SOLDIER: [*Before* ANNAS *had time to admonish the offender, the first blow from the thick hand of a* SOLDIER *fell upon* JESUS' *face. He struck* JESUS *with the palm of his hand. He ran up to* JESUS *and slapped Him, shouting.*] Answer you the high priest so?

SECOND VOICE: Never before had any one dared to speak thus to the aged questioner. The objection was received with open disdain; and one of the officers who stood by, hoping perhaps to curry favor with his superiors, actually struck Jesus a vicious blow.

This was the first blow struck against the Body of Jesus—a blow unreprimanded by the judges. Thus Caiphas and the court really put Jesus outside the sphere of the law. To escape the content of the message, the soldier criticized its form—a common reaction to religion. Those who have not the capacity to criticize Jesus resort to violence.

JESUS: Shakes His head to clear the effects of the blow. Replies with almost superhuman gentleness.] If I have spoken evil, bear witness of the evil: but if well, why smite you me?
(If I was wrong in speaking this way, then prove me wrong; but if I was right, then why do you strike me?—If I have spoken wrongly, testify *legally* about the wrong, but if well, why do you beat me?—If there was harm in what I said, tell us what was harmful in it; if not, why do you strike Me?)

SECOND VOICE: Combined with submissiveness, this constituted another appeal to the principles of justice; if what Jesus had said was evil, why did not the assailant accuse Him; and if He had not spoken well, what right had a police officer to judge, condemn, and punish, and that too in the presence of the high priest? Law and justice had been dethroned that night.

He sought to awaken with a question the conscience of the soldier who smote Him. He did not rebuke the rude churl who struck Him in the face before the assembled court, but tried to make him see his fault.

The assault was a mistake. It gave the impression that the defendant was being deprived of his rights, it brought out sharply the illegality of the whole examination.

FIRST VOICE: With one breath, Jesus might have hurled the offender into eternity, but since He was to be stricken for the transgressions of men and to be bruised for their iniquities, He would accept that first blow in patience.

His foolishness was apparent. Jesus' contemporaries were annoyed when, in the face of insult, His patience turned to gentleness. For Jews and Gentiles alike there were only two ways in which insult could be met with dignity; either it could be repaid or, if that were impossible, it could be proudly ignored. In both cases the feeling of superiority was retained, and there was no third way. The law of Moses made the exact repayment of wrong compulsory.

He condescended to answer even *a servant who had struck Him.* The foolish Son of man! Neither in this respect would He fit in with the ideas of His age as to the meaning of real greatness.

SECOND VOICE: Now the chief priests, and elders, and all the council, sought false witness against Jesus, to put him to death; but found none: Yea, though many false witnesses came, yet found they none. At the last came two false witnesses.

[**THE SANHEDRIN** *all sigh in relief when the examination of witnesses begins.*]

[**WITNESS** *strikes his breast and vows.*] I have heard this Galilean proclaim himself as one sent by Yahweh himself.

CAIPHAS: [*Asks of the prisoner*] Is he speaking the truth or not?

[**WITNESSES** *vow many things.*]

SECOND VOICE: One after another, the stories of the witnesses collapsed.

[**The ELDERS,** *the elect, look at one another.*]

SECOND VOICE: More witnesses were called. The members of the supreme council questioned the witnesses sharply. These contradicted each other so badly that it was not necessary to question them to prove false witness. The high priest and his full council were trying to find a charge on which they could make a claim to the governor that Jesus should be executed. Under their own law any charge had to be supported by at least two witnesses, and they could find nothing serious enough

176

to bring against Him before the Roman governor which could be supported by more than one witness.

Some foundation had to be shown for the accusations against Him. Old Annas, recognizing that he could get no farther on his present line, called witnesses who could testify to the gravest of Jesus' crimes.

FALSE WITNESS: This fellow said, "I am able to destroy the temple of God, and to build it in three days."

SECOND VOICE: Jesus had actually said in connection with the clearing of the temple, "Destroy this temple, and in three days I will raise it up." He spoke not at all of Himself as the one who would destroy; the Jews were to be the destroyers, He the restorer. And Jesus had spoke of the "temple of his body," and not at all of those buildings reared by man.

The words of the witnesses were a perversion of those Jesus spoke in the temple when He referred to what was now beginning to take place. Now the false witnesses claimed that Jesus had said that He would destroy the temple; but what He actually had said was that they would destroy it and the temple would be His Body, which had just received a violent blow.

This statement, misunderstood and misinterpreted, undoubtedly added flames to their wrath; but a charge of this kind, if proved, would have little weight with Pilate. If they could prove, as they *later* attempted, that Jesus had proclaimed himself the Messiah or Christ, Pilate might thereby be led to recognize him as a dangerous conspirator against Rome and, therefore, best put to death.

FIRST VOICE: Divine purposes will be attained now as they were in Joseph, His prefigurement, who told his brethren who sold him that they intended evil, but that God would make good come from it. In his delivery into the hands of evil, Judas delivered Jesus to the Jews, the Jews delivered him to the Gentiles, and the Gentiles crucified Him. But, on the other side of the picture, Jesus said that the Father had delivered His Son as a ransom for many. Thus the evil but free actions of men are overruled by God.

The plan of the conspiring rulers appears to have been that of convicting Christ on a charge of sedition, making Him out to be a dangerous disturber of the nation's peace, an assailant of established institutions, and consequently an inciter of opposition against the vassal autonomy of the Jewish nation, and the supreme dominion of Rome. (Note the accusation reported to Pilate that Jesus was guilty of "perverting the nation.")

CAIPHAS: [*To the prisoner.*] Is he speaking the truth or not?

FALSE WITNESS: We have heard Him say, "I will destroy this temple that is made with hands, and in three days I will build another made without hands."

SECOND VOICE: This was an allusion to His predictions of His resurrection. For many bore false witness against Him, but their witness agreed not. Neither did their witness agree together. Even in this particular their witness or testimony did not agree.

The high priest was forced to call witnesses of high rank, and these testified and joined in declaring—with varying degrees of corroboration. Their failure to find witnesses against Him threatened to delay the carrying out of their nefarious scheme. Haste was necessary. Their purpose was to convict the prisoner in time to have Him brought before the Roman authorities as early as possible in the morning—as a criminal duly tried and adjudged worthy of death.

Even in this particular their witness or testimony did not agree. Surely in a case at bar, such discrepancy as appears between "I am able to" and "I will," as alleged utterances of the accused, is of vital importance. Yet this semblance of formal accusation was the sole basis of a charge against Christ up to this stage of the trial.

Failing to convict Him out of His own mouth on either His doctrine or His disciples, they now hoped to do so by the testimony of false witnesses.

The accusers were required to appear in person; and they were to receive a preliminary warning against bearing false witness. But in the so-called trial of Jesus, the judges not only sought witnesses, but specifically tried to find false witnesses. Though many false witnesses came, yet there was no "witness" or testimony against the prisoner, for the suborned perjurers failed to agree among themselves; and even the lawless Sanhedrists hesitated to openly violate the fundamental requirement that at least two concordant witnesses must testify against an accused person, for, otherwise, the case had to be dismissed.

The lack of two hostile witnesses who would tell the same falsehoods was a serious hindrance.

CAIPHAS: [Calls loudly.] If there are any witnesses in behalf of Jesus, step forward now and testify.

SECOND VOICE: The words rang around the chamber and caromed into silence. No one stood. No one came through the door to say,

178

"This is a good man. This is a man of peace. This is the true Messiah come to save the twelve tribes." No one.

[Again **JESUS** is silent.]

ANNAS: [*Leans forward from among his cushions, pushes aside one of the coverlets, and inquires*] Answer you nothing?

[*No sound breaks the stillness in the thickly curtained room. The* ASSESSORS *look at one another wonderingly.*]

SECOND VOICE: The council thought, *Why does not our venerable chief proceed to count the votes? The accused does not deny the blasphemy with which He has been charged.*

[**CAIPHAS** *finally gets up and moves dramatically forward into the center of the gathering. He rises from his seat to give dramatic emphasis to his question. In full robes and conical hat, he points sternly at* JESUS. *The* HIGH PRIEST, *in order to carry their point, addresses* JESUS *with the language prescribed by Jewish legal procedure for addressing a witness. Slowly he walks out into the middle of the semicircle. He speaks, gently, insinuatingly, with infinite entreaty in his voice, with infinite suffering in his face.*]

SECOND VOICE: He sought to provoke Jesus into incriminating Himself.

CAIPHAS: Have you no answer to make? What about their evidence against you?
[JESUS *makes no reply. The prisoner looks at the man and says nothing. The Incarnate Word is wordless during the false testimony.*]

SECOND VOICE: He scorned to answer the governor's puppet, who thus hypocritically sought to challenge him. There was nothing to answer. No consistent or valid testimony had been presented against Him; therefore He stood in dignified silence.

At last Caiphas and the rest realized that they could never convict Him. There was a time when His word had been powerful and unconquerable, but now His silence was even more unconquerable. Caiphas was in a ridiculous position and saw his case against Jesus dying for lack of witnesses who could testify separately to one charge.

Caiphas was caught. He could not prove the prisoner guilty of a charge, and he could not ask the uncommitted judges to vote for conviction. They wanted to convict Jesus, and they wanted him to suffer death for the peril in which they fancied he had placed the temple, but first of all they wanted two witnesses who, questioned separately, would support the same incriminating evidence.

Everyone in the room, except Caiphas, seemed to forget that the particular charge against the prisoner was, in itself, unimportant; the prime concern was to validate a charge which would make him a criminal in the eyes of the Roman procurator. Of course, even the charge that Jesus claimed to be the Son of God might not do, because the visit of the true Messiah to earth was the last great hope of all Judea; brought up in public it might call forth mockery of a Gentile governor. But, in the absence of other evidence, this would have to do.

But the shrewd old man who presided had been taught by long experience. He wanted firmer ground, for he knew the "yea and nay" of the Pharisees, their fondness for raising objections when a decision had become irrevocable; and he knew the curt and gruff ways of the Roman governor, who always insisted upon having an indisputable warrant before taking action. A frank admission must therefore be extorted from the false prophet, and Annas at length touched upon the most dangerous question of all, using a word of power which must surely tempt Jesus to lay aside the mask of impassivity.

ANNAS: [*He stretches out his silk-clad arms, as if he would touch the threadbare robe of the accused.*] If you are the Christ, tell us.

SECOND VOICE: The high priest gave a new turn to the trial. He asked Jesus whether He was the Messiah, the son of the Blessed. Jesus had made no disclosure to the *people* before Jerusalem about his messiahship. The bribed witnesses knew nothing of the sort to allege. They in no wise charge him with wishing to be the Messiah. His "impious pretension" was in disrespectful words about the temple.

In Jerusalem the scene changes, the entrance into Jerusalem —according to the common acceptance—a messianic ovation. Therefore the people must have had a presentiment of Jesus' dignity. The high priest put to Him the question whether He were the Messiah. Therefore he knew of Jesus' claim.

The witnesses of the Pharisees could adduce nothing that would justify His conviction. When, however, the witnesses had withdrawn, the high priest put the question to Jesus directly: was He the Messiah. To prove such a claim on Jesus' part they could not obtain the necessary witnesses, for there were none. The high priest was here in possession of Jesus' secret. That was the betrayal of Judas! Through him the Sanhedrin knew that Jesus claimed to be something different from what the people held Him to be.

To claim to be Messiah, that was blasphemy! The perfidy of the charge lay in the high priest's insinuation that Jesus held Himself then to be the Messiah, just as He stood there before him. He was to be condemned as Messiah although he had never appeared in that role.

What the Sanhedrin desired all the time was to obtain testimony that Jesus claimed to be the Messiah. As Messiah He would, in their opinion, be a rebel against Rome, and they could accuse Him to Pilate of treason. That He claimed to be the Messiah, Judas had doubtless told them, for Judas knew it, but no one of those whom they could summon as witnesses had ever heard Jesus make this claim; he had spoken of it only within the circle of his Disciples.

JESUS: [With His usual tact—he is content to say.] If I tell you, you will not believe, and if I ask you, you will not answer me, nor let me go!

SECOND VOICE: His cautious answer was in keeping with His answers to His persecutors at other times. Indeed, in the circumstances, it was the only answer He could truthfully make. To assert that he was the Christ would, in the light of the popular interpretation of that term, have been as misleading as to have asserted that He was not the Messiah. Jesus' words reveal the dilemma which confronted Him.

The gulf fixed between their conception of the Messiah and His own was impassable. Once again there was a conflict within Jesus between His faith in His own mission and His contempt for those who questioned it; dignity was at war with loathing; pride was arrayed against pride. Once again He evaded the issue.

This seemed to suggest that He would not reply.

The assessors become ever more wrathful at the forwardness of the accused, and at what seems to them the undue forbearance of their chief. But Annas stuck to his point. With an old man's obstinacy and a priest's cunning, he moved on toward his goal. He set out to force an avowal from Jesus and now he summoned all his energies for this purpose.

Caiphas now demanded an answer from the prisoner, and put the accused under oath, as a witness before the court.

ANNAS: [Slowly the wizened form—little more than a skeleton decked out in silk—rises from among the coverlets and cushions. The ancient lifts his bony hand, and croakingly apostrophizes the accused.]

I adjure you by the living God that you tell us whether you be the Christ, the Son of God.

SECOND VOICE: The fact of a distinct specification of "the Christ" and "the Son of God" is significant, in that it implies the Jewish expectation of a Messiah, but does not acknowledge that He was to be distinctively of divine origin. The charge of sedition was about to be superseded by one of greater enormity—that of blasphemy.

[**CAIPHAS,** *annoyed because thwarted by the contradictions, exclaims.* CAIPHAS *had begun speaking but never finished. Suddenly his face changes and he cries out in a strange voice as if he were not himself but someone else.*]

SECOND VOICE: The high priest was still standing. So long as the prisoner remained silent, the Great Sanhedrin had to acquit.

CAIPHAS: [*In desperation, and almost pleading,* CAIPHAS *shouts.*]
I adjure you by the living God to tell us outright, are you the Messiah, the Son of God?
[Looks directly at JESUS.]

FIRST VOICE: Caiphas here addressed Jesus in his capacity as high priest or minister of God, and put Jesus under an oath to make an answer. Caiphas raised no question about the destruction of the temple or His disciples. The question was: Was He the Christ or the Messias; was He the Son of God; was He clad with Divine power; was He the Word made flesh? Was it true that God, Who has at sundry times and in diverse manners spoken to us through the prophets, in these last days has spoken to us through His Son? *Are You the Son of God?*
Here was heard the cry of all his nation, of all mankind.

SECOND VOICE: He looked directly at Jesus, and had no hope of an answer. He knew that the prisoner too was well versed in the law, and understood that to say no would be to admit to His multitudes of followers that He had lied to them and was an ordinary man with no ministry; to say yes would be to plead guilty to the charge of blasphemy, because, in the eyes of these men, He was not the Messiah and could not hope ever to convince them that He was. Therefore, as He had remained silent all along, it was expected that He would continue to remain silent to this final question, and thus walk out of the palace of Caiphas free.

JESUS: [It is in the tone of humility which characterized Him in the earlier days of His mission that He answers, softly. An instant later He raises an arm, glances round the half circle of his judges, and, in His other voice, the voice proper to His regal dignity, He exclaims. He holds himself erect and speaks distinctly.]

You have said I am he; nevertheless I say to you, hereafter shall you see the Son of man sitting on the right hand of power, and coming in the clouds of Heaven.

(As you say; but I warn you: hereafter you will see the Son of Man enthroned at the right hand of the Almighty and returning upon the clouds in the sky.—Moreover, I tell you this; you will see the Son of Man again, when He is seated at the right hand of God's power, and comes on the clouds of heaven.—I am, and you shall see the Son of Man seated on the right of the Power and coming with the clouds of heaven.)

FIRST VOICE: Jesus could not refrain, at this supreme moment of His life, from asserting that they would soon see the evidence of His divine calling. These words reveal the profound conviction in the mind of Jesus that God in His own good way would quickly vindicate Him.

"Thou hast said" was equivalent to "I am what you have said." It was an unqualified avowal of divine parentage, and inherent Godship. Now Jesus feels that the moment had come when He must, in the heart of His enemies' camp, make the open avowal so solemnly demanded of Him. He yet had to die before achieving His status as the Messiah. This question could only be answered by His life and teachings as a whole.

He passed from His Divine nature to His Human nature. First He affirmed His Divinity, then His humanity; but both under the personal pronoun "I." In the hour when the greatest indignities were heaped upon Him, He gave testimony of being at the right hand of God, whence He will come on the last day. But if He would sit at the right hand of the Father He would ascend into heaven; if He was to have a Second Coming, it would be to weigh on the scales the reception souls gave to His First Coming.

Despite the certain condemnation facing Him, He permitted His glory to shine forth amidst the civil injustice as he proclaimed His triumph, His reign, and the fact that He would judge the world. He is the Messiah—that they will see when He appears as the Son of man upon the clouds of heaven. "Son of man" refers to His future dignity. To Him whoever assumes the role of "the Son of man must suffer and will then rise from the dead." Thus this Messianic consciousness of Jesus appears at the triumph of faith over experience, of the ideal over reality;

it was a faith which surged up from the depths of His being. This is why, as the human outlook became darker, this consciousness increased in force and certainty; this is why He declared it publicly and unequivocally before the Sanhedrin at the very moment when it was evident that his position was desperate. Jesus did not believe that He was the Messiah *although* he had to suffer; he believed that he was the Messiah *because* He had to suffer. This is the great paradox, the great originality, of His Gospel.

SECOND VOICE: But He didn't remain silent. At the most dangerous moment of all, Jesus chose to speak, and thus to save face for Caiphas. To Caiphas He had to answer, for Caiphas spoke the truth. "It is I—I am." These were the same words as written on the reddish gold scroll on the wall. "I am thy God, Israel."

For His accusers the answer sufficed. It gave them the basis they were seeking for their charge before Pilate that Jesus claimed to be the Messiah. That any man should fail to deny vehemently that He was the Son of God, the expected heavenly Messiah, seemed to a Jew presumptuous blasphemy. This was a virtual confession.

[*The* **PRIESTS** *are startled—all are aghast.*]

CAIPHAS: But what further need have we of evidence? For we have heard it ourselves from His own lips.

MEMBERS OF SANHEDRIN: [*All spring to their feet.*] What need we any further witnesses? For we ourselves have heard the confession and blasphemy from His own mouth.

SECOND VOICE: Tension was succeeded by alarm, as if they had expected a different answer. That which for an hour they had been eagerly awaiting, came in the end (when boldly uttered) as a blow. Daniel's words, that the Messiah would sit by God's throne—He had twisted them to His own uses!

A storm broke over His head as the Sanhedrin heard Him admit His Divinity. The clock was about to strike twelve; the first trial ended as the high priest rendered his decision that Jesus was guilty of blasphemy.

What relief the high priest must have felt! When all else had failed Jesus had condemned Himself. He had, in effect, pleaded guilty, though perhaps not *exactly* as Caiphas wished. There was no further need of witless witnesses, even though the law said that the words of a defendant are not to be taken into account.

The entire body of the Great Sanhedrin was witness to the proclamation that Jesus had said that He was sent by God to save Judea.

[*The action of the* HIGH PRIEST *in rending his garments is a dramatic affection of pious horror at the blasphemy with which his ears had been assailed.*]

SECOND VOICE: It was expressly forbidden in the law that the high priest rend his clothes. But the rending of garments as an attestation of most grievous guilt, such as that of blasphemy, was allowable under traditional rule.

CAIPHAS: [*The* HIGH PRIEST *tears his garments.* CAIPHAS *rends from bottom to top as was the custom. With trembling hands old* ANNAS *plucks at his garments, striving to rend them.*

In a great pretense of horror and sorrow at such blasphemous words, he tears his clothes, and cries out to the council. CAIPHAS *places both hands high on the collar of his tunic and pulls down and away, ripping the cloth through the middle.*

At that moment the hall is filled by the sound of rending cloth. CAIPHAS *tears his thin white upper garment of finest flax from top to the bottom, and then both the undergarments, strictly adhering to all the rules required by the Law: to tear across a whole place, not along a seam, and in such a way that the tear could not be sewn up again, that the breast be uncovered as far as the heart, and that the torn pieces shall reach down to the floor. The others follow suit.*]
He has blasphemed!
[*The* **COUNCIL** *all tear their garments.*]

SECOND VOICE: In the tearing off his garments, Caiphas was actually stripping off his priesthood, putting an end to the priesthood of Aaron. The robes of the priesthood were rent and destroyed by the hands of the high priest himself, but the veil of the temple would be rent by the hand of God. Caiphas rent from bottom to top as was the custom; God rent the veil from top to bottom, for no man had a share in it. This rending meant the death sentence for the accused.

Further words might vitiate the plea. Caiphas desired to close the case as quickly as possible. The startling assertion gave the high priest all he wanted. He was sure he could get a conviction from the governor on this statement.

CAIPHAS: Listen, then! You have heard his blasphemy; what is your verdict? Did you hear his blasphemy? What is your decision?

What think you? What further need have we of witnesses? You have heard His blasphemy for yourselves; what is your finding? (He has spoken blasphemy. What further need have we of witnesses? Behold, now you have heard this blasphemy.)

COUNCIL: He is guilty of death. [*Comes the answer from them all. There is no indication that the vote of the judges was taken and recorded in the precise and orderly manner required by law.*[

[JESUS stands, his gentle face turning from face to face again, and He sees that now the judicial faces are contorted with anger. He says nothing.]

SECOND VOICE: There was a general feeling of relief. Hitherto, a flavor of malice, a sinister aroma of partisanship, had clung to the arrest and the trial. Now the prophet was self-condemned by the terms of the prevailing law. He had attempted high treason against the theocracy, and must pay the penalty of failure.

The question was unanimously carried and the council condemned Him to death. This charge of blasphemy they could lay before the governor, since it would seem to him to mean that Jesus meant to make himself king.

His death was determined precisely because He had proclaimed His Eternal Divinity. They now argued that His death was necessary to preserve the spiritual unity existing between God and His people. The Sanhedrin divested itself of the responsibility for the charge by invoking God against God.

They decreed that the Son of God was deserving of death, on no evidence save that of His own acknowledgement. By express provision the Jewish code forbade the conviction, specifically on a capital charge, of any person on his own confession, unless that was amply supported by the testimony of trustworthy witnesses.

FIRST VOICE: He was condemned to capital punishment for what He thought. The idea that this God is a laborer but not a Sovereign was really a revolutionary idea. From the point of view of the idea of God of the Jews, it was a devolution and decline in the idea of the value of God, and so it was a dangerous thought. For God to become a man is to degenerate. But Jesus emphasized such an idea.

The man who spoke such revolutionary words could hardly be pardoned. He was guilty of confusing the supernatural and natural, absoluteness and relativity, piety and impiety, earthly affairs and religion. Therefore people thought that religion was presented by Jesus in a degenerated form. Anyway this carpenter was a man to be questioned. He presented to the world a religion that could not be judged by the standards of value that had been prevalent up to that time.

SECOND VOICE: Jesus stood convicted of the most heinous offense known in Jewry. However unjustly, He had been pronounced guilty of blasphemy by the supreme tribunal of the nation. The high priest's court decided that Jesus was worthy of death, and so certified when they handed Him over to Pilate.

CAIPHAS: The court stands in recess until after dawn.

[*To the* **GUARDS.**] Take the prisoner out and guard him well.

[*The* **JUDGES** *come down from their benches and walk up to* JESUS *and spit in His face. Others in the crowd around Him clench their fists and hit Him.*]

[**JESUS** *says nothing, though some of the blows cause Him to double over.*]

[*The* **GUARDS** *to whom He is now returned also cuff Him as they take Him away.*]

Scene 4

THE COURTYARD OF CAIPHAS'S PALACE (THE STONE COURTYARD)

SECOND VOICE: The servants led him out onto the portico and down the steps into the stone courtyard.

[Bound once more, **JESUS** is taken from the hall of CAIPHAS into another chamber—the place of detention of the condemned.]

SECOND VOICE: Bound once more, the Prisoner was taken from the hall of Caiphas into another chamber—the place of detention of the condemned. They had waited wearily all night and the news of guilt had preceded the prisoner. And they too planned to make sport of the Messiah.

The malignity of his captors manifested itself in the usual indignities

187

an ancient prisoner might expect, being spat upon, and also blindfolded and struck, and asked if He was prophet to tell who had hit Him.

In their excess of malignant hate, Israel's judges abandoned their Lord to the wanton will of the attendant varlets, who heaped upon Him every indignity their brutish instincts could suggest.

GUARDS: [*The* GUARDS *move a brazier full of coals over to the corner where* JESUS *stands. The sad, bearded face is now bathed in red. There is a cry of horror. Some begin to spit on Him, and then others; then the* ATTENDANTS *strike Him. They cover His face and hit him with their fists.*]
They spurted their foul spittle into his face; and then, having blindfolded Him, amused themselves by smiting Him again and again.—They fell to spitting upon His face and buffeting Him and smiting Him on the cheek. *The* GUARDS *dance around Him, cuffing his face* (struck him on the face, buffeted Him) *and simpering.*]
Prophesy to us, you Christ, who is he that strikes you?

[*The miscreant* **CROWD** *mocks Him, and rail upon Him with jeers and taunts, and brand themselves as blasphemers in fact. They call Him cruel names. And obscene names. Then they beat him again. And the* SERVANTS *strike Him with the palms of their hands.*]

SECOND VOICE: If He had not been humble in aspect, if there had been in His bearing that majesty which we attribute to Him, the rabble would have held their distance. No, there was nothing in the Nazarene to impress this cowardly scum from the kitchens. At least not at that moment. Jesus wished to obscure the glory of His august face. His will to efface himself masked on the holy face all that could make the executioners hesitate. It is true that the very purity of a visage sometimes attracts hate and brings down insults. These brutes had God at their mercy, and they made sport of Him to their hearts' content.

The dignity of a court of justice, a dignity whose semblance had hitherto been upheld, was scattered to the winds. Fasting and lamentation, prescribed by the law before every execution, were forgotten. They crowded round the condemned man, derided Him and buffeted Him, as if to assure themselves of His weakness.

The guards were angry because Jesus had not answered any of the questions asked by the priests. It showed lack of respect. So they asked a few questions on their own, and when no answers were forthcoming they slapped Him and repeated their questions.

Someone in the group had a more amusing idea. He got a cloth and blindfolded Jesus. They knew that they were doing nothing reprehensible because this prisoner had already been condemned to death by the Great Sanhedrin, and from experience they knew that a condemned prisoner was legitimate prey for the sadistic pleasures of the guards. So long as He was conscious at the time of stoning or strangling or crucifixion no one would be reprimanded.

The master of the house allowed this to be done because the judges were not completely convinced of the rightness of their decision and wanted further proof. If He was actually the Son of God as He claimed, the Father would never have allowed Him to suffer such indignity. Consequently Jesus was a "Deceiver," a "Seducer." This would at some time become known to Israel, to the whole world, and the decision of the judges would be confirmed thereby.

The servants mocked Him to prove to themselves that there was nothing to be afraid of. The sounds of their slaps convinced them that He was a villain rejected by God and man.

FIRST VOICE: Now that He was condemned as a blasphemer, all things were allowable, for He had no rights. They covered His face. The veil was really on their hearts, not on His eyes. They who were so proud of their earthly temple now buffeted the Heavenly Temple, for in Him dwelt the fullness of the Godhead. They used the title "Christ" sarcastically; but they were more right than they knew, for He was the Messias, the Anointed of God. Here was the worst in man, the disgrace of man is the Glory of God. The world is overturned and everything is revered in the Kingdom of God.

The power of Jesus over souls is rooted in His conformity to the suffering of men. There must never be in the world a prisoner, a martyr, a condemned person, innocent or guilty, who does not find in Jesus, outraged and crucified, his own image and likeness. Since He suffered and died, men have not become less cruel, no less blood has been spilled, but the victims have been recreated a second time in the image and likeness of God—even without knowing it, even without willing it.

[*The* **GUARDS** *thrust* JESUS *forth from the room, to wait outside.*

JESUS bears Himself now with simple, silent dignity. He reviles not again; when He suffers, threatens not. He does not turn away His face when they revile Him and spit upon Him.]

SECOND VOICE: They thrust him contumeliously forth from the room, to wait outside till they could bring him to Pilate's hall of judgment when day dawns. Having sufficiently mocked Him, they locked Him up in the gaol until the morning.

189

Again was the Son alone with the Father. And he prayed for His judgment seat. Jesus hoped to the end, the last gasp. He says at every instant and with every step, "Father, all things are possible to you: take away this cup from me. . . . Nevertheless not what I will, but what you will."

FIRST VOICE: The inquiry was whether or not He was both the Messias and the Son of God, who had been foretold by the prophets. It was Christ the Prophet, therefore, Who was on trial before Caiphas; it would be Christ the King Who would be on trial before Pilate; and it would be Christ the Priest who would be disowned on the Cross as He offered His life in sacrifice. In each instance, there would be mockery of His office. Here the mockery was directed to Christ the Prophet in fulfillment of the prophecy of Isaias.

The religious trial was over. The Son of God was found guilty of blasphemy; the Resurrection and the Life was sentenced to the grave; the eternal High Priest was condemned "by the high priest for a year." It was now the Sanhedrin that mocked Him; next it would be the Roman Empire, and then at the Cross it would be both combined.

But now that the Sanhedrin had found Him guilty, it proceeded to deliver Him over to Pilate, thinking that he who alone had authority to put Christ to death would do so without hesitation. The prophecy that He would be delivered up to the Gentiles was now fulfilled. But as Judas brought on himself the death he had prepared for Christ, so Caiphas in deciding to put Christ to death out of fear of the Romans, merely prepared for the ultimate destruction of the city of Jerusalem and the temple. As the people gave up Jesus to the Romans, so were they later given up to the Roman power.

He was comforted by the Spirit. And the Son answered, "Yea, though I walk through the valley of the shadow of death I will fear no evil: for you are with me." Thus the Lord prayed on this last night before Golgotha, lying on the straw in the prison, beaten, mocked, spat upon.

Scene 5

A DIFFERENT COURTYARD OF CAIPHAS'S PALACE

[*The house of the* HIGH PRIEST, *where the trial is held, is like many oriental houses built around a quadrangular court, the entrance to which is gained by a passage from the front part of the house. This passage or archway is a porch closed to the street by a heavy gate. The gate, on this occasion, is being kept by a* MAID *of the* HIGH PRIEST. *The interior court to which the passage leads is covered with flagstones and open to the sky.*]

SECOND VOICE: Now, after arresting Jesus, they took him and brought him to the house of the high priest. But Peter followed at a distance.

And when they had kindled a fire in the middle of the courtyard and had sat down together, Peter sat down among them. He went in and sat with the servants to see the end.

JOHN: [*At the door the doorkeeper or* MAID *lets in* JOHN *and rudely slams the door in* PETER'S *face.*]

PETER: [*Then the bolt rattles again and* PETER *slips through the open crack of the door. The* MAID *draws the bolt and opens the gate sufficiently to give her a glimpse of the man. She surveys him cursorily.*]

SECOND VOICE: He was assisted in securing admittance by John, who was on terms of acquaintanceship with the high priest. John asked her to admit him when he knocked. He had given her sufficient description to enable her to make an easy identification. Peter had entered into the courtyard, thanks to a disciple who knew the portress of the High Priest.

SERVANTS: [*There, in the anteroom or courtyard, the* SERVANTS, TEMPLE GUARD, *are seated around the fire, discussing the events of the night.*]

[**PETER** *draws near, seeking to glean information.*]

SECOND VOICE: While Jesus was before the Sanhedrists, Peter remained below with the servants. The night air was now very chilly. There was a wet wind out of the west and the temple guards shouldered their cloaks and built a charcoal fire in a brazier. They crouched around it in the courtyard of the high priest, and the glow of the coals painted their faces in brief, ruddy flicks. As the night declined, it grew cold. A great fire lighted by the servants burned in the courtyard. All those who were roaming about outside the palace awaiting the dawn, approached the flames, and from the gloom emerged a circle of figures and of out-stretched hands.

MAIDSERVANT: [*Among the* MENSERVANTS *is a* MAID *laughing and jesting with them. This damsel had seen the prophet and his followers in the* *temple. Now, catching sight of* PETER, *she recognizes him, and exclaims, perhaps teasingly at first.*

In the light of the flame, the MAIDEN *who had let* PETER *in the gate is better able to see his face. Seeing* JESUS *seated by the firelight, she looked at him steadily.*]

SECOND VOICE: This man also was with him. She asked Peter if he was a disciple of Jesus. She knew that Peter's friend was a follower of Jesus; under the circumstances it was no more than passing the time of day. One of the high priest's maids happened to come up, and, seeing Peter warming himself, took a second look at him.

The attendant at the door was a young woman; her feminine suspicions had been aroused when she admitted Peter, and as he sat with a crowd in the palace court she came up and intently observed him. As the maid stood and listened, she turned to Peter.

While these events, so freighted with tragic meaning, were being enacted in the upper room, Peter had been for a time warming himself by the fire below. Peter was *beneath* in the palace. Of course everybody in the palace that night knew what was going on, and why night was being turned into day. The arrest and trial of Jesus would naturally become a topic of conversation among both servants and temple guests. The maid who kept the door drew near the fire at times and listened to the conversation. As these people were all in the service of the priests, we can easily imagine that the remarks made were of a nature hostile to Jesus and his friends.

Peter was thinking of what was happening above in the upper, living, story of the house where the hangman-judges were interrogating Jesus, torturing Him, tormenting, beating, perhaps killing Him. And if they did kill and bury Him, would that be an end of everything? All talk down below was about Him—"sorcerer," "villain," "deceiver," "madman," "devil-possessed," and much more that made Peter long to draw his sword out of the scabbard.

He was not so much afraid for himself as for Him, not so much afraid of these men as sick of them. Everything seemed finished. He waited for the end.

Outside in the courtyard, meanwhile, Peter was still hanging around, waiting to see what the council was going to do with Jesus. To this extent Peter was making good on his loud protestations that he would never forsake Jesus, no matter what the others did. But he was unequal to the demands his presence there was to make upon him.

PETER: Woman, I do not know him. (I know not what you say.—I

192

don't know or understand what you mean.—I know him not, neither understand I what you say.—This man too was with him.—Woman, I know him not.—I neither know nor understand what you mean.—I am not.—It was not me.—I know not this man.)

[THE MAIDSERVANT'S *astonishment is considerable when* PETER *shouts this denial.*]

SECOND VOICE: Now this was Peter's great opportunity to brave his Master's peril and share his probable fate. But he did not stop to think, but under the strong instinct of self-preservation took the safer course. Peter was prompt to deny.

It was a dangerous place for a friend of Jesus. Were he detected, Peter did not know what might happen to him. In Gethsemane his attack upon the temple guard had been ignored in the confusion, but, if caught here, it might go hard with him. His first instinct was one of self-preservation. He had performed a small evil action for a great good—to be with the Lord to the end, to "lay down his life for Him."

Peter would have stood his ground before the Sanhedrin and before the Roman governor, and would have made his confession of faith well and bravely; before the nameless maidservant he had to deny His Master because his courage was not ready and his faith not so strong as he thought.

The Lord Jesus Christ was not to fall upon the field of battle but was to be put to death upon the cross; He was not to die as a martyr but as a criminal; He was not to be admired but despised.

Peter shuddered at this way of the cross, and he had a terror, which no courage and no remedy could subdue, of contempt and ridicule. The prospect of facing them put an end to his dreams of martyrdom and heroism, and finally the only prudent course seemed to be to deny Christ. "One must do in Rome as the Romans do!"

If the challenge to Peter's loyalty had come from a sword or from a man, he possibly might have been stronger; but as he was hampered by his pride, a young woman proved too strong to the presumptuous Peter. Jesus' plan was to conquer by suffering; Peter's plan was to conquer by resisting.

While John was safe, thanks to his acquaintance with the high priest, not so Peter, who had just committed mayhem on the high priest's slave. At best, this was a punishable crime; at worst, Peter might be accused of resistance to Roman authority. Poor Peter was thoroughly frightened.

Thrown off guard by the maid, he made his first denial. The first outburst was a fear that the thing to which he had given his devotion was powerless to sustain the full weight of life. There swept over him a doubt as sinister and engulfing as the darkness.

FIRST VOICE: The ideal of the Kingdom of God, the efficacy of moral love, the healing balm of forgiveness, what had happened to them? Suppose they were after all only the fancy of a dreamer. Were not the boats that had been left idle by the seaside these many months a safer craft in troubled waters than the promises and hopes of a carpenter? Suppose this teacher had misunderstood the nature of man, his greed, his grossness, and his stupidity; and instead of winning men to beauty was to succumb to their cruelty and hate. Suppose! And with the mounting aggregate of doubt rose the potency of fear.

[**PETER** *slips past the* MAID, *pushing his way past her into the safety of darkness.*]

SECOND VOICE: She had cause to be content, having frightened one of "the band of thieves."

[**PETER** *goes out into the porch for safety.*]

SECOND VOICE: Now he drew away from the fire so as not to be recognized. Peter began to feel uncomfortable, so he moved a little distance toward the porch. Anxious to escape from inquiring faces and busy tongues, he felt safer in the retirement of the darkness of the porch.

Then he left the fire and went out into the gateway: perhaps he was thinking about leaving the place altogether, since it was beginning to look dangerous to stay around the palace. But the irrepressible girl caught sight of him out there, and seeing she had annoyed him, started in again.

[**PETER** *returns to the fire.*]

SECOND VOICE: When the panic in Peter's mind subsided, seeing that he was, for a moment, out of the reach of danger, he moved quietly through the shadows to a place where a crowd of rough men were crowded about a charcoal fire, edging for advantage near its parsimonious warmth. To be among strangers was a better defense against fear than to stand alone in the darkness, so he joined them.

Peter sat with others at the fire, thinking, perhaps, that brazen openness was better than skulking caution as a possible safeguard against detection.

A MAN: Did I not see you with Him overnight in the garden?

SECOND VOICE: By a chance, one of the men, seeing the stranger in their midst, asked him if he was not one of those in the recent fracas in the garden. At once the fear of detection that had been laid by the friendly encirclement of a high wall leaped like a flame in the tinder of Peter's mind.

A MAID: [*Another* MAID *sees him and speaks to them that are there, or the* MAID *reappears and she announces in a loud voice so that everyone can hear.*] This fellow was also with Jesus of Nazareth. (This fellow is one of them.—Of a truth this fellow was with him.)

SECOND VOICE: She proudly informed the bystanders. She no longer doubted but was convinced.
[*They all wait for his answer.*]

PETER: [*Shouts.*] I do not know the man. I know nothing of the man. (I know not, neither understand what you say.—I don't know what you are talking about.)

SECOND VOICE: He who had drawn the sword in defense of the Master a few hours before now denied the One whom he had sought to defend. He who had called his Master "the Son of the living God," now calls Him the "man."

FIRST VOICE: If he had questioned the value of an ideal and feared for himself because of his espousal of it, was it not natural, in the company of gross men, to doubt and fear its availability for their kind? He stood aloof for a moment beyond the circle about the fire. These men were salty of speech and boasted of their ruggedness. They dearly loved a brawl, and when not fighting, were noisily recalling their escapades to impress each other. What was a lily of the field to them? Suppose it was more splendid than Solomon? Who cared about Solomon except as the paragon of lusty manhood? Forgiveness seventy times seven? A fist were better and more economical of time and patience.

There are, Peter argued nervously to himself, some to whom lilies and birds and forgiveness and that sort of thing were appealing. Take Nicodemus, for example. He no doubt understood talk about spiritual births and such like. He had time to think about them since he had no worries about food and clothing. He could seek the Kingdom of God without any risk; he had all the other things already. But these insensitive ruffians? If they wanted to pick up such ideals, would not the hard hands of necessity wrest them from their grasp?

The light broke over his face; the question was put to him. It seemed absurd that he should have been taken in by such delicate and impractical nonsense.

[*A* **cock** crows.]

SECOND VOICE: A first hoarse cock announced the dawn; but trembling with cold and fear, Peter did not hear it.

A MAN: [*As venture, but confidently.*] Of a truth, this fellow also was with Him, he is a Galilean.
[*To* PETER.] Your speech betrays you! (So you are with that Galilean. Your speech gives you away.—You certainly are one of them, for you're a Galilean!—Surely you also are one of them, for your speech betrays you.)

SECOND VOICE: He referred to Peter's Galilean dialect as evidence that he was at least a fellow countryman with the high priest's prisoner. He noted the rustic accent. They had detected a Galilean tone in his speech. Even his denial revealed his identity, for his way of pronouncing words told from whence he came. Galilee lacked the polished dialect of Judea and Jerusalem.

PETER: [*Begins to curse and swear.*] May I be damned, may God kill me where I stand, I know not this man! (I know not the man. I know not this man of whom you speak.)

SECOND VOICE: Peter went so far in the course of falsehood upon which he had entered as to curse and swear, and to vehemently declare for the third time, "I know not the man." Peter was at a loss as to what to do. He was wretched.

Peter, having started on a cowardly course, felt compelled to persist in it. He was of a volcanic temperament and was nervous and overwrought by the events of the night, so he began to curse and swear, to give emphasis to the statement. By this time Peter was enraged, so he invoked the Omnipotent God to witness his reiterated untruth. He now swore in order to force belief on the incredulous.

He doubted and feared the ideal as an absolute value; he doubted and feared its practical usefulness among the mass of common men. But there still was a sector where the battle raged. What was he to do now? He had made a conspicuous failure. His more realistic friends were at least out of danger. They might be on their way to their homes. They had talked about such a move. But here Peter was, left by his friends and having denied his allegiance to their leader. He was neither out nor in. Unable to overtake his companions, he was equally unwilling to confront his friend.

What to do? Obviously look out for Number One since his friends were gone and the Master was in the hands of enemies. Take care of himself. The men revolted him by their rude manners. After months of association with the Galilean he had no relish for the obscenities that interlarded their noisy talk. Peter was warming himself at the fire. It was an abandonment of himself to opportunism. The blood that had rushed in hot resentment in the garden, because of his friend's peril, was cooled now.

Was he afraid, if he reflected on it, that his devotion to all that Jesus had stood for would ultimately leave him by a brazier of cold embers, lacking even the spark to kindle it again? The time was passed for kindness. One must repudiate unequivocally all the nonsense about losing one's life in order to save it. *No wench; I don't know what you mean. Never even heard of the man.*

Once again the tongue of fear leaped like a searing flame, blinding him with hot, defensive resentment. He was by now getting concerned, and began to swear with the strongest oaths he could think of, that he was nothing of the kind. And at the amazed men and women he shouted with an oath. Peter, still sedulous to deny, began to curse and swear, and reiterate.

PETER: I know not the man!
No, I don't even know what you are talking about.
I do not know this man you are talking about!
I know not this man of whom you speak.

[**SOLDIERS** *go back to warming themselves.*]

SECOND VOICE: Such were his imprecations that his accusers hesitated and went back to warm themselves, leaving him alone. The heavens grew pale.

More time passed, and his Savior was accused of blasphemy and delivered over to the brutality of the attendants; but Peter was still surrounded.

PETER: [*Withdrawing unobtrusively from the circle by the fire,* PETER *slinks away to the gate.*]

197

COCK: [*Immediately the cock crows.*]

PETER: [*There, through the bars,* PETER *hears the crowing of the cock in the outer court.*]

SECOND VOICE: And Peter suddenly remembered what Jesus had said to him at the supper the night before. The remembrance of Jesus' prediction welled up in his mind. Peter heard it and stopped. Everyone was silent.

Memories of the past rushed in on him. The Lord had called him "blessed" as He gave him the keys of the Kingdom of Heaven, and permitted him to see His glory in the Transfiguration. Now in the chilly morn as the consciousness of guilt mounted in his soul, he heard an unexpected sound: "The cock crew."

Dawn came also to this poor heart. The night was over. All became clear within him, as the roofs of the palace and houses, the tops of the olive trees and the highest palms gradually emerged from the darkness. Before you can see the light you must deny, so that pardon can be granted.

JESUS: [*Then a door opens. Pushed ahead by the* ATTENDANTS, JESUS *appears, his wrists tied together, a jail-and-gallows bird.* JESUS *is led from the scouring, His face covered with spittle. He is still bound. He looks at* PETER.]

SECOND VOICE: He looked at Peter. In his gaze there was held an infinite treasure of tenderness and pardon. A reproachful look. He said nothing; He just looked. The look probably was a refreshment of memory and an awakening of love. The wounded stag was seeking the thicket to bleed alone, but the Lord came to Peter's wounded heart to draw out the arrow.

Then He stood shrouded, derided, taunted between the soldiers in the court of the high priest, surely He might have thought of Himself. But His eyes searched through the hall until they found the corner where a coal fire glowed, and He helped Peter with a single glance.

With horror the Apostle looked upon this face already swollen by blows from fists.

[PETER *turns from the crowd and meets the gaze of the suffering* CHRIST. PETER'S *back had been turned on the* LORD.]

SECOND VOICE: Trembling in wretched realization of his perfidious cowardice, he turned from the crowd and met the gaze of the suffering Christ, who from the midst of the insolent mob looked into the face of His boastful, yet loving but weak apostle.

[**PETER** *leaves the house of* CAIPHAS. *He weeps bitterly. He hides his own face between his hands.*]

SECOND VOICE: Hastening from the palace, Peter went out into the night, weeping bitterly. We see him stumble out of the courtyard, shaken by an agony of contrition, and we weep with him. Here to the sensitive spirit is the epitome of all infidelities, the compendium of all denials. As his later life attests, his tears were those of real contrition and true repentance.

Sorrow for the loss of his Master, and the disappointment of all his high hopes, and most of all the revelation of the poor stuff of his own character, overwhelmed him, and he broke down and cried aloud.

He was no longer cold now, but burning hot as in an unquenchable fire, and tears scalded his heart like molten lead. Peter knew that he would be forgiven but he did not want forgiveness.

FIRST VOICE: Peter was now filled with repentance, as Judea in a few hours would be filled with remorse. Peter's sorrow was caused by the thought of sin itself or the wounding of the Person of God. Repentance is not concerned with consequences, but remorse is inspired principally by fear of consequences. The same mercy extended to the one who denied Him would be extended to those who would nail to the Cross and to the penitent thief who would ask for forgiveness.

Peter had failed the Master. And yet, knowing all, the Son of God made Peter, who knew sin, and not John, the rock upon which He built His church that sinners and the weak might never despair. It was a wretched performance, one which would have been the ruin of a weaker man than Peter.

Nothing in the encounter at the outer portal was provocative of his ill manners or his implausible lies. Nothing in a group of tough-minded and horny-handed men about a fire was terrifying to one inured to the harsher moods of nature, and accustomed to daily contact with fishermen and peasant folk. It was, rather, something Peter carried in his turbulent soul. And it was not until that poison was purged, that dark sea drained, that restless demon exorcised, that he could achieve the poise and the victory of his later years.

The restoration of Peter began when he came within the radiant focus of a face; it continued when he broke his heart in penitence; and it was completed by a life of danger-defying service to the friend he had once denied.

It is easy to see that Jesus was touching with a healing finger the sickness of his faltering friend. In order that fear should be purged, another emotion had to take his place. Fear cannot simply be exorcised; it has to be displaced by an emotion of equal power.

SECOND VOICE: Jesus' gloom at the supper had seemed to him and his companions little more than a momentary weakness, but now events were putting a somber meaning into his strange words. The issue of the story is unaffected by Peter's perfidy. The betrayal was the evil deed of another, and the sentence of death was to be pronounced by Pilate. It is unlikely that anything hapless Peter could have done would have changed the issue already determined by other forces.

How can one account for the out-of-character behavior of this important actor as the play draws to its dénouement?

If it is not weakness, where then is our clue to understanding? We return to the fact of tension which is adduced to explain much that is discussed here. Those days of our Lord's Passion, days that changed the course of history, were electric with fear—fear that appeared in manifestations ranging all the way from misgiving to wild panic. Simon Peter was afraid.

Scene 6

THE HALL OF HERON STONES (TEMPLE SYNAGOGUE)
THE APPOINTED MEETING PLACE OF THE COURT
THE MORNING SESSION

[NOTE: In order to avoid a new scene, the palace of Caiphas could be used.]

SECOND VOICE: The law and the practice of the time required that any person found guilty of a capital offense, after due trial before a Jewish tribunal, should be given a second trial on the following day; and at this later hearing any or all of the judges who had before voted for conviction could reverse themselves; but no one who had once voted for acquittal could change his ballot.

Apparently for the purpose of establishing a shadowy pretext of legality in their procedure, the Sanhedrists adjourned to meet again in early daylight. The requirement was that for every case in which the death sentence had been decreed, the court should hear and judge a second time in a later session. They should have deferred the second meeting till another day. Had they so deferred it, however, it would have fallen on the Sabbath, when a meeting could not be held. They doubtless felt that the urgency of the case justified them in not following the exact wording of the law.

And as soon as it was day, the elders of the people and the chief priests and the scribes came together, and led Him into their council.

The second meeting of the Sanhedrin was held, in order to confirm, in accordance with their oral law, the sentence passed as their meeting held in the night.

And straightway in the morning the chief priests held a consultation with the elders and the scribes and the whole council. They took counsel against Jesus to put Him to death.

They had to find some reason for Pilate to pass judgment against "the king of the Jews," the "disturber of the peace."

The elders had trapped a religious faker, and not only that, they had managed to bait Him into admitting his own blasphemy. In front of all, He had had the brazen effrontery to refer to Himself as the Messiah! This had led a few of the milder members of the Sanhedrin to think that Jesus might be insane, but if this point was admitted they would not be permitted, under law, to put him to death, so they were silenced by the majority.

Jesus had already been found guilty. Now they had only to sentence him by daylight and the job was done. Any member who had the slightest qualms about the possibility of Jesus' being the Messiah had only to walk over to the corner of the courtyard and look at Him. He was not Godlike. He was manlike, and currently, a poor specimen of man. His face was gashed and raw and swollen so that purple welts marked His cheekbones, and both eyes were puffed. His hands shook in the fetters and He was bent over like a person of twice his years.

The Messiah? Not a chance. He was a sinner who had been caught after doing enormous damage to the minds and the faith of the people. The elders knew that if His followers could see Him now, they might revolt and riot in the temple, and anyone who wore the trappings of the high priesthood would be likely to be stoned by the infuriated mob.

The Great Sanhedrin had had an informal meeting and an informal trial; now, when Caiphas was ready, the body of sages would meet in the temple and pass a resolution condemning this poor man to death. This would be *formal*, and the certification of it would be carried to the procurator for endorsement.

No one in the group felt any pity for Him. Pity was an emotion used with economy in that era.

[JESUS shows signs of weakening. The GUARDS walk Him to a column of stone, bind His arms around behind him, and tighten the ropes so that it would be difficult for Him to fall down without increasing His pain.]

SECOND VOICE: They should have examined anew the witnesses against Him.

CAIPHAS: Are you the Christ? Tell us.

JESUS: If I tell you, you will not believe: and if I also ask you, you will not answer me, nor let me go.
Hereafter shall the Son of man sit on the right hand of the power of God.

SECOND VOICE: They should now have inquired into the merit of the claim.

CAIPHAS: [*Calls for a voice vote.*] It is confirmed.

FIRST VOICE: Jehovah was convicted of blasphemy against Jehovah. The only mortal Being to whom the awful crime of blasphemy, in claiming divine attributes and powers, was impossible, stood before the judges of Israel condemned as a blasphemer.

JESUS: [They bind JESUS, and lead Him away. The light of day is strong now and the sun rises over the tops of Olivet.]

A SERVANT: [*If at the palace, comes down off the porch and tells the* GUARDS.] Take the prisoner to the temple, to await the pleasure of the high priest.

SANHEDRIN: [*Thereupon the* SANHEDRIN *all rise and prepare to go to the* GOVERNOR.]

SECOND VOICE: They delivered him up to Pilate the governor.
Jesus was bound, and, escorted by the council, taken to the Roman governor, Pilate. For under the Romans, the Jews had no authority to impose and execute a sentence of death, which is what they demanded.

Upon the governor devolved the carrying into effect of it.

In solemn procession, the seventy councillors made their way to the fortress of Antonia, the condemned man, bound, in their midst. And they led their prisoner away to the praetorium, to make their accusation against him to the Roman governor, Pontius Pilate.

Scene 7

THE COURT OF PRIESTS (A TEMPLE ROOM)

SECOND VOICE: While they dragged Him away to take Him toward the praetorium (no doubt to the Fortress Antonio which overlooked the temple), a terrified man surveyed his handiwork.

Among those who stood waiting outside the home of Caiphas (or the temple) that morning was Judas. He had been paid for his work, but he wanted to know what had happened to his Lord and Master. He waited, and when Jesus came out Judas looked and was sickened by what he saw. The party passed him, and Judas watched the guards push Jesus and kick him when he stumbled. His sorrow grew into horror and he told himself, over and over, that he had not meant this to happen! Perhaps Jesus deserved punishment: perhaps banishment to Galilee or further. But not this.

There are no monsters; Judas had not believed that things would go very far—imprisonment, perhaps several stripes from the scourge, and the carpenter would be sent back to his bench. Very little would have been needed for the tears of Judas to be allied in the memory of mankind with those of Peter. He might have become a saint, the patron of all of us who constantly betray Christ. He was stifled with remorse; he "repented." Then Judas, who betrayed Him, when he saw that He was condemned repented himself.

Before this hour arrived (to accuse Him before Pilate), however, the priests had an unexpected visitor. It was Judas Iscariot. Poor fellow! The events of the night had turned out far otherwise than he expected. Instead of revealing himself as the Messiah, as Judas had thought Jesus would do, Jesus had submitted to his enemies, and had actually been condemned. Instead of trapping the priests, as Judas had intended, he had betrayed his best and most loved friend. His astute management, instead of hastening the Kingdom of God, had wrecked everything that Jesus had through the past months built up. Now Judas saw in its real ugliness the nature of his deed. When Judas Iscariot saw how terribly effective had been the outcome of his treachery, he became wildly remorseful. When the unresisting Sufferer had been delivered up to the Romans, and the fatal consummation had become a certainty, the enormity of his crime filled Judas with nameless horror.

JUDAS: [*To* CAIPHAS. *He rushes into the presence of the* CHIEF PRIESTS *and* ELDERS, *while the final preparations for the crucifixion of the* LORD *are in progress. He is still clutching the bag of silver. He penetrates even to the precincts of priestly reservation.*

He turns into the inner room of the offerings. Several PRIESTS *are in a group, holding a discussion. They know* JUDAS, *because these are the men who had paid him. When they see him, their tongues freeze into still silence and he approaches, bowing and grovelling and smiling, pretending not to notice their aloofness. He wets his lips, determined that he will not shout. He clears his throat and speaks with forced sweetness. He implores the priestly rulers.*]
Take back the money that you paid me.

SECOND VOICE: He may have vaguely expected a word of sympathy from the conspirators in whose wickedly skillful hands he had been so ready and serviceable a tool; possibly he hoped that his avowal might stem the current of their malignancy, and that they would ask for a reversal of the sentence.

THE PRIESTS: [*With a sneer. The* PRIESTS *look at each other and then back to the traitor.*] That is nothing to us; that is your affair.
What is that to us?
See you to that.
What does that matter to us?
That is your worry.
[*They turn away from him.*]

SECOND VOICE: They repulsed him with disgust. They could not be further out of sympathy with this man. They had been ordered to pay to the Apostle thirty pieces of silver out of the temple treasury and they had done this: there had been witnesses to the transaction. What did he want now?

He had served their purposes; they had paid him his price; they wished never to look upon his face again; and pitilessly they flung him back into the haunted blackness of his maddened conscience.

JUDAS: [*Cries in an agony of despair.*] I have sinned in betraying innocent blood. [JUDAS'S *mouth opens to emit sound, then it closes.*]

SECOND VOICE: The shock of their words was beyond bearing. Didn't they understand? The whole bargain was a mistake. To Judas, if he returned the thirty pieces of silver, then the high priest, in justice, would have to return the prisoner.

JUDAS: [*He mumbles.*] This was simply a matter of justice or lack of justice. [*He tries again to speak to them, but they have resumed their conversation.*]

SECOND VOICE: He realized then what their words meant: The entire matter was out of their hands. They proposed to do nothing to save Jesus, and if Judas had, as he protested, betrayed innocent blood, then it was his crime, not theirs.

[JUDAS *stands indecisively a moment, wild-eyed, staring at the* PRIESTS.] SECOND VOICE: Then he made a resolve. He would nullify the agreement by returning the money.
[JUDAS *reaches into his garment and unties the long leather strings around his money apron, and pulls it out. The* PRIESTS *pause in speech to watch him. Nervously,* JUDAS *counts out thirty silver coins, and with an oath casts them to the floor.*
Then he turns, apron in hand, leather strings flying behind him, and flees.]

SECOND VOICE: He cast down the pieces of silver into the sanctuary instead of "in the temple," signifying that he flung the money into the Porch of the Holy House, as distinguished from the outer and public courts. He hated it. He went out a distracted and despairing man.

What did the thirty pieces of silver mean to Judas? Perhaps he would not have delivered Jesus up if he had not loved Him, had not felt himself less loved than the others.

FIRST VOICE: Those who were associated with him in the crime now attempted to shake off the responsibility for the common act. One of the punishments in concerted sin is mutual recrimination; whenever men band together to do evil against a good man, they always end by falling out with one another. However, in the case of Judas, we find a reversal of the usual conduct of evil characters. The greater the wrong, the more reluctant one is to admit that it had no justification.

Evil men, in order to appear innocent, load accusations of guilt on those whom they have wronged. If there was anything that would have justified the sin of Judas, he certainly would have seized on it and exaggerated it in order to cover up his perfidy and his shame. But Judas himself pronounced Jesus innocent. He who had once complained about the waste of Mary's precious ointment now wasted his thirty pieces of silver by throwing them away. Could not the money have been given to the poor? Judas no longer thought of them.

[*The* **CHIEF PRIESTS** *gather the money up from the temple floor.*]

SECOND VOICE: The shekels lay in the temple where Judas had thrown them. The chief priests hated both them and Judas, their miserable tool. He tried to throw responsibility on the Sanhedrin; they tossed it back in his face.

But the money must not be left on the temple floor, and so the chief priests gathered it up.

CHIEF PRIESTS: It must not be put in the treasury, since it is the price of blood.
[*After consultation*] We will use it to buy a potter's field, as a burial place for strangers.

SECOND VOICE: Judas's fellow conspirators were willing to consult about the money, but not about the innocent man. They discarded Judas as a useless tool. He was no longer wanted; neither was the money, so it was used to buy a field of blood.

They killed the Son of God and thought only of not contaminating themselves! Thus, on the eve of the Passover, they did not dare to penetrate into the praetorium for fear of soiling their feet, and the procurator himself was forced to come out and deal with them from the peristyle.

It would be unlawful to add the attainted coin to the sacred treasury. It is upon that account that the field has been called Haceldama, the field of blood, to this day. They bought with it a certain clay yard, once the property of a potter, and the very place in which Judas had made of himself a suicide; this tract of ground they set apart as a burial place for aliens, strangers, and pagans.

FIRST VOICE: Judas was repentant unto himself, but not unto the Lord. He was disgusted with the effects of his sin, but not with the sin. Everything can be pardoned except the refusal to seek pardon, as life can forgive everything except death. His remorse was only a self-hatred, and self-hatred is suicidal. To hate self is the beginning of slaughter. It is salutary only when associated with the love of God. Repenting to oneself is not enough. Conscience speaks lowest when it ought to speak loudest. It is a lamp which sometimes goes out in darkness.

Though death is one of the penalties of original sin and though it is something to be universally dreaded, nevertheless there are some who rush into its arms.

He was blackened with infamy, the thought, that was unforgivable. The evil he had done was past repairing. He felt he could not endure life; he went and hanged himself.

The devil entered Judas. He was on his feet in one instant, and through the door into the night in another. The tremor in his harassed soul shook him menacingly, toppling every dream and ideal about him in chaotic disorder. The violence increased. He made his offer to the agent of the high priest. There was a din as of the rumblings of doom about his ears. For a moment it stopped, breathlessly. There was a moment of incredible calm in a garden—and a kiss. Then the storm again. To the sense of frustration was now added the black cloud of guilt, and the fear of retribution. He had betrayed innocent blood. Then the flight back to the city, the silver coins thrown at the feet of the astonished priests, the panting escape through the city gate, to a field, and to a gallows tree. And driven to the last excess of fear, as his life was choked out of him, the earthquake broke in a tumult of frenzy. It was such a cataclysm as the world had never seen, for it marked the end of an era, and the days that followed brought with them a new destiny for the race.

Then, under the goading impulse of his master, the devil, to whom he had become a bond-slave, body and soul, he went out and hanged himself.

Down the valley of Cedron he went—that valley with all of its ghostly associations. Amidst jagged rocks and between gnarled and stunted trees, he was so disgusted with himself that he would empty himself of self. Throwing a rope over the limb of a tree, he hanged himself. God can be sold, but He cannot be bought. Judas sold Him, but his evil collaborators could not buy Him, for He was present again in risen glory on Easter.

The tree followed Judas and his money apron, like a marionette on a stick, down, down into the Valley of Hinnom. There, the body of Judas landed on the rocks and moved no more.

He was the first of the Twelve to die, and he died before the Messiah he sold.

Jesus tried to save both: Peter through a look, and Judas by addressing him as "Friend." Both repented: Peter went out and wept bitterly; Judas repented by taking back the thirty pieces of silver and affirming the innocence of Jesus.

Why, then, is one at the head of the list, the other at the bottom? Because Peter repented unto the Lord and Judas unto himself. The difference was as vast as Divine-reference and self-reference. Peter knew he had sinned and sought redemption; Judas knew he had made a mistake and sought escape—the first of the long army of escapists from the Cross. Divine pardon presupposes but never destroys human freedom. Supernatural remorse leads to an abiding and salutary change of heart, whereas the world's remorse leads to death.

The tragedy of the life of Judas is that he might have been a true Apostle. While there exists a ray of hope in the most guilty soul, it is separated from infinite love by only a sigh. And it is the mystery of mysteries that the son of perdition did not heave this sigh.

ACT III

TRIAL BEFORE PILATE

Scene 1

THE FORTRESS OF ANTIPAS—THE JUDGMENT HALL

SECOND VOICE: The united claim of the Sanhedrists that Jesus was deserving of death would be ineffective until sanctioned by the emperor's deputy, who at that time was Pontius Pilate, the governor, or more properly, the procurator, of Judea, Samaria, and Idumea. The governor with his attendants was in Jerusalem at this momentous Passover season.

He had had six years of bitter experience as procurator of the province of Judea. He felt more every day that between the indulgence of Rome and the insolence of the Jews, his fate hung in the balance. "He was ever amazed at the cruelty of their piety." To the Jews he was an "uncircumcised dog," "the enemy of God and man," and for him they were a nestful of vipers. He wished to annihilate the whole Jewish race, completely to destroy Jerusalem. Pilate hated and distrusted the Sanhedrin, and Herod Antipas as well, but he feared them. Since he had lost one suit against them, the procurator was wary of these furious people.

His residence was the palace Herod had built for himself in Jerusalem. At the northwest corner of the temple area there had stood a fortress since the time of Nehemiah (444 B.C.). Fortress Antonia was built by the father of King Herod Antipas, the current ruler, Herod the Great. He was a half Jew fond of building elaborate structures and beautiful cities. When the Romans made him king of the Jews, he named the fortress, which kept Jerusalem in subjugation, after his friend Mark Antony.

Adjoining this fortress on the north a praetorium which served as a government building and barracks had been built; it was really an extension of the fortress. The governor resided in the praetorium when at Jerusalem.

Hither at the early hour at which Pilate had arranged to hear the case, the Jewish authorities went with their prisoner. Pilate had set his judgment seat that morning in the open court and there he sat throughout the trial.

Before the entrance in the praetorium, and raised above the square was a circular "stone pavement." It served the purpose of a public pulpit for announcing the sentences of the court. A tribune (dais, platform, rostrum), open to the sky and to the public, was a heritage of Rome.

The trial of the Prophet was over; now began a trial of the King. The religious judges had found Jesus too Divine because He had called Himself God; now the civil judges would condemn Him for being too human.

The approval and sentence of death required the seal of Pilate. There were two ways in which the Sanhedrin could have done this: either by Pilate accepting the judgment of the religious court, or by opening a new trial in the civil court of their conquerors. The second was the method chosen, and shrewdly enough. The Sanhedrin knew very well that Pilate would laugh at them if they told him that Jesus was guilty of blasphemy. They had their God; he had his gods. Furthermore, since this was a purely religious charge, Pilate might have referred it back to their own court without sentencing Jesus to death.

The whole world was to own itself liable for the responsibility of His death. Both Jew and the Gentile condemned Him to death.

Pilate knew that it was from envious hatred that Jesus had been brought before him. He knew about the envy because he was already to some extent acquainted with the case. Jesus' entry into Jerusalem as the "Son of David" five days earlier was known to the Roman governor. The activities of "the prophet from Nazareth," the "King of the Jews," of His "miracles" and His "signs" had reached his ears as well as those of Herod in Tiberias. Also he knew that the people considered this new prophet the "Son of God" or "a son of the gods," as the Roman centurion who saw His death on the Cross was to call Him. The term "a son of the gods" was known to Pilate from the fact that all great men, from Alexander to Caesar to the "divine" Augustine and Tiberius, claimed the title.

Then the whole company of them rose up and led him to Pilate. They led him away, and delivered him to Pontius Pilate, the governor. In the morning, the soldiers belonging to the cohort which had arrested Jesus, and who had led him before the high priest, now brought him before Pilate.

The priests came out of the meeting room first. Then came the guards with Jesus in their midst, then the Levites and the temple hirelings, who made a sizable crowd.

FIRST VOICE: Very early in the morning, all the members of the Sanhedrin—including the priests, elders, and Scribes—decided to bring Jesus to Pilate and ask for the death sentence. He was led away in bonds. The priests were indignant that He had spoken of Himself as the Lamb of God; the elders were offended because, as opposed to their fixed traditionalism, He affirmed that He was the Word of God; the Scribes hated Him because He opposed the letter of the word and promised the Spirit that would illumine it.

Putting Him in fetters for Pilate to see would create the impression that He had committed some fearful crime. Leading Him away to Pilate fulfilled the prophecy that Jesus had uttered. "He will be given up to the Gentiles, and mocked, and beaten, and spat upon; they will scourge Him, and then they will kill Him; but on the third day He will rise again.

[The CROWD, *robed in festal array, has come to the praetorium.*]
[*To either side of the praetorium rose a tower seventy-five feet high, set on the native rock, which had been rendered impossible of escalade by a veering of polished stone slabs, and entered by rock-cut stairs from the outside. Between them, the street entered the courtyard through a double gate under round archways.*]

HIGH PRIESTS: [*At this point, the* HIGH PRIESTS *stopped.*]

A MESSENGER: [*He appears before* PILATE.] The Great Sanhedrin, in its wisdom, has found guilty of blasphemy one Jesus of Nazareth, who deceived the people by pretending to be King of the Jews.

This Man Jesus has been arrested, tried under law, and condemned to death. If it pleases the procurator of his imperial majesty, Tiberius, the supreme council asks that he, Pontius Pilate, endorse the sentence and see that sentence is executed this day before the hour of the coming Sabbath.

SECOND VOICE: They did not wish to enter into the praetorium in order "not to be defiled" at Passover. This to Pilate was "Jewish insolence."

It was about six or seven o'clock in the morning. Roman judges were accustomed to holding their court early in the day.

It must have rudely disturbed the governor's comfortable routine to be called upon so early in the morning by his Jewish neighbors, but he was now used to such calls, as he had already been embroiled with the Jewish population. Messengers had conveyed to the governor as early as possible on Friday morning the fact that they wished to bring such a prisoner before him for trial.

When Jesus was brought to His trial before Pilate, Pilate had to open it to public hearing because Jesus was sent from the Sanhedrin. He was not certain whether Jesus had committed a sufficient offense to be brought to trial: from the first he did not like the accusation that was submitted.

They themselves went not into the judgment hall, lest they should be defiled; but that they might eat the Passover meal. The Jews could not enter the heathen castle, for they would be defiled by doing so at the season of Passover.

They did not dare go farther and enter the praetorium, if they did they would become polluted and thus be unable to eat the approaching Paschal meal. They had to keep themselves pure in order to shed the innocent blood of the Passover lamb. Pilate must therefore come out to meet them. The Sanhedrin—which had scruples about using the Judas money that purchased blood—also had scruples about entering the house of a Gentile, in this case, that of Pilate. These same Jews feared to soil themselves in touching the ground of the praetorium where they had gone to have an innocent man condemned to death.

[**PONTIUS PILATE,** *procurator of Palestine, the highest judge and top administrator of the country, has few of the marks of greatness. He is intelligent, ulcerous, sometimes brilliant in conversation, and has a regal bearing.*

PILATE *has a square, heavy face as if carved of stone, clean shaven, with soft wrinkles like those of an old woman, with a prominent, patrician Adam's apple and a bald patch like Caesar's. He has a fastidious or a thin-lipped, skeptical smile and an arrogant, nonchalant, almost suicidal boredom over all.*]

SECOND VOICE: As governor, Pontius Pilate's attitude was always formal. He was a man of intellectuality; he was also capable of venom and cruelty in equal parts and he never missed an opportunity to lash his subjects verbally, symbolically, or physically.

A list of his evil deeds would include "inhuman cruelty, extortion, robbery, executions without trial," and so on. Pilate was no saint, but neither was he a villain. He was an average man of this time. Almost merciful and almost cruel, almost noble and almost mean, almost wise and almost foolish, almost innocent and almost criminal—everything *almost*, and nothing quite.

Pilate felt sick, his bones ached, his head felt heavy and his body was hot and then cold.

[**PILATE** *screws up his face—a horrible sky, a horrible land, a horrible people.*]

SECOND VOICE: He would have to make a report to Sejanus, to that terrible old man of Capri. An accusation in the matter of "the King of the Jews" might be dangerous for him.

[**PILATE** *rises and wipes the sweat off his bald patch, and slowly, not of his own will but urged to it—by an unknown power, steps out on the lithostraton.*]

Scene 2

THE LITHOSTRATON BALCONY

[**PILATE** *emerges from the praetorium.*]

SECOND VOICE: Here, in white robes so torn that the rags dragged in the dust, he was being awaited by the Seventy . . . and one—the Prisoner.

Hanan was present in the square unseen, directing everything. Those to be directed were the people and the proconsul. Pilate guessed that it would be with Annas that he the judge and the Accused would clash.

[**The PRIESTS** order the CROWD to part to permit JESUS and His GUARDS to come forward. He is brought up to a point inside the arches of Fortress Antonia, slightly forward of the HIGH PRIESTS.]
[*The* PRIESTS *looked up toward the balcony where the* PROCURATOR *stands, flanked by his* AIDES. *He is surrounded by his* OFFICERS *and* LICTORS.]

[*A* **SERVANT** *brings out a regal chair.*]

[**PILATE** *walks down the righthand stairway and sits on the chair which has been placed on a stone landing.*]

[**JESUS** watches this through swollen, purple eyes. He stands alone,

His wrists bound behind Him with a short rope.

JESUS *looks at* PILATE *and sees a short, patrician-looking man of about fifty years of age. His hair is graying (such as he has) and he wears an expensive toga and gilded sandals.* PILATE *holds his right hand aloft.*]

SECOND VOICE: From this time onward, the disposition of the case of Jesus versus temple law was in the hands of Rome.

[**PILATE** *stands to receive* CAIPHAS, *the high priest, a spokesman of the Great Council.*]
(He snapped out—pointing to Jesus. Looking at the bound figure in the midst of the priests, the Roman said curtly. He is cold, blunt, and forbidding.)

SECOND VOICE: When the governor and high priest met unwatched in the former's private apartments, both were wont to be extremely courteous in their demeanor, and sought the best way to a mutual understanding, for Rome wanted willing subjects, and Caiphas wanted a friendly ruler. But today, under the public eye, Pilate has to represent the grandeur of Rome, and is therefore cold, blunt, and forbidding.

PILATE: What accusation bring you against this man? (What accusation are you bringing against this fellow?—What charge do you bring against this man?)

SECOND VOICE: It was still very early. The dawn was cold. Pilate had passed an uneasy night keeping down the disorders incident to the Passover season. Irritated, we may be sure, by the untimely summons which interrupted a sorely needed repose, irritated also by the refusal of those stubborn Jewish high priests to defile themselves by entering *his* palace, though well enough they knew what it meant to his discomfort, the shivering Pilate was in no gracious mood.
Carrying on the Roman tradition of respect for law, he declared that he would not pass sentence unless the evidence showed the accused to be guilty.

[*The* **PRIESTS** *exchange uneasy glances.*]

SECOND VOICE: Pilate's pretended ignorance must mean that the cruel oppressor was planning to have Jesus tried before him—and, in that case, might dismiss the charges against Him for lack of evidence.

The question, though strictly proper and judicially necessary, surprised and disappointed the priestly rulers, who evidently had expected that the governor would simply approve their verdict as a matter of form and give sentence accordingly; but instead of doing so, Pilate was apparently about to exercise his authority of original jurisdiction.

CAIPHAS: [*Gives the insolent reply—with poorly concealed chagrin.*] If he were not a malefactor, we would not have delivered him up to you. (If this fellow had not been a criminal we should not be turning him over to you. If this Man were not a criminal, we should not have handed him over to you.)

SECOND VOICE: This insolent reply did nothing to soothe the procurator's ruffled feelings. These words constituted a legal sarcasm. It did not answer the governor's question, which concerned the nature of the charge.

Sarcasm was a dangerous weapon to use against a man like Pilate, who understood this case thoroughly. Still, his knowledge was unofficial, and as Caesar's deputy it was correct to open a hearing by asking the manner of the charge.

In order to capture Pilate's good will, they invited him to trust the judgment that they had already pronounced. Furthermore, they assured Pilate that they would certainly never do anything wrong to an innocent man.

Nothing was said about blasphemy. They knew that charge would be useless before a Gentile, a conqueror, and one whom they despised; so they used the general term "malefactor."

FIRST VOICE: And here they were more right than they knew, for Jesus was indeed a malefactor or one "bearing the sins of many."

SECOND VOICE: Pilate understood that he was supposed to accept their decision; he was to legalize their verdict without a trial. They wanted him to back them up, but he would be responsible.

Obviously Pilate cared little for the alleged breach of the Jewish law with which Jesus was charged. So far as he could ascertain, Jesus was guiltless of any matters for which a Roman court could condemn Him.

Now ordinarily, one might expect that contempt for a people and their holy law, and confidence in the innocence of one accused of its breach, would result in release of the accused. If legal or humane considerations did not suggest release, the wish to spite a law he despised would operate in the prisoner's favor. But the problem was hardly that simple. Here was a subject race. Here was a member of that race who was not only guiltless but was winsome. But to release him would be to yield to a demand that had been shouted at him from the street, and to yield to a feeling of kindliness toward one of the vassals he despised was unthinkable. On the contrary, to yield Him to death might have two results: it might teach Caiphas and his crowd what would happen to all pretenders to popular following, and it might put a man out of the way who had ideas about sovereignty, which, however fantastic, might prove dangerous.

FIRST VOICE: The Jews presented him not only with a problem in provincial administration; they posed also a spiritual problem. They believe in God. They believed also in humanity. This to Pilate may have been the silliest sort of sentimentality; but it kept alive the fires in a nation's heart, fires that years of bondage to Rome had not put out. To these two great items of faith, this man before him had testified among the people. Upon love for God and one's neighbor, said He, was suspended the whole framework of their law.

Of course Pilate believed in none of this nonsense. Tiberius was all the god he knew, and certainly was the only one to whom he owed allegiance. Mankind, to Pilate, was the pawn of empire. The community in which life was to be endured was an empire that rested not on worship and the humane spirit, but on law and discipline.

SECOND VOICE: Pilate was in Jerusalem because he hated the Jews. Everything the Jew believed in was repugnant to him. Should he yield to his belief that this one man was guiltless? Should he yield to the frantic warning of his hysterical wife? If he did, he would yield to everything that he despised.

PILATE: Take Him, crucify Him! [*It was now* PILATE'S *turn to feel or at least to feign umbrage. Cold and angry*] Take you Him, and judge Him according to your law.
(Oh, very well; if you don't care to present the charge in proper order, take you him, and judge him according to your law; don't trouble me with the matter.—Then, take Him in charge yourselves, and try Him by your law!)

SECOND VOICE: The coldly angry procurator was determined to have the last word. To bring the high priest to his knees, all Pilate had to do was to pretend innocence of the entire matter and walk off the scene. Pilate, knowing their status under Rome was not such as to protect his authority and not wishing to handle the case, told them to judge Him according to their own law.

It was far better from his viewpoint to let this mild pretender to the leadership of the sons of truth be killed by His own people. He could lend a company of soldiers to this. The envy of the leaders would be both satisfied and chastened. Their zeal for the integrity of their holy law was envy. It was a sign of their spiritual decadence.

FIRST VOICE: Rome was to Jesus the antithesis of Israel. Its worship of an emperor-deity was blasphemous; its derogation of the human dignities to the service and aggrandizement of empire was insufferable; its dream of world dominion pressed forward by the edge of the sword was the abomination of desolation. With that there could be no compromise. If death was to be the issue of His ministry, it would be death on the cross. If those who shared His ideals would share His destiny, they too must refuse to compromise with the philosophy of empire, and they too must bear their own crosses. In the long light of history the cross was the answer of the idea of empire to the idea of the beloved community.

Jesus, the emissary of God, the exemplar of love, the agent of redemption, confronted Pilate, the pupil of Sejanus who feared and hated the Jews, the representative of Tiberius whose empire balanced always on the thin Etruscan blade of a Roman sword.

The ideal of the beloved community is Jewry's great gift to human life thought. Her great prophets foretold it; her greatest son died for it.

And obviously it stands in direct conflict with every other social or political ideology that thinks in terms of a derogation of God, man, and society to human ends. Here was the challenge of empire to the beloved community.

Herein originated the religion of the Cross. The religion of Jesus is the religion of crucifixion, that is, of redemption.

SECOND VOICE: Much that took place in and around Jerusalem during the days of our Lord's Passion finds partial explanation in the inflamed and irritable tempers of men. Pilate was disdainful and afraid. Caiphas was envious and anxious. Procula dreamed wildly, and the mob was restive.

FIRST VOICE: Here was a man (Jesus) of passion, intense enthusiasm, and zeal for a cause. He portrayed passion, not only to suffer, but passion itself. He was not just a sympathetic, kind, soft, tender, meek and humble personality but he portrayed all the various facets of personality—he was a man of action of the highest order.

THE PRIESTS: [*Several of the* PRIESTS *cup their hands and shout together.*]
It is not lawful to us to put any man to death.
(We have no power to put any one to death.—It is not allowed us to put anyone to death.)

SECOND VOICE: They then realized that they had been caught in a trap, as the Romans had taken the right of the sword, or to kill anyone, away from them. Their judgment would mean nothing. Furthermore, they did not dare put anyone to death on the feast day when they sacrificed the Paschal lamb.

They did not say that they had no power to condemn a prisoner to death, only that they could not carry out their own sentence. The high priests were not pleased so they implicitly demanded the right of capital punishment.

Pilate was forced to take up the case of Jesus against his will.

There was a determination on the part of the Jews to have Jesus put to death not only by Roman sanction but by Roman executioners. Furthermore, if Jesus had been put to death by the Jewish rulers, even with governmental sanction, and insurrection among the people might have resulted, for there were many who believed in Him. The crafty hierarchs were determined to bring about His death under Roman condemnation. They delivered Jesus up to be crucified, but they would not pronounce the sentence.

SECOND VOICE: And they began to accuse Him, setting forth three charges. The trial began by the presentation of the charge against Jesus on the part of the members of the Jewish Sanhedrin.

[*The* **crowd** *of* TEMPLE EMPLOYEES *is stunned.*]

THE PRIESTS: We found this man perverting our nation, forbidding people to give tribute to Caesar and saying that he himself is Christ the King.
(We caught this Man inciting our nation to revolt. He opposes the paying of taxes to Caesar and passes Himself off as the Messiah—a king. We saw this man stirring up the people and denying to pay taxes to Caesar, and calling Himself Christ the King. We found this fellow leading astray our people, forbidding to give tribute to Caesar and saying that he

218

himself was Messiah King. We have discovered that this Man is subverting the loyalty of our people, forbids the payment of tribute to Caesar, and calls Himself Christ the King.)

SECOND VOICE: The accusing Sanhedrists did not hesitate to substitute for blasphemy, which was the greatest crime known to the Hebrew code, the charge of high treason, which was the gravest offense listed in the Roman category of crimes.

[**PILATE** *does not answer. He pauses and looks around. He turns his back on the* PRIESTS *and starts to walk up the steps.*]

SECOND VOICE: The procurator paused and looked around. The charge against Jesus had been seriously altered. Blasphemy was one thing. Any mentally unbalanced person might call himself God. But when a responsible group of citizens used the words "revolt" and "taxes" and "Caesar," they were charging the prisoner with a high crime against Tiberius and the empire.

Pilate studied the little knot of elegant priests and was forced to show a brief smile of admiration. They had rid themselves of Jesus as a local problem and had thrown Him to Pilate as a menace to the empire.

The accusation was that He was perverting the Jewish nation, that is, undermining their allegiance to Rome, that He claimed to be the expected Jewish Messiah, or king, and that he endeavored to make their state independent so that tribute to Rome should cease.

Before the Sanhedrin the condemnation had been for blasphemy, while here the charge was political. The claim of Jesus to Messiahship appeared in very different aspects when viewed respectively from the point of view of Jewish law and from that of Rome political government. The charge presented before both bodies was the same charge, only in the one case it was considered from the point of view of the Jewish religion, and in the other case, of Roman politics.

By this time, the high priests had learned that they must change their tactics. Pilate had made it perfectly clear that he would not be browbeaten by their bluster. They must present a charge which would terrify the procurator.

This was a downright lie.

The first charge was that which is made against Jesus in the Talmud, namely, that he was a seducer. It is equivalent to the modern term "heretic." From the point of view of narrow Jewish ceremonialism, there was truth in the charge; but with the Roman governor it had little weight. Still no mention of blasphemy, the charge now was sedition; Jesus was unpatriotic, He was too worldly, He was too political, He was anti-Caesar, anti-Rome. In short, He was a deceiver who was inducing people to follow another direction than that dictated by Rome.

The second charge was a deliberate perversion of the facts, for Jesus had taken direct issue with the extremists of his nation and taught the duty of giving to Caesar his due. The charge was well calculated to rouse the suspicions of Pilate, whose chief duty was to see that the rebellious Jews paid their regular tribute to Rome. He was urging the people not to pay taxes to the king or to Caesar. In those days the antitaxation movement was spreading. It pointed out why Pilate should be interested.

And thirdly, He was setting Himself up as a rival king to Pilate; this was an abuse of majesty. The Romans, they said, must be on their guard against this political upstart. The charge they brought against Jesus was evidently that He called himself the Messiah, which to Pilate could only mean that He meant to launch a revolution to make Himself king. To defend the Roman authority against such occasional national outbursts was the prime duty of the governor.

They even spoke of "the loyalty of our people" to Rome, whereas in their hearts they really despised Pilate and Rome.

Every word was a lie. If Jesus had been a ringleader of sedition or if there had been any signs of insurrection connected with His name, Pilate would have heard of it. Never had the slightest complaint been brought against Him previously.

The third charge—that He was king—was not that He had made Himself king of the Jews, but rather that He was a king that challenged Caesar. This too was a lie, because when the people sought to make Him that kind of king, He fled into the mountains alone.

CAIPHAS: [*Imposes silence on them.*] The man calls himself Christ, the king of the Jews!

SECOND VOICE: The high priest was acting on his father's instructions, for the crafty Annas wished the whole affair to be given a new complexion. The religious question, which did not interest their pagan rulers, was to be thrust into the background and its place to be taken by a political one. This was to become a trial of a traitor against Rome.

[**PILATE** *now gives a sign to the* LICTORS, *who separate* JESUS *from the* PRIESTS *and take Him through the gateway into the judgment hall within the castle. He turns back.*]

[*The* **PRIESTS** *shout accusations.*]

[**PILATE** *goes back through the gate to the judgment hall in the praetorium.*]

SECOND VOICE: Pilate, however, was at a loss, and went back through the gate to interrogate the accused. His chief desire was, as always, to avoid espousing the cause of any particular faction of the Jews. It may have been for this reason, or it may have been because he was impressed by the aspect of a prisoner whose doings had long been known to him by repute, that he now went back to the judgment hall within the castle.

[**JESUS** answers nothing.]

FIRST VOICE: To the vociferous accusations of the chief priests and elders, the calm and dignified Christ deigned no reply. To them He had spoken for the last time—until the appointed season of another trial, in which He shall be the Judge, and they the prisoners at the bar.

Scene 3

THE JUDGMENT HALL (IN THE PRAETORIUM)

[**JESUS** stands in the hall of judgment. This inner hall is a fine stone structure, richly ornamented. Beyond it is a pleasure garden, with attractive paths, and a turreted open reservoir, over and around which doves are wheeling. JESUS is examined by PILATE at his comfort in his residence, the southeast tower, which from the height of a hundred and five feet affords an unequalled view of both city and temple.]

SECOND VOICE: That the accused would thereby become polluted troubled the high priests not a whit; He would not be alive, they hoped, to eat the Paschal meal.

[**PILATE** *comes in, and questions* JESUS *in the abrupt way usual in inquiries of this sort. Entering the judgment hall,* PILATE *has* JESUS *called.*]

[**JESUS** is brought in and stands in the center of the room. PILATE orders His hands untied.]

[*The* **ROMANS and SYRIANS** *study Him for the first time.*]

SECOND VOICE: They wanted to see the greatness that had frightened the high priests. But they saw only the pathetic figure of a Man, shorn of dignity.

Anyone was at liberty to enter, for publicity was an actual and a widely proclaimed feature of Roman trials.

PILATE: Hear you not how many things they witness against you?

[<u>JESUS answers nothing</u>.]

SECOND VOICE: And when He answered not a word, the governor marvelled greatly. Pilate was surprised at the submissive yet majestic demeanor of Jesus; there was certainly much that was kingly about the man; never before had such a one stood before him. The charge, however, was a serious one; men who claimed title to kingship might prove dangerous to Rome; yet to the charge the accused answered nothing.

Pilate, no doubt exasperated, but prudent, went back into the praetorium. He did not know what question to put to this wretched man, safe for the moment from the clutches of the filthy rabble. It would be too much to say that the procurator yielded to pity. He knew already it was best to flatter the mania of madmen.

The procurator looked at the accused and felt a doubt; this simple fellow did not have the appearance of a dangerous rebel.

PILATE: [*Scornfully he demands.* PILATE, *plainly without animosity or prejudice against* JESUS, *asks.*] Are you the king of the Jews?

SECOND VOICE: Pilate suspected their sincerity because he knew how much the Jews hated him and Caesar. But one charge worried him slightly. Was this prisoner before him a king?

The charge was only that He was a king. Pilate knew that if Jesus was setting Himself up as a rival king to the Romans, the Gentiles would be there to testify against Him. So He asked if He were King of the Jews.

The pride of Rome was in that question. "Is it for a miserable creature like this to think of a kingdom, to dispute it with the Divine Augustus Tiberius?" This was equivalent to asking Him to plead guilty or not guilty to the charge brought against Him.

In asking the question, Pilate was perhaps less formulating a question than indicating the motive for the sentence he intended to pronounce, without paying attention to anything the accused might say. The fate of Jesus was sealed not at the praetorium but at the moment when the Jewish authorities denounced Jesus as an agitator and as an aspirant to the Messiahship, and when the procurator decided to arrest him.

JESUS: [The swollen lips begin to move.] Say you this thing of yourself, or did others tell it you of me? (Do you ask this question from personal observation, or have others spoken to you about me?—Of yourself do you say this or did others tell you about me?—Say you this of yourself, or did others tell it you concerning me?)

SECOND VOICE: Jesus' counter-question meant, Do you ask this in the Roman and literal sense—as to whether I am a king of an earthly kingdom—or with the Jewish and more spiritual meaning? "Do you use the word 'king' in the Roman sense, or have the Jews been talking to you, and do you mean by it the Jewish Messiah?"

A direct answer yes would have been true in the Messianic sense, but untrue in the worldly signification.

Jesus in answer to the question penetrated the conscience of Pilate; He asked him if he was saying that because his suspicions had been aroused by the false charge of His enemies.

Pilate's reference to Him as a "king" meant nothing to Him.

PILATE: [*With a twinkle in his eye, the* GOVERNOR *rejoins, quite in the style of a Jewish disputation. With yet deeper contempt. But no, this is not a madman!* PILATE *fumes.*] Am I a Jew?

GENTILES: [*This brings chuckles from the* GENTILES *in the room.*]

PILATE: [*Resuming his official manner, he goes on.*] Your own nation and the chief priests have delivered you to me. What did you *do?*

SECOND VOICE: Pilate was humiliated at being mixed up in the affair of this fanatic. Pilate misunderstood Jesus. All Pilate needed was a denial. He was giving Jesus a chance to save His life.

JESUS: [Explains.] My kingdom [says slowly] is not a worldly one. Were my kingdom of this world, my attendants would be struggling so that I should not be handed over to the Judaeans. But now my kingdom is not from here. (My kingdom is not of this world. Had my kingdom been of this world, my servants would have fought that I should not be delivered to the Jews. But no, my kingdom is not hence. . . .—If Mine were a worldly kingdom, My subjects would exert themselves to prevent My being surrendered to the Jews. As it is, My kingdom is not of an earthly character.—My Kingdom does not belong to this world. If my Kingdom were one which belonged to this world, My servants would be fighting, to prevent My falling into the hands of the Jews; but no, My Kingdom does not take take its origin here.)

FIRST VOICE: Again Jesus is impelled to explain to the pagan a thing which his fellow countrymen who are his enemies have never understood. In the tone of the old Nazareth days, with the gentle, melting voice of that vanished time, he says (and it sounds like a sublime avowal): "My kingdom is not of this world. . . ."

He could not have indicated more clearly that *his* kingdom was of the Spirit, that he made no claim to be the Messiah whom the Jews, as Pilate only too well knew, expected to restore an independent Jewish kingdom on earth.

Pilate had expected a direct answer. Jesus now made clear that a distinction had to be made between a political and religious kingship; political kingship, which was the only interest Pilate had in the case, the Master rejected; religious kingship, which meant that He was the Messias, Jesus admitted. To the skeptical Pilate, Jesus had to make clear that His kingship was not that of an earthly kingdom obtained by military power; it was rather a spiritual kingdom to be established in truth. He would have only moral subjects, not political ones; He would reign in hearts, not in armies.

Pilate's worry about a challenge to Roman power was, for the moment, put at ease. Jesus' kingdom was not of this world. If His kingdom were of the world, Jesus argued, He would need the help of armies of men, but a Heavenly kingdom was sufficient unto itself, for its power came from above. His kingdom was in the world, but not of it.

SECOND VOICE: The governor listened to him with astonishment. Maybe a use might be made of him! The Jews were often refractory, and Jesus might help to keep them in order.

PILATE: [*Asks with lively interest. He glances at his staff helplessly.* PILATE *cannot restrain his sarcasm.*] Are you a king, then?

SECOND VOICE: Pilate repeated his question. Pilate, satisfied that Jesus was not a political rival, in wonderment prodded a little deeper into the mystery of His kingly claim. The quiet and dignified bearing of the one before him so helplessly bound with ropes—His face marred with the beatings after the first trial, His assertion that His kingdom was not of this world, that He had servants who would not use the sword, and that He was to establish a kingdom without fighting—all this puzzled Pilate, who changed his question. The first time Pilate had asked, "Are you king of the Jews?" Now he asked: "You are a king, then?"

The civil trial revolved about Jesus' kingship.

Pilate was vexed. Why did this pious faker not take advantage of his generosity? He glanced at his staff helplessly. There was no accounting for the obstinacy of Jewish religious fervor.

JESUS: [Answers quietly.] You say that I am a king.

SECOND VOICE: Jesus was saying, "You are right, I am a king. Yes, I am what you said." Jesus evidently understood Pilate's question as referring to His being the Messiah.

In the mind of Pilate, Jesus' answer was equivalent to saying, "Judge for yourself." It left the charge to be proved by the evidence. To have answered no might have resulted in His acquittal, but He could not do so and remain true to his convictions.

FIRST VOICE: In the house of Caiphas He confessed Himself before all Israel—"I am the Son," and in the praetorium of Pilate before all mankind—"I am the King."

JESUS: [JESUS nods assent.] You say that I am a king. To this end was I born, and for this cause came I into the world, that I should bear witness (give testimony) to the truth that I should reign. Everyone that is of the truth hears my voice. (Only he who is open to the truth gives ear to My voice). It is your own lips that have called Me a king. What I was born for, what I came into the world for, is to bear witness of the truth. Whoever belongs to the truth listens to My voice.)

FIRST VOICE: Never before had He described his mission in such mundane terms. When He said that He was born, He was acknowledging His human temporal origin as the Son of man; when He said He came into the world, He affirmed His Divinity. Furthermore, He who came from heaven came to bear witness, which meant to die for the truth. He laid down the moral condition of discovering truth and affirmed that it was only an intellectual quest; what one discovered depended in part on one's moral behavior.

When Jesus said that everyone that is of the true would hear His voice, He enunciated the law that truth assimilates all that is congenial to itself. "Any one who acts shamefully hates the light . . . whereas the man whose life is true comes to the light. . . ."

If therefore, the impulse toward truth was in Pilate, he would know that Truth Itself stood before him; if it was not in him, he would sentence Jesus to death.

SECOND VOICE: Jesus, having already avowed His kingly state, acknowledged the inference which Pilate had somewhat scornfully drawn and answered.

After such an avowal from the lips of the prisoner Himself, it was the duty of the judge, according to the letter of the law, to stop all further examination and to pronounce the sentence. For, as the Jews acknowledged at that time, "they had no other king but Caesar."

Pilate did not consider the law as final for he could not find sufficient guilt to justify a sentence as Jesus had not done anything to possess Himself of the kingdom. He therefore continued the interrogation of the mute prisoner.

It was clear to the Roman governor that this wonderful man, with His exalted views of a kingdom not of this world, and an empire of truth in which He was to reign, was no political insurrectionist; and that to consider Him a menace to Roman institutions would be absurd.

Pilate was reassured. He was convinced that before him was no "villain," "sedition-monger," no "adversary of Caesar," but merely an innocent "dreamer." He was harmless, laughable, and even pitiable. In his mind he was mentally preparing a report for Rome: "In this affair I have found nothing but ignorant superstition."

PILATE: [*Somewhat disdainfully, and yet not wholly in contempt, he rejoins. He asks ironically. He sneered the question. Those last words—about truth—were of all the most puzzling; Pilate was restive, and perhaps a little frightened under their import. "What is truth?" he rather exclaimed in apprehension than inquired in expectation of an answer, as He starts to leave the hall. He turns his back upon the Logos Incarnate.*] What is truth?

SECOND VOICE: But Pilate thinks: *Merely a philosopher, after all! Nothing to be done with Him in that case!*

For a moment they stand face to face, the Jewish prisoner and the Roman governor, in the judgment hall of the fortress, surrounded by swords and helmets. One of them is armed, and clad in a short toga; the other is weaponless, and wears a long, gray mantle. They confront one another, exchanging thoughts; as though they were not accused

226

and judge, beggar and lord, as though one of them were not fighting for the life which the other weighs in his mailed hand; rather as though the beggar were a king, and the governor an emperor's envoy, but nothing more than the poor servant of his duty. Thus do Jesus and Pilate confront one another, reflective, waiting on one another's words, questioning—until one of them speaks of "truth," and thereby the man of the world and the prophet are torn asunder.

FIRST VOICE: Pilate evidently caught the idea that moral conduct had something to do with the discovery of truth, so he resorted to pragmatism and utilitarianism, and sneered at the question.

Then he turned his back on truth—better not on it, but on Him Who is Truth. It remained to be seen that tolerance of truth and error in a stroke of broadmindedness leads to intolerance and persecution; "What is truth?" when sneered, is followed up with the second sneer, "What is justice?" Broadmindedness, when it means indifference to right and wrong, eventually ends in a hatred of what is right. He who was so tolerant of error as to deny an absolute truth was the one who could crucify Truth. It was the religious judge who challenged Him, "I adjure you"; but the secular judge asked, "What is truth?" He who was in the robe of the high priest called upon God to repudiate the things that are God's; he who was in the Roman toga just professed a skepticism and doubt.

Pilate was one of those who believed that truth is not objective but subjective, that each man determines for himself what is to be true. It is often the fault of practical men, such as Pilate, to regard the search for objective truth as useless theorizing. Skepticism is not an intellectual position; it is a moral position, in the sense that it is determined not so much by reason as by the way one acts and behaves.

SECOND VOICE: Pilate's desire to save Jesus was due to a kind of liberalism which combined disbelief in absolute truth with a half-benevolent unwillingness to disturb such dreamers and their superstitions. Pilate asked the question, "What is truth," of the only person in the world who could answer it in all its fullness.

Pilate was a hard-bitten Roman official. At many a trial over which he had presided, he had seen the strict letter of the law triumph over simple justice.

[<u>JESUS</u> does not answer.]

FIRST VOICE: It was not only Pilate who spoke these words, but

Rome and the world who were behind them. Jesus did not answer. He could not as He himself was the answer, "the Word was made Flesh." No human words can measure up to this divine act. He is an existing truth.

If he had had the heart of a beggar, of a lost woman, of a publican, He might have received this reply: "I am the truth, who speaks with you." But he was a serious man, a great official; he would have shrugged his shoulders. A secret virtue was acting within him, nevertheless; this man "had something," he could not say what. He no longer took him for a madman. It was envy that had exasperated the Sanhedrin; one could not deny the power of the prisoner's look, of his voice. This Roman distrusted the Jews, but he was superstitious. One never knew; the Christ was full of dangerous divinities.

PILATE: [*To the* HIGH PRIESTS *and the* CROWDS.] I find nothing criminal in this man.

Scene 4

THE SQUARE IN THE PRAETORIUM

PILATE: [*Goes out again to the* JEWS.]
I find in Him no fault at all. (I can detect no guilt in this man.) You have brought this man to me, as one that perverts the people: and, behold, I, having examined Him, have found no fault in this man touching those things whereof you accuse him.
(There is nothing in this man with which I can find fault. He may claim to be a king, but it is not in a sense which makes it necessary to punish him.)

SECOND VOICE: Strangely enough, Pilate did not seem to think this settled it. He was haunted by the suspicion that the Sanhedrin was jealous of Jesus, and was trying on that account to put an end to Him. Pilate did not think this specially a crime, so he said to the high priests and the crowd that he did not find any crime in Him, and dismissed the case. To the Jews without he announced officially the acquittal of the prisoner. "I find in Him no fault at all" was the verdict.

It is noteworthy that Jesus did not deny the charge that He was a king, but claimed kingship in such a peculiar way that Pilate was convinced that there was no political danger in it.

The Roman governor's decision was doubtless based on the impression made upon him by the accused and by his knowledge of the character and reputation of His accusers.

Pilate's policy at this time reveals that vacillation, combined with selfish cruelty, which marked his career. He was entirely willing to cruelly scourge Him whom he pronounced innocent; but his innate Roman sense of justice made him eager to release Jesus.

Nevertheless, Pilate had been persuaded that Jesus was nothing but a religious fanatic, that He was preaching no nationalistic uprising which could be a danger to the Roman government. By now he was satisfied that the high priests, for devious reasons of their own, were determined to send an innocent man to His death. Pilate did not like Jews, least of all the high priestly crowd, as the ten years of his procuratorship amply showed, and for this reason if for no other he would make up his mind to block their designs.

But there was a much more pressing reason for his reluctance to accede to their demands. Pilate was a procurator, a governor of the second rank, but of an imperial province and so directly responsible to the emperor. Tiberius had far excelled Augustus in his stern adherence to duty; he had repeatedly and in direct contrast to his predecessor shown his determination to protect the native population of his empire against grafting officials and overzealous tax collectors. Pilate was an honest man and as an official responsible to a stern master, the procurator had no desire to be a party to a miscarriage of justice.

Pilate now began the first of several attempts to rescue Jesus, such as a declaration of His innocence, a choice between prisoners, a scourging, an appeal to sympathy, a change of judges.

If there was no fault in Him, Pilate should have released Him.

FIRST VOICE: His enemies condemned Him for qualities that seem to us now His virtues.

THE JEWS: [*There is a moment or two of stunned silence, and then a riotous babble of voices arises. The* HIGH PRIESTS *strike their foreheads repeatedly and turn to the people in mute appeal. The roar becomes louder. The* CHIEF PRIEST *and* SCRIBES *and* ELDERS *of the people are undeterred. Their thirst for the blood of the* HOLY ONE *has developed into mania. Wildly and fiercely they shriek. A nightmare swarm of eyes glints all around, while a whole world roars for death. Intermittently, that inhuman crowd sound arises.*] He stirs up the people, teaching throughout all of Judea, beginning from Galilee and coming even here (beginning from Galilee to this place). (He rouses sedition among the people; He has gone round the whole of Judea preaching, beginning in Galilee and ending here.)

SOLDIERS: [*Some of the off-duty* SOLDIERS *run into the garrison room and get their cuirasses and swords.*]

FIRST VOICE: He was a "Disturber of the world," just as later it was to be said of His disciples, "These have turned the world upside down."

SECOND VOICE: Jesus' accusers accused Him again. On hearing the Roman governor's declaration that the prisoner was innocent, the members of the Sanhedrin became more violent in their accusation that He was an insurrectionist and revolutionist.

[**PILATE** *sits and smiles.*]

SECOND VOICE: Caiphas and the others of the Sanhedrin knew that the procurator was turning the man loose not on the legalities but to confound them.

This Herod was Herod Antipas, the son of Herod the Great, who had caused all the male Jewish children under two years of age to be murdered at Bethlehem. Herod was a sensual, worldly man; he had murdered John the Baptist because John condemned him for divorcing his wife and living with his brother's wife. Herod had an uneasy conscience, not only because he had slain the announcer of Jesus but also because his superstitions made him believe that John the Baptist had risen and was haunting his soul.

Herod Antipas, the degenerate son of his infamous sire, Herod the Great, was at this time tetrarch of Galilee and Perea, and by popular usage, though without imperial sanction, was flatteringly called king. He ruled as a Roman vassal, and professed to be orthodox in the observances of Judaism. He had come up to Jerusalem, in state, to keep the feast of the Passover.

PILATE: [*Hearing this*] Is the man a Galilean?

SECOND VOICE: Why not set him free? Unfortunately, the members of the Sanhedrin had placed themselves on political grounds. Jesus declared himself king and Messiah, and it was just this kind of agitator who was most detested in Rome. Pilate's enemies knew it would turn a powerful arm against him. An insignificant affair, but one which might prove his undoing. He was a politician, and like all politicians who are playing both sides, he sought a subterfuge. Suddenly, he struck his forehead: he had found it! A Nazarene? Well, then, Jesus was of Herod's jurisdiction. Since without permission from Herod, Pilate had massacred some Galilean revolutionaries, he had been at odds with the tetrarch, but he would show him this mark of deference and would kill two birds with one stone. He would get rid of Jesus and would reconcile himself with Herod, who happened to be in Jerusalem for the feast.

Galilee? Amid the clamour, this word gave a clear lead to the Roman. The period of communing upon abstract topics was over. Once more he was dominated by the wish to find a course that would most effectively gratify the numerous and conflicting demands that were voiced in this amazing theocracy. As soon as he heard that Jesus was a Galilean, he saw a way of escape from his perplexities.

Pilate caught them up; was the fellow a Galilean? The harried procurator, unwilling to condemn an innocent man, but beginning to fear that he could not save Him, was delighted to learn that the accused was a subject of a vassal tetrarch; most fortunately Herod Antipas, for political if not for purely religious reasons, actually was present at the great feast. He had been terribly angered at Pilate when the procurator had massacred his Galilean subjects at the preceding Feast of Tabernacles; here was the golden opportunity for Pilate to make his peace by an act of courtesy.

By so doing, he would also wash his hands of this whole, unpleasant problem. The mention of Galilee suggested to Pilate a new course of procedure. Pilate thought of another expedient. He saw an escape from judging Christ. By sending the prisoner to Herod, Pilate hoped to rid himself of further responsibility in the case, and moreover, Herod, with whom he had been at enmity, might be placated thereby. He hoped of getting Herod to employ his influence with the Jews to persuade them to drop their charge.

PILATE: [*Suddenly, he strikes his forehead: he has found it!*] Well, then, this case should be under the jurisdiction of Herod, Tetrarch of Galilee. Take Him to Herod.

SECOND VOICE: He directed that Jesus should be taken across the city to Herod's palace. He accordingly adjourned his court for a time. He sent Jesus to Herod with a message which secured the desired examination of the prisoner by the tetrarch.

As the Sanhedrin had changed the charge from blasphemy to sedition, so Pilate would turn over jurisdiction of the trial to one who had power in Galilee.

The Priests could hardly believe their ears when Pilate told them to take Jesus before Herod. The governor had been aware of this troublemaker and His origin, and if it were a matter of jurisdiction, could have told Caiphas last night that the prisoner properly belonged to

Herod, who was in Jerusalem for the Passover.

This amounted to dangerous meddling in the internal affairs of Palestine. The mock Messiah was a Jew, charged with a religious crime in Jerusalem, to which was added a crime against the empire. How then could He be brought before Herod, whose jurisdiction was confined to Galilee?

He had, he thought, done a bright thing. The Roman was now making a gesture of friendship, or respect. Herod could not interpret it in any other way, and he would be forced by custom to reciprocate in some way. Thus the breach between the two would be healed over the worthless body of a Galilean.

Further, the gesture forced Herod to become part of the trial of Jesus. Now, no matter what happened, the king could hardly write any lying, poisonous letter to Tiberius about Pilate and the case of Jesus.

In one brilliant stroke Pilate had removed himself from a highly sensitive case, had embroiled Herod in it, had at the same time made a gesture of high regard to Herod, and had placed Annas and Caiphas in a dangerous, almost untenable position. The procurators returned to his office well pleased.

FIRST VOICE: Pilate's supreme interest was the peace of the state; hence the supreme interest of the Sanhedrin was to prove that Christ was a disturber of the peace.

[**PILATE** *stands. The* PROCURATOR *nods to the* SOLDIERS *to take the* MAN JESUS *in charge and deliver Him to* KING HEROD. *He begins to look pleased. Goes back into the fortress or praetorium.*]

SECOND VOICE: Pilate stood. He would not entertain an argument about the matter. By a postern gate, Pilate sent the prisoner in charge of a centurion and a few soldiers to Herod, with an inquiry whether the tetrarch would not like to take over the case, since the Galilean came within his jurisdiction.

Scene 5

THE PALACE OF HEROD ANTIPAS

SECOND VOICE: At the gate of Fortress Antonia the priests argued among themselves about what should have been said to Pilate, and what had been said. They were very worried. The more time that passed, the more of Jesus' sympathizers might find out what was happening.

There was nothing to do, however, but proceed to Herod. According to his custom when he was in residence in Jerusalem, he was using the Hasmonean Palace. Caiphas dispatched a courier to run ahead and acquaint the tetrarch with the circumstances. The big party of marchers arrived at the gates of the palace of Herod, and the servants told the high priests to keep the crowds outside. Only the priests, Jesus, and the Roman guards were admitted.

The high priests wanted to waste as little time as possible with Herod. They hoped solely to get the vindictive support of Herod so that they could hurry back to Pilate.

Herod Antipas was the man whom Jesus had called "that fox." Now at last the two stood face to face.

The appellation "fox" was apt. Herod was crafty, a schemer. He was not cruel, as Pilate could be cruel, or mercenary, as Annas could be mercenary. All the Herods changed political allegiance as a weathercock changes direction in a variable breeze.

Now when Herod saw Jesus, he was greatly delighted, for he had long wished to see Him on account of what he had heard of Him. And he also hoped to see some sign performed by Him. So he questioned Him with many words. This was a means of gratifying Herod's curiosity to see Jesus, of whom he had heard so much, whose fame had terrified him, and by whom he now hoped to see some interesting miracle wrought.

Now he confronted the Man who, in Herod's eyes, resembled John the Baptist. He could atone partially for what he had done to the Baptist by sparing the life of this one. In any case, he was as eager to see Jesus as a child would be to watch a fire-eater.

Herod had long been on friendly terms with Pilate, but the compliment Pilate paid him in sending Jesus for him to examine disarmed his enmity, and made him Pilate's friend.

[**HEROD** *is a medium tall man with a paunch and a square-cut beard. He wears the trappings of his office—crown, royal cape, scepter—at all possible times. Looking at* JESUS *with mingled curiosity and uneasiness.*]

SECOND VOICE: Whatever fear Herod had once felt regarding Jesus was replaced by amused interest when he saw the far-famed Prophet of Galilee in bonds before him, attended by a Roman guard, and accompanied by ecclesiastical officials.

Antipas was quite willing to let things take their course about Jesus.

He was relieved to see that Jesus was not John the Baptist, risen from the dead, as he had feared, but another man altogether.

Now, when the prophet was brought in, Herod looked at him with mingled curiosity and uneasiness. No, Jesus was not in the least like John! Still, this Galilean seer might well be able to utter some wise saying, might be able with a single phrase to dispel the feelings of horror with which the tetrarch was afflicted whenever thoughts of the murdered Baptist invaded his mind.

Jesus could not be impressed. The things He knew about Antipas were engraved deeply in His mind. He knew the king would do nothing in this case except ask for a show of power.

HEROD: If you Jesus of Nazareth have indeed been sent by God, I will be happy to witness a few simple demonstrations of this power. Would you mind performing?

SECOND VOICE: The murderer of John the Baptist had long sought to see this famous Jesus, and received him at first with some pomp, surrounded by his guards and his court. Although the aspect of the unhappy man must have confounded him, he proceeded to ply him with questions.

JESUS: [There is no answer. JESUS stands in quiet dignity and refused to answer questions.]

HEROD: A small feat of magic, perhaps? A little miracle? Can you make water pour from the walls or thunder roll through the sky?

[JESUS remains silent. He changes into a statue.]

SECOND VOICE: Jesus who had never worked a miracle on His own behalf would certainly not work one now to release Himself. But the frivolous tetrarch, who regarded the prisoner in the way an audience might regard a juggler, looked for the thrill of some brief moment of magic. He did not believe in a future life; and as a man entirely devoted to licentiousness, he identified religion with magic.

Herod was the type of man who was curious about religion, studying, reading, and sometimes knowing it well, but he also kept his vices. That is why he asked Jesus many questions.

For penitent sinners, weeping women, prattling children, for the scribes, the Pharisees, the Sadducees, the rabbis, for the perjured high priest and his obsequious and insolent underling, and for Pilate the

234

pagan, Christ had words—of comfort or instruction, of warning or re-buke, of protest or denunciation—yet for Herod the fox He had but disdainful and kingly silence.

[*The* **CHIEF PRIESTS** *and* SCRIBES *stand and vehemently accuse Him.*]

SECOND VOICE: But the Son of Man had changed into a statue, and despite the vehement accusations of the scribes, he answered naught to this fox, as he had one day called Herod. The tetrarch and his court about him represented the world for which Jesus did not pray. The priests were less repugnant to him than these futile criminals, these parrots, these scum, who believed themselves the flower of the world.

JESUS: Jesus would give no answer. Brought before Herod, His only thought was that this was the man who killed the forerunner, John. Was He to answer such a man's questions, read the stars, foretell the future?

FIRST VOICE: He was silent, though a few carefully chosen words might have saved His life; was silent because He no longer thought of being rescued by human hands; was silent, because both the Jewish tetrarch and the pagan governor were but phantoms before the eyes of One whose vision could pierce the clouds of heaven.

HEROD: [*He stands up and reviles* JESUS. *He mocks* JESUS *and taunts Him.*] You are a king of nothing and a monarch of no one.
[*The* TETRARCH *walks around the prisoner.*]
No! Is this Jesus? What a disappointment! He merits death for this if for nothing else. But they told me He was handsome! He is frightful! He certainly does not look like a Prophet! What a trumpery affair. Strange how reputations are made!
At least John the Baptist had been somebody. Beside John the Baptist this man does not exist. He is a nobody in comparison. He is an imposter!
No, but look at his air! Who does He think he is, the poor devil. . . . He thinks he is impressing us with His silence.

SECOND VOICE: From the dregs of memory, he brought up epi-thets recalled only in unreasoning anger. He mocked Jesus and taunted Him. He made personal remarks about His shabby appearance, His lacerated face, His dirty garments, the now-unwashed feet, the swollen eyes.
The silence of Jesus so irritated Herod that his insulted pride turned to scoffing and mockery.

235

HEROD: It might help His case if He were more cooperative.

[*The* PRIESTS *fill the gap of silence with recitations of all the crimes* JESUS *had committed.*]

FIRST VOICE: Although the scribes and the chief priests joined Herod in goading Jesus, He refused to speak to Herod. If He had spoken, He would only have added to the guilt of the moral trifler.

The temptation to accept all the kingdoms of the world by compromising the Cross was once more presented to Jesus. Pilate He could have won—and Herod too with a word—but He refused to speak. He had warned about preaching to those who were insincere in the Sermon on the Mount.

Truth is not to be given to everyone, but only to those who are "of the truth." Though Herod was glad to see Jesus, his gladness did not arise from noble motives of repentance. Hence, Jesus, who spoke to a penitent thief and to Magdalen and Judas, would not speak to the Galilean king, for Herod's conscience was dead. He was too familiar with religion. He wanted miracles, not as motives of credibility, but as delights to his curiosity. His soul was so blinded by appeals, including even the Baptist's, that one more appeal would have only deepened his guilt. It was not his soul for salvation that Herod offered Jesus, but his nerves for tittilation. So the Lord of the world spoke not a word to the worldling.

Herod had seen men gain the ascendancy in his court by words, but he saw something utterly new when Jesus gained the moral command of the situation in the court by silence—a silence that hurt.

Jesus held his peace—before the High Priest, before Pilate, before Herod—always there was the same silence. Truly the natural man cannot find the way of His glorification in His silence. The result was that the world (Herod) held to its opinion—"here we have no wise man, no noble man, no man of discernment after the flesh."

HEROD: A king indeed! Pray, king of what?

[*He calls one of his* ASSISTANTS *and whispers to him. Then he winks at the* PRIESTS, *and everyone waits in silence.*]

[*In a few minutes the aide returns with a beautiful cloak. It is a garish red garment such as might be worn by the king of a nomadic tribe. It is more theatrical than kingly.*]

[**HEROD** *takes it in his hands and shakes the dust from it. Then, with a friendly smile, he swings it over the shoulders of* JESUS *and ties the red ropes at the collar. It is comic.*]

[*Even the* HIGH PRIESTS *are forced to smile.*]

SECOND VOICE: Jesus made the most sorrowful and ridiculous king any of them had seen.

[**HEROD** *and his* ATTENDANTS *make a jest of Him, arraying Him in festal attire*]

SECOND VOICE: Herod and his attendants made a jest of Him, arraying Him in festal attire out of mockery. Thus Herod intimated that the pretend king was worthy of contempt. Thoroughly piqued, Herod turned from insulting questions to acts of malignant derision. He and his men-at-arms made sport of the suffering Christ. In travesty they arrayed him in a gorgeous robe. Herod had his revenge.

Herod, therefore, came to the conclusion that He was no more than a fool, one who had assumed John's mantle without inheriting any of that prophet's sardonic wisdom. He was an object for mockery.

FIRST VOICE: Authority, fame, recognition by the people, these make up the sunshine which the man of wisdom seeks. He should be proudly conscious of his merits and bask in his own admiration. What about Jesus? Was He to put princes out of countenance? He stood before the king, and Herod and his courtiers jeered at the lowly Man who seemed so easy a subject for their mockery.

Exaggerated renunciation always attracts attention among men of the world. Jesus was "like other men" and His poverty never became a source of vanity. He was never engaged in big business, but was untiringly faithful in little things. "The Greatest of all chose everyday life as His working place." His humility came from the heart, but to His contemporaries this was synonymous with lack of dignity. No one looked for "the man of wisdom" in this garb.

HEROD: [*Waves his hand to the* SOLDIERS *and the* PRIESTS *to take the* PRISONER *back.*] Take him back to Pilate. Tell Pilate that nothing against the accused can be found. We find in Him no crime against Galilee.

SECOND VOICE: And he sent him again to Pilate, thus dressed as a witless imbecile. Herod had no jurisdiction over Him now. The time had been when Herod would have put Jesus to death could he have Him in his power, but, now that he had been arrested in Pilate's province, it was impolitic to do so. Had he yielded to his desires he might have offended the government at Rome.

Herod was played out, and unable to get a word out of Jesus. Much as Antipas appreciated the courtesy, it was a ticklish task which had been handed him. Jesus was indeed his own subject, but right now he was in Jerusalem, for the moment official headquarters of the procurator; no wise vassal prince violated Rome's jurisdiction.

[JESUS staggers with weakness as He starts still another journey. He has been standing for many hours.]

SECOND VOICE: And the same day Pilate and Herod were made friends; for before they were at enmity between themselves.

FIRST VOICE: It is the way of the world for those who have small hates to bury them for the sake of a higher hate. Nazism and Communism united because of a common hatred of God; so did Pilate and Herod. Pharisaism and Sadduceeism, which were enemies, united in the Crucifixion. The Cross of Christ unites His friends—that is obvious; but the Cross also unites His enemies. The worldly always drop their lesser hates in the face of the hatred of the Divine.

SECOND VOICE: It was a good joke, this prisoner, covered with His own Blood, hated by His own people, claiming to be a king. Herod could trust Pilate to see the humor of it. When Pilate and he would laugh over it together, they would no longer be enemies—even when the butt of the humor was God. The only time laughter is wicked is when it is turned against Him Who gave it.

FIRST VOICE: These two judges would be mentioned together; so would the Jews and Gentiles, for the whole world that shared in His condemnation shared or would share in His Redemption.

Scene 6

A COURTYARD OF FORTRESS ANTONIA AT THE PRAETORIUM—THE CURRULE CHAIR

SECOND VOICE: The high priests were in a dilemma, and their only consolation was that Pontius Pilate was in an even worse one. He had refused to dispose of Jesus' case, and had sent it to Herod, the king of the Galileans. Now the case was coming to his doorstep and he would be forced to judge, one way or another.

On the way back to Fortress Antonia the priests discussed the best way of handling the procurator. The ranking Sadducees agreed that Pilate would not be persuaded to confirm Jesus' sentence by any eloquence on their part. Perhaps the answer was to stage a violent demonstration of public opinion. If Pilate thought that, by making the case bigger than it really was, he was embarrassing the high priests, they in turn could make it outlandishly bigger by instructing their crowd to scream for the blood of Jesus.

Pilate, they were quite sure, would hardly dare to defy public opinion in an internal affair which was in reality a small one. So the word was passed from mouth to mouth to wait for signals from the high priests and then to demand the death of the prisoner as loudly as possible.

The party arrived under the double arch of the fortress.

A MESSENGER: [*A message is sent in by* MESSENGER *to the Roman governor.*]

SECOND VOICE: Word was sent in to the Roman governor that Herod had interviewed the prisoner and had found in Him no crime against Galilee.
[*In a few moments* PILATE *comes out with his* MEN. *He again sits in the currule chair. The graying, cantankerous little man is about to speak when he notices the* PRISONER.]

SECOND VOICE: He realized at once that Herod had made a spurious king of Jesus, and had mocked Him by returning Him with a red robe. The procurator interpreted this as meaning that, to Herod, Jesus was comical. A clown among kings. He finds that he can not evade further consideration of the case.

PILATE: [*He calls together the* CHIEF PRIESTS *and the* RULERS *and the* PEOPLE.) You brought this Man before my tribunal [*said loudly*] on the ground that He incited the nation to revolt. In your presence I conducted this hearing, but detected no guilt in Him regarding the charges you preferred against Him.
(You have brought this man to me, as one that perverts the people: and, behold, I, having examined him before you, have found no fault in this man touching those things whereof you accuse him (I examined Him in your presence, and could find no substance in any of the charges you bring against Him).

SECOND VOICE: Pilate resumed the judgment seat and made another effort not to have the Sanhedrin press its charges.

239

PILATE: Nor did Herod either! [*The* PROCURATOR *shouts, and then, subsiding*] for he referred His case back to us. This, then, is the verdict: He has done nothing to deserve the penalty of death.

(Nor could Herod, when I referred you to him. It is plain that He has done nothing which deserves death.—No, nor yet Herod, for I sent you to him; and, lo, nothing worthy of death is done to him.)

SECOND VOICE: He pointed out that Herod had found nothing worthy of death in Jesus; his claim to Messiahship was rather to be made sport of. Apparently both judges were convinced that, regardless of the report that had been circulated, the prisoner was guiltless. For a second time, He was declared innocent.

[The PEOPLE *listen, but they are already muttering.*]

SECOND VOICE: But the crowd did not want Jesus to be released.

PILATE: I will therefore chastise Him, and release Him.

SECOND VOICE: Scourging was indeed the Roman equivalent of our third degree, but it was also Roman practice to seize troublemakers, as happened later to Paul and Silas, scourge them as a warning, and let them go, assured that the troublemakers would not again risk arrest. Such was the punishment Pilate proposed for Jesus.

Herod's scourging was a precedent which seemingly was what the people wanted. Perhaps such would be sufficient to satisfy the desires of the Jews.

The crowd did not want Jesus to be released. So Pilate asked the crowd to let Him off with the punishment of scourging of forty stripes save one, because He had not been guilty. But in vain!

Pilate's desire to save Jesus from death was just and genuine; his intention of scourging the prisoner, whose innocence he had affirmed and reaffirmed, was an infamous concession to Jewish prejudice.

He knew that the charge of sedition and treason was without foundation; and that even the framing of such an accusation by the Jewish hierarchy, whose simulated loyalty to Caesar was but a cloak for inherent and undying hatred, was ridiculous in the extreme; and he fully realized that the priestly rulers had delivered Jesus into his hands because of envy and malice.

He was annoyed by the importunity of these self-seeking priests, who wished, for the advantage of school or sect, to sacrifice one who might be their rival in popular favor.

[**The CROWD,** *on signal, begins to cry for vengeance.*]

SECOND VOICE: Thus the issue hung in the balance, as the Jews and the governor faced one another.

Scene 7

CLAUDIA'S ROOM OR APARTMENT

SECOND VOICE: It is felt that Pilate's appointment to the position of procurator was due to the ties of his wife, Claudia Procula, to the Roman throne. She is said to have been the granddaughter of Caesar Augustus. When Pilate married into the emperor's family, it assured his political future. On the strength of his marriage, Pilate was made the procurator of Judea.

Unlike her husband, who was an atheist, she was superstitious in matters religious; although she worshiped the many gods of the emperor, she feared to interfere with the practices of any other cult, including that of the Jews.

We may reasonably conclude that Claudia must have heard of Jesus and heard His message. During the years spent among the Jews, she had pondered deeply concerning the things she had heard both from philosophers in Rome and Alexandria, and from Hebrew teachers here in Palestine.

The wife of Chise, a steward of Herod Antipas, was so earnest a Christian as not to desert Jesus when He was crucified. It seemed that she had entered into the faith when her child had been cured by Jesus. The wife of Pilate, the governor-general of Judea, had been a friend of the steward's wife, and had perhaps been influenced by her friend to some extent; at all events she seems to have had a sympathy for the teachings of Jesus.

There was almost a Prussian submission to law among the Romans. No woman was allowed to interfere in the processes of law, nor even to offer a suggestion concerning legal procedure.

At this moment Claudia, the wife of Pilate, sent her message to her husband. To send a message to a judge while he was in court was a punishable offense, and only the awfulness of the deed she saw about to be done could have moved Claudia to it. The nightmare rose before her, the face of the doomed, the crowd, the death cries, the memory of Pilate jabbing his thumb downward.

241

[**CLAUDIA** *sits at a desk writing.*]

SECOND VOICE: Claudia had heard about Jesus and the miracles He had performed. She did not want the fate of such a man to rest in Pilate's hands. This morning, hearing the noise from the courtyard below, she wrote to her husband a short note. She remembered her dream of the night before, and told him to have nothing to do with the business.

While the women of Israel were silent, this heathen woman bore witness to the innocence of Jesus, and asked her husband to deal with Him in a righteous way.

FIRST VOICE: The message of Claudia was the epitome of all that Christianity would do for pagan womanhood. She is the only Roman woman in the Gospels and she was a woman of the very highest rank. This dream was an epitome of the dreams and longings of a pagan world, its agelong hope for a righteous man—a Savior.

While Pilate was sitting on the judgment seat, His wife sent to him a message.

CLAUDIA: [*Seated at the window of her room, she looks down at the* PROPHET. *She turns around and motions to a* SLAVE GIRL. *The* SLAVE GIRL *comes forward and* CLAUDIA *hands her the note.*] Go quickly and give this note to Pilate.

SECOND VOICE: She looks down at the prophet of whom during those days she had heard many tales of wonder. Superstition was at work in her as well as knowledge, and the sympathy aroused to all women who set eyes on the Nazarene doubtless played its part.

Scene 8

A COURTYARD OF FORTRESS ANTONIA—THE CURRULE CHAIR OR GABBATHA

[A SLAVE GIRL *comes up from behind and hands* PILATE *two wax tablets joined together—the letter of* CLAUDIA. PILATE *is no less surprised than the mob when a* SLAVE GIRL *suddenly appears beside him in the bright sunlight. Her eyes are wide with fear and burning with the fire of excitement. She plucks his sleeve and drops on her knees before him.*]

[**PILATE'S** *heavy face twists in a scowl of annoyance and he lifts his hand as if to strike her when she speaks.*]

SLAVE GIRL: I bring you word from my mistress. She sent me here to say to you "Have nothing to do with that innocent man, for during the night I have suffered terribly in a dream through him! (Have you nothing to do with that just man: for I have suffered many things this day in a dream because of him.—Have you nothing to do with that just man. Last night I suffered many things in a dream because of him!—Do not have anything to do with the righteous man, for I have had a painful experience in a dream about Him.)

[**PILATE** *looks from the girl into the darkened corridor. He sees* PROCULA *standing half concealed behind a curtain. She looks at him appealingly, but as he starts to speak, disappears and is gone.*]

SECOND VOICE: Pilate's opinion of Jesus was strengthened by a message from his wife.

[**PILATE** *waves the* SLAVE GIRL *away and she is gone.*]

SECOND VOICE: There happened at that very time to be lying in prison at Jerusalem a Jew named Barabbas. He had engaged in armed rebellion and in the struggle that followed had committed murder. He had done the very things the Jews were trying to persuade Pilate that Jesus was likely to do.

[**PILATE** *sees that the square, which just now had been almost empty, is filling with people. From below, from the temple square, the multitude is ascending.*]

SECOND VOICE: Pilate saw that this was a mob-rule crowd gathered for a purpose. Hanan's motley crew consisted of the guardians of the temple, the noble families of Levi, and partly of the temple servants and slaves of the chief priests, a rabble taught beforehand what to do at a given signal to please their masters. The chief priests had persuaded the multitude to destroy Jesus.

[**PILATE** *stands, having pronounced a second verdict. But the bedlam of venom from the crowd is so shattering that, for an instant, Pontius Pilate loses his poise and becomes a frightened man. Out of the roar of sound,* PILATE *hears snatches of words, parts of phrases, and becomes aware that some are asking a Passover pardon for a prisoner named* BARABBAS. *He had forgotten about it. These are political friends of the man now in the dungeon below Antonia—a rebel and a murderer.*]

SECOND VOICE: At this juncture, there arrived on the scene a rabble of persons who had come to celebrate a popular custom. Year by year at the Passover the Romans granted amnesty to one condemned Jewish criminal, whose liberation was regarded as symbolic of the deliverance of the Israelites out of Egypt—with the added implication that thereby the strictness of Roman rule and the indignity of Hebrew servitude are mitigated. Having run through the streets, they reached the gate of the fortress, and clamored there like children, rather for the granting of an established right than because they had any wish to save a life.

It was the custom for the governor at the Passover season to pardon and release any one condemned prisoner whom the people might name. Now at that feast the governor was wont to release to the people a prisoner, whom they would choose.

On that day there lay in durance, awaiting execution, "a notable prisoner, called Barabbas. Now Barabbas was a robber." He was scheduled to die that day, along with two thieves.

FIRST VOICE: His full name was Jesus Barabbas. Barabbas was a nickname for Bar-Abba, which in Aramaic means "the son of the father." Two "rebels," two "deliverers," two "Christs," Jesus and Barabbas. The namesake of the Son of God is the son of the devil.

THE CROWD: It is Passover! Deliver up to us a prisoner!
[*In a few minutes, two figures stand before the multitude on the white marble floor of the praetorium.* PILATE *sits on a raised platform, surrounded by the* IMPERIAL GUARD. BARABBAS, *on one side, blinks in the sunlight. He has not seen it in months. On the other side stands* JESUS. *The trumpets sound. Order is restored.*]

SECOND VOICE: Here were two men accused of revolution. Barabbas appealed to national grievances; Jesus to conscience.

PILATE: [*When they are gathered together. He holds both hands high for quiet. He steps forward and addresses the mob.*] Whom will you that I release to you? Barabbas, or Jesus which is called Christ? (Which do you want me to release as your choice, Bar-Abbas or Jesus called the Messiah?)

SECOND VOICE: For he knew that for envy they had delivered him.

Pilate was very clever; he sought to confuse the issue by choosing a prisoner who was guilty of exactly the same charge they brought against Jesus, namely, sedition against Caesar. This high official had to find another way out, and believed that he had found it when someone reminded him that it was the custom on the feast of the Passover to release a prisoner selected by the multitude.

FIRST VOICE: The question of Pilate had all the air of democracy and free elections, but it was only its cheap facsimile. Ponder his question. Consider first the people to whom it was addressed, then the question itself. The people themselves were not inclined to put Jesus to death. He was holding a fair, democratic election. He was assuming that a vote means the right to choose between innocence and guilt, goodness and evil, right and wrong.

SECOND VOICE: Pilate had a notion how to circumvent Hanan, to snare him. He would leave the choice between the "two Jesuses" up to the people. Pilate thought to pacify the priests and people by releasing Jesus as the subject of Passover leniency; this would be a tacit recognition of Christ's conviction before the ecclesiastical court, and practically an endorsement of the death sentence, superseded by official pardon. The Passover pardon would close the case against Jesus. He would give the people their choice of freeing Bar-Abbas, a known murderer, or Jesus, a man of obvious gentleness. Pilate was certain that they would choose to free Jesus.

This was a fatal question to a crowd composed only of enemies of Jesus and friends of Bar-Abbas. The crafty high priests knew the weakness of the man, and played upon it. In his extremity he apparently appealed to the crowd, in the hope that the sympathizers with Jesus would support him in refusing the demands of the leaders of the nation.

PILATE: Do you want me to set the king of the Jews free for you?

SECOND VOICE: This was Pilate's inspiration. He had noted the enthusiasm shown by the pilgrim crowds for Jesus and to them he turned.

The governor was naive. More than that, he was inconsistent. First, he had acquitted the prisoner from the currule chair, which made the acquittal official; then, confused by the tumult of the high priests and the people, he had permitted himself to send Jesus to a Jewish king to be judged according to Jewish law.

This, in effect, had canceled the first verdict, or at least had thrown it into doubt. Next, to appease the Sanhedrists, Pontius Pilate had offered to have Jesus "disciplined"—scourged. Now, still temporizing, he proposed to give them a choice of the murderer or the Teacher.

[*There is a brief interval between* PILATE'S *question and the* PEOPLE'S *answer, during which the* CHIEF PRIESTS *and* ELDERS *busy themselves among the multitude, urging them to demand the release of the insurrectionist and murderer.*]

PILATE: Which of the two will you that I release to you? (Which of the two do you want me to release for you?)

THE CROWD: [*They all cry out together. The* HIGH PRIESTS *did not have to prompt the people this time. The masses thunder back.*]
Away with him! Release for us Barabbas!
Barabbas! Barabbas!
Not this man, but Barabbas.
No! No! Not him but Barabbas.

SECOND VOICE: Some demagogues had persuaded the multitude to ask for Barabbas. The people can be misled by false leaders; the very ones who shout "Hosanna" on Sunday can shout "Crucify" on Friday. What happened on that Good Friday morning was that through propagandists the people became the masses. A democracy with a conscience became a mobocracy with power.

The chief priests and elders had persuaded the multitude that they should ask for Barabbas, and destroy Jesus.

The priests knew the fickle humor of their own people. A phrase, an exclamation, multiplied a thousandfold by the many-throated crowd, and the dangerous prophet (whom Rome seems inclined to protect) would be set at liberty.

One of their number hit upon an idea. There was another prisoner, Barabbas by name, the most recent of the champions of Jewish freedom, who were thorns in the side of the priesthood, but ever the darlings of the mob. A disciple of Judas the insurgent, a zealot like his great forerunner, he had last autumn invaded the capital at the head of a handful of Galileans, and had been arrested after he and his followers had insulted and molested the Roman watch.

As a catchword, this priest threw out the name of Barabbas. "Barabbas!" The members of the Great Council, grasping the significance of the utterance, were quick to echo it. Those who stood nearest, took up the cry. In a moment every one was shouting, "Barabbas," including many who now heard of him for the first time.

FIRST VOICE: A crowd is almost blind. They are easily stirred up by an agitator. Jesus knew this crowd psychology very well. So He did not trust Himself to them.

SECOND VOICE: Pilate's attempt, however, was futile. The high priests had taken good care that their agents and supporters should be present in goodly numbers.

This would of course have defeated the plans of the high priests, and they instigated the newcomers to stick to their original purpose of getting him to set Barabbas free. The scribes and the priests spread their orders everywhere: the people must demand the release of the robber Barabbas. When Pilate put it to a *viva voce* vote, without hesitation they cried, "Barabbas!"

From the Roman viewpoint, Barabbas was indeed a robber, but to the people he was a hero.

Pilate had put the name of one condemned to death along with Jesus, and indirectly admitted Him as meriting death.

[**PILATE** *can hardly believe his ears.*]

SECOND VOICE: Pilate could hardly believe his ears.

[**BARABBAS** *can hardly believe his ears either! He turns his swollen, burning face toward the* NAZARENE. *He means to measure his rival from head to foot, but his glance no longer dares to rise.*

SECOND VOICE: Barabbas could hardly believe his ears, either! Was he about to be a free man? For the first time, he became aware that he might now carry on his revolt.

He turned his swollen, burning face toward the Nazarene. He meant to measure his rival from head to foot, but his glance no longer dared to rise. There was something about His eyes which read his soul, as if that Nazarene was really sorry for him because he was free.

THE CROWD: [*The whole concourse raises the cry.*] Away with this Man; we must have Barabbas released.

PILATE: [*Again addresses them.* PILATE *is surprised, shocked, disappointed, and angered.*] What shall I do then with Jesus which is called Christ?
[Then what am I to do with Jesus, called the Messiah?—What am I to do with Jesus, the so-called Christ?—What will you then that I should do to him whom you call the King of the Jews?—What would you have

me do, then, with the King of the Jews?]

SECOND VOICE: Pilate wished to release Jesus. He pursued this play-acting at democratic action, hoping he could still get them to vote for releasing Jesus too.

PILATE: [*He sneers.*] Do you wish therefore that I should release to you the king of the Jews?

SECOND VOICE: Pilate then realized he had done a foolish thing. He had committed himself. He was hoping that they would shout an affirmative answer. But he had miscalculated their temper. However much they had been impressed by His teaching and signs, Jesus had alienated them by His tacit admission that tribute should be paid to Caesar. Pilate's sneering title "king of the Jews" applied to one who had refused their offered throne, roused their antipathy.

PILATE: [*A lapse of time occurs.* PILATE *has returned to the praetorium. The* PROCURATOR *comes out again and the* PEOPLE *cease their cries in order to hear him.*]
I have not found any guilt in this man, but you have a custom. Will you, therefore, that I release to you the king of the Jews?

SECOND VOICE: What stupidity to call Jesus thus, even in irony! Even yet, Pilate would fain save Jesus from the priests, but if he was to decide the case against them he needed the support of the people. The festal season would justify a second act of clemency, and he disclosed this possibility by asking those to whom he was leaving the decision.

THE CROWD: [*They keep shouting. They yell.*] Crucify Him! Crucify Him! Have Him crucified!

SECOND VOICE: He offered to set Jesus at liberty, but they continued to answer with shouts of "Crucify Him, crucify Him!" "Crucify Him!" shouted the priests with one voice. "Crucify him!" came in chorus from the crowd—though many of those that joined in the demand did not even know for whose crucifixion they clamored. Such is the universal cry of the mob.

PILATE: [*Once again he raises his voice. He, for the third time, appeals to them.* PILATE *insists.*] Why, what evil has this man done?

248

SECOND VOICE: Pilate was shocked himself at such ferocity, and tried to labor with them.

Pilate had become convinced early in the examination that, although the charge brought against Jesus by the Jews was technically correct, so far as the safety of the State was concerned, Jesus was harmless; hence his efforts to persuade the Jews to withdraw their charge, or accept the release of Jesus.

PILATE: I have found nothing worthy of death in Him. I will therefore chastise Him and release Him.

SECOND VOICE: Pilate beat a retreat, seeking to save the innocent Christ from these furious men. As he could hit upon nothing, his Roman indulgence inspired him with a horrible stratagem: to reduce the man to such a state of abjection and misery that no one would any longer attach the slightest importance to his derisory kingdom. It was to save him from the band of wolves that he delivered him over to the soldiers. He knew how the latter would acquit themselves of their task. When he had left their hands the king of the Jews would disarm even the members of the Sanhedrin; he would fill even the bloodthirsty priests with pity.

Pilate proposed to inflict a punishment in the hope of moving the crowd to pity. Naturally it was no surprise to Jesus, who had foretold that He would be scourged and crucified.

Pilate had made four attempts thus far to free Jesus; one by declaring Him innocent, another by sending Him to Herod, another by releasing a prisoner at the Passover, and the final one by scourging.

Pilate tried to strike a balance between satisfying the Sanhedrin and his own conscience. But Pilate was wrong in thinking that the drawing of blood would calm their passions and melt them to pity. Such compromises in the face of justice rarely achieve their ends. If he were guilty, Pilate should have condemned Him to death; if innocent, he should have released Him.

THE CROWD: [*They cry out the more exceedingly.*] Crucify Him!

SECOND VOICE: *But they were insistent, loudly demanding that He be crucified.*

PILATE: [*He releases* BARABBAS, *and hands* JESUS *over to the* SOLDIERS *to be scourged. To the* CENTURION.] Release Barabbas at once. Proceed with the scourging. [*Motions with his hand. He silently waves his hand to the*

LICTOR *on leaving the lithostraton, and the* LICTOR *knows what has to be done.*]

SECOND VOICE: Then Pilate decided to yield to the clamor of the crowd. Pilate correctly judged the temper of the people to be getting out of hand. So he ordered the centurion to release Bar-Abbas at once, and to proceed with the scourging of Jesus.

Although the sentence had not yet been pronounced, Pilate gave the order for Jesus to be scourged.

THE SOLDIERS *drag* JESUS *away. It was probably a* manipula *of 120 men, or a* centuria *of sixty. A cohort was 600 men, which could not have collected in the inner courtyard of the praetorian camp.*]

SECOND VOICE: And the soldiers led him away into the hall, called the praetorium; and they called together the whole battalion.

Scene 9

THE PRAETORIUM CAMP

SECOND VOICE: Roman scourging was called the "halfway death" because it was supposed to stop just this side of death. It was a great deal more severe than Hebrew scourging, which was known as the "intermediate death." The custom in Palestine was to administer to the prisoner "forty stripes save one." It was done by a paid executioner, who, armed with a long, supple rod, beat the prisoner thirteen times on each shoulder and thirteen times on the loins.

The Roman scourge was administered by a trained man, called a lictor—and he used a short, circular piece of wood to which were attached several strips of leather. At the end of each strip, he sewed a chunk of bone or a small piece of iron chain. This instrument was called a *flagellu.*

The prisoner seldom died but, although in time the scars might fade, the shame and humiliation seldom did.

"The scourge," according to Roman law, had to precede the cross. This may have been more terrible than the cross itself. The scourging should not be misunderstood. In reality, it was intended as an act of mercy. By inflicting the lesser punishment, Pilate still was hoping to satisfy Jesus' enemies and thus save his life. It was a terrible ordeal, but apparently inflicted in mercy on those who were condemned to be crucified, that their physical strength might be in part exhausted, so that they would not have to endure so long the more awful tortures of the cross.

[JESUS is tied to a slightly inclined post, quite naked, with His hands bound tightly behind His back. The SOLDIERS, therefore, take hold of him; they are going to amuse themselves well.]

THE LICTOR: [*The* SOLDIER *who performs flagellations for the Jerusalem garrison approaches and, out of curiosity, bends down to see the face of the victim. He then moves to a position about six feet behind* JESUS, *and spreads his legs. The* flagellum (flagella) *is brought all the way back and whistles forward and makes a dull drum sound as the strips of leather smash against the back of the rib cage. The bits of bone and chain curl around the right side of the body and raise small, subcutaneous hemorrhages on the chest.* JESUS' *back is covered with blood.*

Several of the "more experienced" lictors deal blows from all sides with scourges that consist of leather thongs with sharp globules of bone or lead, which not only beat the flesh but enter into it. He is whipped with lashes of leather loaded with lead, or spikes, or bones, which lacerate the back and chest and face. The fresh coolness of the morning breeze comes down on His back, and the muscles of His legs tremble involuntarily.

JESUS: a moan escapes the lips of JESUS and He almost collapses. The flagellum comes back again, aimed slightly lower, and it crashes against skin and flesh. The lips of JESUS seem to be moving in prayer. The flagellum now moves in slow, heavy rhythm.]

[The TRIBUNE, *whose responsibility it is to stop the "discipline" when he thinks that the guilty one might not be revived, stops the* EXECUTIONER *and goes over to examine* JESUS. *The* MESSIAH *is unconscious. The scourging has not taken more than about three minutes.*]

[**The TRIBUNE** *sends* TWO MEN *for cloths and cold water. The washing of the body is hardly an act of mercy because it returns the prisoner to gasping consciousness. They wash His body. The* TRIBUNE *orders a* SOLDIER *to help* JESUS *to stand.* JESUS *held in this position until He feels a slight return of strength. Then He is permitted to sit on the stone column.*]

SECOND VOICE: Little by little, His entire body began to throb with pain. It began as a pulsing thing, dull and enervating, and it worked up until the entire body screamed with agony.

The Roman soldiers had given Him His baptism of blood. He, meanwhile, has been transformed.

SOLDIERS: [*Several of the* SOLDIERS *approach* JESUS. *They are carrying the scarlet cloak, a heavy reed, and a hat cleverly fashioned out of thorns. As they come nearer, the victim, naked and shivering in spasms which shake His whole body, looks up into the sun and waits. When He was about to clothe Himself again, the fancy had taken them to dress him up as the king he was fabled to be. The* SOLDIERS *carry out into the yard from the barracks the traveling chair of the* CENTURION *and, placing it in the middle, seat* JESUS, *naked and streaming with blood after the scourging. One of them throws a military cloak round His shoulders, and fastens the clasp; another puts a reed sceptre in His hand; a third, cutting some thorns from the garden hedge, plaits them into a crown to surmount the victim's long hair. Again they throw the purple robe of* ANTIPAS *over his bleeding shoulders, they improvise a crown of cruel thorns and press it upon his head.*]

SECOND VOICE: In accordance with the brutal customs of the time, Jesus, weak and bleeding from the fearful scourging He had undergone, was given over to the half-savage soldiers for their amusement. He was no ordinary victim, so the whole band came together in the praetorium, or great hall of the palace, to take part in the diabolical sport.

[*It was the custom after scourging for the soldiers at the fortress to play pranks on the prisoner.*

This Man had pretended to be king, and they were going to costume Him like a king—a comic king. Their joke would be similar to Herod's, but an even better one.]

FIRST VOICE: As they came near, His mutilated face masked the compassion and the strength that would redeem the world. The Lord fulfilled the Last Supper: "This is my body, this is my blood."

THE SOLDIERS: Wait until I make a crown for the king! Here, put this reed into His hands. . . . Hail to the king of the Jews!

Long live the king of the Jews!

SECOND VOICE: The blood with which He was covered enveloped Him first with a scarlet mantle over which the soldiers were to cast another, this one made of cloth, which stuck to the raw flesh.

Of course in a time when one emperor, Augustus, in his shows had set ten thousand men to fighting each other to death to entertain the Roman public, life counted for very little.

FIRST VOICE: This was done to Him by people and yet they believed that God set Him at his own right hand in the heavenly places.

[The **SOLDIERS** *sometimes smite Him and sometimes bow their knees to Him in mock humility. They bow the knee before Him and begin to salute Him. They spit upon Him, and take the reed and smite Him on the head. And bending their knees and jostling one another they worship Him; and fists beat down upon the face that was now an open wound. They knelt down before Him in feigned adoration.*]

SECOND VOICE: These men whose trade was war, whose natures like their occupation were unrefined, whose sport was coarse, and who supposed Jesus to be an unsuccessful rebel, amused themselves by insulting Him.

During this interval the soldiers, appointed for the execution, invented the game of "King of the Jews." "Everything was done as in theatrical performances."

"He was dressed in a fool's crown and seated on a fool's throne, bowed down to, obeyed in every whim." They called out in mock reverence, in mockery of His royalty.

They opened his flesh in violent stripes.

Pilate, losing his none-too-patient temper, had deliberately insulted the high priests by asking the crowd if they wished to liberate the king of the Jews; the Roman soldiers were only imitating their commander, and their mockery was not so much at the expense of the innocent victim as that of the hierarchy.

How they sneered when the crown of thorns crowned His brow!

In the courtyard of Caiphas the Jews mocked the Son of God, the King of Heaven, and here in the courtyard of Pilate the Romans mocked the Son of Man, the King of the World. Thus, in derision, Jesus is treated as a king.

FIRST VOICE: And all the while it was for our sins. He was wounded, it was guilt of ours crushed Him down; on Him the punishment fell that brought us peace, by His bruises we were healed. He carried and bore the weight of our weakness and our miseries. And we thought of Him, as a man God had smitten and brought low.

THE SOLDIERS *take off the purple cloak and put His own clothes back on Him. They bring Him back to the lithostratum or courtyard.*]

Scene 10

A COURTYARD OF FORTRESS ANTONIA—THE PAVEMENT OR GABBATHA—THE CURRULE CHAIR

SECOND VOICE: He is before Pilate, crowned with thorns, a stick in His hand, and a mock robe of royalty about His shoulders—an object of abject pity. But is He? There shines through this abjectness a regal dignity. Pilate knew that the prisoner was judging the judge, and "he was the more afraid."

[**PILATE,** *preceded by* ABENADAR *and a* SQUAD OF SOLDIERS, *comes down the steps for the third time. He has* JESUS *brought forth. He sits down in the judgment seat. The crowds around the Fortress Antonia arches have thinned.*]

SECOND VOICE: Pilate had watched from afar off and put an end to the punishment as unworthy of the "Majesty of Rome." Pilate had been a silent observer of this barbarous scene (the scourging). He stopped it, and determined to make another attempt to touch the springs of Jewish pity, if such existed.

[**The PRIESTS** *stand in front and converse in whispers. At once the deep growl of many men talking in low voices is hushed.*]

SECOND VOICE: The high priests were certain that when Pilate had completed the flagellation of the prisoner he would tell them that this was punishment enough. He would try to free Jesus on the premise that He was now a broken and pathetic figure. Caiphas was nettled by this type of reasoning.

On this preparation of the Passover, it was about the sixth hour.

PILATE: [*Once more, the* GOVERNOR *sits in his chair. This time he seems to be impatient. He glances angrily at the remaining crowd and, raising his right hand high, he goes out to speak to them in person (with an air that says: "You will see what you will see!")*] Now, look! I am bringing this so-called Messiah out to you, and you must understand that I find no guilt in Him! (Behold, I bring Him forth to you, that you may know that I find no fault in Him. See, I am bringing Him out to you, to show that I cannot find any fault in Him. . . . See, I am bringing Him out to you, so that you may realize that I find in Him no *crime* at all. [*He points across the lithostrotos to the left and sees a* CENTURION *and some* SOLDIERS *leading* JESUS *out.*]

254

SECOND VOICE: This was the governor's third definite proclamation of the prisoner's innocence.

[**JESUS** comes out through the gate, still silent—Or PILATE goes in to find JESUS and reappears, pushing before him that puppetlike figure, covered with red and faded finery, His head crowned with thorns, His face a mask of spittle, of sweat and blood, in which are matted the meshes of His hair.]

[**The CROWD** *utters shouts of ribald laughter.*]

SECOND VOICE: Then Pilate, the man of the world, was once again aware of a feeling of respect for this man of the spirit. Even Pilate felt his strength and courage. The two men offered a strange contrast standing there—the Roman governor whose lips were so soon to speak the sentence of death, and the silent, self-possessed ex-carpenter—accused and doomed—yet bearing Himself with so much majesty, as though He were somehow beyond the reach of manmade law, and safe from the hurt of its penalties.

PILATE: [*He points to the crowned figure dramatically.* PILATE *looks on the prisoner. He looks at the crowd, and sees the natural pity of common people for suffering. Their eyes also show horror and some turn away.* PILATE *raises his hand; the shouting and the tumult die; a deathly stillness descends upon the crowd. He turns and faces the figure at his side. Then he seizes His hand and holds it aloft.*] Behold the man.

FIRST VOICE: From Pilate's coarse lips there burst a sentence which is a truer portrait than any painter has ever given us. It was the involuntary testimony of the flabby Roman, "Behold the Man." Thus said a Roman in the presence of perfect strength, perfect assurance, perfect calm: "Behold," he cried, "the man!"

SECOND VOICE: Pilate was determined to the last to save Jesus if possible, so he came out once more. This simply means: "Here is the individual in question. You see the kind of man that you are accusing. Behold Him not decorated with ermine, with no other crown but thorns, with no other mark of kingship than red blood and with no other sign of authority than a reed. Be assured that He will never again assume the title of a king which has cost Him so dearly. I had hoped to find some spark of humanity in you, and that is why I yielded to your wishes. See he is just an ordinary man, not a king." The Roman wanted to capitalize on the pity and the revulsion. Pilate seems to have counted on the pitiful sight of the scourged and bleeding Christ to soften the hearts of the maddened Jews. If the procurator had hoped that the sight of the bleeding, humiliated victim would awaken pity, he had underestimated the fury of the accusers.

FIRST VOICE: But the effect failed. Think of the awful fact—a heathen, a pagan, who knew not God, pleading with the priests and people of Israel for the life of their Lord and King!

[**The CROWD:** *looks, and sucks in its breath. This man is a shocking sight. The face is so marked that individual features are almost indistinguishable. The top of the garment under the cloak is stained.*]

SECOND VOICE: His accusers were determined. They thronged the courtyard before the palace, clamoring for his blood, yet even they felt a momentary awe when He appeared before them on the balcony.

FIRST VOICE: It was not courage but a conviction in His purpose that carried Him to the end. This conviction gave him strength, energy and if you must—courage.

SECOND VOICE: When the Roman saw what remained of the Jew he was reassured. The soldiers had done their work well; this lamentable creature would put to shame those who had delivered Him up.

THE PRIESTS: [*They cry with increasing vindictiveness, a tremendous cry.*] Crucify Him, Crucify Him.

SECOND VOICE: This disconcerted the procurator. The appearance of Jesus did not correspond with Israel's hopes? Jesus made quite a different impression. His people were aware that He laid claim to the Messianic title; in fact, at the last this claim was made openly, and He became an offense, provoking their contradiction. This Man the Messiah?

PILATE: [*Not daring to look into the face of the accused, the* JUDGE *raises his hand.*] Behold your king.

THE PRIESTS: Away with Him, away with Him, Crucify Him. To the cross! To the cross!

THE CROWD: [*They are excluded from the blame. Some of them weep.*

Others smite their breasts—then cry them all.] Liberate not this man, but Barabbas.
[*Shocked,* PILATE *drops the prisoner's hand.*]

SECOND VOICE: He could not believe that, even under the tutelage of Caiphas, the crowd could be so callous in the face of what was left of this human being.

Did they not realize that, at the snap of his fingers, he could have freed this man at any stage of the hearing? Why did they press for crucifixion when it was obvious that he did not want to countenance capital punishment in this case? Did they not realize that he could order the immediate arrest of them all?

He saw now—too late—that he should not have argued with either the priests or the people. It would have been much better if he had exercised the *ius gladii,* the power of the procurator, and ordered Jesus to be freed for lack of evidence.

PILATE: Why? What evil has He done?

THE PRIESTS: Crucify Him, crucify Him.

PILATE: [PILATE *tries to cry out louder than they.*] But he is innocent. [*This he adds with bitter emphasis. Disgustedly,* PILATE *glares at the people and makes two or three false starts to say something. Finally he says bitterly.*] Take Him *yourselves* and crucify, for I do not find in Him a crime. (Then take Him in charge yourselves and crucify Him! I find no guilt in Him!)

SECOND VOICE: This of course they could not do; they did not possess the legal authority. Caiphas knew, and so did Pilate and everyone present, that the Jews had no power to crucify.

A PRIEST: [*Comes apart from the multitude. A great silence falls because he speaks in the name of all.*] We have a law, and according to the law He must die, because He has made Himself Son of God (and according to that law he ought to die for pretending to be the Son of God).

SECOND VOICE: They had failed to prove their charge that Jesus was a potential rebel; they could only fall back on the earlier accusation. Then a priest came apart from the multitude.

Now that sentence of crucifixion (to be done by the Jews) had been extorted from Pilate, they brazenly attempted to make it appear that the governor's mandate was but a ratification of their own decree of death;

therefore they said: ". . . Because He made himself the Son of God."

PILATE: (Such an argument had no validity under Roman law and Pilate continued to urge dismissal of the case.)

SECOND VOICE: What did it mean? That awe-inspiring title, Son of God, struck yet deeper into Pilate's troubled conscience. Here was something new! It will be remembered that the only charge preferred against Christ before the Roman governor was that of sedition; the Jewish persecutors had carefully avoided even the mention of blasphemy, which was the offense for which they had adjudged Jesus worthy of death.

Pilate was troubled. *Son of God*—what did this mean? When Pilate hears the words, *Son of God*, he begins to be afraid. Until that moment, he has regarded Jesus as an innocent man; now he has a vague sense that he is possibly in the presence of someone with supernatural powers.

FIRST VOICE: Pilate said that He was a "man"; they said, "the Son of God." Pilate had declared that He was innocent before the Roman law. They answered that He was guilty before their law.

Superstition goes hand in hand with skepticism. Herod did not believe in the Resurrection; nevertheless, when he heard of Jesus preaching in his territory, he thought that Jesus was John the Baptist who was risen from the dead. Pilate did not believe that He was the Son of God; nevertheless, he wondered at this strange being before him, who spoke no words in His own defense.

The governor was at his wit's end. He was worried. For he remembered that Procula had begged him please not to do anything about this man—that she had suffered a great deal in a dream about Him.

Pilate believed in none of it—from divinity to dream—but he was strangely troubled.

PILATE: [*He is more afraid than ever. He turns away on his gilded sandals and walks back into the praetorium. To Abenadar:*] Bring the prisoner to me.

Scene 11

THE JUDGMENT HALL IN THE PRAETORIUM

PILATE: [*He makes* JESUS *come forward. In trepidation. Inside, it is* PILATE *who appears to be harried. Now a cold fright takes hold of him and he cannot* *understand what frightens him. He studies the wounded man standing before him and says gently.*] Where do you come from? (What is your origin?)

SECOND VOICE: The inquiry or surprising question was as to whether Jesus was human or superhuman. In the mind of the procurator there was no question of Jesus' earthly origin. No doubt the Roman sensed in this derelict an immense force which escaped him. He was deeply shaken and fearful that probably Jesus was some messenger from the gods.

Jesus' Galilean origin did not interest him, for he had already sent Jesus as the Galilean to Herod. He perceived Jesus to be something more than a man. If He was really from heaven he would not crucify Him; therefore, he asked privately for His real origin. Pilate had already asked six questions. There remained only one more which he would ask.

[**JESUS** seems to gather a little strength. He studies the Roman briefly, then lowers His head and does not answer. CHRIST is silent.]

FIRST VOICE: A direct avowal of the Lord's divinity would have frightened but could not have enlightened the heathen ruler; therefore Jesus gave no answer.

A victim? Yet He himself bows to the stroke; no word comes from Him. Sheep led away to the slaughter house, lamb that stands dumb while it is shorn.

Pilate had treated Jesus as a subject of speculation for he availed Him not of the truth before Him. To such men there is no response from the heavens. In the depths of his own mind, Pilate had reached the conviction of innocence, but he did not act upon it. Therefore Pilate deserved no answer and received none. He had forfeited his title to any further revelation from the prisoner. Every soul has its day of visitation, and Pilate had his.

At last Jesus had to realize that no further blessing could be brought about by His words; He held His peace.

Jesus' love was humble, that is, directed downwards, willing to abase itself and to serve. Service is the opposite of ruling, it is help given in lowliness and weakness. It is true that it thus took on strength, for it is not mere endurance or quiet acceptance, but the humility of action, that actually does something. His humility was a heroic sense and power; He willed to stoop, to use all His power in sacrifice and in lowly service.

This Jesus did not think meanly of Himself, for He knew that He was the Master and Lord, the one green tree in the midst of all the dry wood, ripe for judgment. He had no sense of being a miserable sinner; while we can hardly speak of any humility shown by Him toward God.

And yet this unique personality, reigning in solitary state high above mankind, stooped and still stoops to serve in lowliness, undisturbed and unwearying.

SECOND VOICE: Pilate was further surprised, and perhaps somewhat offended at this seeming disregard of his authority. He demanded an explanation.

PILATE: [*Says through set teeth.* PILATE *grows impatient and irritated.*] Speak you not to me? Know you not that I have power to crucify you, and have power to release you?
(What, have You no word for me? Do you not know that I have power to crucify You, and power to release You?—that I have power to set You free and power to crucify You?)

JESUS: [The dry, broken lips move. The voice is hoarse.]
You could have no power at all against me, except it were given you from heaven.
(You would have no power over me, were it not given you from above.—You have no power whatever to harm Me, unless it is granted to you from above.—You would not have any power over Me at all, if it had not been given you from above.)

FIRST VOICE: The positions were reversed; Christ was the judge, and Pilate the subject of His decision. Jesus was saying that Pilate had no power at all because it would be overruled.

Pilate spoke of his power to release or to condemn. The judge is judged. Jesus spoke at once, reminding Pilate that any judicial authority which he had came not from Caesar but from God. Pilate had boasted of the arbitrariness of his power, but Jesus referred to a power that is delegated to men.

The power that Pilate boasted was "given." Whether a governor, king, or ruler know it not, all earthly authority is derived from on high. He told Pilate that his authority as a judge came from Him, yet He would accept a false judgment.

Divinity and a suffering Savior were both repugnant to unregenerated men; Divinity, because man secretly wants to be his own god; suffering, because the ego cannot understand why a seed must die before it springs forth into new life. The Son of God became a stumbling block when He humiliated Himself to the human level, taking on the form and habit of man. It is hard on the intelligentsia to believe that Greatness can be so little. On the other hand, the Son of Man became a scandal when He took upon Himself the weakness and even the guilt of man and did not use His Divine power to escape the Cross.

JESUS: <u>Therefore he that delivered me to you has the greater sin.</u> (He who surrendered Me to you is guilty of a graver offense.—That is why the man who gave Me up to you is more guilty yet.)

FIRST VOICE: Though not found guiltless, the Roman was pronounced less culpable than he or those who had forced Jesus into his power, and who had demanded of him an unrighteous committal. Jesus immediately ascribed a greater sin to both Judas and the high priest. Pilate, the Gentile, did not know that his power came from God, but Caiphas did; so did Judas. This superior knowledge made each more guilty than the Roman. Pilate sinned through ignorance; Caiphas sinned against knowledge; so did Judas. All the world had delivered Him.

He reminded the Roman governor, boasting of his power, of the One above who was mightier still, but at the same time sought to take some of the responsibility from him.

SECOND VOICE: And from now on Pilate sought to release him. Pilate saw that he would be lost (his prestige and authority vanish, if he was unable to persuade them), if he did not save Him.

In the minds of the Jews of that day there loomed faith in the one God. "He will return as king of the Jews and Lord of the world!"

Pilate's heart was hot within him. The pride of these Jews was the pride that apes humility! Rome had subjugated half the world. Would she never be able to conquer this small and weakly people? Five years and more he had ruled here in the name of the emperor, and although in his reports he spoke of tranquility and obedience, he knew that beneath the surface a spirit of revolt was seething, ready at any moment to burst forth.

How preposterous it was that he could have the emperor's image stamped on the Jewish coins! What harm would the portrait of the emperor do to these lunatics? Though the emperor be honored as a god, he was but emperor; where else in the world was a people whose god was king? What did they mean by their "City of God?" No one interfered with their customs in the temple; Rome had never forced her own gods upon the barbarians. Why, then, should there be this perpetual uproar about a few images, a few ideas?

If there were any further disturbances in Jerusalem, if there was more rioting in Galilee, if the Romans should be worsted in some street affray, when the news of these matters reached Rome it would go hard with the governor.

Pilate's thoughts turned to Rome. He wondered whether his powerful patron, Sejanus, was still alive. Who could tell? The governor mused. He thought of the emperor.

Tiberius, a lonely, old man, dwelt at Capri. The lord of the world, the Roman emperor, had for years now been living in this little aisle, far from the capital, neglecting the affairs of government, gloomy, morose, inactive. A somber dictator was Tiberius, entrusting his powers into the hands of others, withdrawing these powers without notice—suspicious, dour, melancholy. Feelings of hatred were universal. The praetorians distrusted Sejanus; the emperor distrusted the praetorians; everyone distrusted the emperor. Only on this island of Capri could he be safe! Where else could the lord of the world seek refuge?

Seneca, in his last epistle, had written of Diogenes: "It is worth a kingdom to be, in a world of cheats, murderers, and kidnappers, the only person whom no one can injure!" The emperor sent for Seneca's new discourse and read: "We have all erred, and on into our old age we shall continue to fail in our duty. The evil does not lie outside us; it is intertwined with our own entrails. The body is nothing but the burden and punishment of the spirit. The soul strives to return to the place whence it came. There waits eternal calm, and there, after the confusions of the world, lucidity prevails. The day is coming which will free you from the tabernacle of this hateful life. To be fettered, mutilated, crucified—these are the signs of virtue."

The emperor's thoughts turned to the Jews. This all sounded akin to the strange faith of Jerusalem!

As he turned these things over in his mind, Pilate's thoughts flitted to and fro between Capri and Rome. Pilate was no worse than any other governor—though cruel at times, arrogant, and ill-tempered, as was natural to a man in the dull seclusion of colonial life. What did it matter to him that the country groaned under the exactions of the tax-gatherers and the usurpers? Pilate's own hands were clean.

Scene 12

THE COURTYARD—THE GABBATHA

SECOND VOICE: The governor, though having pronounced sentence (conditional sentence), yet sought means of releasing the submissive Sufferer. Jesus' bold rebuke of Pilate, reminding him of his dependence upon God and charging him with the lesser but nonethe-lesss real, sin, stirred his efforts more than ever toward "releasing Him." Pilate went outside to meet the mob and reaffirm the innocence of the prisoner.

THE JEWS: [*Tumultuous cries. They shout ever louder.*]
If you release this man, you are no friend of Caesar's; everyone who makes himself a king sets himself against Caesar.
(If you let this man go, you are not Caesar's friend: whoever makes himself a king speaks against Caesar.—You are no friend of Caesar, if you do release Him; the man Who pretends to be a King is Caesar's rival.) [*Repeats*] Don't release this man. Anyone who declares himself a king renounces allegiance to Caesar.

SECOND VOICE: The mob had their clever answer ready. Pilate's first evidence of wavering was greeted by the Jews with a cry. The tumultuous cries of the Jews rendered, however, further argument with them useless. They would not withdraw the accusation against Jesus, but were bound to press it.

That was the crux of the case. Jesus had admitted that He, in a sense, was a king. Technically, the Jews were right. If they pressed the case, Pilate was bound to condemn Jesus, or run the risk of having to explain at Rome why he had not rid the province of one who was planning rebellion.

At long last the high priests had discovered how to force Pilate's hand. Violation of Jewish law meant nothing under Rome, but now a definite crime was charged. Jesus was accused of treason against the person of the emperor.

Accusation of treason left Pilate no alternative. Jesus must be con-demned or the procurator's numerous enemies would be only too glad to report his failure to the always suspicious Tiberius.

Pilate was frightened! If he released the prisoner, complaint would be made to the already suspicious emperor that he was guilty of con-spiracy and treason. If so, he might lose both his governorship and his head.

This is the way they forced his hand. It was very strange that the mob who despised Caesar for his massacres, for all the harm that he had done them, and his prostitution of the temple, now proclaimed that they had no king but Caesar. The mind of man can easily be diverted or changed by a cause. By proclaiming Caesar as their king, they re-nounced the idea of a Messiah and made themselves vassals of the empire, thus preparing for the Roman armies that swallowed up Jeru-salem within a generation.

It was now no longer a question of saving Jesus, He had to save himself. Pilate dashed about between the Gabbatha and the praetorium, all the while the majesty of Roman justice slowly ebbing away.

FIRST VOICE: The terrors of Tiberius seemed more real to Pilate than the denying of justice to Jesus. But in the end, those who fear men rather than God lose that which they hoped men would preserve for them. Pilate later was deposed by the Roman emperor on a complaint by the Jews—another instance of men being punished by the very instruments in which they confided.

PILATE: [*When* PILATE *hears these words he brings* JESUS *out, and sits down on the judgment seat. Once more he seats himself on the currule chair, surmounted by the Roman eagle over a bundle of spears. There is a sudden hush in the square. He formally takes his place on the tribunal which has been set up on the pavement.*]

SECOND VOICE: There was a sudden hush in the square, for they all knew that when a judge took his seat on the judgment chair the sentence was about to be pronounced. The hour was about the sixth, not far from noon.

Beset by constant worry in the effort to keep the peace during the most dangerous week of the year, the procurator had been compelled to waste six (or five) precious hours, interrupted only by the futile effort to persuade Antipas to take over the case, on the trial of an obscure Gailiean villager. By this time, Pilate had completely lost his temper.

By the very fact that he had finally surrendered (conditionally) Jesus to the demands of the high priests, Pilate had freed himself from their further pressure. Without danger of reprisal, he could insult them to his heart's content.

PILATE: [*Pointing to* JESUS, *he exclaims with unveiled sarcasm.*] Behold your king! [*He mocks them.*] Look, there is your king!

SECOND VOICE: He was resentful against those Jews who had dared to intimate that he was no friend of Caesar, and whose intimation might lead to an embassy of complaint being sent to Rome to misrepresent him in exaggerated accusation.

THE JEWS: [*The* JEWS *answer in threatening and ominous shouts.*] Away! Away! Crucify Him! Away with Him, away with Him, crucify Him!

PILATE: Shall I crucify your king? [*With cutting irony.*] (Am I to crucify your king?—What, shall I crucify your King?)

SECOND VOICE: Here was a stinging reminder of their national subjugation.

Pilate smiled inwardly. So they wanted to talk about Caesar. With a prompt change of front, he endeavored to secure a yet more open expression of this remarkable display of friendship for Rome on the part of the Jewish people. It would be something he could report, with an excellent effect on his own prospects. To spur on the multitude to the direction he wanted them to pursue, he inquired: "Shall I crucify your king?"

THE CHIEF PRIEST: [*Smugly the* HIGH PRIESTS *assure him.*]
We have no king but Caesar.
[*This angers the* HIGH PRIESTS *and the* PEOPLE *and, in a jumble of sound,* PILATE *makes out the words.*]

SECOND VOICE: It would have been impossible to have played better into the hands of Hanan than Pilate did by himself exciting the people. Remembering the already too long list of Jewish revolts, Pilate smiled cynically.

FIRST VOICE: And the king took them at their word! As once before, in the days of Samuel, they rejected the government of God in order to have a king which God gave them in anger, so now, as they rejected the kingship of Jesus Christ they would be ground to the earth under the kingship of Caesar.

The people who had by covenant accepted Jehovah as their king now rejected Him in person, and acknowledged no sovereign but Caesar. Caesar's subjects and serfs have they been through all the centuries since. Pitiable is the state of man or nation who in heart and spirit will have no king but Caesar! With this cry Judaism was, in the person of its representatives, guilty of denial of God, of blasphemy, of apostasy.

Why did Pilate waver, hesitate, vacillate, and at length yield, contrary to his conscience and his will? He was in servitude to his past. He was the Roman ruler, but the people over whom he exercised official dominion delighted in seeing him cringe, when they cracked, with a vicious snap above his head, the whip of a threatened report about him to his imperial master, Tiberius.

Pilate knew what was right but lacked the moral courage to do it. He was afraid of the Jews, and more afraid of hostile influence at Rome. He was afraid of his conscience, but more afraid of losing his official position. He realized that his tenure was insecure, and he dreaded exposure. Such wrongs had he wrought that when he would have done good, he was deterred through cowardly fear of the accusing past.

Ironically, this group of Palestinians had now turned the political table askew so that they appeared to be more loyal to the cause of Tiberius Caesar than Caesar's hand-picked governor. At that point, Pontius Pilate gave up the fight.

[*It was a Roman custom when a criminal was condemned to death to take a long stick, break it in two, and throw it at the prisoner's feet.* PILATE *follows this custom, and the broken pieces on the marble floor form the figure of a cross.*]

SECOND VOICE: Pilate saw that he could prevail nothing, but rather a tumult was made, and that he was only adding fuel to the fire. He found that he could not prevail, and foresaw a tumult among the people if he persisted in the defense of Christ.

Pilate understood that he had gone too far, that he could not spare this miserable man without being denounced in Rome.

[**PILATE** *calls for water and washes his hands before the multitude. He dips both hands into it.*]

SECOND VOICE: This was a symbolic act of disclaiming responsibility, which they all understood. Pilate was so shocked at the upshot of his slipshod efforts to get somebody else to take the responsibility for letting Jesus go that he called for water and solemnly washed his hands before the crowd.

PILATE: [*He looks directly at* CAIPHAS.] I am innocent of the blood of this just person: see you to it. (I am not responsible for this man's death; you must see to it yourselves. I have no part in the death of this Innocent Man: it concerns you only.—I am innocent of the blood of this just Man. The responsibility is yours!)

SECOND VOICE: The judge refused to argue further, and would permit the contender to have his way. The man found a subterfuge to acquit himself of legal responsibility. This was to wash his hands in public, and to proclaim himself innocent of the blood of this just man. He protested that it was not his hand that shed this blood, nor that his eyes had ever witnessed the deed. Now the role was reversed. It was Pilate who declared himself innocent; it was the followers of Moses who did the opposite. Though the cowardly governor washed away symbolically the responsibility for his perversion of justice, history has run with the cry: "Suffered under Pontius Pilate."

From the perspective of history we need no official or miraculous confirmation of Jesus' innocence. His condemnation was the result of the murderous hate of a group of unprincipled men and of a gross disregard of the Roman traditions of justice.

THE JEWS: [*The rabble cries out.*] His blood be on us and on our children.

SECOND VOICE: History bears an appalling testimony on the literal fulfilment of that dread invocation.

FIRST VOICE: Jesus hated mother earth, and that is what was mortally to wound Him. The Son of man "must suffer," that He already knew, but He did not know that it was from His own people that He was to suffer and not from strangers. He was still to hope, and to hope to the end, to the Cross, that it would be the strangers who would reject Him, and His own people would accept Him. In this anguishing torture by hope was His inward cross, more difficult for Him to bear than the outward one.

That blood could be upon them for destruction, but it was still redeeming blood. Though they attached a curse to themselves, the One whom they crucified had not ratified their sentence. In the end they will repent. Before the end, there is always the remnant that will be saved.

[**The JEWS** *were insistent, loudly demanding that He might be crucified.*]

PILATE: Let their request be granted. I condemn you. You will go to the cross. (He is sentenced to hang on the Cross.)

SECOND VOICE: Pilate, therefore, yielded and passed sentence upon Jesus. Pilate resisted the pressure of the Jews for a long time. It was now about the sixth hour, that is, at noon.

Their voices prevailed. Their voices carried the day; Pilate gave his assent that their request should be granted.

PILATE: [*He looks at the rage-distorted faces, at the eyes flaming with a light that was hardly human. He calls out in a stifled rage.*]
Away with Him, away with Him! [PILATE *hands* JESUS *over to be crucified.*]

SECOND VOICE: Meaning away with such a fellow from the earth: for it is not fit that he should live.

Looking at the rage-distorted faces, at the eyes flaming with a light that was hardly human, it must have seemed to him that they were devils.

FIRST VOICE: The majority is not always right. Majority is right in the field of the relative, but not in the absolute. Majority is a legitimate test so long as voting is based on conscience and not on propaganda. Truth does not win when numbers alone become decisive. Numbers alone can decide a beauty queen but not justice. Beauty is a matter of taste, but justice is tasteless. Right is still right if nobody is right, and wrong is still wrong if everybody is wrong. The first poll in the history of Christianity was wrong!

Barabbas was freed because of Jesus, political freedom though it was. But it was a symbol that through His death men were to be made free. It happened at Passover time when a lamb was substituted for the people and went to death in atonement for their sins. The Savior should suffer and the sinner go free. The Book of Exodus had proclaimed that the sinner was to be redeemed with a lamb, but the Lamb could not be redeemed. The Savior could not be released, but the sinner could.

The good weep, "smiting their breasts" or "sleeping for sorrow," and the evil keep awake, act and cry, "Crucify him!" So it always was, and so it always will be.

Jesus was condemned *justly* for his teaching was contrary to the existing order of things. In order to acquit him one must believe that the order of things desired by Him is better than the "existing order of things." According to all the laws, according to all the truths excepting His, He was and always will be condemned. In other words the world must be judged and its prince cast out.

[**PILATE** *delivers Him to the Roman* CENTURION *that the sentence might be carried out.* ABENADAR *orders the royal cloak taken from* JESUS *and His own garments put on Him.*]

FIRST VOICE: He would go forth in His own garments and be identified as the One who had preached to His people and walked among them as the Messias.

[**PILATE** *walks to the praetorium slowly. If he looks back, it is to take another glance at the strange prisoner over whom he had fought so hard and so uncleverly.*]

SECOND VOICE: When Claudia Procula asked him about this, Pilate would say, in honesty: "I did not intend to condemn the Man.

His crime was religious, so I surrendered Him to Caiphas."

PILATE: [*Almost as an afterthought, the procurator calls* ABENADAR *to him and orders that a heavy wooden sign be made to nail to the top of the cross, listing the crime of* JESUS *in three languages: Hebrew, Latin, and Aramic—in that order.*] The sign should read, Jesus of Nazareth, king of the Jews.

SECOND VOICE: That was His name and His crime.

ABENADAR: What about clothing, should He be allowed to wear something?

PILATE: Follow the custom.

SECOND VOICE: On the cross, He would be allowed to wear a breech clout.

ABENADAR: Were there any special orders from his excellency?

PILATE: No special orders. Proceed, and be done with it.
[*He walks back up the stone steps and into the fortress.*]

SECOND VOICE: The signs listing the crimes of the three prisoners were hastily painted, and when the high priests saw the one for Jesus, marked "King of the Jews," they became excited and upset.

THE PRIESTS: [*They come running back into the pavement. To the* LICTOR *on guard.*] We want an immediate audience with Pontius Pilate.

Scene 13

THE JUDGMENT HALL

THE PRIESTS: [*They are admitted. They say as politely as they can.*] We beg of you a final favor. The sign must be changed. Write not, The King of the Jews; but that He said, I am king of the Jews.

SECOND VOICE: They did not want the public to see Jesus proclaimed king of the Jews. He wasn't, and He did not pretend to be. Still, they did not dare say this. They asked that the superscription over the

Cross be changed. This was the one shadow over their pleasure. They wanted it to be corrected.

PILATE: [*He smiles grimly.*] What I have written, I have written. My inscription stands.

SECOND VOICE: The sign was made as Pilate wanted it made. The procurator's patience had reached the end, he was perhaps torn with anguish. He proved how stubborn he could be. He refused to modify what he had written.

Pilate had strongly resented the trick by which he had been compelled to sacrifice an innocent man; now by his grim joke he had his revenge.

FIRST VOICE: The incident of the *titulus* confirms the view that Jesus was condemned as an aspirant to royal power, that is to say, as the Messiah. It was a Roman custom to publish abroad the reason for the condemnation by an inscription which was sometimes carried before the condemned person on the way to execution, and sometimes fixed to the instrument of torture itself.

It was not by chance, but by a providential arrangement, that Pilate thus proclaimed the truth of the royalty of Jesus against which the Jews protested in vain.

The enemy of the Pharisees was no dreamer, but a soul of prodigious power, with twelve young men around him to whom he was saying that the present age must pass away and a new order come, that Jerusalem would be destroyed and they be persecuted, but that the Kingdom would arrive, and that at all costs and hazards they must be loyal to the Cause.

Thus crafty ecclesiastics, the Roman politician, the corrupt tetrarch, and the hardened soldiery all had their part in this supreme tragedy.

ACT IV

THE TRIUMPH

Scene 1

A STREET IN JERUSALEM—THE ROAD TO GOLGOTHA

[*When the cross is ready the* SOLDIERS *place the beams on* JESUS' *shoulders. When the column is fully formed, the* CENTURION *walks the length of it and finds it satisfactory. He calls a forward march, and the little parade starts through the archway. The few* HIGH PRIESTS *move aside and watch* JESUS *stagger as He starts out under his burden.*

According to Roman law the condemned man was bound to carry the cross himself, consisting of a post and the crosspiece tied together with a rope. He bore the full weight of the Cross on His back and shoulders, which were already raw.

The hands of all three are tied, held aloft athwart the wooden beams which rest on their right shoulders. These are the horizontal pieces of the crosses on which they will die. The uprights already are in place on Calvary. The crosspiece and the upright are hollowed out, so as to dovetail into one another. Roughly done, but strong enough to bear a man's weight.]

SECOND VOICE: They started for the place of execution, which was a spot called Golgotha, or "Place of a Skull." This was north of the city, by a gate near the present Damascus gate. Toward Golgotha Jesus, escorted by soldiers, now took His way.

The sentence of death by crucifixion required that the condemned person carry the cross upon which he was to suffer. The bearing of the crossbeam (*patibulum*) by the condemned person was an integral part of

271

the penalty. Jesus started on the way bearing His cross. The terrible strain of the preceding hours, the agony of Gethsemane, the barbarous treatment He had suffered in the palace of the high priest, the humiliation and cruel usage to which He had been subjected before Herod, the frightful scourging under Pilate's order, the brutal treatment by the inhuman soldiery, together with the extreme humiliation and the mental agony of it all, had so weakened His physical organism that He moved but slowly under the burden of the cross. The road from the arch to Golgotha was almost exactly one thousand paces—about three thousand feet. The first part of the march was by a narrow road, hardly more than twelve feet wide, up a slight incline, then sharply down into the valley below.

FIRST VOICE: They willed now that He should die, but what He was and what they hated could never die. The Jerusalem that had saluted Him on the previous Sunday was now the Jerusalem that disowned Him. Since the temple priests had found him accursed, they exiled Him from Jerusalem. Christ, the ultimate in sin offering, was driven like the scapegoat outside the city. It now became clear that the Cross was His government or law of life.

THE PROCESSION: [*A body of* ROMAN SOLDIERS *have the condemned* CHRIST *in charge; and as the procession moves out from the governor's palace, a motley crowd comprizing* PRIESTLY OFFICIALS, RULERS OF THE JEWS, *and* PEOPLE OF MANY NATIONALITIES, *follows.*

TWO CONVICTED **CRIMINALS,** *who had been sentenced to the cross for robbery, are led forth to death at the same time.*

The procession of the cross was usually preceded by a TRUMPETER *to clear the road; then followed a* HERALD *announcing the name of the criminal who was being led to execution. Sometimes the name of the criminal and the reason for his condemnation was hung about his neck. Two* WITNESSES *of the council that sentenced the one condemned to death were also to accompany the procession.*

A CENTURION *mounted on horseback, along with a considerable* DE-TACHMENT OF SOLDIERS, *form part of the procession. The* CENTURION *in charge of the execution leads the procession carrying the white board of wood with the inscription written on it in big letters in Roman, Greek, and Hebrew characters, in order that all may read:* "The King of the Jews." *Behind trudge the* PRIS-ONERS, *prodded along by four* SOLDIERS. *Others march at the rear, their orange-colored capes rippling at their backs. The* CENTURION *moves at the side of the column, occasionally snapping orders.*

JESUS' face is scratched, blood-streaked, and puffed with ashen bruises. His arms bear the jagged gashes of the metal- and bone-tipped

lash. Neither of the other TWO MEN, both burly, vicious-looking ruffians, show any signs of a flogging. Only the one appears gravely hurt and weakened. Red stains soak the back of His robe.]
[*Like many another tourist,* SIMON *sees the martial procession coming down the hill from the Fortress Antonia. Curious, he stops to watch it. The crowd has thickened, but when the big man from Africa steps forward a bit, the others edge aside, opening a path. He had not intended to move closer, but the action comes involuntarily.*]

SECOND VOICE: There was to be a triple execution; and the prospective scene of horror attracted the morbidly minded, such as delight to gloat over the sufferings of their fellows.

It was the Roman custom to make the execution of convicts as public as possible, under the mistaken and antipsychological assumption that the spectacle of dreadful punishment would be of deterrent effect.

Yet, with all the marks of abuse and injury, there was about Jesus a formidable strength. He was broken, crushed, but somehow, still relentlessly determined in His walk to doom. One felt a surge of admiration.

THE ONLOOKERS: [*Simon's ears pick up scatterings of talk now, and some of the* ONLOOKERS *point their fingers.*] The Nazarene. The disturber, Jesus. The other two men are the bandits, Dysmas and Gestas.
[*Along the sides of the road,* PILGRIMS *press against the walls and argue loudly for guilt or innocence as the parade moves by. The* LEGIONNAIRES *move the crowds back, when necessary, with their spears.*]

THE CENTURION: [*The* SOLDIER *who leads the procession on a horse shouts continuously to the people.*] Make way for the soldiers of Rome.

SECOND VOICE: Some of the throng that followed were priests who went from hatred; others went from idle curiosity; they wanted to enjoy the horror of seeing the torture.

How heavy the cross was, and the way seemed long. The day was hot, and this cedar wood was heavy.

[**SIMON'S** *eyes narrowed resentfully as he watches the agonized progress of the* NAZARENE.]

[*At the bottom of the hill,* **ABENADAR** *turns his column to the left.*]

[**JESUS** makes the turn, following those in front, but He is so faint

He cannot take the next step forward. The MESSIAH feels that He is falling, but He cannot free His bound hands from the beam and, in a moment, He has pitched downward. He lands on His right knee and both elbows, and the crosspiece hangs standing for a split second, and then falls away from Him.

His breath comes in light, rapid gasps, and He totters uncontrollably each time He advances a foot. Then, just as the PRISONERS come abreast of SIMON, the NAZARENE stumbles on a jutting cobblestone and pitches forward on the pavement. The board slams against His back.]

A SOLDIER *curses.* ANOTHER ONE, *muttering, slides the board free, and the* CENTURION *comes running up to get the* PRISONER *back on his feet. Once He is up, the* OFFICER *surveys Him dubiously and shakes his head.*]

SECOND VOICE: The centurion wanted everything to be orderly. But after a quick glance at the muddy face and the fresh rivulets of blood starting from the thorns on the right side of Jesus' head, he knew that it was useless, in front of a crowd, to order this Man to stand up and again shoulder the beam.

It was the killing; the stag was delivered over to the dogs. How was He to carry his cross, He who could scarcely drag Himself along?

Jesus was weakened by the fearful flogging or scourging He had undergone, and it was not possible for Him to keep up and carry the crossbeam of His cross to the place of execution, as the prisoner was expected to do. By the time they reached the gate of the city through which they had to pass, Jesus, weakened by the terrible ordeal of scourging, sank under His cross, no longer able to carry it. And the Romans were not supposed to touch "the accursed tree."

FIRST VOICE: Two robbers walking with him, dragging the same wood, could not be distinguished from God.

[**The CENTURION** *does the next best thing. Someone else has to be found to carry it. Then the* OFFICER'S *irritated gaze sweeps the crowd. He studies the people in the crowd to find a man strong enough to shoulder the tree for the rest of the journey. He sees a* FARMER *with brown, bulging biceps, a man with a big dome of a head and a black beard.* SIMON *stands out, a natural physical specimen for a heavy load.* ABENADAR *beckons to him and orders him to pick up the crossbeam and carry it.*]

ABENADAR: Pick up the crossbeam and carry it. [*He jabs a finger at him.*] You!

[The **SOLDIERS** *seize and impress into service* SIMON *to carry the cross.* SIMON *eyes the* SOLDIER *warily. They lay the cross upon him, and compel him to turn around and carry it to Golgotha. He wipes his lips and strolls over beside the crossbeam. With a quick, easy dip of powerful arms, he swings it to his shoulder.*

SIMON OF CYRENE *does as he is told. He picks the crossbeam up out of the dust and, with a grimace, throws it over his shoulder. Then he turns and for the first time his eyes meet those of* JESUS.]

SECOND VOICE: The soldiers laid hold upon one Simon, a Cyrenian, coming out of the country, and on him they laid the cross, that he might bear it for Jesus. No Roman or Jew would have voluntarily incurred the ignominy of bearing such a gruesome burden; for every detail connected with the carrying out of a sentence of crucifixion was regarded as degrading. The farmer cursed the moment he had permitted his curiosity to bring him to the front of the crowd. He was on his way from his farm to the city. He was a prosperous man who did not want to be a party, however unwilling, to the problems of the Romans or the Jews.

Simon eyed the soldier warily. He didn't like jumping to Roman command. Then he glanced at the battered prisoner, and that puzzling attraction, another sort of command, rang at him.

FIRST VOICE: When his eyes met those of Jesus, it was only an instant, but to Simon it held an eternity of affection received. Those eyes, despite all the man's mistreatment, swam with a strangely rich animation, with a deep knowledge and immense love.

There was something else, too, a sort of brotherliness, as if in the flash of a single look. He knew you utterly, through and through, and made you a cherished companion. There were no guarded reservations, no barriers in those eyes.

Never before had Simon felt so fully wanted, so genuinely needed and approved of. It wasn't so much gratitude that he saw in that look, but a limitless understanding that smiled approval and kinship.

Simon bore the cross upon which the Savior of the world was to consummate His glorious mission.

[**SIMON** *is ready. But* JESUS *lies on His right side, gasping.* ABENADAR *reaches down and lifts Him by the arm. Then he orders the column forward. The pathetic parade moves down the street to the south, then turns right. Ahead is a formidable hill leading to the Gannath Gate. The walk to the cross is a little more than half finished.* SIMON *steps along beside the prisoner.*]

FIRST VOICE: At a barked order, the procession resumed, and Simon stepped along beside the prisoner, hardly aware of the weight on his shoulder. He had an urge to thank this condemned man, Jesus, for the chance to carry the beam. It just didn't make sense, this feeling he had of being especially good and worthy, because he walked with this man to Calvary.

It was a strange experience for Simon thus against his will to be brought into such close association with the most tragic experience of the Christ. It was the first time the Savior laid His Cross on anyone; to Simon belongs the privilege of first sharing the Cross of Christ.

Simon did not undertake this task willingly. Simon was probably one of the curious thousands who were interested in seeing a man go to death, and who stood on the roadway until the long arm of the Roman law forced him to share the ignominy of a cross.

He had received the new message in his heart though he had never heard it with his ears. Thus in the last hour there came a new disciple. But where were the others?

[JESUS walks more steadily now, and Simon hears Him sigh with relief. While the cross is thus borne forward on a young man's powerful shoulders, there totters along behind it the pale figure of the PROPHET, suddenly grown old, pushed and jostled by the SOLDIERS of the escort. The CENTURION in command rides beside the train in gloomy silence.]

SECOND VOICE: The officer and his men were out of humor, for they regarded such executioner's work as beneath a soldier's dignity, and they loathed the tedium of waiting. Last time they had had to spend two days under the cross before the victim died.

And there followed him a great company of people, and of women, which also bewailed and lamented him.

[As JESUS drags His feet up the long hill, He is in such acute pain that His breathing can be heard by the citizens who watched, and among them are these charitable WOMEN. They weep, wail, and lament.]

SECOND VOICE: Under the law, sympathy toward an accused was permitted; sympathy toward one condemned was forbidden. However, there was a society of charitable women of Jerusalem. They bewailed and lamented the fate to which Jesus was going. They wept aloud at his impending fate. We read of no man who ventured to raise his voice in protest or pity; but on this dreadful occasion, as at other times, women were not afraid to cry out in commiseration or praise. Their

276

hearts were moved and, when one of them burst into tears, all began to sob.

JESUS: [JESUS turns to the PEOPLE. The MESSIAH stops. His gaze turns shakily from one woman to the next until He has seen them all and has seen the reality of the tears—the first shed for His death. In a strained voice He says slowly and with massive effort.] Daughters of Jerusalem, weep not for me, but weep for yourselves, and for your children.

For, behold, the days are coming, at which time they shall say, blessed are the barren, and the wombs that never bare, and the paps which never gave suck. Then shall they begin to say to the mountains, Fall on us; and the hills, Cover us.

SECOND VOICE: Then in a strained voice He warned the women of the impending pillage of their city. For the final time, Jesus was a prophet and He had reserved His last warning for the women who were good of heart and who could bear to look upon a strange man reduced almost to the last breath of life.

Jesus, who had been silent under the inquisition of the priests, silent under the humiliating mockery of the sensual Herod and his coarse underlings, silent when buffeted and beaten by the brutal legionnaires of Pilate, turned to the women whose sympathizing lamentations had reached His ears, and uttered these pathetic and portentous words of admonition and warning.

During His last week the children shouted, "Hosanna," the men cried "Crucify," but the women "wept."

It was the Lord's last testimony of the impending holocaust of destruction that was to follow the nation's rejection of her king.

In the terrible scenes which many of those there weeping would live to witness, barrenness would be accounted a blessing, for the childless would have fewer to weep over, and at least would be spared the horror of seeing their offspring die of starvation or by violence; for so dreadful would be that day that people would fain welcome the falling of the mountains upon them to end their sufferings.

FIRST VOICE: Even at that hour He had sympathy for his wayward kinsmen, and, seeing clearly the awful woe which their course must bring on them (a fate which actually came forty years later), He had leisure from Himself, even in His exhaustion and suffering, thus to address them. As for Himself, at this moment He measured beyond His own sufferings the chastisement of His city and of His people, and He trembled for them.

As in the garden He had told the soldiers to take Him and let the Apostles go their way, so too He told the women not to mourn over Him, for He was innocent, but to mourn over the destruction of Jerusalem, which was a symbol of the destruction of the world at the end of time.

Such fearlessness under such conditions can have but a single end, and to that end the Master went with utter steadfastness. And this is the final condemnation of man and his refusal to accept the invitation offered to him. And this virtue of fearlessness, not gentleness, was what the disciples remembered most.

JESUS: [Yes, He says, nodding His head slowly.]
For if they do these things in a green tree, what shall be done in the dry?

FIRST VOICE: Jesus was the green, the new word. The sinners were the dry wood. If they would do this to Him, what would they do to the jaded and the callous? If Israel's oppressors could do what they were then in process of doing to the "Green Tree," who bore the leafage of freedom and truth and offered the priceless fruit of life eternal, what would the powers of evil not do to the withered branches and dried trunk of apostate Judaism?

The dry tree is the whole human race. These unforgiving words are in contrast to the previous forgiving ones.

The green tree was Himself; the dry tree the world. He was the green tree transplanted from Eden; the dry tree was Jerusalem first, and then the unconverted world. His warning meant that if the Romans so treated Him who was innocent, how would they treat Jerusalem that had condemned Him to death? If He was so bruised because of the transgression of others, how in the final judgment would the guilty be punished for their own iniquities? If He who had no sin suffered, how would they suffer who were rotten with sin!

No tears of Delilah would keep this Samson from His work today; no superficial wailings of the women of Jerusalem would weaken Him in His predetermined purpose of sacrifice; their dowry of tears could not make them the brides of His heart. If He were just a good man going to His death, then let them open the fountain of tears; but because He was a priest going to sacrifice, then let them weep only if they availed themselves not of its fruits. As He would purge death of death by rising from the grave, so He now purged tears of lamentation by showing that sin alone was worth tears. They were weeping for Him as a good man, but no such tears would He have at His deathbed. By rejecting their

278

grief, He showed that He was not a good man sent to death, but a God-man saving sinners.

Hidden in His words was a plea for faithfulness to avert the doom of Jerusalem; its destiny was in the hands of women, would they but repent. On this as on many other occasions, He bade His hearers look to the state of their own souls. He diverted attention from Himself, who was sinless, to those who needed redemption. When Peter said he would die for Him, Jesus told the Apostle how weak his soul was; so now the women were told not to have misplaced sorrow; let them look to their souls, their children, their city. He needed no tears; they did.

This was the Passion sermon of the Savior, or rather the first part of it; the second part consisted of His seven last words from the Cross.

He bade the women to shed no tears for Him. He who wept at Bethany and Whose Blood now wept on the road to Jerusalem, bade them not to weep for Him, for His death was a willed necessity—willed freely by Him, but a necessity for men. Furthermore, since He had promised to wipe away all tears, tears for Him were needless.

SECOND VOICE: And there were also two others, malefactors, led with Him to be put to death.

[**ABENADAR** *comes running back and urges the column to continue its march.*

The MARCHERS *start up again.* JESUS *lifts a foot and brings it forward and sets it down. Then, mechanically, He begins the effort of lifting the other one and trying to move it ahead.*]

FIRST VOICE: Beyond the horseman up ahead, Jesus could see the Gannath Gate. It had been a long difficult road for the Galilean, and it was almost a consolation to know that a few more steps would bring Him to the pinnacle of His promise—the chance to die for everyone.

SECOND VOICE: Along the city streets, out through the portal of the massive wall, and thence to a place beyond but yet nigh unto Jerusalem, the cortege advanced. The destination was a spot called Golgotha, or Calvary, meaning "the place of a skull."

Scene 2

THE GOLGOTHA HILL—THE CRUCIFIXION

THE CENTURION: Halt.

SECOND VOICE: Outside the Gannath Gate Jesus and the two thieves were led on for some thirty yards to the small, rocky hill of Golgotha. At the crossing of several main roads, and visible from them, lay the favorite place of execution of the Romans, called Golgotha—"a skull." Legend has it that it was the burial place of Adam.

Executions took place in public. Usually they took place near towns, by the roadside or at crossroads, in order that passersby might see the gibbet. This was in order that those passing by should see the crucified and be frightened by very salutary example.

Till three in the afternoon when He died, passersby never ceased walking past the Crucified and "railed at Him."

FIRST VOICE: The cross of the Master, in which is symbolized all the sacrificial endurance of His life, has done more than all else put together to win the world to Him. Nothing is so powerful as love that is willing to suffer to achieve its object. In this consuming devotion which identifies an individual with a cause, and makes Him ready to give up everything selfish for the people whom He loves, lies the consummate perfection of character.

And so the vertical bar of God's will is negated by the horizontal bar of the contradicting human will. An unsuffering Christ who did not freely pay the debt of human guilt would be reduced to the level of an ethical guide.

He said to them: "Destroy," and they said to him, "Crucify."

SECOND VOICE: No temple was ever more systematically destroyed than was His body. The dome of the Temple, His head, was crowned with thorns; the foundations of it, His sacred feet, were riven with nails; the transepts, His hands, were stretched out in the form of a Cross; His Heart was pierced with a lance.

FIRST VOICE: By the agonizing death upon the Cross, what He had foreseen was accomplished, and God's supreme message was spoken to the world. He knew that in giving up His life He was consummating His service to the world. He paid the price it could not pay. Love is the bond of perfectness. Jesus laid down His life for a hostile world that had treated Him cruelly and to which He owed no gratitude; for a strange world to which He had really been as alien as it was to Him; for a humanity which might well have disgusted Him for its pettiness and vulgarity, its baseness and spitefulness. It was then that His love experienced its coronation.

For Jesus the performance of atonement, Jesus' death, is of the utmost importance. It is (the final doctrine) realization of the Kingdom. The coming of the Kingdom of God with power is dependent upon the atonement that Jesus performs. There is a bridge between earth and heaven. Jesus, the son of God, is that bridge. For those who are on the way to destruction the story of the Cross is nonsense, but to us who are being saved, it means all the power of God.

Jesus' consciousness of being the Son remained unshaken in the most difficult hours of His life. Here again in the days of the Passover God reenacted the scene, the sacrifice becoming the fundamental act in establishing the new Covenant. Jesus had given the Cross as the final argument. Up to the point of Calvary, men had been taught by preaching. After Calvary, they would be taught by His Resurrection and Ascension. The principle of universality became effective. It took Golgotha to universalize the mission of Christ. It was only by this key—the Cross—that the "great door" would be opened to the Gentiles. The Kingdom of God is an overturned world, and the lever that overturns it is the Cross.

The difficulty with the world is that death is overemphasized. True to the human world of flesh, death looms as a gigantic shadow; it is something to fear and be in awe of. But actually, what is it but that the body is returned to dust. It is something that is not desirable to keep. True, the human emotions go through anguished torment while one is killed on the cross. But one goes to better things, the universal spirit of God only draws nearer. And so the sacrifice of an innocent Son is of no moment after it has passed. And this is the truth which Christ preached. It is the soul that counts. Jesus Christ came to set an example, to show us that to follow the spirit is of utmost importance, the only essential thing; even unto death, as He did.

They suppose Jesus just to have lived and died so that men can go on sinning. That they can go on having their sensibilities without thought to their sins and the welfare of other people. His death was to save men from their sins, but it also pointed to the day when they could sin no more.

When He died few men mourned, but a black crepe was hung over the sun. Though men trembled not for their sins, the earth beneath shook under the load! All nature honored Him; sinners alone rejected Him.

SECOND VOICE: Crucifixion represented the acme of the torturer's art; atrocious physical sufferings, length of torment, ignominy, the effect on the crowd gathered to witness the long agony of the crucified. Nothing could be more horrible than the sight of this living body, breathing, seeing, hearing, still able to feel, and yet reduced to the state of a corpse by forced immobility and absolute helplessness. The penalty of crucifixion combined all that the most ardent tormentor could desire: torture, the pillory, degradation, and certain death, distilled slowly, drop by drop. It was an ideal form of torture.

The agony of Jesus lasted for three hours, from the sixth until the ninth hour (from noon unto three o'clock).

In all, there were seven distinct bloodsheddings: the Circumcision, the Agony in the Garden, the Scourging, the Crowning with thorns, the Way of the Cross, and now the two that are to follow, the Crucifixion and the Piercing of the Heart.

They crucified Him. And with Him they crucified two thieves; the one on His right hand, and the other on His left.

(PLACE OF EXECUTION: A stranger could not mistake the fact that this was a place of execution, because three upright beams stood naked against the sky. These were ordinary cypress beams, like those carried by the condemned men, except that, at the top, they had been planed down so that the mortises in the crossbeams would fit across them.)

THE CENTURION: *He consults with the* EXECUTIONER. *To the* THREE SOLDIERS *who had carried the signs.*]
Assist the executioner and stand guard beneath the crosses.

[ABENADAR *had assigned four soldiers to each of the thieves, and they await a signal.*]
[*Golgotha is crowded. The* PEOPLE *press in upon the* SOLDIERS *and, with the shouted orders of the* SOLDIERS *to stand back and the sobbing of* WOMEN SPECTATORS, *there is considerable noise.*]

SECOND VOICE: The most awful moment had come; the cloth of the mantle stripped from His wounds, the blows of the hammer upon the nails, the raising of the tree, the weight of the human fruit, thirst quenched with vinegar, with myrrh and with gall, nakedness, the shame of the poor, butchered flesh.

This cross we must see as it was, so different from the throne which we have built since, and which raises the Lamb of God high above the world!

The first Christians had a horror of seeing Christ shown upon a cross, because with their own eyes they had seen those poor bodies, completely naked, attached to a heavy stake surmounted in form of a T, by a transverse bar, hands nailed to this gibbet, feet also fixed with nails, the body sinking beneath its own weight, the head hanging, dogs, drawn by the odor of blood devouring the feet, buzzards wheeling over this scene of carnage, and the sufferer exhausted by torture, burning with thirst, calling on death with inarticulate cries. It was the punishment of slaves and bandits. It was that which Jesus suffered.

[**The SOLDIERS** *give him and the other* TWO *condemned* PRISONERS *to drink wine mingled with myrrh.*]

SECOND VOICE: Preparatory to affixing the condemned to the cross, it was the custom to offer each a narcotic draught of sour wine or vinegar mingled with myrrh for the purpose of deadening the sensibility of the victim. To myrrh or incense was also sometimes added the essence of poppy, opium. This was to deaden sensibility to pain. This was no Roman practice, but was allowed as a concession to Jewish sentiment. It was an act of mercy which the Romans permitted.

[When the drugged cup is presented to **JESUS** He puts it to His lips, but having ascertained the nature of its contents refuses to drink. JESUS refuses the stupefying drink. With a silent motion of the hand he thrusts away the cup.]

SECOND VOICE: Jesus, when it was brought to His lips, knowing it to be a sedative, refused to sip. He demonstrated His determination to meet death with faculties alert and mind unclouded. He did not want to lose his consciousness to ease His suffering. Though His body, already exhausted, cried out for water, He would not drink that which would dull His role as mediator.

FIRST VOICE: At His birth, His mother was given the gift of myrrh and accepted it as a sign of His ransoming death. At His death, He would refuse the myrrh which would deaden the reason of His coming. He told Peter the night before that He would drink the cup His Father had given Him. But to drink that cup of Redemption He must not drink of the cup that would drive a wedge between His Body and His Spirit.

[**ABENADAR** *waits patiently until they have finished. He gives the signal.*]

[**FOUR SOLDIERS** *move in closely around the* PRISONERS *and begin to strip them of their clothes. They strip Him of His garments, opening new wounds in His Body. They hang a piece of cloth in front. When the* PRISONERS *are naked, a cloth is wound around their loins and between the thighs with the loose end tucked in at the back. Their clothes and sandals are set in a loose pile before each of the three. It is a few minutes after noon. The sun is high and warm.*]

SECOND VOICE: Being stripped of His garments meant that He was no longer localized by dress. In His nakedness He became the Universal Man. Exiled outside the city, He now gave up country as well as life. The Sacred Heart was confined by no frontiers. Many church teachers affirm His absolute nudity—"Naked was the second Adam on the cross, as the first in Paradise."

PEOPLE: [*A murmurous sound comes up from the* PEOPLE *below.*]

SECOND VOICE: The crucifixion had begun.

[**More LEGIONNAIRES** *are already at work and delving, for there are two other crucifixions today. The crosses were usually made low, just high enough for the feet of the crucified not to touch the ground. The* THIEVES *are crucified on such low crosses. However, for important criminals, higher crosses were made. The upright beam was long enough to permit the infixing of an inscription above His head, and his feet seem not to have been lifted far from the ground.*]

SECOND VOICE: Up there on the hill, more legionnaires are already at work hammering and delving, for there are two other crucifixions today, Jews expiating the crimes of theft and murder.

While some of the soldiers are digging holes in the ground, others are nailing the criminals to the crosses as these lie flat upon the soil.

A number of soldiers working together, they lower the base of the cross into the hole which has been prepared, and shovel in earth and stones to make it stand firmly.

SOLDIERS: [*While the beams of the cross are being prepared, the* SOLDIERS *mock and torture* JESUS.] [*First the upright wood is firmly planted in the ground.*

284

Next the crossbeam is placed on the ground, the VICTIM *laid upon it, his arms extended and bound to it. The* EXECUTIONER *lays the crossbeam behind* JESUS *and brings Him to the ground quickly by grasping His arm and pulling Him backward. As soon as Jesus falls, the beam is fitted under the back of His neck and, on each side,* **SOLDIERS** *quickly kneel on the inside of the elbows.*]

SECOND VOICE: He whose turn is now to come sees all this as if in a dream. He suddenly becomes aware that His arms have been seized by pitiless hands, and that He has been stretched on the cross. He watches a nail, which looms gigantic before his eyes. Horror overwhelms Him; pain racks Him; He faints.

[JESUS gives no resistance and says nothing, but He groans as He falls on the back of His head and the thorns press against His torn scalp. Once begun, the matter is done quickly and efficiently. *The* EXECUTIONER *wears an apron with pockets. He places two five-inch nails between his teeth and, hammer in hand, kneels beside the right arms. The* SOLDIER *whose knee rests on the inside of the elbow holds the forearm flat to the board.*

With his right hand, the EXECUTIONER *probes the wrist of* JESUS *to find the little hollow spot. (The nails were never put in the hands.) When he finds it, he takes one of the square-cut iron nails from his teeth and holds it against the spot, directly behind where the so-called lifeline ends. Then he raises the hammer over the nail head and brings it down with force.*

The EXECUTIONER *jumps across the body to the other wrist. As soon as he is satisfied that the condemned Man could not, in struggling, pull Himself loose and perhaps fall forward off the cross, he brings both of his arms upward rapidly. This is the signal to lift the crossbeam.*

Disrobed, the condemned was put on his back, and four men held down His hands and feet to prevent struggling, while a fifth hammered in long 'cross nails' into the soft part of the palm (wrist), first of the right hand and then of the left. The long black nails pierced the white flesh. The knocking of the hammer could be heard, and the echo reverberated.

Then, by means of ropes or by the use of ladders, the sufferer is raised and the crossbeam bound or nailed to the upright. Two SOLDIERS *grab each side of the crossbeam and lift. As they pull up, they drag* JESUS *by the wrists.*]
[With every breath, JESUS groans.]

FIRST VOICE: The rough nail was applied. Blow followed blow and was quickly re-echoed from the city walls beneath. Every detail of prophecy was being fulfilled. A thousand years before, David looked forward to the role hammer and nails would play in greeting the Messias, as carpenters would put to death Him who carpentered the universe.

"My enemies ring Me round, packed close as a herd of oxen . . . so might a lion threaten Me with its jaws, roaring for its prey. . . . Prowling about Me like a pack of dogs, their wicked conspiracy hedges Me in . . . and they stand there watching Me, gazing at Me in triumph."

SOLDIERS: [*When the* SOLDIERS *reach the upright, the four of them begin to lift the crossbeam higher until the feet of Jesus are off the ground.*]

[<u>JESUS' body writhes in pain.</u>]

SOLDIERS: [*The four* SOLDIERS *push forward until the mortise hole is over the upright. A rest or support for the body is also fastened to it. The* VICTIM *is seated astride on a horn-shaped pummel nailed to the post, or His feet are allowed to rest on a small plank, slightly inclined and also nailed to the post. The feet are supported by the projecting board to which they are nailed, and the fork of the legs by a little seat slanting backwards, which prevents the body from falling forwards, and, with its weight, rending the hands from the nails.*

The EXECUTIONER *kneels before the cross. Two* SOLDIERS *hurry to help, and each one takes hold of a leg at the calf. Last, the feet are extended and either a nail hammered into each, or a large spike driven through them both. The ritual was to nail the right foot over the left, and this was probably the most difficult part of the work. If the feet were pulled downward, and nailed close to the foot of the cross, the prisoner always died quickly. Over the years, the Romans learned to push the feet upward on the cross, so that the condemned man could lean on the nails and stretch himself upward.*]

FIRST VOICE: Jesus was crucified. He was left to die of exhaustion and hunger. He faced the Holy City for the last time.

SECOND VOICE: In one respect, Jesus was fortunate. He no longer enjoyed the tough resistance of youth. His strength was that of a village artisan, not of the peasant. His temperament was high-strung, not dull; His suffering would be more intense but more quickly over. Last night, He had been allowed no sleep. For the last twelve hours he had been badgered by constant questioning. Jesus was exhausted when He was nailed to the cross. His death could be only a matter of two or three hours.

The pulpit was lifted slowly off the ground, wavered in midair for a moment, tearing and lacerating His flesh; then suddenly with a deep thud that seemed to shake even hell itself, it sank into the pit prepared for it.

[**The EXECUTIONER** *moves to the others, and goes through the same* *ritual with each one. One of them resists; but strong hands hold him fast, his yells are ignored, and the huge nails are driven home.*]

THE CENTURION: Nail them firmly, so that no cord need be wasted on the malefactors! Now, up with the cross!

THIEVES: [*Thus almost simultaneously the two crosses with the* THIEVES *nailed to them are set up in the scorching sunlight, and the air is rent with the screams of the tortured men.*]

SECOND VOICE: Death by crucifixion was at once the most lingering and most painful of all forms of execution. The victim lived in ever-increasing torture, generally for many hours, sometimes for days. The spikes so cruelly driven through hands and feet penetrated and crushed sensitive nerves and quivering tendons, yet inflicted no mortal wound. The welcome relief of death came through the exhaustion caused by intense and unremitting pain, through localized inflammation and congestion of organs incident to the strained and unnatural posture of the body.

[*To the watching* CROWD *in front, death appears to come slowly astride the shoulders of fatigue.*]

SECOND VOICE: The four wounds, in themselves, were not fatal. But the constant pain forced the dying men to move in agony.

To the strangers, Jesus looked like any other pain-racked criminal they had ever seen. To the casual viewer there was nothing different about Him, or unusual.

<u>**JESUS:** [Like the others', His head at times is lowered, with chin touching chest. Again, moved by sudden spasms, His head tosses from one shoulder to the other and his eyes look directly up into the sun as His lips move. When His body sags, in fatigue, its weight hangs on the nails in His wrists and His knees bend far forward.</u>]

SECOND VOICE: His arms were now in a V position, and Jesus became conscious of two unendurable circumstances; the first was that the pain in His wrists was beyond bearing, and that muscle cramps knotted His forearms and upper arms and the pads of His shoulders; the second was that His pectoral muscles at the sides of the chest were momentarily paralyzed.

This induced in Him an involuntary panic; for He found that while He could draw air into His lungs, He was powerless to exhale.

287

At once, Jesus raised Himself on His bleeding feet. As the weight of His body came down on the insteps, the single nail pressed hard against the tops of the wound. Slowly, steadily, Jesus was forced to raise Himself higher until, for the moment, His head hid the sign which told of His crime.

When His shoulders were on a level with His hands, breathing was rapid and easier. Like the other two, He fought the pain in His feet in order to breathe rapidly for a few moments.

Then, unable to bear the pain below, which cramped legs and thighs and wrung moans from the strongest, He let His torso sag lower and lower, and His knees projected a little at a time until, with a deep sigh, He felt Himself to be hanging by the wrists. And this process was repeated again and again.

When He came to his senses again and grew aware of the fiery smart in his wounds, He turned His head to right and to left, and the sight of the other crosses recalled Him to an understanding of what had happened. Certainly He had not awakened in heaven! On the ground, the soldiers had settled down for their long vigil. Some were drinking, others dicing.

THE CENTURION: Fix the placards at the top of the Cross.

SOLDIER: [*A thickset little* SOLDIER, *the one who had kicked him just now, is nailing a placard to his cross. When the cross beam is set firmly, the executioner or* SOLDIER *reaches up and sets the board which listed the name of prisoner and the crime. It is written in black letters on a white board, now nailed on over His head. Other* SOLDIERS *nail similar ones to the crosses of the two* THIEVES.]

SECOND VOICE: The titles were read by many of the Jews, for the place where Jesus was crucified was nigh to the city. They were written in Hebrew, and Greek, and Latin so none of the passers-by would fail to understand. The three world languages were all represented.

FIRST VOICE: Above the head of each a placard or titulus has been affixed, declaring in three languages the nature of the offenders' crimes. This placard indicated the reason for the crucifixion of the victim. It was written: "Jesus of Nazareth, the King of the Jews."

His death and also His Kingship were proclaimed in the name of the three cities of the world: Jerusalem, Rome, and Athens; in the language of the Good, the True and the Beautiful; in the tongues of Sion, the Forum, and the Acropolis.

His Kingship remained proclaimed, though, for the moment, a Cross would be His throne; His Blood, the royal purple; the nails, His sceptre; the crown of thorns, His diadem. Truth was made to speak when men ridiculed.

THE CROWD: [*Comment was aroused. The* CROWD *derided Him, wagging their heads, so also the chief priests mocked Him.*]

SECOND VOICE: If literally construed, the inscription was an official declaration that the crucified Jesus was in fact king of the Jews. The inscription stands in history as testimony of a heathen's consideration in contrast with Israel's ruthless rejection of Israel's king.

FIRST VOICE: Jesus used many pulpits during His public life, such as Peter's barque pushed into the sea, the mountaintop, the streets of Tyre and Sidon, the temple, the country road near a cemetery, and a banquet hall. But all faded into insignificance compared to the pulpit which He mounted now—the pulpit of the Cross. Jesus had mounted His pulpit for the last time.

[**The AUDIENCE** *is straining its eyes to see Him. At the edge of the crowd are timid* FOLLOWERS, *ready to flee in case of danger.*]

SECOND VOICE: Like all orators, He overlooked His audience. Far off, in Jerusalem, He could see the gilded roof of the temple, reflecting its rays against the sun which was seen to hide its face in shame. He could catch a glimpse of those who were straining their eyes to see Him. At the edge of the crowd were timid followers, ready to flee in case of danger; there, too, were the executioners getting their dice ready to shake for His garments. Close to the Cross was the only Apostle present, John; Magdalen was there too—and His own mother.

FIRST VOICE: Mary, Magdalen, John; innocence, penitence, and priesthood; the three types of souls forever to be found beneath the Cross of Christ.
[*The people passing along pause to jeer at the dying man.*]

THE CROWD: This man has been judged of God. What need we further proof?

SECOND VOICE: The people were convinced. The Jewish authorities, priests, Pharisees, scribes, whom Jesus had denounced in such vigorous language in the temple only two days before, now had their revenge. They could not forbear taunting Jesus in his suffering.

[The SOLDIERS *jest among themselves, and deride the* CHRIST, *pledging Him in their cups of sour wine in tragic mockery.*]

SECOND VOICE: It was the duty of these soldiers to guard the crosses, until loitering death would relieve the crucified of their increasing anguish.

FIRST VOICE: Jesus spoke seven times from the Cross; these are called His Seven Last Words. Humans are always anxious to hear of the state of mind of anyone at that very common, and yet very mysterious, moment called death.

Jesus left His thoughts on dying, for He was representative of all humanity. In this sublime hour He called all His children to the pulpit of the Cross, and every word He said to them was set down for the purpose of an eternal publication and an undying consolation. There was never a preacher like the dying Christ; there was never a congregation like that which gathered about the pulpit of the Cross; there was never a sermon like the Seven Last Words.

SECOND VOICE: Some never remain near the Cross long enough to absorb the mercy which flows from the Crucified.

THE CROWD: [*They blaspheme against Him, tossing their heads. They rail on Him, wagging their heads.*] Come now, You who would destroy the temple and build it up in three days, rescue (save) yourself; come down from that cross, if You are the Son of God. [*One, cupping his hands, yells.*] You are the one that can pull down the sanctuary and lift it up in three days!

[*Another shouts*] Help yourself if you are the Son of God, and come down from the cross! [OTHERS] Aha! You who would tear down the temple and build one in three days! Come down from the cross and save yourself!

FIRST VOICE: Jesus was no sooner on the Cross than they asked Him to come down. This is the most typical demand of an unregenerated world in the face of self-denial and abnegation: a religion without a Cross.

If He had obeyed their taunt "Come down," in whom would they believe? How could Love be Love if it costs not the Lover? If Jesus had come down, there would have been the Cross, but not the crucifix. The Cross is contradiction; the Crucifixion is the solution of the contradiction of life and death by showing that death is the condition of a higher life.

But mockery is an ingredient of the cup of sorrow, and how else would His followers draw strength in similar trials, if He had not borne it patiently? The cruelty of lips which sneer is part of the heritage of sin as much as the cruelty of hands which nail. On the mountain of temptation, Satan used the same technique when he asked the hungry Jesus to change stones into bread. It was so unbecoming the Son of God to be hungry! Now it was so unbecoming for the Son of God to suffer.

Skeptics always want miracles such as stepping down from the Cross, but never the greater miracle of forgiveness.

SECOND VOICE: Mount Cavalry was near the road, and many people came and went under the cross of Jesus, making mock of Him. The spectators observed Jesus closely because the high priests had passed the word that this was a mock Messiah, and that part of His crime was saying that if the great temple were destroyed He could raise it in three days. The elders could not refrain from pouring some scorn onto the pain. The multitude milled around this gibbet, so close to the earth that the condemned man could still be spat upon. Even the false witnesses, walking up and down in front of the cross, wagged their heads.

THE CROWD: [*They look at the title affixed above the* SUFFERER'S *head, they bellow forth the devil-inspired challenge. They exchange satisfied comments upon the situation. They speak ironically.*]
[*One*] Let Christ the King of Israel descend now from the cross, that we may see and believe!

THE CHIEF PRIESTS: [*They gloatingly exalt and cry aloud.*] He saved others, He cannot save Himself. If He is the King of Israel, He has but to come down from the cross, here and now, and we will believe in Him. He trusted in God; let God, if He favors Him, succor Him now; He told us, I am the Son of God.
(If he be the King of Israel (Messiah), let him now come down from the cross, and we will believe him. He trusted in God; let him deliver him now if he will have him: for he said I am the Son of God. Let this Christ, the King of Israel, come down from the cross now, so that we may see and believe!)

SECOND VOICE: They derided Him with laughter. The "offense

291

of the cross," "shame," "disgrace," "laughter," "blasphemy," that was all that was left at that moment of the Kingdom of God. A delegation from the Sanhedrin was also in attendance, to see that their wishes were carried out. A crucifixion was no such frightful novelty to them as it would be to us.

CAIPHAS: He helped others! He cannot help Himself!

FIRST VOICE: This word came from the intelligentsia of the time, the chief priests, scribes, and Pharisees. The intelligentsia always know enough about religion to distort it, hence they took each of the three titles which Jesus had claimed for Himself—"Savior," "King of Israel," and "Son of God," and turned them into ridicule.

Now they would admit He had saved others. They could afford to admit it now, for the Savior Himself stood in need of salvation. The conclusive miracle to them was still lacking.

Of course, He could not save Himself! The rain cannot save itself, if it is to bud the greenery. The sun cannot save itself, if it is to light a world; the soldier cannot save himself, if he is to save his country. And Jesus cannot save Himself, if He is to save His creatures!

"King of Israel": that title the crowd gave Him after He fed the multitude and fled into the mountains alone. They repeated it again on Palm Sunday, when they strewed branches beneath His feet. Now that title was mocked as they sneered.

Must all the kings of earth be seated on golden thrones? Suppose Israel's king decided to rule from a cross, to be king not of their bodies through power, but of their hearts through love? Their own literature suggested the idea of a king who would come to glory through humiliation. How foolish to mock a king because He refused to come down from His throne. And if He did come down, they would be the first to say, as they had before, that He did it through the power of Beelzebub.

Why is it that in time of trouble, God is always put on trial, and not man? Why in war, should the judge and the culprit change places as man asks: "Why does not God stop the war?"

Thus did Jesus hear Himself mocked! They did not know they were already lost. They thought He was. Therefore they, the really damned, mocked One whom they believed to be damned. Hell was triumphing in the human!

They said they would believe if He came down. But they did not believe when they saw Him raise Lazarus from the dead. Nor would they believe when He would rise from the dead. Then they would prohibit the Apostles from preaching the Resurrection which they knew to be a fact. No descent from the Cross would have won men. It is human to come down; it is Divine to hang there! The Death on the Cross is the greatest negation of the external miracle, and affirmation of the internal miracles.

If He had come down from the Cross and not risen from the dead, only an external miracle would have been performed. Christ as a man must die for the sins of mankind, but as Christ shall rise from the dead and thus the sign is shown that death has been conquered.

Nothing put an end to the hate of the scribes and the priests. They were still there, before the living wound, laughing, wagging their heads, mocking; their triumph knew no end. The dominant note in all the railings and revilings, the ribaldry and mockery, with which the patient and submissive Christ was assailed while He hung, "lifted up," as He had said He would be, was that awful "if" hurled at Him by the devil's emissaries in His time of mortal agony; as in the season of the temptations immediately after His baptism it had been most insidiously pressed upon Him by the devil himself.

That "if" was Satan's last shaft, keenly barbed and doubly envenomed, and it sped as with the fierce hiss of a viper. Was it possible in this, the final and most dreadful stage of Christ's mission, to make Him doubt His divine sonship, or, failing such, to taunt or anger the dying Savior into the use of His superhuman powers for personal relief or as an act of vengeance upon His tormentors? To achieve such a victory was Satan's desperate purpose. The shaft failed. Through taunts and derision, through blasphemous challenge and diabolical goading, the agonized Christ was silent.

SECOND VOICE: There was little interest in the fate of Jesus after the first hour. Only a few high priests remained; the others had hurried back to the temple. Most of the curious had left because they were afraid of the midday darkness. The birds were hushed. The little olive trees and the wild flowers held a steady pose in the still air.

The only sounds were the deep moans of pain wrenched from the throats of the dying. Each had come a long way in pain; each had a long way to go. It is likely that one or the other of the condemned fainted from time to time. But never for long, because the moment the sweetness of unconsciousness embraced him he could not breathe. If death did not overcome him quickly, the return to consciousness was acutely painful.

SOLDIERS: [*Behind the crosses, the* SOLDIERS *roll knucklebones on the slope of rock and argue loudly. They insult each other at play.*]

293

A SOLDIER: Let us divide the clothing.

ABENADAR: Take your midday rations first.

THE SOLDIERS: [*They drink cheap wine, toast* JESUS, *and, raising their cups:*] Toast us in return. How about your state of health? How are you feeling?
[*Four* SOLDIERS *take His garments, and make four parts, to every* SOLDIER *a part; and also His coat.*]

ABENADAR: [*He walks around the cross and picks up the garments of* JESUS. *To one, he tosses the worn sandals. To another, he gives the bloody cloak. To a third he throws the broad white band which was worn as a hat. For himself, he keeps the girdle. He nods to the other* SOLDIERS *to portion out the clothing of the* THIEVES. *They jump to their feet.*]

SECOND VOICE: Then the soldiers, when they had crucified Jesus, divided His garments. There had been one article of clothing left over after the garments of Jesus were divided. This was a tunic—an under-garment made like a long petticoat. It was stained with the Savior's blood. The coat was without seam, woven from the top throughout.

The garments of Jesus, like those of every Jew of the time, consisted of five articles—a shirt-coat, a cloak, a waist-cloth, a head kerchief, and sandals.

Each cross was guarded by four lictor-executioners. Under the law, the effects of all condemned persons were confiscated by the State. The spoils of drawing this particular duty were that the four soldiers assigned to each prisoner were permitted to divide his clothes among them.

ABENADAR: [*ABENADAR has the coat in his hand. He stands on the rock with his fingers inside the neck band, turning it around and around trying to find a seam. There isn't any.*] Let us not rend it, but cast lots for it, whose it shall be. (Let us not tear it, but instead throw dice for it, whose it shall be.)

[*The* SOLDIERS *pass it around, feeling and looking for a seam, but find none. They throw dice. They hear the ring of the dice thrown into the brass helmet.*]

SECOND VOICE: Under Roman rule, the clothes worn by a con-demned person at the time of execution became the perquisites of the executioners. The shirt-coat could not be shared. To rend the coat would be to spoil; so the soldiers cast lots to determine who should have it.

The centurion was just. He wanted the garment. When it was washed, it would be worth more than the other items, but he decreed that he and his friends should have a little more wine and then roll the cubed bones for the tunic.

FIRST VOICE: That was done that the Scripture might be fulfilled, which says, "They parted my raiment among them, and for my vesture they did cast lots. These things therefore the soldiers did. All is to happen as it must," point for point, line for line.

True success for Jesus was to complete one's life. It is to attain to eternal life; all else is failure. Thus people who seem to be successful are in most cases failures. But truly Jesus Christ was a failure of failures according to the standards of men. When He died He had nothing but a coat, a girdle, and a seamless gown; and the Roman soldiers divided these, and cast lots for the gown.

[THE SOLDIERS *sit down.*]

SECOND VOICE: They sat down to keep watch, and see that no one tried to release Him. According to the Roman custom, the soldiers sent out to execute a criminal were responsible for his death. They therefore remained until the end.

FIRST VOICE: The executioners expected a word, but not the kind of word that they heard. The scribes and Pharisees awaited His reaction, and they were quite sure that He who had preached, "Love your enemies," and "Do good to them that hate you," would now forget that Gospel with the piercing of His feet and hands. Every one expected a cry. Like some fragrant trees which bathe in perfume the very axe which gashes them, He on the Tree of Love poured out from its depths the prayer of pardon and forgiveness.

Forgive whom? Forgive enemies? The soldier in the courtroom of Caiphas who struck Him with a nailed fist? Pilate, the politician, who condemned God to retain the friendship with Caesar? Herod, who robed Wisdom in the garment of a fool? The soldiers who swung the King of Kings on a tree between heaven and earth? Forgive them? Forgive them, why? Because they know what they do? No, because they know not what they are doing. If they knew what they were doing and still went on doing it; if they knew what a terrible crime they were committing by sentencing Life to death; if they knew what a perversion of justice it was to prefer Barabbas to Christ, his prayer might never have been uttered.

They were unmindful of the fact that the very Blood which they shed was capable of redeeming them; if they knew what they were doing, they would never be saved! Rather they would be damned! It was only the ignorance of their great sin that brought them within the pale of the hearing of that cry from the Cross. It is not wisdom that saves: it is ignorance!

Men on dying either proclaim their own innocence, or condemn the judges who sentenced them to death, or else ask pardon for sins. But Perfect Innocence asked no pardon; as Mediator between God and man He extended pardon. As High Priest who offered Himself in sacrifice, He pleaded for sinners. In a certain sense, the words of forgiveness were spoken twice: once in Eden, as God promised Redemption through the "seed of the woman" who would crush the serpent of evil; now as God in the form of the Suffering Servant who fulfilled the promise. Forgiveness was identified with His sacrifice. Thus He interceded and offered Himself for the guilty.

Abel's blood clamored for the wrath of God to avenge the murder of Cain; the new Abel's blood spilled by jealous brethren of the race of Cain was raised to lift the wrath and to plead for pardon.

[The **SOLDIERS** *proceed with their awful task, with roughness and taunts, for killing was their trade and to scenes of anguish they have grown callous through long familiarity. The* SOLDIERS *gamble, and the* CROWD *gawks.*]

JESUS: Father, forgive them; for they know not what they do.

SECOND VOICE: Jesus heard the taunts. Loud were the taunts. Bitter the mockery.

FIRST VOICE: Jesus did not pray forgiveness for all, He only prayed for those who would repent knowing that there was no forgiveness except through Him. All cannot be saved but only those who are "chosen" through repentance. Instead of asking for mercy at the hands of the mob, He commends them to mercy at the hands of the Father. He once more prayed aloud for His debtors, many of whom were standing mocking beneath Him. He implied that they were simply the victims of their own ignorance of spiritual truth.

Though He loved righteousness, He strove to find some excuse for His enemies, so long as it did not offend against the truth. He never was angry at a private wrong. He attributed to ignorance the enmity of those who crucified Him. He is incomparably the most magnanimous soul that ever lived.

He is called crazy, deceitful, devilish; is betrayed, beaten, crowned with thorns, spat upon, crucified, while Barabbas, a robber, is released? That one with such an estimation of Himself and His mission, subjected to such contumely and suffering, should live a life of unspoiled good-will toward all men! An insult or a blow seemed to him a signal of moral need flung out from his enemy's heart. Jesus thought first not of the wrong done to him, but of the pitiable need of the man who was so ignorant and perverted as to do it. Whenever a man did him a wrong, He looked upon the wrong as a sure sign of a deep need in the man's life.

The ancients clung to the idea of revenge. The man who did not seek revenge rendered himself contemptible. Revenge was a part of righteousness. But the religious man had discovered another way of proving his superiority over His enemy. Where His own hand was impotent, He left revenge to God.

Selfishness in receiving other people's actions on us is more common than refusal to serve them. *Touchiness, petulance, supersensitiveness, readiness to have one's pride hurt and to be insulted, keeping a chip on one's shoulder, all these are forms of selfishness.* They reveal vanity, self-consciousness, a desire to be noticed, and an irritable and peevish fear of being slighted.

That spirit wrested the offensive from their hands and turned the tragedy into a triumph. The ejaculation asked pardon for the high priests, the Pharisees, Sadducees, the people, the world. Love. This is what He meant by love.

[**THE SOLDIERS** *stop the game briefly.*]

SECOND VOICE: It was so unexpected that the soldiers stopped the game briefly—for even in their half-drunken state the extraordinary words must have brought a moment of wonder.

And with Him they crucified two thieves, the one on His right hand and the other on His left.

FIRST VOICE: And thus was fulfilled the Scriptures which said: "And he was numbered with the transgressors."

[**One of the THIEVES** *folds his hands in prayer.*]

[**The CROWD** *jeers.*]

SECOND VOICE: The watchers noted that the three were failing.

SOLDIERS: [*Some of the* SOLDIERS *look at the sky. Others, fairly full of wine, pull their helmets off and doze on the big rock.*]

SECOND VOICE: Some of the soldiers looked at the sky and wondered what had delayed the storm so long in coming.

Each minute required sixty slow steps to cross the faces of the condemned. With each second, the pain mounted. But death was not ready. The arms, the limbs, the torso screamed with pain; the nerves were pulled across the bridge like that on a violin, and the nerve ends were screwed tighter and tighter and tighter.

FIRST VOICE: All the things He had undergone might well have driven Him from the hitherto unsubdued fortress of His patient love. But so many lives were ransomed and made intercession for the guilty.

THE THIEF CESTAS: [*The selfish one. Now from the cross on the left, the political robber to the left of Jesus glares at Him. It is as though he has a secret grievance against the stranger who was dying with him. He keeps glowering across his right shoulder, and at last explodes in anger.*]
Save Yourself and us too, if You are the Christ!
(If you be Christ, save Yourself and us.—Yes, if you be Christ, save yourself and us.—Are You not the Messiah? Save Yourself then, and us!—Are not you the Christ? Save yourself and us!)

SECOND VOICE: Even the wretched man crucified with him found some relief in joining in His abuse. From the cross on the left came another voice, rancorous with hate.

FIRST VOICE: The typical selfish man who is never conscious of having done wrong asks: "Why did God do this to me?" He judges the saving power of God by release from trials. He was saying, "Religion is the opiate of the people. If it cannot give relief from trial, what good is it?" A religion that thinks of souls when men are dying, which bids them look to God at the moment when the courts are inflicting injustice, which talks about Paradise or "pie in the sky," when stomachs are empty and bodies racked with pain, which discourses about forgiveness when social outcasts, two thieves and a village carpenter, are dying on a scaffold—such a religion is "the opiate of the people."

"Save what? Our souls? No! Man has no soul! Save our bodies! What good is religion if it cannot stop pain? Step down from a gibbet! Rescue a class! Christianity is either a social gospel or it is a drug." Such was his cry.

Men can be in identical circumstances and react in totally different ways. Both thieves were alike in the depravity of their hearts, and yet each reacted differently to the man in their midst. No external means, no good example, of and by itself, is enough to convert unless the heart itself is changed. This thief was certainly a Jew, for he based his acceptance of the Messias or Christ solely on His power to take him down from the cross. If Jesus were only a man who had to sustain His reputation, He would have had to show His might then and there; but being God, who knows the secrets of every heart, He kept silence. God answers no man's prayer merely to show His power.

He trembles. Are these wayfarers right after all? When will the saving miracle be wrought?

JESUS: [For a while JESUS keeps silence. JESUS looks toward the man whom pain has conquered. He says nothing.]

DYSMAS THE OTHER THIEF: [*He rebukes the other* THIEF. *The silent one raises himself high on his bloody feet and looks across Jesus to reprove his friend.*]
Do you not fear God, seeing you are in the same condemnation? And we indeed justly, for we receive the due reward of our deeds; but this man has done nothing amiss. (Have you no fear of God even when you are suffering the same penalty? And we are suffering it justly, for we are only getting our deserts, but this man has done nothing wrong.—What, have you no fear of God, when you are undergoing the same sentence? And we justly enough; we receive no more than the due reward of our deeds; but this Man has done nothing amiss.—Are you not ashamed? We are justly condemned, and receive due reward of our deeds, being malefactors! This man has done nothing amiss!—Do you not even fear God, seeing that you are under the same sentence? And ourselves indeed justly, for we are receiving the fitting reward of our deeds; but this man hath done naught amiss.—Do not you even fear God, though you have been condemned to the same punishment. We suffer justly and are getting what we have deserved for our crimes. But this Man has done no wrong.)

FIRST VOICE: A robber is dying by the most fiendish mode of torture that the ingenuity of man has ever contrived. This man has led a hard and bloody life. He has been a highwayman, a knight of the road. He has swooped down upon his fellows as ruthlessly as a beast of prey. But now he has reached the end of the trail. He is suffering the pangs of death. But, as he thus suffers, he declares that it is just, that he is receiving the due rewards of his deeds. How has he come to make such a confession? None such is being made by his fellow in crime. What has happened? This man has seen himself and his deeds against the white background of the personality of Jesus.

As we see Jesus, we see ourselves.

The world has room only for the ordinary; never the very good or the very bad. The good are a reproach to the mediocre and the evil are a disturbance. Hence on Calvary, Goodness is crucified between two thieves. That is His true position: among the worthless and the rejects. He is the right man in the right place. He who said He would come like a thief in the night is among the thieves; the Physician is among the lepers; the Redeemer is in the midst of the unredeemed.

SECOND VOICE: Then one of the crucified thieves, softened into penitence by the Savior's uncomplaining fortitude, and perceiving in the divine Sufferer's demeanor something more than human, rebuked his railing fellow. He reproved him. The one abused Jesus and the other defended him and said, "Hold your tongue!"

[CESTAS, *the political robber, has sunk to the bottom of his cross, and can no longer hear. There is no reply. The robber is groaning in anguish.*]

DYSMAS: [*He says in humble desperation.*] Lord, remember me when You come into Your Kingdom.
(Jesus, remember me when You return in Your glory.—I know you are an innocent man, but I am a great sinner. But will you remember me when you come into your kingdom?)

SECOND VOICE: The good thief, touched by Jesus, now spoke to the Savior on the Cross.

FIRST VOICE: This was the only work spoken to the Cross that was not a reproach. While passersby were judging the Divinity of Jesus by deliverance from pain, the good thief was asking for deliverance from sin. The believer asks no proofs.

Hardly had he spoken when a great grace was given to him, that of believing that this dying man, this miserable and rejected man of whom even the dogs wished no more, was Christ, the Son of God, the Author of life, the King of Heaven.

His confession of guilt and his acknowledgement of the justice of his own condemnation led to incipient repentance, and to faith in the Lord Jesus, his companion in agony.

300

These words show the same division in the two thieves, in human hearts here in Golgotha, as in the yard of Caiphas or in the praetorium of Pilate. The whole of mankind is divided in two by the Cross.

In spite of his crimes, he now had a sort of blind faith, not in the goodness of Jesus,but in the ultimate triumph of good over evil. He was a Jew and expected a supernatural kingdom to be established in which he could share, although he must now die.

There have been leaders who call forth enthusiasm when their fortunes runs high. But He, when His enemies had done their worst, so bore Himself that a crucified felon looked into His dying eyes and saluted Him as king.

Then, throwing himself upon Divine mercy, the thief asked for forgiveness. A dying man asked a dying man for eternal life; a man without possessions asked a poor man for a kingdom; a thief at the door of death asked to die like a thief and steal Paradise. One would have thought a saint would have been the first soul purchased over the counter of Calvary by the red coins of Redemption, but in the Divine plan it was a thief who was the escort of the King of kings into Paradise. If Jesus had come merely as a teacher, the thief would never have asked for forgiveness.

[The ROMAN SOLDIERS *laugh to hear these crucified Jews wrangling.*]

FIRST VOICE: To Jesus, the words were like a ray of light. No matter that the Roman soldiers laughed to hear these crucified Jews wrangling. What Jesus heard was the voice of one who believed in him. This thief and murderer felt the power of the Son of man, whose sinking hopes revived. Through the mouth of one of the lowliest of His brethren, God was exhorting Him to be steadfast in the faith. Once more there had been a word about his kingdom, a word from on high, out of the firmament, though only spoken on a cross.

The conduct of everyone around the Cross was the negation of the very faith the good thief manifested; yet he believed when other disbelieved. The penitent thief called Him "Lord" or One who possessed the right to rule; he ascribed to Him a Kingdom which certainly was not of this world, for Jesus bore no outward mark of kingship. Victim and Lord were to the good thief compatible terms. A dying thief understood it before the Apostles. This is the only deathbed conversion mentioned in the Gospels, but it was preceded by the Cross of suffering. What the good thief asked for was to be remembered. But why be remembered, except that the pardon Jesus offered to His executioners could also be offered to him? Nor was there a word of smiting or reproach to the thief, for he was already bruised and broken. This was the only word spoken to the Cross that received an answer, and it was the promise of Paradise to the thief that very day.

SECOND VOICE: But since the thief's request touched the reason of His coming to earth, namely, to save souls, the thief heard the immediate answer.

JESUS: [The MESSIAH raises Himself, breathes painfully and says] I promise you, this day you shall be with Me in Paradise. (Today, you shall be with Me in paradise.—Truly I say to you, today shall you be with me in paradise.—I tell you, you will be in Paradise with me today!—Truly I say to you, be of good cheer, today shall you be with me in paradise.—This very night you shall be with me in paradise.)

SECOND VOICE: Pangs of body and tortures of mind become interwoven one with another, simultaneously confusing Him and enlightening Him. His thoughts were like arrows, fiery arrows, resembling the shafts of the noonday sun, descending mercilessly out of the blue upon burning forehead and scorched limbs.

FIRST VOICE: The Last Judgment was prefigured on Calvary: the Judge was in the center, and the two divisions of humanity on either side: the saved and the lost, the sheep and the goats. When He would come in glory to judge all men, the Cross would be with him then too, but as a badge of honor, not shame. It was the thief's last prayer, perhaps even his first. He knocked once, sought once, asked once, dared everything, and found everything. When even the disciples were doubting and only one was present at the Cross, the thief owned and acknowledged Him as Savior.

Practically everything about the Body of Jesus was fastened by nails, or tortured by whips and thorns, except His Heart and His tongue—and these declared forgiveness that very day. But who can forgive sins, but God? And who can promise Paradise except Him who by nature is eternal to Paradise? What does that mean? It means that the moment this criminal looked to Jesus to be his friend, that moment he received everlasting life. Even on the cross, here was a man who saw the truth, who believed in Him.

What about the future? What about the Day of Judgment? Only the word of Jesus counts here. And what is His word? Here it is. He died for you and is now in heaven interceding for you. This is the question

302

in the school of everlasting life. Have you passed from death unto life?

In His last hour on earth Jesus gave one of the two thieves the assurance of mercy. Mercy is a divine perogative, and when we see Jesus thus exercising it we recognize again the royal freedom of one who is the Son.

Jesus knew that when He should be exalted into heaven, He would still carry on His work—He, Himself, only by new methods and with a wider scope. He would be everlastingly present in person, and the power and glory of God were to be His. At the last He was to come again to satisfy the desire of His people, as the bridegroom satisfies the longing of the bride on the wedding day.

He knows the art of grafting a sound tree, and making man a new creation. The novelty is this: He leads men to the Father and Himself helps them to a higher righteousness than that of the Pharisees.

He began to judge while He was still on earth. Finally, as He was dying, *the thief on the cross.* He was indeed a judge who took His judgments to heart, condemning with tears. Yet His condemnation remained. It was also a condemnation when He kept silent over men's lack of a sense of truth.

"Be of good cheer!" brings the lights of infinite hope that "You can be saved." Jesus promised him that love and mercy awaited him in paradise. Jesus wiped away past errors and mistakes, he inherited what was good in him. There was no cause to be worried or afraid or burdened by a sense of guilt.

This very night! He still hopes. Soon, very soon, the Father will deliver him. He had wrestled for faith ever since the dove and the voice of God came to tell him that He was to forsake His handicraft and to proclaim the kingdom of the Father. Was this faith a deception? Was the vision an illusion? Why, then, should he have been put to such a test? Why should he have been seized and nailed to a cross, iron nails driven through hands that had never struck a blow? If all this were but transitory suffering, why should it be so agonizing, and why should it last so long?

FIRST VOICE: He was to be the new Adam, beginning a new humanity, changing the water of sin into the wine of life. He knew that the world would not tolerate His Divinity. He knew that when He was no longer known among men as the son of the carpenter, but as the Son of God, that would be His first step toward Calvary. The moment that He proved His Divinity by His works and His miracles, He began the royal road to the Cross.

THE PATIENT: [*Now there stands by the cross of Jesus his* MOTHER, *and his mother's sister* MARY, *the wife of Cleophas, and* MARY MAGDALENE. *They weep.*]

SECOND VOICE: At 2:00 P.M. Jesus found Himself in a multiplicity of pain. Slowly, steadily, He was being asphyxiated as though two hands were on His throat.

The loss of blood had not been fatal. No arteries in wrists or feet had been severed, though there was considerable loss from thorns and wounds.

The thieves were weaker, too; the whole scheme of crucifixion was progressive weakness under increasing pain. But their weakness did not keep pace with that of Jesus because He had been beaten and had been given no food or water since eleven the night before—almost fourteen hours. Jesus was closer to death than the robbers.

The mouths and throats of all the condemned men cried for water and, as the victims went deeper into shock, they lost more fluids and their skin became increasingly moist to the touch.

Jesus began His final hour on the cross. The cluster of people around Golgotha was composed of hardly more than the few who loved Him and the few who despised Him. The sky remained under a dark veil, and some said that it must be an eclipse of the sun, although the more learned knew that this could not be, because the sun was now in the western side of the sky and the moon would rise in the east after sun-down.

Among the spectators of this, the greatest tragedy in history, were some who had come in sympathy and sorrow. John the Apostle and certain women were present. They first at a distance, and then close by the cross, wept in the anguish of love and sorrow.

[JESUS' eyes rove in search of disciples and friends. From the cross JESUS looks at the little party of loved ones who stand only twenty-five feet away.]

FIRST VOICE: All His disciples and friends have fled except John. There is not one to give the Master a last consolation (except John), and, in His secret need, to strengthen Him with His own teachings. Only one to hear the prophet's last words, and hand them down to posterity.

Just as overnight they had fallen asleep at Gethsemane, and had taken flight when His enemies had seized him, so now, it would seem, their zeal had fallen asleep. His influence was at an end; their faith had vanished; His message had fallen on deaf ears; the springs of brother love had dried up. All had been in vain! The only onlookers were two or three women, thickly veiled, standing a long way off. They seemed to be weeping. Were they afraid to call a greeting?

These strangers who have followed Him in His wanderings—they, at least, have understood the message of love. But where were the thousands? Would any vestige remain of His teaching? If the disciples scattered, who would record His message? If that message passed without leaving a trace, must He not have been rating Himself too high? Perhaps, after all, He was just such a man as His own brothers, who deemed Him possessed!

SECOND VOICE: And many women were there beholding from afar, who had followed Jesus from Galilee, ministering unto Him: among whom was Mary Magdalene, and Mary the mother of James and Joses, and the mother of the sons of Zebedee. Standing also by the cross of Jesus were His mother, his mother's sister Mary, wife of Cleophas, and Salome.

The finest in womanhood, as well as in manhood, has looked to Him for its ideal and has responded to His appeal for loyal devotion. These devoted women stood at a distance and kept with aching hearts such watch as only patient, loving women know how to keep.

Only as far as Golgotha is the Gospel masculine, from there on it is feminine. The male disciples had run away and only the female ones remained. The masculine in love proved itself powerless, and the feminine strong. Feminine love rose in the Resurrection whereas masculine love was hindered by His death. Only women (except John) stood by Him to the end. And this, we must remember, was no peaceful deathbed; it was just as far from it as possible.

JESUS: [He draws Himself up on the cross, so that He can speak. He clenches His teeth against the pain until His knees are straight again and He can breathe. Now he looks down from His Cross to JOHN and MARY. With a gesture of His dust-filled eyes and His thorn-crowned head, He looks at her. Then, in an economy of words.] Woman, this is your son.
[Gestures with His eyes toward JOHN. JESUS first looks at his MOTHER and then turns His eyes to the disciple as He speaks.]

[**MARY** looks at JOHN.]

FIRST VOICE: He did not call him John. In his anonymity, John stood for all mankind.

JESUS: [To JOHN. JESUS looks steadily at JOHN. Gestures with his eyes toward MARY.] This your mother.

[JOHN looks up into the eyes of his MESSIAH and nods. JESUS assigns a spiritual motherhood for redeemed humanity. JOHN understands.]

SECOND VOICE: This was said when Jesus saw his mother and the disciple standing by, whom he loved. And from that hour that disciple took her into his own home. He immediately assumed the new relationship established by his dying Master.

FIRST VOICE: The mystery came to an end on Calvary. He was asking her to love men as He loved them. He beheld love triumphant and eternal and raised it above the personal to the divine. The bitterness of Eve's curse—that women would bring forth children in sorrow—was now fulfilled. John's mother was present at the Cross. He needed no mother from a human point of view.

Mary the mother, at last she emerged from the silence and shadows, with that sword in her heart. That He fulfilled the part of a dutiful son to the very last is shown in his dying provision for His mother (all humanity).

FIRST VOICE: At noontide the light of the sun was obscured, and black darkness spread over the whole land. The terrifying gloom continued for a period of three hours. This remarkable phenomenon has received no satisfactory explanation from science. In the eyes of the evangelists there is no doubt that something supernatural took place at this moment. The darkness was brought about by miraculous operation of natural laws directed by divine power. It was a fitting sign of the earth's deep mourning over the impending death of her Creator. For nature, in sympathy with its Creator, refused to shed its light upon the crime of deicide. Mankind, having condemned the Light of the World, now lost the cosmic symbol of that Light, the sun. At Bethlehem, where He was born at midnight, the heavens were suddenly filled with light; at Calvary, when He entered into the igominy of His Crucifixion at midday, the heavens were bereaved of light. The darkness was such that it seemed as though nature sympathized with the Holy Victim and veiled her face at his suffering.

A WOMAN: [To her HUSBAND] It is becoming difficult to see. [He looks into the sky, and others look.]

A MAN: A storm is coming.

THE CROWD: [*They look into the sky. There are no clouds. But the heavens have deepened from a pale azure to a deeper hue. The sky continues to darken. The crowd begins to break up, and many hurry toward the gates to get to shelter before the storm breaks. The people are afraid.*]

[**MANY**] What is this?

[**SOME,** *calmer than others*] It must be a gigantic dust storm which has flung millions of tons of sand between the land and the sun.

[**OTHERS**] Not even the oldest living Jew has ever seen a sandstorm of more than minor proportions over Jerusalem.

SECOND VOICE: There was no sound of thunder. There was no lightning flashes. There were no clouds. But the heavens had deepened from a pale azure to a deeper hue. The sky continued to darken. The sky deepened until the sun could be stared at with the human eye. The blue deepened until the darkness of dusk descended over all. The darkness, which was like looking through extra strong sunglasses, seems to have pervaded the world at this hour. Tertullian said later that he found in the records of Rome a notation of worldwide darkness which the statesmen of the empire could not explain. Phlegon wrote that there was a great darkness over Europe, surpassing anything that had ever been seen.

And when the sixth hour was come, there was a darkness over the whole land until the ninth hour, from midday until three o'clock. And some of the people remembered the prophecy, "I will cause the sun to go down at noon, and I will darken the earth in the clear day, says the Lord."

For three hours the pall hung over the land until Jesus expired, but through its gloom the soldiers and the faithful women watched.

SECOND VOICE: Jesus entered into the second phase of His suffering. At times the crucified were known to live for forty-eight hours and would only die from thirst and starvation if the executioners did not break the bones of their legs with an iron club. The terribly slow coming of death was the chief suffering of the crucified.

Owing to inflammation and swelling, the blood from the wounds in the hands and feet soon stops flowing, and a numbness of all the members sets in, accompanied by a shivering ague, a burning thirst, and a mortal anguish which is worse than any torture. His blood congealed where it could not flow freely; fever consumed the body; the thorns which were the curse of the earth now were covered with blood poured out as a curse of sin.

As the slow minutes ebbed away, pain chased pain through His tortured frame, as if it were being seared with fire, devoured by beasts of prey.

An unearthly stillness, which was rather normal in darkness, now became frightening in the abnormal darkness of high noon.

The Galilean was close to death.

JESUS: [For a time, JESUS hangs down.]

SECOND VOICE: For a time, He hung down, and the vision of His loved ones and the wall of the city and the high priests dimmed before His eyes. The dusk deepened and Jesus felt the chill shock of the imminence of death.

FIRST VOICE: The catastrophe of being fixed to the Cross was followed by the passion of being crucified. Jesus knew its agony but knew also that nothing could be compared with the final agony He would suffer when forsaken by the Father.

When Judas came with the band to arrest Him in the garden, Jesus told him that it was His Hour and "the power of darkness." But this darkness not only signified that men were putting out the Light who illumined every man coming into this world, but also that He was denying Himself, for the moment, the light and consolation of His Divinity.

At length, when ages as it seemed, had passed, when he felt that the heart in His frail body was breaking; when intelligence and imagination were clouded, and faith and hope are obscured; when all His consciousness was filled with pain—he broke the silence He had kept throughout these dreadful hours. The doubts which had assailed Him yester eve in the garden had been multiplied a thousandfold in His dolorous situation on the cross. The craving to escape from this sacrificial death took the form of a complaint. In these seconds of the final agony, dreams of a life transcending that of mortals no longer sustained him. The Father, to whom he had given himself with such devout faith, had turned away from the most loving of sons. No longer did God look down from his palace above the clouds into this world of suffering men. His spirit was remote from earth, and His heart beat only in heaven. The world was a lost world; the Son was alone; the Father was no Father. Lonely and helpless, a human body was parching, and a human heart was breaking.

Suffering now passed from the body into the mind and soul, as He spoke with a loud voice.

[JESUS struggles valiantly for another breath and pulls Himself up on His wrists. When He reaches the top, He pants and looks again at the world of men. Speaks with a loud voice. At three o'clock JESUS gives a great cry. Suddenly comes the unexpected cry, which still chills our blood. A loud voice, surpassing the most anguished cry of physical suffering, issued from the central cross, rending the dreadful darkness.]

SECOND VOICE: He struggled valiantly for another breath and pulled Himself up on His wrists to stop His vision of the world from fading. When He reached the top, He panted and looked again at the world of men.

JESUS: My God, My God, why have You forsaken Me?

SECOND VOICE: He repeated the Psalm of David which prophetically referred to Him, though written a thousand years before.

FIRST VOICE: Here is a recollection of his spiritual agony; for the sense of being abandoned by God must have caused unfathomable pain to Him whose whole life had been supported by the experience of the presence of God. So real was Jesus' humanity that during these hours of gloom His feelings ebbed again as they had in Gethsemane, only now in a more terrible way. It seemed to him as though God had forsaken Him—as though all His ideals were to end in disaster. His blank despair was such that He cried out.

What mind of man can fathom the significance of that awful cry? It seemed that in addition to the fearful suffering incident to crucifixion, the agony of Gethsemane had recurred, intensified beyond human power to endure. In that bitterest hour the dying Christ was alone, alone in most terrible reality. That the supreme sacrifice of the Son might be consummated in all its fullness, the Father seems to have withdrawn the support of His immediate Presence, leaving to the Savior of men the glory of complete victory over the forces of sin and death.

In quoting the first verse He was thinking of the last ones, where the righteous man, suffering innocently, is temporarily abandoned by God and is later again taken into favor. Death prevented their utterance. He uttered words of the utmost despair, though the Psalm goes on to end with deliverance. The remainder of the verse ends in a paean of joy and praise.

This not only underscored His faith and trust in the Father but recorded His joy in having His mission finished and fulfilled. This poem is rather a song of triumph that His prayer had been heard. And when the darkness of deluded humanity hung over Jesus, it was not surprising that He should have spoken these words, as He thought of the distance between God and mankind.

"My God, My God," thus He clung to the Father with tenacious belief even in this darkest hour of His life. Indeed, the Cross of Jesus is the greatest of triumphs. Jesus' cry was of abandonment which He felt standing in a sinner's place, but it was not of despair. The soul that despairs never cries to God.

This emptiness of humanity through sin, though He felt it as His own, was nevertheless spoken with a loud voice to indicate not despair, but rather hope that the sun would rise again and scatter the darkness.

Not to have drunk the cup of death to the end meant for Jesus not to have drunk it at all. That he should taste of death for every man *outside God*.

Not to have drunk the cup of death to the end, meant for Jesus not to have drunk it at all. That he should taste of death for every man.

Only on the cross, for the first and only time in His life, does the Son call the Father no longer "Father" but "God." Here He was in doubt of being the Son of the Father, the cup did not pass Him, for which He had prayed. The Son was forsaken by the Father. It was necessary for the Son to know that ultimate horror: abandonment by the Father.

His dying thoughts were fixed upon another Psalm that were accomplished in Him to the letter, at that very moment. "But I am a worm, and no man: the reproach of men, and the outcast of the people. All they that saw me have laughed me to scorn: they have spoken with the lips, and wagged the head. He hoped in the Lord, let him deliver him: let him save him, seeing he delights in him . . . they have dug my hands and feet . . . they parted my garments amongst them; and upon my vesture they cast lots."

In taking upon Himself the sins of the world He willed a kind of withdrawal of His Father's face and all Divine consolation. Sin has physical effects, and these He bore by having His hands and feet pierced; sin has mental effects which He poured forth in the Garden of Gethsemane; sin also has spiritual effects such as a sense of abandonment, separation from God, loneliness. This particular moment He willed to take upon Himself that principal effect of sin, which was abandonment.

Man rejected God; so now He willed to feel that rejection. Man turned away from God; now He, who was God united personally with a human nature, willed to feel in that human nature that awful wrench as if He Himself were guilty. Earth had already abandoned Him by lifting His Cross above it; heaven had already abandoned Him by veiling itself in darkness; and yet suspended between both, He united both. This was the moment when leaning on nails He stood at the brink of hell in the name of all sinners. As He entered upon the extreme penalty of sin, which is separation from God, it was fitting that His eyes be filled with darkness and His soul with loneliness.

The darkness gave expression to that burning curse which He would remove by bearing it and triumphing in the Resurrection. As mediator and pleader for the emptiness and darkness of sinful hearts, He would deny Himself that primitive gift of light.

The history of God's dealings with man began in the Old Testament when light was made, and history will come to an end in the final judgment, when the sun and moon shall be darkened and the stars withdraw their shining, and all the heavens will be clothed with blackness. In this particular midday, He stood between the light which was created and the ultimate darkness where evil will be condemned.

The tensions of history He felt within Himself: The Light came into the darkness but the darkness did not comprehend the Light. As a dying person sometimes sees his whole life summarized, so now He saw all history recapitulated in Himself when the darkness of sin had its moment of triumph.

Evil cuts off every thread connecting man with God, setting up barriers against all the avenues that open unto Him and closing all the aqueducts that might strengthen man to go to God. He now felt as if He Himself had severed the cord that bound human life to the Divine. Children can make crosses, but only sin can make the darkness of soul.

Death is the Creator's curse on all creatures. Having once accepted death, the Son had to accept the Father's curse. He alone died that in Him all should rise from the dead. The answer is the Resurrection, without which, then Jesus died in vain. The Resurrection can never be proved, it must be known.

SOLDIERS: [*And sitting down the* SOLDIERS *watch Him there.*]

THE CROWD: [*Some of those who stand by say;*] Why, He is calling upon Elias.

SECOND VOICE: Here is mockery. They mistook Eloi for Elias. It was a belief of the Jews that Elias must come before the Lord came. Their words meant that He certainly could not be the Lord, for Elias had not yet come. Thus they made the self-vaunted Messiah appear as if He summoned a man who was to precede His coming. Actually, Elias had come in spirit in the person of John the Baptist.

The cry from the cross, though heard by all who were near, was understood by few. This was the final mockery, a play upon words.

FIRST VOICE: Jesus had told them during His public life that to accept John as Elias meant the acceptance of the repentance John was to bring about in souls. He told the messengers from John that the reception of any truth He taught depended upon one's state of will. If their consciences were right, He told them, they would have accepted John in the spirit of Elias. Two years had passed, and now their consciences were revealed as Jesus hung on the Cross. They reproached John with asceticism and self-denial; they now reproached Jesus for hanging on the Cross. As the people expected a different Elias as His forerunner, so they expected a different Christ.

All through the Crucifixion, the one unifying motif was: "Come down from the Cross." Satan did not want Him to mount it, Peter was scandalized at the very mention of it. Even those who believe Christ was a human person do not want His Cross. The world is always waiting for Elias to take Him down.

The uncrucified Christ is the worldling's desire. The refusal to come down will forever be the reproach to those who want a lily Christ with hands unscarred and white.

SECOND VOICE: There now came a point in the discourse of the Seven Last Words from the Cross which indicate that Jesus was speaking of Himself, whereas in some of the previous words He was speaking to others.

It is, indeed, true that the loss of blood through the sufferings, the unnatural position of the body with the extreme tension on hands and feet, the overstretched muscles, the wounds exposed to air, the headache from the crowning of thorns, the swelling of the blood vessels, the increasing inflammation—all would have produced a physical thirst. It was not surprising that He thirsted; what was surprising was that He said so. He who threw stars into their orbits and spheres into space, He who shut up the sea with doors, He who made waters out of the rock smitten by Moses, He who had made all the seas and rivers and fountains, He who said to the woman of Samaria, "The man who drinks the water I give him will not know thirst any more," now let fall from His lips the shortest of the seven cries from the Cross.

JESUS: I am thirsty.

312

[The words make a hollow sound on the little hill. The muscles of His upper arms dance in spasms as He tries hard to hold Himself high on His cross.]

SECOND VOICE: The period of faintness, the conception of utter forsakenness soon passed, and the natural cravings of the body reasserted themselves. The maddening thirst, which constituted some of the worst of the crucifixion agonies, wrung from the Savior's lips His one recorded utterance expressive of physical suffering.

When He was crucified, He refused to take a concoction which was offered Him; now He avidly asked for a drink. With such words He openly acknowledged His suffering to friends and foes alike. But there was considerable difference between the two drinks.

FIRST VOICE: The words made a mockery of hollow sound on the little hill. Who could help Him? He was there to die, not to drink. Nevertheless the Man of Sorrows went over his part, verse by verse. He spoke again: "I thirst!"

Jesus had once said to those who thirsted, "If any man thirst, let him come to me, and drink. . . . Whoever drinks of the water that I shall give him shall never thirst." Now he was to thirst Himself. Only life everlasting—the Resurrection—would quench it. His triumph of spirit over matter was in spite of the fact that He had the same bodily limitations and requirements as we.

Thus Jesus twice asked for a drink in circumstances in which the noble, high-minded man would rather have expired of thirst; He asked a Samaritan woman, and He asked His executioner. We are often aware in other great men of an endeavor to shed what is human, or at least to repress it. He who came down among us from above was never ashamed of being a man. His spirit was strong enough to have sealed His lips from giving utterance to the feeling of desolation which beset Him, and to the request that His thirst should be assuaged; but instead, He acknowledged His need. Jesus chose to be man, and repressed nothing in Himself of that which we call human. As a man of truth and candor, Jesus was not ashamed of His need.

Here Jesus thirsted for righteousness. Jesus, knowing that all things are now finished, that the scripture might be accomplished, says, "I thirst." And now Jesus knew well that all was achieved which the scripture demanded for its accomplishment; and He said, I am thirsty Jesus here expressed a deep yearning, "ardent desire; a craving or longing." Now that His work was done his attention returned to God. He desired the speedy return of His all-conquering spirit to its divine source.

He Who had turned water into wine at Cana could have used the same infinite resources to have satisfied His own thirst, except for the fact that He never worked a miracle in His own behalf.

[JESUS groans.]

SOLDIER: [Behind Him, a SOLDIER has heard the words. He stirs and stands and looks up at the dark sky. He groans, one of them looks up, ANOTHER gives a sign. The SOLDIERS bring a vessel containing vinegar. He fills a sponge with vinegar (the ordinary beverage of the soldiers), places it on a reed (a short javelin or spear or a stalk of hyssop). Stabs it into a sponge, then dips it into a jar of posca. Posca was made of sour wine, water and beaten eggs. The dripping sponge on the spear is lifted up to the lips of the MESSIAH. He presses it to the LORD'S fevered lips.]

SECOND VOICE: They wanted to give the crucified to drink in order that He should die more quickly, and that they might be set free the sooner from their watch by the cross. They believed that the death of a person who is crucified is hastened if something is given him to drink.
The cry denoted such suffering that even one of the soldiers was touched by it and offered Jesus a stupefying drink, such as was sometimes given to render sufferers somewhat insensible to the agony of their tortures.

FIRST VOICE: When the soldiers mockingly gave Jesus the vinegar at the end of hyssop, they intended to ridicule one of the Jewish sacred rites. When the blood of the lamb was sprinkled by the hyssop, the purification through a symbol was now fulfilled as the hyssop touched the Blood of Christ.

THE SOLDIER: [*Speaking in Greek*] Drink, it will dull your pain.

[JESUS utters a loud cry but He does not drink. He shakes his aching head in refusal. The vinegar mixture glistens on His cracked lips and rolls down off His beard.]

SECOND VOICE: But, after tasting it, Jesus declined to drink.

FIRST VOICE: Not until then does He fully realize the situation. Summoning up His last reserves of energy, He shook his aching head in refusal. Jesus did not wish to benumb himself. Was He to miss the moment for which He had so long been waiting, simply in order to ease the pain in His hands? If only the disciples were here, to see God's grace about to be manifested!

But the disciples were far away (except John), and there were very few spectators, for everyone was celebrating the Passover in that harsh city couched upon its hills of stone. Jerusalem! Something shone brightly in the distance to the left. That was the temple. There He had hoped to gain a victory. What had He achieved? Had He not made a deadly onslaught upon the priests? No doubt they had felt that He was the herald of a new order, before whose words the old temple would crumble.

No. He would bear to the end what He had to bear in full possession of all His powers.

That which takes place last in the life of men held by intention the first place in His, for He came to suffer and die. But He would not give up His life until He had fulfilled details of the Scriptures that men might know that it was He, the Christ, the Son of God, who was dying on the Cross. He was taking out of the Scriptures the idea that the Messias of the promise must not accept death as a fate, but perform it as a deed. Exhaustion accounted not for His thirst. As High Priest and Mediator it was the prophecies concerning Him that prompted the cry of thirst. The bystanders at the Cross who knew well the Old Testament prophecies were thus given another proof that He was the suffering Messias. His fourth word, which expressed His sufferings of soul, and His fifth word, which expressed sufferings of body, were both foretold.

Thirst was the symbol of the unsatisfying character of sin; the pleasures of the flesh purchased at the cost of joy of the spirit are like drinking saltwater. Making complete atonement for sin demanded that the Redeemer now feel the thirst even of the lost before they are lost. But for the saved, too, it was a thirst—a yearning for souls. Some men have passion for money, others for fame; His passion was for souls! "Give me to drink" meant "give Me your heart."

The tragedy of Divine love for mankind is that in His thirst men gave Him vinegar and gall.

THE CROWD: [*Sarcastically. They smirk elatedly.*] Let us see whether He calls for Elijah. Let him alone; let us see whether Elijah will come to save him.
(Let be, let us see whether Elias will come to save him. Elias is to come and save him.)

SECOND VOICE: Many at this time believed Elijah to be a sort of guardian spirit of all good Israelites, and this sarcastic speech was an allusion to that.

They not only wished to make His anguish more bearable but there was also curiosity and fear—"What if he does come?" There was a thirst for mockery of what is most sacred.

THE CROWD: [*All the* PEOPLE *depart, beating their breasts.*]

SECOND VOICE: And they wondered in their hearts, "What is this? Who is this? What have we done?"

But Jesus had not called the prophet. He had called His Father. And, in His agony, which had not reached the point where the human nervous system will refuse to accept more and short-circuits itself into unconsciousness, Jesus prayed these words of the psalm.

JESUS: [Full consciousness returns, and JESUS looks around Him]

SECOND VOICE: Full consciousness returned, and He looked around Him. The world before Him was clear. He saw the anguish of His friends. He saw the triumph of the priests, who reasoned that He could not be the Son of God if, in His pain, He was calling for help from one who was only a prophet.

THE SOLDIERS: If You are the King of the Jews, save yourself.

SECOND VOICE: These men were not Jews, nor citizens of conquered Israel; they were proud legionnaires of Rome. Why then did they refer to Him mockingly as the King of the Jews? Because in keeping with the spirit of paganism, they thought all gods were national gods. Babylon had its gods; the Medes and Persians had theirs; the Greeks had theirs; and so did the Romans have their own. The implication was that of all the national gods, none seemed poorer and weaker than the God of Israel who could not save Himself from a tree.

The soldiers' ridicule was also inspired by the inscription on the Cross in three languages which read: "This is the King of the Jews."

Others had asked Him to come down from the Cross or to save Himself. The soldiers, too, were interested in salvation, but only physically, not spiritually.

The soldiers had already shaken dice for His seamless robe. Caiphas rent his priestly robes, but the robes of the High Priest on the Cross were not rent. He left to His military revilers His seamless robe and their belief that He could not save Himself. They would be stationed at the

316

tomb on Easter morning to see how wrong they were and why He would not save Himself.

FIRST VOICE: These soldiers belonged to an empire where a general who sacrificed thousands of soldiers for temporal glory was held in high repute, but they scorned the Captain of salvation who Himself died that others might live. Little did they see that His refusal to save Himself was not weakness but obedience to the law of sacrifice. They could see events only in succession, but He had ordained all from the beginning. He came to "give His life as a ransom for many." If in obedience to their command He had saved Himself, man would have been left unsaved.

[<u>JESUS</u> is silent for a while.]

FIRST VOICE: From all eternity God willed to make men in the image of His Eternal Son. Having perfected and achieved this likeness in Adam, He placed him in a beautiful garden. In some mysterious way the revolt of Lucifer echoed to earth, and the image of God in man became blurred. The Heavenly Father now willed in His Divine mercy to restore man to his pristine glory, in order that fallen man might know the beautiful image to which he was destined to be conformed. God sent His Divine Son to this earth, not just to forgive sin but to satisfy justice through suffering.

In the beautiful Divine economy of Redemption, the same three things which cooperated in the Fall shared in Redemption. For the disobedient man Adam, there was the obedient new Adam, Jesus; for the proud woman Eve, there was the humble new Eve, the Virgin Mary; for the tree of the Garden, there was the tree of the Cross.

SOLDIER: [*One of the* SOLDIERS *comes around to the front of the cross to take another look. Then he goes back and lies down on the rock.*]

SECOND VOICE: The slow hours dragged on.

JESUS: [<u>From</u> JESUS' <u>lungs comes a final cry in a loud voice.</u>] <u>It is finished.</u>
[<u>And He bows His head and gives up the ghost.</u>]

FIRST VOICE: Looking back on the Divine plan and after having tasted the vinegar which fulfilled the prophecy, He now uttered what in the original was only one word.

The despairing cry of Jesus was not in vain. God sent him a comforting consciousness of a Father's presence, and sympathy, and love. Fully realizing that He was no longer forsaken, but that His atoning sacrifice had been accepted by the Father, and that His mission in the flesh had been carried to glorious consummation, He exclaimed in a loud voice of holy triumph.

"It is finished" means ended, the end of the Son means the end of the world. And the Son rested, having finished His work. And this is the meaning of "the Cross was before the world began."

There was something in the face and in the voice of the dying which, in the words "It is finished" was correctly divined by the hearts and impressed itself on the memories of those who head that voice and saw that face.

"It is accomplished," that is, "My work is finished, the redemption of the elect is assured." He was announcing the completion and perfection of his mission, the canceling out of the material and transmuting it into the divine, the spiritual. In the midst of the misery of the world, His own great suffering and the breakdown of His work, He showed that inwardly He could prevail against all such tribulation, and when His plans seemed to have miscarried He could cry triumphantly, "It is finished!" His trust in God quite openly celebrated its greatest triumph in that hour. Jesus came down from heaven to accomplish a preordained task.

This does not mean that everything was ended, but rather that matters were accomplished. That is, that He had walked the full length of the path that had to be covered. Here He was praying for others, but there was no prayer for His own salvation. In Israel a man hanged on a tree was from time immemorial cursed of God. Must not such a curse have given Jesus much cause for self-examination? But He not only died in the assurance that He would be that day in Paradise, and that He was going to the Father, but in the hours when conscience made her reckoning He could put forward His own purity as the power which should redeem sinners from their most secret need. His soul required no ransom, so was free from all guilt that He could offer it as a ransom for others.

We are faced by a fact of His inner life which is unique in history: His conscience never separated Him from the Divine God. What we see in Jesus has only been seen once in the world, a great riddle—a Man who was the first to teach others what sin really means.

We are endowed with a proclivity to sin, but He was not. We make the force of circumstances our excuse. In the midst of sinners, His development was steadfastly accomplished. Sin was not inherent in Him, yet perfection was not laid as a gift in His cradle. There is a moral progress which does not proceed from bad to good, but which rises from perfection to perfection. It is no less difficult than the other, but it is more glorious, and it is what God originally intended.

When it looked as though everything were lost He cried, "It is finished!" He was absolutely convinced that the Kingdom was to come with Him and that He was to overthrow all hostile forces. He, the outcast, was yet the cornerstone. He, the Crucified One, had conquered the world. Now He might set Himself down at God's right hand; for after He had given His life as a ransom for sin, He would assuredly "reign." He was always able to live without care in the present just because He was so sure of the future. He will live and He will conquer—not only His cause, but He Himself, as He has already conquered.

Here is expressed a great truth: It is finished. Indeed, everything seemed finished. The attempt made by Jesus to lead Judaism beyond itself had failed. Judaism had lost the opportunity of realizing all the latent possibilities and capacities it possessed. Henceforth it was to be a religion which had survived itself. The Sanhedrin and Pilate thought that they have finished with one whom they believed—or pretend to believe—to be a Messianic agitator.

The word also means: "All is accomplished." The work of Jesus was finished. The faith which He had been able to plant in the hearts of a few men, feeble and hesitating as it was, had roots which were too deep to be ever eradicated. Nothing was finished; in reality, everything had just begun. The faith in the Resurrection was about to be born, and with it that Christianity which was destined to conquer the Ancient World and to march through the centuries.

Christ, one with the Eternal Father in the work of creation, had perfected Redemption. It was not after preaching the beautiful Sermon on the Mount that He said that His work was perfected. It was not to teach that He came; it was, as He said, to give His life as a ransom for many. Now the work which the Father had given Him to do was finished. All this came to pass that He might suffer on the Cross. What was achieved was Redemption.

It was not an utterance of thanksgiving that His suffering was over and finished, though the humiliation of the Son of Man was now at an end. It was rather that His life from the time of His birth to the time of His death had faithfully achieved what the Heavenly Father sent Him to do.

Three times God used that same word in history: first, in Genesis, to describe the achievement or completion of creation; second, in the Apocalypse, when all creation would be done away with and a new heaven and earth would be made. Between these two extremes of the beginning and the accomplished end, there was the link of the sixth utterance from the Cross. Jesus in the state of His greatest humiliation, seeing all prophecies fulfilled, all foreshadowings realized, and all things done which were needful for the Redemption of man, uttered a cry of joy.

The life of the Spirit could now begin the work of sanctification, for the work of Redemption was completed. In creation, on the seventh day, after the heavens and the earth were finished, God rested from all the work that He had done; now the Savior on the Cross, having taught as Teacher, governed as King, and sanctified as Priest, could enter into His rest. There would be no second Savior; no new way of salvation; no other name under heaven by which men might be saved. Man had been bought and paid for. A new David arose to slay the Goliath of evil, not with five stones but with five wounds—hideous scars on hands, feet, and side; and the battle was fought not with armor glistening under a noonday sun, but with flesh torn away so the bones could be numbered. The Artist had put the last touch on his masterpiece, and with the joy of the strong He uttered the song of triumph that His work was completed.

FIRST VOICE: Now the new Abel, Jesus Christ, slain by the race of Cain, prepared to go home. His sixth word was earthward; the seventh was Godward. The sixth was the farewell to time, the seventh, the beginning of His glory. The prodigal Son was returning home; thirty-three years before, He had left the Father's house and gone off into the foreign country of this world. There He began spending His substance, the Divine riches of power and wisdom; in His last hour, His substance of Flesh and Blood was wasted among sinners. There was nothing left to feed upon except the husks and the sneers and the vinegar of human ingratitude. He now entered into Himself and prepared to take the road back home into His Father's house and, as He did so, He let fall from His lips the perfect prayer.

JESUS: [JESUS again pulls Himself up to the top of His cross.] Father, into your hands I commend my spirit.

FIRST VOICE: In the agony of the crucifixion He turned to the Psalms for expression of His Anguish and his trust. "My God, my God, why have you forsaken me?" "Father, into your hands I commend my spirit."

The Master's mind was saturated with the Old Testament.

In reverence, resignation, and relief, He addressed the Father, thus replacing a cry of despair by a cry of filial confidence. Can you easily imagine anyone facing what the Master faced without *becoming cynical and discouraged*? Think of the patience, the persistent faith, the unconquerable goodwill of the Master. Would you not expect anyone, enduring what He endured in a good cause, to have his *faith in God shaken*?

By committing His spirit into the hands of God he exemplified obedience, faith, and trust and now awaited His further will or order. His eye was on God, the good. For Him the meaning of the cross is not one of destruction and death but of dynamic, ever-resurgent life. For Jesus death was a transition—nothing but a move to God.

[JESUS cries again with a loud voice in delirium and yields up the ghost. The body sags on the cross and, bowing His head, He dies.]

FIRST VOICE: Jesus willed Himself to die. He voluntarily gave up His life. Jesus the Christ was dead. His life had not been taken from Him except as He had willed to permit. Sweet and welcome as would have been the relief of death in any of the earlier stages of His suffering from Gethsemane to the cross, He lived until all things were accomplished as had been appointed.

His last words were not spoken in an exhausted whisper, as men do as they breathe their last. He had already said that no one would take away His life from Him, but that He would lay it down of Himself. Death did not lay its hand on His shoulder and give Him a summons to depart; He went out to meet death. In order to show that He would not die from exhaustion, but an act of will, His last words were spoken, "crying with a loud voice."

It is the only instance in history of a dying one who was a living one. He was not singing the song of death to Himself; He rather proclaimed the onward march of Divine life. He was not taking refuge in God because He must die; rather His dying was a service to man and the fulfillment of the will of the Father.

JESUS: [And His spirit went up to heaven.]

FIRST VOICE: And His spirit went up to heaven, for Christ is entered into the heaven itself now to appear in the presence of God for us.

Man thinks that it is his dying that decides his future state; it is rather his living that does that. Some of the choices he has made, the opportunities that were in his hand, the graces that he accepted or threw

321

away, are what decide his future. The peril of living is greater than the peril of dying.

So now it was the way He lived, namely, to ransom men, that determined the joy of His dying and His union with the Heavenly Father. The Word Incarnate, having completed His earthly mission, now returned again to the Heavenly Father who sent Him on the work of Redemption.

[*There is* **an earthquake.** *The sky turns black and the earth shakes.*)

SECOND VOICE: And, behold, the veil was rent in two from the top to the bottom; and the earth did quake, and the rocks rend; and the graves were opened, and many bodies of the saints which slept arose, and came out of the graves after His Resurrection, and went into the holy city, and appeared to many.

A sound went through the air as though a herd of animals had stampeded underground. The earth trembled and a small rock fissured the earth from the west toward the east and split the big rock of execution and went across the road and through the gate of Jerusalem and across the town and through the temple, and it split the big inner veil of the temple from the top to the bottom and went on east and rocked the big wall and split the tombs in the cemetery outside the walls and shook the Cedron and went on to the Dead Sea, leaving fissures in the earth, the rocks, and across the mountains. The death of Christ was accompanied by terrifying phenomena. There was a violent earthquake; the rocks of the mighty hills were disrupted, and many graves were torn open.

FIRST VOICE: An intervention of God in the course of nature took place in the hour when the Savior's earthly life came to a close. Thus to the greater events in the world of the spirit were added counterparts in nature, confirmatory and complementary. God did not allow these great events in the spiritual world to leave no trace on the material world. God is no one-sided idealist; external as well as internal things belong to Him.

When Christ was crucified, the sun hid its light; when He died, the earth shook in grief. If the earth gave signs of recognition when God was delivering His people from the slavery in Egypt by the parting of the waters of the sea, with how much greater reason now did it manifest recognition as the Lord liberated man from the slavery of sin. Though the hearts of the people could not be rent, the rocks could.

When the veil of the temple was rent in two it was a prophecy of the destruction of the temple. "Christ is entered into the heaven itself," and from now on man also can enter within the *veil*. Can enter into the holiest by the blood of Jesus, by a new and living way, which He has consecrated for us, through the *veil*, that is to say, His flesh.

The interior of the Holy of Holies, which none but the high priest had been permitted to see, was thrown open to common gaze. It was the rending of Judaism, the consummation of the Mosaic dispensation, and the inauguration of Christianity under apostolic administration.

The very fact that it was torn from top to bottom was to indicate that it was not done by the hand of man, but by the miraculous hand of God Himself, Who had ordained that, as long as the Old Law should endure, the veil should stand before the Holy of Holies. Now He decreed that it should be torn asunder at His death. That which of old was sacred now remained opened and manifest before their eyes, uncovered like any common and ordinary thing, while before them on Calvary, as a soldier pierced his Heart, was revealed the new Holy of Holies containing the ark of the New Testament and the treasures of God. The death of Jesus was the deconsecration of the earthly temple, for He would raise up the new temple in three days. Only one man, once a year, could enter into that old Holy of Holies; now that the veil was rent which separated holiness from the people, and separated the Jew from the Gentile, both would have access to the new Temple, Christ the Lord.

What was holy was made manifest. The Holy Spirit meant us to see that no way of access to the true sanctuary lay open to us, as long as the former tabernacle maintained its standing. . . . Meanwhile, Christ has taken His place as our High Priest. . . . a more complete tabernacle, which human hands never fashioned, it does not belong to this order of creation at all. It is His own Blood, not the blood of goats and calves, that has enabled Him to enter, once for all, into the sanctuary; the ransom He has won lasts for ever.

We can enter the sanctuary with confidence through the Blood of Christ. He has opened up for us a new, a living approach, by way of the veil; I mean His mortality.

As the Psalmist looked back on the sacrifices of slain beasts, the burnt offerings to attain Divine favor, and the sin offerings to make reparation for wrong, His mind dwelt upon them only to cast them aside. For he well knew that these slaughtered bulls, goats, and sheep could not really affect man's relationship with God. He saw in a future day God having His Divinity enshrined in a human body as in a temple, and coming with only one purpose, namely, to surrender His life in accordance with the Divine will. Now the figure was fulfilled as the spotless Lamb of God offered Himself to His Heavenly Father. The old promise made to Israel in Egypt still held good and could be claimed, in a higher sense, by all who invoked the Blood poured out on the Cross.

When Christ came into the world to be the fulfillment, Judea denied Him welcome. But, as the veil of the temple was torn, the priesthood came into its own, and with it the true Holy of Holies, the true Ark of the New Covenant, the true Bread of Life—the Christ, the Son of the Living God.

When He died He . . . "vanquished death by death." He has broken the gates of brass, and cut the bars of iron in sunder.

The earth shall reel to and fro like a drunkard, and shall be removed like a cottage; and the transgression thereof shall be heavy upon it, of the greatest of all transgressions—the murder of the Son of God by man.

It was here on Golgotha that began to be fulfilled the Lord's word about the end of the world, for when the end of the Son came, the end of the world began.

With Jesus' death upon the cross a new world era dawned.

And when Matthew speaks about the many bodies of the saints who slept and arose, and came out of the graves after His resurrection, he speaks no longer in the tongue of time but in that of eternity, joining the past with the future. (Mystery and history are intermingled and combined.) They are now one.

Then the darkness lifted and the sun came out. And in this way were fulfilled the words of the Lord: "And I, if I be lifted up from the earth, will draw all men to me."

[ABENADAR *and some of the* SOLDIERS *jump to their feet in alarm. They come to the front of the cross and look at Him and at the darkened sky and the crack across the big rock.*]

SECOND VOICE: The Roman centurion and the soldiers under his command at the place of execution were amazed and greatly affrighted. They had probably witnessed many deaths on the cross, but never before had they seen a man apparently die of his own volition, and able to cry in a loud voice at the moment of dissolution.

THE CENTURION: [*He bows his head.*] This was the Son of God. (Assuredly, this Man was the Son of God. Certainly this was a righteous man. This man was certainly a son of God. No doubt but this was the Son of God.)

SECOND VOICE: The centurion, who had charge of the soldiers, noting the earthquake and recalling the manner in which the Man on the central cross had died, began to reflect. Then this sergeant in the Roman army gave testimony, not in the realm of dreams as did Claudia, the other pagan, but with the expression of an honest and reasonable man.

The Christ who had been utterly abandoned and who had no one to come forward courageously to acknowledge Him—He was finally owned in His death by the battle-scarred soldier who had commanded and presided over the execution.

Doubtless the centurion had crucified many before, but he felt there was something mysterious in this Sufferer, who prayed for His enemies and was so strong in His last breath as to prove that He was Master of the life He was surrendering. Seeing all nature become animated and vocal, his mind saw the refutation of the foul calumnies and the innocence of the righteous man; aye, even more, he proclaimed His Divinity. He had observed Jesus' bearing through all his suffering, and exclaimed when all was over.

What astounded the Roman centurion was just this which caused him "to stand over against him" and to look closely at the dying face. He had seen many deaths, but none like this one. (There are various ways and measures of knowledge, either more external or more internal. They are all equally authentic and indispensable to us.)

A fitting conclusion is the testimony of the Roman centurion. Jesus' manner, his unflinching endurance, and, above all, the loud cry that proclaimed a physical and spiritual strength that defied death, impressed this heathen soldier so that he declared involuntarily, "Truly this man was a Son of God."

The Roman sergeant, who had his own gods and was hardened both to war and death, came to the answer during the Crucifixion, when both his reason and his conscience affirmed the truth. He answered the cry of the Dying One involuntarily, not thinking of the consequences that he was making himself the accomplice of the "malefactor," "an Adversary of Caesar."

The actual death of Jesus appeared to all who were present to be a miracle, as in fact it was. This marvel, coupled with the earthquake and its attendant horrors, so impressed the centurion that he prayed to God, and solemnly declared "Certainly this was a righteous man."

FIRST VOICE: A Roman eye saw and a Roman ear heard that which Jewish eyes and ears did not see and did not hear. A stranger understood better than one of His own. All heathendom, all mankind, was present here, on Golgotha, in the person of the centurion. Here there was one man who believed. Here on Golgotha the world was saved just as when in Caesarea Philippi, Peter answered the question of Jesus: "Who am I?" by, "Thou art the Christ, the Son of God."

Judas confessed that he had betrayed "innocent blood"; Pilate repeatedly "found no fault" in Him; Herod neither; Claudia Procula regarded Him as a "just man"; the thief on the cross later would say that He had done no wrong; and the centurion would finally proclaim: "No doubt but this was the Son of God."

The centurion did not hear in the last cry of the Lord death; it was victory over death. "He will swallow up death in victory."

The Cross was beginning to bear fruit: a Jewish thief had already asked for and received salvation, and now a soldier of Caesar bowed in adoration of the Divine Sufferer. That strange combination which was everywhere in the public life of Jesus was now manifested on the Cross: humiliation and power. While others condemned Him of blasphemy, the centurion worshiped Him as the Son of God.

SOLDIERS: [SOLDIERS *join in fearsome averment.*] Truly this was the Son of God. [*Leave beating their breasts.*]

SECOND VOICE: The terrified ones who spoke and those who heard left the place in a state of fear, beating their breasts, and bewailing what seemed to be a state of impending destruction.

WOMEN: [*A few loving* WOMEN, *however, watch from a distant point, and see all that takes place until the* LORD's *body is laid away.*)]

SECOND VOICE: The minutes moved on. The high priests were worried. The water clocks were nearing the ninth hour and it was not seemly that Jesus and the robbers should continue to struggle. The priests did not want to appear to be callous about the matter of time, but, in a little more than three hours the Sabbath would be upon all.

[**The HIGH PRIESTS** *have some discussion.*

The CENTURION *sees that* TWO OF PILATE'S GUARDS *are now conversing with the* HIGH PRIESTS.

The HIGH PRIESTS: [*to the* MESSENGER] Hurry to Pilate and ask him to order the centurion to dispatch these three, so that they might be interred before sundown.
Ask Pilate that their legs might be broken.

[**A MESSENGER** *is seen hurrying back into the city.*]

326

SECOND VOICE: It was now late in the afternoon; at sunset the Sabbath would begin. The Jewish officials, who had not hesitated to slay their Lord, were horrified at the thought of men left hanging on crosses on such a day, for thereby the land would be defiled; so these scrupulous rulers went to Pilate and begged that Jesus and the two malefactors be summarily dispatched by the brutal Roman method of breaking their legs, the shock of which violent treatment had been found to be promptly fatal to the crucified. The added suffering to be endured by the criminals was in their sight as nothing in comparison to the danger of polluting an especially holy day. They wanted them taken down from the cross.

[**The CENTURION** *has only begun to wonder the presence of* PILATE'S GUARDS, *however, when the two come across the rock to tell him.*]

PILATE'S GUARDS: The high priests sent word to Pilate that if the crucified were still on the trees at sundown, all of Golgotha would be defiled, and no Jew could set foot on it henceforth.
Pilate says, apply the *crurifragium.*

[**The CENTURION** *motions to the* SOLDIERS. ABENADAR *nods toward the three crosses and orders the* GUARDS *to do their duty. One of the* GUARDS *is armed with a spear. The other carries a board, about one inch by three inches and about four feet long. The two men confer and decide to begin at the left, with the silent one.*]

[**A CRIMINAL ON THE CROSS** *sees them coming and knows that the crurifragium means the breaking of both legs to hasten death. When the* ROBBER *sinks to the bottom of his cross and shows no sign of trying to pull himself up again; the pair moves on to the* POLITICAL ROBBER, *who has exhausted himself with protests.*

The POLITICAL ROBBER *can only stare in mute horror as the man with the board takes a stance beside him. He is struck upon the leg by a Roman soldier to see if he is dead, is crying out in a sudden access of agony, and writhing, tears one foot loose from the nail that pierces it.*

MARY *and* JOHN *weep with averted eyes, unable to endure the sight.*]

THE SOLDIERS: [*They break the legs of the* TWO CRIMINALS *first with an iron club or cudgels, and then they come to* JESUS.] This man is dead.

SECOND VOICE: When the soldiers saw that Jesus was dead already, they broke not His legs.

[**A SOLDIER** *waves the* OTHER *away, then steps back a pace. He holds his lance midway down the shaft and draws it back, aiming for the right side of the* MESSIAH's *chest. With a spear he pierces* JESUS' *side. And there comes out blood and water.*

JESUS: <u>The body of the MASTER hangs limp and dead.</u>]

[**MARY MAGDALENE**, *in passionate grief, is trying with vain hands to ward away the* SOLDIER *who from horseback drives the spear into the* SAVIOR's *side.*]

SECOND VOICE: He would make certain that this one was not feigning death. One of the soldiers, to make sure that Jesus was actually dead, or to surely kill Him if He was yet alive, drove a spear into His side, making a wound large enough to permit a man's hand to be thrust thereinto. Thus was accomplished two prophecies: "Neither shall you break a bone thereof;" "Shall look upon me who they have pierced."

Though the executioners pierced His side, they did not break a bone of His Body as was prophesied. This prophecy was accomplished in spite of His enemies, who asked for the contrary.

The spear jumped forward and rove inward between the fifth and sixth ribs. It went through the pleura and the thin part of the lung and stopped in the pericardium.

The dead do not bleed, ordinarily, but the right auricle of the human heart holds liquid blood after death, and the outer sac holds a serum. When the soldier withdrew the spear, blood and water were seen to emerge and drip down the side of the body. The physical rupture of the heart was the direct cause of death.

FIRST VOICE: The Divine Miser had hoarded up a few precious drops of His Blood to pour forth after He gave up His spirit, to show that His love was stronger than death. Blood and water came forth; blood, the price of Redemption and the symbol of the Eucharist; water, the symbol of regeneration and baptism.

Water stood at the beginning of Jesus' ministry when He was baptized, blood stood at the close of it when He offered Himself as a spotless oblation. Both became the ground of faith, for at the Baptism the Father declared Him to be His Son, and the Resurrection witnessed again to His Divinity.

The messenger from the Father was impaled with the message of love written on His own Heart. The thrust of the lance was the last profanation of God's Good Shepherd. Though He was spared the brutality that was arbitrary, such as the breaking of His legs, nevertheless, there was some mysterious Divine purpose in the opening of the Sacred Heart of God. At the Deluge Noah made a door in the side of the ark, by which the animals entered, that they might escape the flood; now a new door is opened into the heart of God into which man might escape the flood of sin. When Adam slept, Eve was taken from his side and was called the mother of all living. Now as the second Adam inclined His head and slept on the Cross under the figure of blood and water there came from His side His bride, the Church. The open heart fulfilled His words: "I am the door; a man will find salvation if he makes his way in through me."

Sorrow does not come first, then the look at the Cross; rather sorrow for sins spring from a vision of the Cross. All excuses are cast aside when the vileness of sin is most poignantly revealed. But the arrow of sin that wounds and crucifies brings the balm of forgiveness that heals. As those who looked on the brazen serpent were healed of the poison bit; now the figure passes into reality, and those who looked at One who seemed like a sinner, but was not, were healed of sin.

All must look whether they like it or not. The pierced Christ stands emblazoned at the crossroads of the world. Some look and are softened to penitence; others look and go away regretfully but not sorrowfully, as did that mob on Calvary "who went home beating their breasts." The beating of the breasts here was a sign of impenitence; it was their refusal to look on Him whom they had pierced.

SECOND VOICE: Nothing remained of this dark adventure of three years but the bodies of three executed criminals at the entrance to a city, under a stormy sky, on a dark spring day.

It was the custom to leave the bodies of the guilty exposed to the gaze of all and to the outrage of beast, at the city gates. But on the day of the preparation it was not permissible for these corpses to remain. The soldiers finished off the two thieves by breaking their legs. As Jesus was already dead, it was enough to pierce His side with a lance which opened His heart.

FIRST VOICE: Two veils were rent: one, the purple veil of the temple which did away with the Old Law; the other, the veil of His Flesh which opened the Holy of Holies of Divine love tabernacled among us. In both instances, what was holy was made manifest; one, the Holy of Holies, which had been only a figure; the other, the true Holy of Holies, His Sacred Heart, which opened to the guilty access to God.

The psalmist had sung long before in dolorous measure according to his inspired vision of the Lord's passion. "Reproach has broken my heart; and I am full of heaviness: and I looked for some to take pity, but there was none; and for comforters, but I found none. They gave me also gall for my meat; and in my thirst they gave me vinegar to drink."

PILATE'S GUARDS: [*They stand before the crosses and their glances move back and forth across the* CONDEMNED, *to watch for signs of life. All three hang quietly toward the bottom of their crosses. To the* CENTURION] With your permission we will return to Fortress Antonia.

THE CENTURION: I will leave with the platoon as soon as I collect all the gear. [*He notices a* MAN—*one who is attired as a wealthy person—walking rapidly toward the city gate.*

JOSEPH OF ARIMATHEA *walks rapidly toward the city gate.*]

SECOND VOICE: Abenadar did not know the man, but he had seen him in the last hour standing apart from the others, watching the face of Jesus with obvious compassion.

[*Then* **the SOLDIERS** *take the bodies down.*]

FIRST VOICE: It was over. The rabble had sickened quickly of its revenge and scattered; His friends were hiding. There was nothing left of the external influences that fire men's imaginations or grip their loyalty. Surely the victory of His enemies was complete; He could do no miracle there, hanging on a cross.

The tragedy was ended. Jesus had endured atrocious suffering and was dead because He had excited the bitter hatred of the unprincipled high-priestly gang. Not a voice can be raised in their defense. Josephus has repeatedly and rightly blackened their reputation. Jewish fathers of a later generation remembered their names only to curse their rapacity and greed. Mark and Luke but more especially Matthew have bracketed with them the good Pharisees and even the whole people.

Without his death His life was meaningless to the world or to God.

SECOND VOICE: Directly after the death of Jesus the Jews begged Pilate to take down the bodies of all the three crucified. To this Pilate agreed, acting probably on the usual Roman theory of never interfering with local customs.

Scene 3

THE JUDGMENT HALL OF PILATE—FORTRESS
ANTONIA—JOSEPH'S AUDIENCE WITH PILATE

SECOND VOICE: And now when evening came, because it was the Preparation, the day before the Sabbath, Joseph of Arimathea, a councillor of honorable position, who was also himself looking for the kingdom of God, took courage and went to Pilate and asked for the body of Jesus. Joseph was a man of wealth, station, and influence. He went in boldly unto Pilate and begged the body of Christ. He it was who had not consented to the counsel and deed of them.

He was a Sanhedrist and had been opposed to the action of his colleagues in condemning Jesus to death, or at least had refrained from voting with the rest.

A man known as Joseph of Arimathea, who was at heart a disciple of Christ, but who had hesitated to openly confess his conversion through fear of the Jews, desired to give the Lord's body a decent and honorable interment. But for some such divinely directed intervention, the body of Jesus might have been cast into the common grave of executed criminals.

Joseph was anxious to receive it, because at sunset the Sabbath would begin, and to have a dead Jew hanging on a cross by the high road on the Sabbath would be very highly offensive to Jewish sensibilities. The Jews also had strong views on the defilement produced by contact with the dead.

The Jews were accustomed to burying their dead immediately, on the day on which they died. The Roman custom was to permit the bodies to remain on the cross until the carrion birds, the dogs, and other small animals and insects had had sufficient time to reduce the body to bones.

He hurried to Antonia and requested an audience of Pontius Pilate. It was granted.

JOSEPH OF ARIMATHEA: May I have your permission to bury Jesus of Nazareth at once? May I take away the body of Jesus?

SECOND VOICE: This was an embarrassing interview for Joseph. In asking for the body for burial, he was making known to the procurator

331

that he, a member of the Great Sanhedrin, the head of the well-known Sadducean family, was a secret disciple of Jesus.

It required courage of Joseph to dare to do this, to rise up alone against many, to take the body of his Friend from the enemy, and give his own tomb to one "hanged on a tree, accursed of God."

To bury the unclaimed Jewish dead had long been a pious practice among the Jews. He now made himself responsible for Jesus' burial.

PILATE: [*He is startled.*] I cannot believe that Jesus is dead.

JOSEPH OF ARIMATHEA: I saw Him die with my own eyes.

PILATE: Dead so soon? [*Motions to a* SOLDIER—*the* CAPTAIN.] Is it really so? Get a report from Abenadar.

SECOND VOICE: To settle the matter, the Roman ordered a horseman to Golgotha at once to get a report from Abenadar.

[JOSEPH OF ARIMATHEA waits.]

A SOLIDER: [*Comes hurrying in.*] The Galilean has died after no more than a few hours on the cross. The Man Jesus died first, just prior to the work of the guard with the plank.

PILATE: [*He shrugs. He bows pleasantly.*] You have permission to take the body down, in conformity with Jewish custom, and to bury the body before the onset of the Sabbath.

I give you leave.

SECOND VOICE: And Pilate marvelled that He was already dead. And calling the centurion, he asked him if He had been dead for a long time. Learning the facts from the centurion, he granted the corpse to Joseph.

Surprised at the quick death of which the centurion had informed him, Pilate gave instructions for the corpse of Jesus to be given to Joseph, fulfilling thereby a paragraph of the known Roman law: "The bodies of the executed must be given for burial to those who claim them."

Perhaps the procurator felt pity and blame and granted the only restitution possible, proper burial for the poor, mangled corpse; perhaps he had in mind only further irritation of the high priests.

FIRST VOICE: It is ironic that when Jesus died His burial would be arranged not by the stalwart Peter nor the beloved John nor any of the men who had been close to Him, but by a Sadducee, a Pharisee, and a pagan.

Scene 4

THE GOLGOTHA HILL—THEY TAKE DOWN HIS BODY

SECOND VOICE: Joseph came therefore and took away the corpse. But Nicodemus came also, he who visited Jesus by night at the first; he was bringing a mixture of myrrh and aloes, about a hundred pounds.

FIRST VOICE: Nicodemus, a politician, had also been afraid. It was the hour of the timid. The two men who had not dared to confess the living Christ, and who came to see him secretly in the night, now that He was dead showed more faith and tenderness than those who had expressed themselves in words.

Nothing now meant anything to them, these ambitious men, for they had lost Jesus. What did they fear? The Jews could no longer harm them. Everything could be taken from them, now that they had lost everything; those honors to which they cleaved more than anything in the world were as nothing to them now that Jesus was dead.

JOSEPH AND NICODEMUS: [*When they arrive at Golgotha,* JOSEPH *and* NICODEMUS *approach the* FRIENDS OF JESUS *and tell* JOHN.]

JOSEPH OF ARIMATHEA: The Romans have given the body to me for burial.

[JOHN *searches their faces.*]

SECOND VOICE: John searched their faces, and saw love and pity. [*They all are in discussion.*]

SECOND VOICE: They discussed the need for haste so that the Sabbath would not be profaned.

[JOSEPH *points to the proximity of the sepulchre which was newly hewn from rock.*]

SECOND VOICE: Joseph had a rock-cut tomb in the broken ground north of the city and not far from the place of the crucifixion. He had a new tomb in a garden upon the slope of Golgotha, in which no one as yet had been placed.

There they laid the body of the Lord. They buried Jesus. The sepulchre consisted of two cells hewn out of the thickness of the rock, an outer and an inner one, having so low a doorway that it was necessary to bend in order to enter it, and then a descent of two or three steps.

In the interior was hewn also out of the rock, under an arch, a long and narrow bench or shelf of the dimensions of a man, a sort of "manger."

A heavy, flat, circular stone rolled into an orifice in the rock, closed the cave, and rolling out of it opened the entrance. The entrance was less than five feet high and was closed by a millstone sixty inches in diameter and nine inches thick. The weight of this stone was beyond the strength of one person to move.

It sat in a curved groove and, when two or more men tried to rock it away from the entrance, an extra man had to crouch below with a heavy stone to use as a chock. The tendency of the stone was always to roll back into place before the aperture.

A thin ledge of rock separated the vestibule from the main sepulchre. The doorway between was about forty inches high, and loved ones always had to bend deeply to enter.

FIRST VOICE: Born of a virgin womb, He was buried in a virgin tomb, "And a Joseph did betroth them both."

Nothing seems more repelling than to have a Crucifixion in a garden, and yet there would be compensation, for the garden would have its Resurrection.

Born in a stranger's cave, buried in a stranger's grave, both human birth and death were strangers to His Divinity. Stranger's grave, too, because since sin was foreign to Him, so too was death. Dying for others, He was placed in another's grave. His grave was borrowed, for He would give it back on Easter, as He gave back the beast that he rode on Palm Sunday, and the Upper Room that He used for the Last Supper. Burying is only a planting. Paul would later on draw from the fact that He was buried in a garden the law that if we are planted in the likeness of His death, we shall rise with Him in the glory of His Resurrection.

THE GROUP: [*The* TWO MEN *with a few devout* FOLLOWERS *prepare to take* JESUS *down, to unfasten the nails and to take off the crown of thorns. The* MEN *move on to the cross. It is not a simple feat, but they manage to rock the*

334

patibulum loose. Once JESUS *is free of the patibulum, the* THREE MEN *lift Him and move Him to a flat rock for bathing.*]

SECOND VOICE: He lay on the rock as though He were still on the Cross.

FIRST VOICE: All had changed. He was no longer white as He came from the Father; He was red as He came from the hands of men.

[JOSEPH *kneels behind the head of* JESUS *and, with a wet cloth, wipes the face softly, soothingly. With his thumb, he closes the eyes tight. When the neck and shoulders have been washed, he takes a dry strip of linen and ties it tightly around the head, closing the mouth.*

NICODEMUS *unrolls some linen sheeting and places it on the rock beside the body.*

The THREE MEN *lift* JESUS *and set the corpse on the linen. Parts of the body are anointed with perfumed spices.*]

JOSEPH: Let us take the body into the vestibule of my tomb to complete the obsequies.

SECOND VOICE: The men knew that the arms would have to be brought down and the legs laid flat. They did not want to proceed in the presence of the Mother. Joseph solved the dilemma.

[**The WOMEN** *do not object.*]

The THREE MEN *lift the body on the linen and carry it slowly and tenderly 120 feet north-northwest to the middle of the low garden.*]

Scene 5

A GARDEN—THE PLANTING—THE BURIAL—THE SEPULCHRE

[*In the vestibule of the sepulchre, the body is laid on a slab of stone. On the right side of the vestibule is a flat slab of stone for the use of visitors who might want to sit. It is on this stone, in cramped quarters, that the* THREE MEN *hurriedly prepare* JESUS *for final entombment. They light tapers and stick them*

335

in the walls. The body faces Jerusalem and the rock is chipped so that the head-rest is slightly higher than the remainder of the shelf.

NICODEMUS: [*When the body of* JESUS *has been laid flat,* NICODEMUS *places the downy feather under the nose of the deceased for a specified length of time, which was about fifteen minutes.*]

SECOND VOICE: Nicodemus was well versed in these matters. If after fifteen minutes, the feather had not moved, the soul had left the body. The feather did not move.

[**The MEN** *work quickly and quietly. One anoints the body with balm oil, rubbing it in with the ball of the thumb; another tears the big bolt of cloth into strips; a third winds the strips around the legs and the arms.*

JOHN: [**From the vestibule** JOHN *brings the rolls of linen back to the* MARYS.]

JOHN: Will you impregnate these with the aromatic spices?

[**The WOMEN** *ease their grief in work.*]

SECOND VOICE: The Marys (or women) were grateful to be asked, and in performing this service for the Redeemer they eased their grief in work.

Nicodemus brought a large quantity of myrrh and aloes, about a hundredweight. The odorous mixture was highly esteemed for anointing the embalming, but its cost restricted its use to the wealthy.

They therefore took the body of Jesus and wound it with linen bandages, with the spices, as was the custom to bury.

[**The THREE MEN** *roll a stone to the door of the sepulchre.*]

SECOND VOICE: Joseph bought fine linen, and took Him down, and wrapped him in the linen, and laid Him in the sepulchre and rolled a stone to the door of the sepulchre.

This was the last sight of the Dead. The "roller" rolled into its orifice and closed the entrance.

Because of the nearness of the Sabbath the interment had to be made with haste; the door of the sepulchre was closed, a large stone was rolled against it; and thus laid away, the body was left to rest. It was not meant for a permanent burial, but to give the body temporary shelter over the Sabbath. After the Sabbath, they would arrange for an interment in due form. All they wanted today was to make sure of a provisional burial, without interference on the part of the priests. That is why they were so speedy, as if in flight. Enough to roll a great stone to the door of the sepulchre, for the evening star was already shining, and no more work must be done till the Sabbath was over.

As the sun was beginning to set over the western hills and the Jews were completing their preparation for the approaching Passover meal, the body of Jesus was temporarily laid to rest.

[The **WOMEN** *behold where He is laid*.]

SECOND VOICE: And Mary Magdalene and Mary the mother of Jesus beheld where he was laid.

The faithful Galilean women who had followed Jesus from Galilee, Mary of Magdala, and Mary, Joseph's mother, witnessed Joseph's action and followed Jesus' body to the tomb. They watched the entombment from a distance. They noted the spot, for they meant to come back after the Sabbath to bring spices and anoint His body.

And the women beheld the sepulchre and how the body was laid.

FIRST VOICE: "Sleep in the grave, O deceased, until the resurrection of the dead" is the hopeless meaning of such a burying.

The elaborate embalming rather suggested that these secret disciples, as the Apostles themselves, were not expecting the Resurrection. Physically, they were mindful of Him; spiritually, they knew not yet who He was. Their concern about His burial was a token of their love for Him, not of their faith in Him as the Resurrection and Life.

Merely a few frightened and despondent souls in whom the divine power of this death was making itself felt, a few souls who, vanquished by the love that had made Christ give up his life for man, of their own free will professed their faith in Him as He hung dying upon the Cross and so became heralds of His Resurrection after the crucifixion was over.

SECOND VOICE: When the entombment was completed they returned, and prepared spices and ointments; and rested the Sabbath day according to the commandment.

337

ACT V

THE PROOF OF THE RESURRECTION
(Death Could Not Conquer Him)

Scene 1

AN INNER ROOM OF THE TEMPLE—IN CONFERENCE

FIRST VOICE: In the history of the world, only one tomb has ever had a rock rolled before it, and a soldier guard set to watch it to prevent the dead man within from rising: that was the tomb of Jesus on the evening of the Friday called Good.

What spectacle could be more ridiculous than armed soldiers keeping their eyes on a corpse? But sentinels were set, lest the Dead walk, the Silent speak, and the Pierced Heart quicken to the throb of life.

SECOND VOICE: The few high priests who remained were shocked to the point of momentary muteness when they saw two of the great Jewish leaders of the temple with the kin of the blasphemer. And when they understood that Jesus would be buried in Joseph's own crypt they hurried, muttering, into Jerusalem to confer with the old patriarch Annas.

FIRST VOICE: An account was settled, the business was finished; and so much hate, henceforth useless, fell back upon the hearts of the scribes. The immense sadness of their race crushed down upon them; enough to fill century after century with dissatisfaction, with a sense of

338

unfulfillment. The Pharisees were still anxious concerning the agitation going on about the body, even one so dishonored as this had been. Those who had always seen things clearly sneered at those who had been impressed by the impostor. But the Passover was at hand and each went back to his house.

Crucified, dead, and buried! The destiny of Jesus of Nazareth has been fulfilled, and everything had happened as it had to happen. For no nation will allow its religion, its own peculiar piety, its chosen faith, to be destroyed. And here implied is that no nation was more proud than the Jewish. And the threat of destruction to all these things was, of course, the trouble on that Good Friday—as we look at the human motives. Here we see a people proud of its history and of its blood—a nation proud of its piety and of its temple.

This people had carried out reprisals and vengeance on the man who set His face against its pride, proclaiming the approaching sovereignty of God which orders all human arrogance to repent, but who did not offer any real or tangible substitute.

"Believe in the gospel!" What does the gospel or "good news" really mean on the lips of Him who takes away from us all wherein we find pleasure and destroys all whereon we pride ourselves?

On the evening of Good Friday the high priests and the Pharisees heaved a sign of relief. Public peace and safety had been restored; the unity of the church and of the religion of the Jewish nation had been preserved; the national faith had gained a complete victory. The old hope might now awake to new life; the nation could again proclaim and believe: "We are Abraham's seed; we are the heirs according to the promise; ours is the everlasting kingdom."

The people had spoken, and its words had condemned the Teacher of Nazareth to eternal silence. Is not the voice of the people the voice of God?

They said He was dead; they knew He was dead; they would say He would not rise again; and yet they watched! They openly called Him a deceiver. But, would He still deceive? Would He, Who "deceived" them into believing they'd won the battle, Himself win the war for life and truth and love? They remembered that He called His Body the Temple and said that three days after they destroyed It, He would rebuild It; they recalled, too, that He compared Himself to Jonas and said that as Jonas was in the belly of the whale for three days, so He would be in the belly of the earth for three days and then would rise again. After three days Abraham received back his son Isaac, who was offered in sacrifice; for three days Egypt was in a darkness that was not of nature; on the third day God came down on Mount Sinai. Now, once again, there was worry about the third day.

[ANNAS *sits in informal discussion with* CAIPHAS *and the* HIGH PRIESTS *who had seen the* MAN JESUS *die.*]

SECOND VOICE: Annas was old and wise and he listened to the ranking priests as they told, in tones of horror, about the apostolic actions of Joseph and Nicodemus. The old man could hardly have been less moved. The heresies of a few members of the Great Sanhedrin were matters that he had witnessed again and again over a span of years.

What worried Annas was that the faker Jesus had said, in His teachings, that He would rise again in three days. Now that He was dead, there was one more chore to do.

ANNAS: We will have to go to Pontius Pilate in the morning and ask for guards to be posted over the tomb of Joseph of Arimathea. We do not want the scheming disciples of this Man to come and steal the body and claim later that He has risen from the dead.

SECOND VOICE: The importance of this was twofold: first, it would have the same effect as having the Romans participate in the original raid on Gethsemane—once they became a part of it, the Romans would have to protect their interests by not permitting anyone to steal the body; second, the word of the Romans would have more weight with the people of Jerusalem at this time.

If the priests said that Jesus did not rise from the grave, the thousands of followers of the Galilean would say that the priests were lying to cover the darkness of their deed in having Him crucified; if the Romans said it, the people would believe, understanding that the Gentiles had no interest in the matter one way or the other.

CAIPHAS: [*Praises his father-in-law.*] You are a man of great wisdom.

Scene 2

THE JUDGMENT HALL OF FORTRESS ANTONIA—THEY SET A WATCH—THE TOMB IS GUARDED

THE CHIEF PRIESTS: [*The* CHIEF PRIESTS *and* PHARISEES *come in a body to* PILATE.] Sir, we remember that that deceiver said, while He was yet alive, "After three days I will rise again." Command therefore that the sepulchre be made secure until the third day, lest His disciples come by night and steal Him away, and say to the people He is risen from the dead: so the last error shall be worse than the first. Sir, we have recalled it to memory that this deceiver, while He yet lived, said: I am to rise again after three days. Give orders, then, that His tomb shall be securely guarded until the third day; or, perhaps, His disciples will come and steal Him away. If they should then say to the people, He has risen from the dead, this last deceit will be more dangerous than the old.

SECOND VOICE: On Saturday, the Sabbath and "high day," the chief priests and Pharisees came in a body to Pilate. Early Saturday morning, therefore, the chief priests and the Pharisees broke the Sabbath and presented themselves to Pilate. It is evident that the most inveterate of the human enemies of Christ remembered His predictions of an assured resurrection on the third day after His death.

Their request for a guard until the "third day" had more reference to Jesus' words about His Resurrection than it did to the fear of the Apostles stealing a corpse and propping it up like a living thing in simulation of a Resurrection. Whence came the terror which drove the victors back to Pilate, when they had scarcely won the victory, to beg him for protection against the dead man?

FIRST VOICE: By how comes it that this Jesus does not remain silent? How comes it that He—who has just been laid in the tomb—again begins to speak?

It is a futile undertaking for a man, indeed for a whole nation, to try to get rid of the living God. It is of no use whatever to brand the Lord Jesus Christ as an enemy of the people and put Him to death and lay him in the tomb among the dead. Anyone who has once met Him, anyone who has listened to His words and seen His work, anyone who has felt His omnipotence, has heard God pass sentence upon himself, and that sentence remains in force.

It was a delusion on the part of Jesus' enemies to think that they could escape the sentence He had passed upon them by the sentence they passed on Him. On the contrary, God's judgment begins in the terror with which the dead Christ inspires his enemies; that is the judgment of the living God on all efforts made by man to regain his peace of mind.

In ordinary circumstances people are not afraid of a dead man. People do not as a rule seek police protection against someone who has been buried. Here it is otherwise. This Jesus of Nazareth is given up to universal contempt. He is condemned and executed, he is buried—and yet we are not done with Him.

Conscience knows well that He has spoken the truth. And more than that, conscience knows that it was God who spoke to Him. And whether we bow to His judgment now and believe in Him, or whether we resist His judgment and refuse to accept Him, our self-assurance is at an end; the Jesus who has been put to death proves to be as dangerous as was the living Jesus. But that is an uncanny situation; and that is why the attempt to get rid of Him, to silence Him by every method within human power, continues to meet with no success. He has been put to death, yet the terror remains; His followers have been persecuted up till the present day, but the unrest has not abated.

The fact is that it is useless for us to fight against God. Our resistance serves only to show forth His might and His Truth.

No, the reason is that the crucified, dead, and buried Christ gives us no peace, that the execution of Jesus was a vain effort on the part of men, and that we ourselves must either fight against the dead Christ or bow down to Him, because humanity has achieved only one result with Golgotha: its resistance has brought it up against God Himself and it is now forced to see that its work was altogether in vain.

And even if men have refused to see and still call Him a deceiver in spite of the voice of their conscience, even if they succeed in again getting the state to intervene—we see in their attitude the unwilling confession of the vanquished victors: "We are at the end of our resources and can do no more; you have conquered, O Galilean!"

We men tried to sit in judgment upon God, and now we discover that He has sat in judgment upon us, and all that is left for us to decide is whether we will bow to God's judgment or to resist it, whether we will acknowledge God's authority or persist in our iniquity.

PILATE: You have a watch: go your way, make it as sure as you can. (You have guards; away with you, make it secure as you best know how.)

SECOND VOICE: The procurator refused to be a party to the scheme, and ordered the high priests to set their own guard over the body.

But Pilate was in no mood to see this group, for they were the reason he had condemned Innocent Blood. He had made his own official investigation that Jesus was dead; he would not submit to the absurdity of using Caesar's armies to guard a dead Jew.

Scene 3

AT THE SEPULCHRE

[**The CHIEF PRIESTS** *put a seal on the stone*.]

SECOND VOICE: So they went, and made the sepulchre sure, sealing the stone, and setting a watch. (And they went and made the tomb secure, putting a seal on the stone and setting a guard over it.)

[**The GUARDS** *stand on guard and watch*.]

FIRST VOICE: The king lay in state with His guard about Him. The most astounding fact about this spectacle of vigilance over the dead was that the enemies of Jesus expected the Resurrection, but His friends did not. It was the believers who were the skeptics; it was the unbelievers who were credulous. His followers needed and demanded proofs before they would be convinced.

It is no wonder that this Jesus ends upon the cross; indeed, that cross is the last, supreme attempt to turn aside judgment from us and to win back our human freedom.

But for us, how are we to continue to live our selfish lives if Jesus is right, if God lives and if He claims dominion over us? How are we to continue to live by selfishness and self-deception if it is not we who have the last word, but God? The answer is that it appears we cannot. That is why the life of this Jesus of Nazareth must be an episode; that is why He must die by the hand of man; that is why the story of His life must end with a full stop.

SECOND VOICE: And when the Sabbath was past, Mary Magdalene, and Mary the mother of James, and Salome, had bought sweet spices, that they might come and anoint him.

Scene 4

THE UPPER ROOM

FIRST VOICE: The death of Jesus brings another message. It not only tells that all human pride, all human assurance, all human power

343

here collapse under God's judgment and are reduced to nought; it also speaks of how God gives grace to the humble, how he comforts the despondent heart and strengthens those who are weak and helpless.

To be sure, the Cross is the work of human hands, and as such it is an attempted rebellion against God which was bound to fail. But this same cross is also the free act of obedience and the free act of love of Jesus Christ. So His death then becomes a miracle. Behold, the master has let himself be slain for his servant!

"It is worth a kingdom to be, in a world of cheats, murderers, and kidnappers, the only person whom no one can injure!"

Seneca discourses: "The body is nothing but the burden and punishment of the spirit. The soul strives to return to the place whence it came. There waits eternal calm, and there, after the confusion of the world, lucidity prevails. The day is coming which will free you from the tabernacle of this hateful life. To be fettered, mistreated, crucified—these are the signs of virtue."

It had been a long day. A very long day.

The grief among the followers of Jesus would be poignant, a volatile fuel which, in its own fierce flame, burned itself out quickly. They did not understand. To their way of thinking, this was now a tragic defeat. It was not.

It was victory beyond their most exalted imaginings. He had come here to die. And He had died. He had come to preach a new covenant with His Father, and He had preached it. He had come to tell man that the way to everlasting life was love—each for the other, each for Him, and His love for all—and He had proved this by laying down His life in a torrent of torment—for them.

He died for man. All mankind. He came to Palestine to lay the foundations of His new covenant because He and His Father were dissatisfied with the old. The Father had never made a covenant with the Romans, or the Greeks or the Egyptians. He had made it, through Moses, with the Jews.

And the leaders of Judea had, over the centuries, perverted that covenant until worship became a matter of externals in which all inner love was missing. If a new covenant was to replace the old, it would be negotiated with the same people.

That is why He had to die in Palestine; that is why, of all the cities in Palestine, He had to die in the Holy City—and city of His Father.

Inside the sepulchre now, Jesus was not dead. His body was to be rent and its functions were to cease. In this immolation, His soul would be glorified and in this too He was pointing the way to man.

The Resurrection was a messianic event which signified the dawn of the glory that was to come. He was immersed as by baptism by the death on the Cross and the burial in the tomb, only to emerge triumphantly in the Resurrection.

He died as a rebel against the all-powerful Roman Empire, but less than three centuries later, this very Roman empire revered Jesus as its Lord and Master. How did this miracle come to pass?

His death on the Cross squared all accounts. His resurrection from the dead vindicated all His claims. And His intercession at the right hand of God is their security for that blessed inheritance they are to receive.

This world with all its pleasures is only sham in comparison with the glory that comes through Christ! The pleasures of this world soon turn to ashes. They are trinkets that fascinate for only a season. But they can never compare with the "inheritance that is incorruptible and undefiled and that fades not away."

Flesh and blood, whether quick or dead, can in no wise have part in the Kingdom. Therefore when the hour strikes and the dead are raised incorruptible, the living also shall be changed, putting on incorruption and immortality.

The Resurrection of the dead is the bridge from the "Now" to the "Then." Life is greater than we are; and Easter brings us news of this ungovernable life which laughs at death and which can be checked by no grave. Easter brings us news of life eternal. Yes, how comes it that the Easter message of the omnipotence of life in the end leaves us utterly empty so that we rebel against it in our innermost hearts? Is it only because it does not satisfy our claims that we want more than a universal message of life, that we long for personal survival beyond death and the grave, for a new life free from the shackles of human and earthly imperfections?

And now to crown all comes Easter, the resurrection of Jesus from the tomb; and we hear that henceforth He will not die and that death can nevermore wield power over Him.

Death is not the last word even with regard to the individual human life. There is a personal, eternal life of perfection, free from all earthly toil and travail, a life in which "there shall be no more death, neither sorrow, nor crying, neither shall there be any more pain: for the former things have passed away."

If God is the supreme and decisive reality behind all life and death, what then? Such things as the miracle of life, or belief in immortality for the human soul, are all very well; *but what of God*? If He exists what is our position? We speak of God as though we know Him; we sing and pray as though we were on the best of terms with Him; we worry about life and death as though we took it for granted that God agrees with our ideas.

And in so doing we forget that when we are dealing with God all our talking, singing, thinking and doing become of questionable value, because it is God who passes judgment on them and not we, and because all depends on what He decrees with regard to our life and our death.

God! That means our life rests on a new foundation and our arrogance is at an end. Man wills, believes, and thinks—*but God*! Everywhere and always this last "but"—*but God*!

And we run against it and of necessity resist it; for we cannot bear that another should be lord over us. "You will be as God!"—that remains our goal even though we may not admit it; therein do we seek the fulfillment of our life. There is no getting away from the fact that we should be like God—however Godlike we may conceive Him to be—to do what we want. And that desire is what the Scriptures call "sin"; and because of this sin, because we refuse to recognize His authority, God places us under the dominion and under the law of death.

Now we yearn for life. Now we dream of life. Now we may even hope for immortality. Yet death stands in our way and sin hangs between us and this immortality: *but God*!

How much of Easter have we left, if it is true that "the wages of sin is death," if we must see ourselves as those who are "dead in their sins?"

This one thing remains: now we know at last that what troubles us is not a flaw in the beauty of life, but a deep and yawning chasm that runs through the whole of life.

Our desire is not for a life which endures longer than death; we yearn for the life which vanquishes death, which knows not sin, behind which there can be seen no menacing "but God."

The old question crops up again and again: "How can we find a gracious God; how can we make our peace with God; where shall we find forgiveness of sin?" For where there is forgiveness of sin there life and happiness are also to be found, and there alone the agonizing "but God" is at last silenced.

For there, in the crucifixion of Jesus, sin is revealed as a conscious and intentional rebellion against God. And so Jesus has to die because the sovereignty of God is revealed in Him; so Jesus has to die because we do not want the sovereignty of God. And then we can go no further; we do not want God and yet we cannot live without Him!

What else does the cross mean but that we pronounce our own death sentence! It must necessarily be so, in order that we may hear the real, true message of Easter, which brings us news of an act of God that takes place when we are absolutely at the end of our resources, when nothing is left but damnation or grace.

But God is rich in mercy for He loved us with His great love.

When we hear these words, then even in the midst of our death, in the midst of our resistance, we feel that there is a possibility, a divine possibility, that grace may have the last word and that it may break down our resistance and overcome our death.

The message tells of death that has been vanquished, of a new life and an eternal perfection—but, of course, "together with Christ."

SECOND VOICE: For a little while the cruel death of Jesus must have seemed to those who loved and followed him the bitter, chilling end of all their hopes. It is one of the paradoxes of history, indeed the chief such paradox, that it was just the opposite.

FIRST VOICE: Biblical scholars accept as truth the claim of the disciples to having had visions of the Master after His death. But the scholars agree that those visions were purely subjective and not objective. (Scholars have never been prone to accept anything that hints even at the supernatural.) But if the Christ came to subdue death and death eventually will be overcome, then seeing the Master after death is not necessarily supernatural or subjective, it could be the most natural thing in the world.

To even dream that such a hoax could have been perpetrated or put over on the intelligence of the people even in those days or that such a so-called untrue story could have been devised and believed even to this day! Truth will out or else all is nihilism.

SECOND VOICE: Jesus, accepted by his followers as the long-awaited Messiah, was dead, a criminal executed by Roman orders, condemned to the horrible sufferings and public ignominy of the cross. Only a few devoted women and personal friends had witnessed His tragic end. One of His favorite Disciples had denied His very acquaintance, the other Disciples had fled. The little group of converts He had collected in his lifetime cowered at Jerusalem in an upper room.

THE GROUP: [DISCIPLES *and* WOMEN *cower in an upper room. Out of all the Disciples and followers there are only five "watching":* THREE WOMEN *and two men,* JOHN *and* PETER. *They are mourning and weeping.*]

SECOND VOICE: Their doors shut in fear of the Jews, who had contrived the judicial murder of their Master and might now be expected to attack his followers. And in the meantime they were grieving and wounded in their hearts. They hid themselves, because they were sought for as malefactors, and setters of fire to the temple. And they ate no bread, and wept all day and all night through the Sabbath.

FIRST VOICE: They had "hoped that He was the one to redeem Israel," but they had been bitterly disappointed and were utterly discouraged.

And where were the friends of the vanquished one? What remained of their faith? The Son of Man had entered into death, and by what a gate! To the Jews His memory would be not only abominable, but ignoble. His heritage, of which He had said so much? A sign of abjection. His victory over the world? Those who hated Him had trapped Him, convicted Him of lack of power and therefore of fraud before all the people. No, there was nothing for His friends to do but to hide themselves, to conceal their tears, their shame, to keep silence and to wait. All of them were without suspicion of the Resurrection.

SECOND VOICE: Nevertheless they waited, remembering certain words, leaning upon them; their faith vacillated, but not their love. Perhaps among them some hearts burned, prey to the folly of confidence, which was already the folly of the cross. The women, especially, those Marys . . . As for the mother of Jesus there was no need for her to have confidence, she *knew*. But the Passion went on within her. The blows continued to rain down, the spittle to stain the adored face. In her heart she could not stop the shedding of the Divine Blood. Each cry still vibrated through her, and the least sign that escaped from the bloodless lips. The Virgin was but the indefinitely prolonged echo of the Passion. She felt her brow for the marks of the thorns, she clasped the palms of her hands, except when she had to turn her care to the prostrated John.

The women then remembered: "I will not leave you comfortless: I will come to you." "I will see you again, and your heart shall rejoice, and your joy no man takes from you." And they returned home, and prepared spices and ointments. He had already been anointed before the burial; they only knew they wanted to see Him once more and in case, prepare themselves for "the third day." And they rested the Sabbath day.

FIRST VOICE: He lay motionless in the grave and the world went on as before. And the question was, would He rise again or not.

348

Scene 5

A GARDEN—THE SEPULCHRE

THE GROUP: [*By late afternoon the place had become deserted, and with public curiosity waning, guard had been reduced to a regular two-man detail. The* ROMAN SOLDIERS *were put under the command of the Jews by the proconsul. The* SERGEANT *pulls his hooded paenula closer about his neck and slumps against a tree.*]

SECOND VOICE: What a weird business this was—guarding a corpse!

[**The SERGEANT** *glances at the face of the tomb. A huge, circular stone, above five feet in diameter, completely covers the opening.*]

SECOND VOICE: He glanced at the face of the tomb. It was dug into a fourteen-foot bluff, gray and cold-looking in the gloom.
To the sergeant, the extraordinary activity about the case—all this ado over a dead man—seemed ridiculous. And that babble about rising to life again! Great Caesar's ghost!

[**The SERGEANT** *picks up a stone and flings it at the face of the tomb. It bangs against the rock wall and clatters down into the blackness of the ground. Then, all at once, everything becomes quiet. He stands as if rooted. The stars still shine brightly. Then he rubs his eyes.*]

SECOND VOICE: Silence reigned totally.
He felt an obscure uneasiness. He thought of moving about, scuffling his feet, to break the spell, but stood as if rooted. All life, himself too, seemed momentarily suspended, halted, pausing on the verge of . . . he knew not what.

[**The SERGEANT** *flings his arm over his eyes, a strangled cry in his throat.*]

SECOND VOICE: The stars still shone brightly, though. In fact, they seemed brighter than before. They *were* brighter. They were a great deal brighter. What was happening? What was wrong with his eyes? That light . . . that light in the sky.

349

It appeared as if a fissure was forming on the roof of the world, with a white brilliance pouring through, a celestial door opening. Its blinding purity flashed downward, shimmering, cascading in a flood.

[**The ANGEL** *of the Lord descends from heaven. There is a great earthquake. It is near midnight.*]

SECOND VOICE: A shattering blast rent the sergeant's eardrums, although he was not sure it was a sound at all, but as if lightning had burst in his own head. A violent shaking seized the earth, and he felt himself falling.

[*As* **the ANGEL** *approaches there is another thunderous roar, a laughing roar, like a whole army shouting a triumph.*]

[**The SERGEANT** *hits the ground, flat on his belly. His face twists to one side in the dirt, his eyes looking at the mouth of the tomb.*]

SECOND VOICE: The sergeant had no sensation at all of hitting the ground, but he realized he was there, flat on his belly, his face twisted to one side in the dirt, his eyes registering the gaping mouth of the tomb. "For fear of the angel the keepers did shake, and became as dead men." The soldiers were as dead men. They were paralyzed with fear.

[**An ANGEL** *comes and rolls back the stone from the door, and is upon it. His countenance is like lightning, and his raiment white as snow. The place shines like dazzling snow. The outlines of* TWO FIGURES *take shape, like men but not like men, radiant, glowing heights of perfect light, and* ANOTHER *appears between them, taller, more resplendent still.*]

[**The SERGEANT** *stands, his arms still folded at his chest, staring blankly into the flickering flames of the campfire.*]

SECOND VOICE: Then he could see no more. He didn't know how long he lay there. An instant, an hour . . . or had he lain there at all? All he knew was that he suddenly found himself standing again, his arms still folded at his chest, staring blankly into the flickering flames of the campfire.

FIRST VOICE: They put royal soldiers on guard at the tomb, and a royal seal on the tomb, but what can royal soldiers and royal seals do before a regal spirit? The final result of the issue between the two was this: "The soldiers were as dead men," but he could say, "I am the resurrection and the life." Is this power? It is the only power!

[The SERGEANT *shakes his head dazedly.*]

SECOND VOICE: Everything was just as it had been before. Except . . . he shook his head dazedly.

WOMEN: [*Over in a garden path stand some* WOMEN, *and a* MAN, *or someone, talking to them.*]

SECOND VOICE: The sergeant saw over there in a garden path stood some women, and a man, or someone, talking to them, and he heard what sounded like, "Be not afraid."

SOLDIERS: [*When they have partially recovered from their fright, the* SOLDIERS *flee from the place in terror. The night preceding Sunday is well-nigh spent. Fearfully then, the* SERGEANT *raises his head and looks at the tomb. With a cry, he bolts.*]

SECOND VOICE: Even the rigor of Roman discipline, which decreed summary death to every soldier who deserted his post, could not deter them. Moreover, there was nothing left for them to guard; the seal of authority had been broken, the sepulchre was open, and empty.

FIRST VOICE: Easter begins with the earthquake; the angel of the Lord rolls away the stone from the door of the sepulchre and seats himself upon it.
"Now what about the man who was put to death upon the cross?" The question remains open, for His tomb stands open—and all the answers which we try to give are empty and devoid of meaning, for His tomb is empty.
Here we are at the end of all our resources; here one thing becomes obvious: that our last word is no last word and we cannot possibly escape from the living God! The Resurrection of Jesus is not what we call a historical fact. It can be neither proved nor refuted by any method of historical research. What remain are the empty tomb, the fact that the dead man who lay in that tomb gives us no peace, that we are haunted by the knowledge that Good Friday, as a human effort and as an attempt to get rid of Jesus of Nazareth, was a futile venture.
This is anything but a message of "glad tidings to all men." This

is an earthquake sent by God, which shatters the last remnants of our human security and opens before us a yawning void. The empty tomb and the stone which was rolled away put an end to all piously happy, romantic notions of Easter. Here we are told plainly, "Make no mistake: it is the living God who speaks the last word!"

This message reveals the division in men's minds. To some Easter is good news and to some it is not.

On that first Easter morning no joyous bells rang out to an astonished humanity the news of life's victory over death. What happened then brought fear and alarm upon men, and by no means only upon the keepers of the tomb who "for fear did shake and become as dead men."

The Easter terror is universal, because it is of vital interest to the whole world that Jesus should be dead and that the full stop which we wrote on Good Friday after his life should remain. The stone must stay before the tomb so that we may have peace. We will gladly tend and care for the sepulchre; we will gladly mourn and revere the dead man, and perhaps even lament the tragic fact that He was too good and too great for us to be able to bear Him. Only He must leave us in peace; He must not ask us to hear, in His words and deeds, in His sufferings and death, the voice of the living God calling us to a sense of our responsibility. That is the reason for the stone, that is the reason for the full stop after His life and work.

SECOND VOICE: At the end of the Sabbath, as it began to dawn toward the first day of the week, came Mary Magdalene and the other Mary to see the sepulchre. At the earliest indication of dawn, the devoted Mary Magdalene and other faithful women set out for the tomb, bearing spices and ointments which they had prepared for the further anointing of the body of Jesus.

Mary Magdalene would anoint the corpse, as before she had anointed the feet of the living man. Mary Magdalene, from whom Jesus had cast out seven evil spirits, came to the tomb. She came not to greet the Risen Savior, but to anoint His dead Body. The Resurrection never occurred to them as a possible thing; it was foreign to their thoughts.

THE WOMEN: [*In the dim dawn of Sunday morning several women approach the tomb. They speak among themselves.*] Who shall roll away the stone from the door of the sepulchre? (Who is to roll the stone away for us from the door of the tomb?)

SECOND VOICE: On the way as they sorrowfully conversed, they seemingly for the first time thought of the difficulty of entering the tomb. Evidently they knew nothing of the seal and the guard of soldiery.

It was the cry of hearts of little faith. Strong men had closed the entrance to the tomb by placing this huge stone against it; their worry was how to remove the barrier in order that they might carry out their errand of mercy. The men would not come to the tomb until they were summoned—so little did they believe.

THE WOMEN: [*And when the* WOMEN *look, they see that the stone is rolled away; for it was very great.* MARY MAGDALEN, *who had in the darkness moved ahead of her companions, notices that the stone has already been rolled to one side while the entrance stands wide open.*]

SECOND VOICE: But when they reached the sepulchre, they found that the stone had already been rolled away, and that the body had vanished. Though it was yet dark, Magdalen could see that the round stone which closed the entrance had been rolled away.

They did not immediately jump to the conclusion that His Body had risen. Their conclusion could be that someone had removed the body.

THE WOMEN: [*They enter into the sepulchre. They see a* YOUNG MAN *sitting on the right side, clothed in a long, white garment; and they are affrighted.*]

SECOND VOICE: At the tomb they saw the angel, and were afraid.

THE ANGEL: Fear not you: for I know that you seek Jesus, which was crucified. (No need to be dismayed; you have come to look for Jesus of Nazareth, who was crucified.—Be not affrighted: you seek Jesus of Nazareth, which was crucified:) He is not here: for He is Risen, as He said. Come, see the place where the Lord lay.
(He is risen: he is not here: behold the place where they laid him.)

FIRST VOICE: The whole of the Last Supper is to be found in the words "this is my Body," and the whole of the Resurrection in "He is not here."

For like Paul we shall all be changed in a moment, in the twinkling of an eye. No laws are to be broken but laws will be accomplished and completed by the "transformation" of mortal man into the immortal.

To an angel, the Resurrection would not be a mystery, but His death would be. For man, His death was not a mystery, but His Resurrection would be. What had been natural to the angel, therefore, was now made the subject of the announcement. The angel was one keeper more than the enemies had placed about the Savior's grave, one soldier more than Pilate had appointed.

The angel's words were the first Gospel preached after the Resurrection, and it is the one that went back to His Passion, for the angel spoke of Him, as "Jesus of Nazareth who was crucified." These words conveyed the name of His humanity, the humility of His dwelling place, and the ignominy of His death; in all three, lowliness, ignominy, and shame are brought in comparison with His rising from the dead. Bethlehem, Nazareth, and Jerusalem are all made the identifying marks of His Resurrection.

The angel's words: "Here is the place where they laid Him," confirmed the reality of His death and the fulfillment of the ancient prophecies. Tombstones bear the inscription "Here lies." Then follows the name of the dead and perhaps some praise of the one departed. But here in contrast, the angel did not write, but expressed a different epitaph: "He is not here."

The angel called on the women to behold the place where Jesus' Body had been laid, as though the vacant tomb was evidence enough of the fact of the Resurrection. It was to a virgin woman that the birth of the Son of God was announced. It was to a fallen woman that His Resurrection was announced. It was appropriate because the Resurrection was accomplished for sinners and those who were subject to death.

The risen Christ does not face the world saying, "Do you want me or not?" His cross stands before the world, and it is there that we must decide whether we, guilty and condemned sinners, confess our faith in Christ, acknowledging the supremacy of God's truth and desiring to live by His Grace. Before the world lies the empty tomb, mutely asking us whether we are ready to let God have the last word. He who wishes to have the last word himself, he who thinks that he has gotten rid of the crucified Christ, must barricade himself against the message of Easter. But he who stands silent before the cross of Christ, he who knows or suspects that he, as one of humanity, has been condemned by God and who because of that knowledge cannot part from the crucified Savior, will hear the words "He is risen" as truly a message of joy.

No one can be happy in the certainty of the risen Christ unless his heart has been won by the crucified Jesus.

The risen Christ is no historical personality with regard to whom, after consideration of the facts, we can make a positive affirmation or denial; He is entirely removed from the sphere of all human and practical methods of research. Since Easter He has been called the Lord and since Easter He has been the Lord. As the Lord of faith He comes only to those who believe in Him as their Lord or who would like to believe in Him. After His Resurrection He ignored His murderers; He would not stoop to show Himself to them, but bided His time for revenge.

THE ANGEL: And go quickly, and tell His Disciples that He is risen from the dead; and, behold, He goes before you into Galilee; there shall you see Him. Lo, I have told you.
(But go your way, tell his disciples and Peter that he goes before them into Galilee; there shall you see him, as he said to you (there you shall have sight of Him as He promised you.)

SECOND VOICE: Those who saw the empty grave were bidden to go to Peter who had tempted Jesus once from the Cross and had three times denied Him. Sin and denial could not choke Divine love. It was to the denying Peters and the persecuting Pauls to whom the most persuasive entreaties of love were sent. To the man who was named a rock and who would have tempted Jesus from a Cross, the angel now sent through the women the message, "Go tell Peter."

THE WOMEN: [*And they go out quickly, and flee from the sepulchre.*]

SECOND VOICE: And they went out quickly, and fled from the sepulchre; for they trembled and were amazed; neither said they anything to any man; for they were afraid.
The women, though favored by angelic visitation and assurance, left the place amazed and frightened.
And they departed quickly from the sepulchre with fear and great joy; and did run to bring His Disciples word. Magdalen ran therefore to Peter and the other Disciple whom Jesus loved.

Scene 6

THE UPPER ROOM

MARY MAGDALEN: [*To* PETER *and* JOHN] They have carried the Lord away from the tomb and we cannot tell where they have laid him. (They have taken away the Lord out of the sepulchre, and we *know not* where they have laid him.—They have taken away the Master from the tomb and I do not know where they have placed him.)

SECOND VOICE: Her first thought was of the Apostles, Peter and John, to whom she ran in excitement. According to Mosaic Law a woman was ineligible to bear witness. But Mary did not bring them tidings of the Resurrection; she was not expecting it. She assumed that He was still under the power of death. She had failed to comprehend the gladsome meaning of the angel's proclamation, "He is risen, as he said." In her agony of love and grief she remembered only the words "He is not here," the truth of which had been so forcefully impressed by her own hasty glance at the open and tenantless tomb.

[PETER and JOHN *hurry out of the room.*]

SECOND VOICE: Peter and the other Disciple hurried forth to the sepulchre. Alarmed by the startling news, Peter therefore and the other disciple rushed out and started for the tomb.

Scene 7

A GARDEN—THE SEPULCHRE

SECOND VOICE: They set forth in haste, running together toward the sepulchre. So they ran both together: and the other Disciple did outrun Peter, and came first to the sepulchre. Mary was left far behind.

[JOHN *comes running up. Stoops down, and looks in. He does not go in.*]

SECOND VOICE: John saw the linen clothes lying; yet went he not in. He courteously awaited the arrival of his older companion. Through the low entrance of the burial cave, in the dim darkness, he saw white, the linen clothes, on the bench, or couchlike shelf. He caught a glimpse of the linen cerements lying on the floor.

[PETER *comes running following* JOHN. *He goes into the sepulchre followed by* JOHN. *They look around. The two observe the linen grave-clothes, and lying by itself, the napkin that had been placed about the head of the corpse.*]

SECOND VOICE: The bold and impetuous Peter rushed into the

sepulchre, and was followed by the younger Apostle. He saw the linen clothes there, and the napkin that was about his head, not lying with the linen clothes, but wrapped together in a place by itself. It was folded in one place to the side. They entered and found not the body of Jesus.

FIRST VOICE: What had taken place was done decently and in order, not by a thief nor even a friend. The Body was gone from the tomb; the original bindings around His Body were found in their con-volutions. If the Disciples had stolen the Body, they would not in their haste have unwrapped it and left the linen cloths. Jesus had risen out of them by His Divine power.

John frankly affirms that having seen these things, he believed, and explains in behalf of himself and his fellow Apostles, that they "had not yet mastered what was written of Him, that He was to rise from the dead." They had the facts and the evidence of the Resurrection; but they did not yet understand its full meaning.

History and religious experience approach from two opposite sides. In the case of the empty tomb, one says, "He is dead, disappeared," and the other, "He has changed, has risen." The Divine cannot be expressed in any words or known by any knowledge.

MARY MAGDALEN: [*While* PETER *and* JOHN *are within the sepulchre,* MARY MAGDALEN has stood without, weeping.]

SECOND VOICE: Finding the tomb empty, she broke again into a fountain of tears.

PETER AND JOHN: [*The two* DISCIPLES *leave.*]

SECOND VOICE: The disciples therefore went off to their abodes. This is the story of the empty tomb—told by an undoubted eyewitness.

By the order of the clothes they could see it all—how He rose, unwrapped the linen, took the napkin from His head and folded it carefully.

Peter departed, wondering to himself at that which was come to pass.

SECOND VOICE: Jesus now began the first of His eleven recorded appearances between His Resurrection and Ascension: sometimes to His Apostles, at other times to five hundred brethren at once, at some other times to the women.

The sorrowful Magdalene had followed the two Apostles back to the garden of the burial. No thought of the Lord's restoration to life appears to have found place in her grief-stricken heart; she knew only that the body of her beloved Master had disappeared. The idea of the Resurrection did not seem to enter her mind either, though she herself had risen from a tomb sealed by the seven devils of sin.

MARY MAGDALEN: [*After the men have left she stoops and looks into the rock-hewn cavern. She sees* TWO ANGELS *in white, sitting.*]

SECOND VOICE: And as she wept, she stooped down, and looked into the sepulchre, and saw two angels in white sitting, the one at the head, and the other at the feet, where the body of Jesus had lain.

TWO ANGELS: [*They are in white; one sits at the head, and the other at the feet, where the body of Jesus had lain.*] Woman, why do you weep?

SECOND VOICE: With her eyes cast down as the brightness of the early sunrise swept over the dew-covered grass, she vaguely perceived someone near her who asked: "Woman, why are you weeping?"

FIRST VOICE: She was weeping for what was lost, but His question took away the curse by bidding her to stop her tears. There was no terror at seeing the angels, for the world on fire could not have moved her, so much had grief mastered her soul. She was not terrified at the appearance of the angels for her thoughts were only on the body of the Beloved.

MARY MAGDALEN: [*With eyes cast down.*] Because they have taken away my Lord, and I know not where they have laid Him. (They have taken away my Master and I do not know where they have placed him.)

SECOND VOICE: In reply she could but voice anew her overwhelming sorrow. The absence of the body, which she thought to be all that was left on earth of Him whom she loved so deeply, was a personal bereavement. There is a volume of pathos and affection in her words.

MARY MAGDALEN: [*Suddenly she turns herself back, and sees* JESUS *standing.*]

SECOND VOICE: She knew not that it was Jesus. Turning from the vault, which, though at that moment illumined by angelic presence, was to her void and desolate, she became aware of another Personage, standing near.

JESUS: Woman, why do you weep? Whom seek you?
(Why are you weeping? Whom are you seeking?)

MARY MAGDALENE: [*She goes down on her knees.*] Sir, if you have borne Him away, tell me where you have laid Him, and I will take him away.
(If it is you, Sir, that has carried Him off, tell me where you have put Him, and I will take Him away.)

SECOND VOICE: She supposed Him to be the gardener. Scarcely lifting her tearful countenance to look at the Questioner, but vaguely supposing that He was the caretaker of the garden, and that He might have knowledge of what had been done with the body of her Lord, she exclaimed. She knew that Jesus had been interred in a borrowed tomb; and if the body had been dispossessed of that resting place, she was prepared to provide another.

It was Jesus to whom she spoke, her beloved Lord, though she knew it not.

Poor Magdalen! Worn from Good Friday, wearied by Holy Saturday, with life dwindled to a shadow and strength weakened to a thread, she would "take Him away."

JESUS: [He has the red, livid marks on His hands and feet.] Mary.

MARY MAGDALENE: [She turns herself and looks again. Her eyes open wide.] Rabboni!

SECOND VOICE: And the eyes of the holy woman opened wide, she answers with the Aramaic title of deep respect. One word from His living lips changed her agonized grief into ecstatic joy.

The voice, the tone, the tender accent she had heard and loved in the earlier days lifted her from the despairing depths into which she had sunk. She turned, and saw the Lord.

FIRST VOICE: That voice was more startling than a clap of thunder. Jesus had uttered "Mary" and all heaven was in it. She had once heard Jesus say that He called His sheep by name. And now to that One, who individualized all the sin, sorrow, and tears in the world and marked each soul with a personal, particular, and discriminating love, she turned, seeing the red, livid marks on His hands and feet, she uttered but one word: "Rabboni!" (which is the Hebrew for "master"). It was only one word she uttered, and all earth was in it.

After the mental midnight, there was this dazzle; after hours of hopelessness, this hope; after the search, this discovery; after the loss, this find. Magdalen was prepared only to shed reverential tears over the grave; what she was not prepared for was to see Him walking on the wings of the morning.

Only purity and sinlessness could welcome the all-holy Son of God into the world; hence, Mary Immaculate met Him at the door of earth in the city of Bethlehem. But only a repentant sinner, who had herself risen from the grave of sin to the newness of life in God, could fittingly understand the triumph over sin.

MARY MAGDALEN: [*In a transport of joy she reaches out her arms to embrace Him.*] (Or she threw herself at His feet to embrace them. They came and held him by the feet.)

JESUS: [With a restraining gesture.] Touch me not (Take not hold on me), for I am not yet ascended to my Father. (Do not cling to Me thus; I have not yet gone up to my Father's side.)

SECOND VOICE: Jesus restrained her impulsive manifestation of reverent love. Her tender tokens of affection were directed to Him more as the Son of Man than as the Son of God. Hence He bade her not to touch Him.

FIRST VOICE: Paul gave the same lesson to the Corinthians and Colossians: "Even if we used to think of Christ in a human fashion, we do so no longer." "You must be heavenly-minded, not earthly-minded; you have undergone death, and your life is hidden away now with Christ in God."

Her tears, He suggested, were to be dried not because she had seen Him again, but because He was the Lord of heaven. When He had ascended to the right hand of the Father, which signified the Father's power; when He would send the Spirit of Truth, who would be their new Comforter and His inner Presence, then indeed would she truly have Him for Whom she yearned—the risen, glorified Christ. It was His first hint, after his Resurrection, at the new relationship He would have with men, of which He spoke so fluently the night of the Last Supper. He then gave the same lesson to His disciples, who were too preoccupied with His human form, by telling them that it was expedient for Him to leave.

Magdalen wished to be with Him as she was before the Crucifixion, forgetting that the Crucifixion was endured for glory and for the sending of His Spirit.

JESUS: <u>Return to my brethren and tell them this; I am going up to Him Who is My Father and your Father who is My God and your God.</u> (<u>But go to my brethren, and say to them, I ascend to my Father, and your Father; and to my God, and your God.</u>)

FIRST VOICE: This was the first time He ever called His Apostles "My Brethren." Before man could be an adopted son of God, he had to be redeemed from enmity from God. He took the Crucifixion to multiply His Sonship into other sons of God. But there would be a vast difference between Himself as the natural Son and human beings, who through His Spirit would become the adopted sons. Hence, as always, He made a rigid distinction between "My Father" and "Your Father." His relation to the Father was unique and incommunicable; Sonship was by nature His; only by grace and adoption were men sons of God. The Son who sanctifies and the sons who are sanctified have a common origin, all of them; He is not ashamed, then, to own them as His brethren.

Nor did He tell Mary to inform the Apostles that He was risen but rather that He would ascend. The Resurrection was implied in the Ascension, which was as yet forty days off. His purpose was not just to stress that He who had died was now alive, but that this was the beginning of a spiritual Kingdom which would become visible and unified when He sent His Spirit.

SECOND VOICE: To other favored women did the risen Lord next manifest Himself, including Mary the mother of Joses, Joanna, and Salome the mother of the apostles James and John. These and the other women with them had been affrighted by the presence of the angel at the tomb, and had departed with mingled fear and joy. They were not present when Peter and John entered the vault, nor afterward when the Lord made Himself known to Mary Magdalene.

[*The* WOMEN *return. Some of them enter the sepulchre and see that the Lord's body is not there. As they stand wondering in perplexity and astonishment, they become aware of the presence of* TWO MEN *in shining garments. The women bow down their faces to the earth.*]

361

TWO ANGELS: Why seek you the living among the dead? He is not here, but is risen: Remember how He spoke to you when he was yet in Galilee, saying, "The Son of man must be delivered into the hands of sinful men, and be crucified, and the third day rise again."

[**THE WOMEN** *nod in acknowledgment.*]

SECOND VOICE: And they remembered His words.

[**The WOMEN** *start to return to the city to deliver the message to the disciples.*]

JESUS: [He meets them.] All hail.

[**The WOMEN** *come and hold Him by the feet, and worship Him.*]

JESUS: Be not afraid: go tell my brethren that they go into Galilee, and there shall they see me.

FIRST VOICE: His coming means joy and comfort for the fact that He is risen and lives means that God has frustrated our human action of Good Friday; the crucified Christ died for us, and God has accepted his sacrifice. So now there is a truly happy message: "Christ was delivered for our offenses and was raised again for our justification."

SECOND VOICE: One may wonder why Jesus had forbidden Mary Magdalene to touch Him, and then, so soon after, had permitted other women to hold Him by the feet as they bowed in reverence. We may assume that Mary's emotional approach had been prompted more by a feeling of personal yet holy affection than by an impulse of devotional worship such as the other women evinced. There was about Him a divine dignity that forbade close, personal familiarity.

Scene 8

A ROOM IN THE TEMPLE—A MEETING OF THE SANHEDRIN

SECOND VOICE: At the time the women were going into the city, the guards came also. After the women had gone to notify the Apostles,

362

the guards, who had been standing about the tomb and who were witnesses to the Resurrection, came into the city of Jerusalem and told the chief priests all that had been done.

When the Roman guardsmen had sufficiently recovered from fright to make their precipitate departure from the sepulchre, they went to the chief priests, under whose orders they had been placed by Pilate, and reported the supernatural occurrences they had witnessed.

And so it happened that in the gray dawn of that long-ago morning, there were two soldiers racing, indeed, they seemed flying, out of the grove of Joseph of Arimathea and along the road to Jerusalem.

THE SERGEANT: [*To the* PRIESTS.] We were very much afraid, and lay like dead men. [*He says haltingly.*] Afterward we heard the voice of the angel saying to the women at the tomb, "Be not afraid."

THE PRIESTS: [*They demand.*] To what women did he speak?

THE SERGEANT: We do not know who they were.

THE PRIESTS: At what time was this?

THE SERGEANT: At midnight.

THE PRIESTS: And why did you not lay hold of them?

THE SERGEANT: We were like dead men from fear, not expecting to see the light of day again, and how could we lay hold of them?

THE PRIESTS: As the Lord lives, we do not believe you.

THE SERGEANT: Assuredly you have done well to swear that the Lord lives, for indeed He does. [*The* SERGEANT *pauses, his expression stubborn. He adds quietly.*] And Jesus is risen.

SECOND VOICE: The chief priests were Sadducees, of which sect or party a distinguishing feature was the denial of the possibility of resurrection from the dead. A session of the Sanhedrin was called.

[The PRIESTS *assemble with the* ELDERS, *and take counsel.*]

SECOND VOICE: The disturbing report of the guard was considered. They now conspired to discredit the truth of Christ's resurrection by bribing the soldiers to lie. For worse than the Master saying "I will arise," would be the Disciples saying, "He has risen." The Jews had already told Pilate: "The last error shall be worse than the first."

If the body of Jesus had remained in the tomb, how could the faith of the Disciples been born and how could they have proclaimed it there, in Jerusalem, where it would have been easy to prove that the body of the pretended Resurrected One was still in the grave.

No one was to accuse Peter of lying when later he would say that "Jesus Christ whom you crucified, God raised from the dead." And they searched long and diligently to find the body and those who had buried it. If they could have pointed to His body, they could have destroyed Christianity at the very beginning but to no avail.

CAIPHAS: [*They give a large amount of money to the soldiers. They offer a rich bribe.*] Here, take this. Say you, "His disciples came by night, and stole Him away while we slept." And if this comes to the governor's ears, we will persuade him, and secure you from blame.
(Let this be your tale, His disciples came by night and stole Him away, while we were asleep. If this should come to the ears of the governor, We will satisfy him, and see that no harm comes to you.)

SECOND VOICE: For the falsehood they were offered large sums of money.

The bribery of the guard was really a stupid way to escape the fact of the Resurrection. First of all, there was the problem of what would be done with His Body after the Disciples had possession of it. All the enemies of Jesus would have had to do to disprove the Resurrection would be to produce the body.

It was very unlikely that a whole guard of Roman soldiers slept while they were on duty, it was absurd for them to say that what had happened, happened when they were asleep. The soldiers were advised to say they were asleep; and yet they were so awake as to have seen thieves and to know that they were Disciples. If all of the soldiers were asleep, they could never have discovered the thieves; if a few of them were awake, they should have prevented the theft. It is equally improbable that a few, timid disciples should attempt to steal their Master's Body from a grave closed by stone, officially sealed, and guarded by soldiers without awakening the sleeping guards.

The orderly arrangement of the burial cloths afforded further proof that the Body was not removed by His Disciples.

The crime was certainly greater in the bribers than in the bribed; for, the council was educated and religious; the soldiers were untutored and simple. The council had bought the kiss of Judas; now it hoped it could buy the silence of the guards.

The mendacious fiction was framed by the chief priests and elders of the people. Not all the priestly circle were parties to it however, for a few months later a great company of the priests were obedient to the faith.

THE SOLDIERS: [*They take the money.*] Right.

SECOND VOICE: They did as they were taught. The soldiers accepted the tempting bribe, and did as they were instructed; for this course appeared to them the best way out of a critical situation. If they were found guilty of sleeping at their posts, immediate death would be their doom; but the Jews encouraged them by promising to intervene with Pilate. Since the soldiers had been put at the disposal of the chief priests they were not required to report the details of their doings to the Roman authorities. The soldiers, if they valued their necks, dared not talk in public.

And this saying is commonly reported among the Jews until this day.

Next day, all Jerusalem had heard the news. A hundred rumors chase one another through the city. Some said that Pilate has regretted giving Jesus' body to His friends, and had had it hidden. A second story was that the priests had stolen the corpse, lest the multitude should idolize it. A third notion was that the gardener must be at the bottom of what had happened, being afraid that a great concourse at the tomb would trample his flowers. According to a fourth version, some of the rascals who plundered tombs of anything they could get money for must have been at work. A fifth theory was that of those who said that no one had ever died after only three hours on the cross, that the Nazarenes' disciples had revived Jesus from apparent death, and gotten Him away into safe hiding.

The priests went to Pilate, berated him for being so pliable, and foretold a peck of troubles, now that the prophet's followers had been allowed to steal the body, in order to tell the people that their Master had risen from the dead.

FIRST VOICE: The Sanhedrin did not deny the Resurrection; in fact, they bore their own unbiased testimony to its truth. And that same testimony they carried to the Gentiles through Pilate. They even gave the money of the temple to the Roman soldiers whom they despised; for they had found a greater hate. The money Judas had returned they would not touch because it was "blood money." But now they would buy a lie to escape the purifying Blood of the Lamb.

Scene 9

THE UPPER ROOM

[The **WOMEN** *converse with the* DISCIPLES *in perplexity and doubt.*]

MARY MAGDALENE: I have seen the Lord. He asked me to tell you that He ascends to my Father, and your Father; and to my God, and your God. And all the rest.

THE WOMEN: He said, "Be not afraid." Also that you should go into Galilee, and there you will see Him. [ANOTHER WOMAN] And the angels told us to remember what He said in Galilee about how on the third day after the Crucifixion He would rise again.

SECOND VOICE: The women returned from the sepulchre, and told all these things to the eleven, and to all the rest. But their words seemed to them as idle tales, and they believed them not.

None of the disciples except Peter and John had even troubled to look at the empty tomb, so "idle" did the tales of the women seem to them. Mary Magdalene and the other women told the wonderful story of their several experiences to the Disciples, but the brethren could not credit their words. To their minds the Resurrection was some mysterious and remote event, not a present possibility.

There was neither precedent nor analogy for the stories these women told—of a dead person returning to life, with a body of flesh and bones, such as could be seen and felt.

The grief and the sense of irreparable loss that had characterized the yesterday Sabbath were replaced by profound perplexity and contending doubts on this first day of the week. But while the Apostles hesitated to believe that Christ had actually risen, the women, less skeptical, more trustful, knew, for they had both seen Him and heard His voice, and some of them had touched His feet.

THE DISCIPLES: [*They receive the tidings with skepticism, doubt, and unbelief.*] You know women!

[**ANOTHER**] Always imagining things.

[**ANOTHER**] It's an idle tale.

[**ANOTHER**] The story seems like madness.

[**ANOTHER**] The whole story is a delusion.

FIRST VOICE: When the Disciples were told that He was alive and that Mary had seen Him, they could not believe it. (When they had heard that he was alive and had been seen by her, they did not believe.) Eve believed the serpent; but the Disciples did not believe the Son of God. The skeptics were anticipated by the Disciples themselves. Modern incredulity in the face of the extraordinary is nothing compared to the skepticism which immediately greeted the first news of the Resurrection. What modern skeptics say about the Resurrection story, the Disciples themselves were the first to say, namely, it was an idle tale. With one assent the Apostles dismissed the whole story as a delusion.

Something very extraordinary must happen, and some very concrete evidence must be presented to all of these doubters, before they overcome their reluctance to believe.

Their skepticism was even more difficult than modern skepticism to overcome because theirs started from a hope that was seemingly disappointed on Calvary; this was far more difficult to heal than a modern skepticism, which is without hope.

No agnostic has written about the Resurrection anything that Peter and the other Apostles had not already had in their own minds. In the case of Jesus, there was a readiness to believe that He had died, but a reluctance to believe that He was living. But perhaps they were permitted to doubt, so that the faithful in centuries to come might never be in doubt.

It was a forecast of the way the world would receive the news of redemption.

Scene 10

ON THE ROAD TO EMMAUS

SECOND VOICE: The third appearance was to Peter. He was the first of the Disciples to whom Jesus showed Himself. "How did He appear, when, what did He look like?" was sacred and because he, Peter, was afraid, he said nothing to anyone.

After that the fourth appearance was when he appeared in another form to two of them, as they walked, and went into the country.

TWO DISCIPLES: [*They talk together of all the things that had happened.*]

[**ONE**] His death means that our hopes for the Messianic reign are lost.

[**THE OTHER**] Yet I am unable to understand the testimony of the women concerning His reappearance.

SECOND VOICE: About sixty furlongs off, or two or three hours' march, on the road to Joppa, directly west of Jerusalem, lay the village of Emmaus, "the colony of Vespasian." During the afternoon of that same Sunday, two disciples, not of the apostles, left the little band of believers in Jerusalem and set out for Emmaus, a village between seven and eight miles from the city.

The two disciples, from among the Seventy, were Cleopas (Cleopater), the brother of Joseph, the nominal father of Jesus, and the second was Nathaniel of Cana in Galilee or the son of Cleopas, Simeon, a cousin to Jesus and future bishop of Jerusalem, a martyr crucified in the days of Trajan.

There could be but one topic of conversation between them, and on this they communed as they walked, citing incidents in the Lord's life, dwelling particularly upon the fact of His death through which their hopes of a Messianic reign had been so sadly blighted, and marveling deeply over the incomprehensible testimony of the women concerning his reappearance as a living Soul.

It was not so long ago that their hopes had been burning brightly, but the darkness of Good Friday and the burial in the tomb caused them to lose their gladness. No subject was more in men's minds that particular day than the Person of Christ.

[JESUS Himself draws near, and goes with them.]

SECOND VOICE: While they communed together and reasoned, Jesus himself drew near, and went with them. As they went, engrossed in sorrowful and profound discourse, another Wayfarer joined them; it was the Lord Jesus. Then they heard a light footstep behind them, somebody was catching up with them, somebody was walking beside them. Judging by his clothes one would say this was a Passover pilgrim on his way from Jerusalem and by the blue tassels on the edge of the cloak, a rabbi or scribe.

As they were discoursing with sad and anxious hearts on the awful incidents of the last two days, a Stranger drew near to them. Their eyes, however, were held fast so that they did not recognize that it was the risen Savior; they thought Him to be an ordinary traveler. But their eyes were closed so that they would not know him.

FIRST VOICE: Who among us does not know the inn at Emmaus? Who has not walked on this road one evening when all seemed lost? Christ was dead within us. They had taken Him from us—the world, the philosophers and sages, our passions. There was no Jesus for us on the earth. We followed a road, and Someone walked at our side. We were alone and we were not alone. Two of Jesus' disciples, who had already heard of the empty tomb, were on their way to Emmaus when a stranger caught up and walked along with them.

As the story unfolded, it became clear that what blinded their eyes was their unbelief; had they been expecting to see Him, they might have recognized Him. Because they were interested in Him, He vouchsafed His Presence; because they doubted His Resurrection, He concealed the joy and knowledge of His Presence. Now that His Body was glorified, what men saw of Him depended on His willingness to reveal Himself and also on the disposition of their own hearts.

SECOND VOICE: Though they did not know Jesus, they nevertheless were ready to enter into discussion with the Stranger concerning Him.

JESUS: <u>What manner of communications are these that you have one to another, as you walk, and are sad?</u>
(What talk is this you exchange between you as you go along, sad-faced?)

FIRST VOICE: The Savior with His infinite wisdom did not begin by saying, "I know why you are sad." His technique was rather to draw them out; a sorrowful heart is best consoled when it relieves itself. If their sorrow would have a tongue and speak, He would have an ear and reveal. If they would but show their wounds, He would pour in the oil of His healing. [*Suddenly grown silent, "they stop with downcast faces."*]

369

CLEOPAS: [*Replies with surprise tinged with commiseration for the* STRANGER's *seeming ignorance.*] Are you only a stranger in Jerusalem, and have not known the things which are come to pass there in these days? (What, are you the only pilgrim in Jerusalem who has not heard of what has happened there in the last few days? Are you a stranger in Jerusalem, and have not known the things which are come to pass there in these days?)

SECOND VOICE: Cleopas expressed amazement at the ignorance of the Stranger who was apparently so unfamiliar with the events of the last few days.

JESUS: [The unrecognized CHRIST asks.] What things?

SECOND VOICE: Jesus was intent on drawing from the men a full statement of the matter by which they were so plainly agitated.

FIRST VOICE: He called their attention to *facts*. They apparently had not gone deeply enough into the facts for proper conclusions. The cure for their sorrow was in the very things that disturbed them, to see them in their right relations. As with the woman at the well, He asked a question, not to get information, but to deepen knowledge of Himself.

TWO DISCIPLES: [*They could not be reticent. In sorrowful mood, they walk on and talk.*] Concerning Jesus of Nazareth, which was a prophet mighty in deed and word before God and all the people: and how the chief priests and our rulers delivered him to be condemned to death, and have crucified him.
We trusted that it would be He which should have redeemed Israel: and beside all this, today is the third day since these things were done.

SECOND VOICE: Obviously, the reason these disciples were sad was their bereavement. They had been with Jesus; they had seen Him arrested, insulted, crucified, dead, and buried. Sorrow afflicts a woman's heart when she loses the beloved; but men generally become perplexed in mind rather than heart at a similar loss; theirs was the sorrow of a shattered career.
Did he not know how the high priests had contrived a shameful death for that mighty prophet, Jesus of Nazareth?

TWO DISCIPLES: [*With brightening countenances, yet still perplexed.*] Yea, and certain women also of our company astonished us. When they went early to the sepulchre they found not his body. They came back saying that they had also seen a vision of angels, which said that He was alive.

And certain of them which were with us went to the sepulchre, and found it even as the women had said: but Him they saw not.
(Some women, indeed, who belonged to our company, alarmed us; they had been at the tomb early in the morning and could not find His Body; whereupon they came back and told us that they had seen a vision of angels, who said that He was alive. Some of those who were with us went to the tomb, and found that all was as the women had said, but of Him they saw nothing.)

SECOND VOICE: In the conversation of the disciples at Emmaus we see clearly enough that they did not care to believe in the testimony of the women. It was defying the world to permit a woman to be the first to see the risen Lord. Thus it was Jesus who first brought woman to honor.

FIRST VOICE: "Empty tomb—foolish words of women about the dead being alive. Could the Lord judge the dead? Could the dead come to life and glorify Him? Could His mercy and His truth be announced in the grave—the place of corruption? And we hoped . . ."

These men had hoped great things, but God, they said, had disappointed them. Man draws a blueprint and hopes that God in some way will rubberstamp it; disappointment is often due to the triviality of human hopes. Original drawings now had to be torn up—not because they were too great, but because in the eyes of God they were too little. The hand that broke the cup of their petty desires offered a richer chalice. They thought that they had found the Redeemer before He was crucified, but actually they had discovered a Redeemer crucified.

They had hoped for a Savior of Israel, but were not expecting a Savior of the Gentiles as well. They had heard Him say on many occasions that He would be crucified and rise again, but they could not fit catastrophe into their idea of a Master. They could believe in Him as a teacher, as a political Messias, as an ethical reformer, as savior of the country, a deliverer from the Romans, but they could not believe in the foolishness of the Cross; nor did they have the faith of the thief hanging on the cross. Hence they refused to regard the evidence of which the women had told them. They were not sure even that the women had seen angels. Possibly it was only an apparition. Furthermore, it was the third day which had come and gone, and He had not been seen. But all the while they were walking and talking with Him.

371

With these disciples as with all of the Apostles, there was no pre-disposition to accept the Resurrection. The evidence for it had to make its way against doubt and the most obstinate refusals of human nature. They were among the last people in the world to credit such a tale. One might almost say that they were resolved to be miserable, refusing to enquire into the possibility of the truth of the story. Resisting both the evidence of the women and the confirmation of those who had gone to verify their story, the final word was that they had not seen the risen Lord.

JESUS: O fools, and slow of heart to believe all that the prophets have spoken, ought not Christ to have suffered these things, and to enter into His glory?

SECOND VOICE: He made it appear as if He were about to continue His journey along the same. (Too slow of wit, too dull of heart, to believe all those sayings of the prophets! was it not to be expected that the Christ should undergo these sufferings, and enter so into his glory?)

FIRST VOICE: He rebuked the disciples at Emmaus for their lack of faith. Jesus gently chided His fellow travelers as foolish men and slow of heart in their hesitating acceptance of what the prophets had spoken.

They were accused of being foolish and slow of heart, because if they had ever sat down and examined what the prophets had said about the Messiah—that He would be led like a lamb to slaughter—they would have been confirmed in their belief. Credulity toward men and incredulity toward God is the mark of dull hearts; readiness to believe speculatively and slowness to believe practically is the sign of sluggish hearts. Then came the key words of the journey. Previously, Jesus had said that He was the Good Shepherd, that He came to lay down His life for the Redemption of many; now in His glory, He proclaimed a moral law that in consequence of His sufferings men would be raised from a state of sin to fellowship with God.

The Cross was the condition of glory. The risen Savior spoke of a moral necessity grounded on the truth that everything that happened to Him had been foretold. What seemed to them an offense, a scandal, a defeat, a succumbing to the inevitable was actually a dark moment forseen, planned, and preannounced. Though the Cross seemed to them incompatible with His glory, to Him it was the appointed path thereto. And if they had known what the Scriptures had said of the Messiah, they would have believed in the Cross.

[JESUS expounds and interprets the Scriptures.]

FIRST VOICE: And beginning at Moses and all the prophets, He expounded to them in all the Scriptures the things concerning Himself. He showed to them all the types and all the rituals and all the ceremonials that were fulfilled in Him. Quoting from Isaias, He showed the manner of His death and Crucifixion and His Last Words from the Cross; from Daniel, how He was to become the mountain that filled the earth; from Genesis, how the seed of a woman would crush the serpent of evil in human hearts; from Moses, how He would be the brazen serpent that would be lifted up to heal men of evil, and how His side would be the smitten rock from which would come the waters of regeneration; from Isaias, how He would be Emmanuel, or "God with us"; from Micheas, how He would be born in Bethlehem; and from many other writings He gave them the key to the mystery of God's life among men and the purpose of His coming.

SECOND VOICE: And they drew nigh to the village, where they were going.

[**JESUS** makes as though He would have gone farther.]

SECOND VOICE: He made it appear as if He were about to continue His journey along the same road, just as once before when a storm was sweeping the lake, He made it appear as though He would pass by the boat of the Apostles. The two disciples begged Him, however, to stay with them. Those who have good thoughts of God in the day will not readily surrender them at nightfall. They had learned much, but they knew that they had not learned all. They still did not recognize Him, but there was a light about Him which promised to lead to a fuller revelation and dissipate their gloom.

TWO DISCIPLES: [*They constrain Him.*] Abide with us; for it is toward evening, and the day is far spent.

[And **JESUS** goes into the inn to tarry with them.]

Scene 11

THE INN AT EMMAUS

[*It is evening. Here is an open door, the obscurity of a room where the flame from the fireplace lights only the trampled earth and makes the shadows move.*

373

They are seated at a table where a meal is prepared.]

JESUS: [He takes bread and blesses it.] Father, bless this bread. [He looks up to heaven. He breaks it and gives to them.]

SECOND VOICE: Their invitation to be a guest He accepted, but immediately He acted as the Host.

[**TWO DISCIPLES** *look intently upon their guest. And their eyes are opened, and they know Him—they recognized Him.*]

SECOND VOICE: There may have been something in the fervency of the blessing, or in the manner of breaking and distributing the bread, that revived memories of former days; or, possibly, they caught sight of the pierced hands; but, whatever the immediate cause, they looked intently upon their Guest.

FIRST VOICE: The eyes of their souls were opened. As the eyes of Adam and Eve were opened to see their sin after they had eaten the forbidden fruit of the knowledge of good and evil, so now the eyes of the disciples were opened to discern the Body of Christ.

The scene parallels the Last Supper: in both there was a giving of thanks; in both, a looking up to heaven; in both, the breaking of the bread; and in both, the giving of the bread to the disciples. With the conferring of the bread came a knowledge which gave greater clarity than all the instructions. The breaking of the bread had introduced them to an experience of Jesus. Then they knew Him.

[**JESUS** vanishes out of their sight.]

TWO DISCIPLES: [*They rise from the table.*] Did not our heart burn within us, while He talked with us by the way, and while He opened to us the Scriptures?
(Were not our hearts burning within us when He spoke to us on the road, and when He made the Scriptures plain to us?)

SECOND VOICE: In a fulness of joyful wonderment they rose from the table, surprised at themselves for not have recognized Him sooner.

FIRST VOICE: His influence upon them was both affective and intellectual: affective, in the sense that it made their hearts burn with love; and intellectual, inasmuch as it gave them an understanding of the hundreds of pre-announcements of His coming. Christ veiled His Presence in the most ordinary roadway of life. Knowledge of Him came as they walked with Him; and the knowledge was that of glory that came through defeat. In His glorified life as in His public life, the Cross and glory went together. It was not just His teachings that were recalled; it was His sufferings and how expedient they were for His exaltation.

SECOND VOICE: And they rose up the same hour and returned to Jerusalem. They forgot the purpose of their journey to Emmaus and went back to the Holy City.

Scene 12

THE UPPER ROOM

THE TEN DISCIPLES: [*They are gathered together, and them that were with them. They are assembled in solemn and worshipful discourse within closed doors.*] The Lord is risen indeed, and has appeared to Simon.

SECOND VOICE: In the Chamber of Sion the ten were then gathered, as on the night before His death. They arrived back in Jerusalem about nine or ten. It was Easter Sunday evening.
The place where the Disciples were assembled that Easter Sunday evening was the upper room where Jesus had given the twelve the Eucharist only seventy-two hours before. The doors were closed and bolted because there was a dread that possibly the people might storm, as they often did the houses of those who were unpopular. Precautions of secrecy had been taken "for fear of the Jews."

TWO DISCIPLES: [*They tell what things were done in the way.*] He was known to us when He broke the bread.

SECOND VOICE: Cleopas and his fellow traveler told of the Lord's companionship with them on the Emmaus road and of the things He had taught them.

TWO DISCIPLES: He was known to us when He broke the bread.

SECOND VOICE: And none believed them. They supposed that they had been deceived by a phantom. But now Jesus would show them His wounds; He flooded them with His peace and joy and gave them the power to remit sins.

FIRST VOICE: Even the Apostles had been scattered by the arrest, arraignment, and judicial murder of their Master; but they and the disciples in general rallied anew at the word of His resurrection, as the nucleus of an army soon to sweep the world.

JESUS: [As they speak, JESUS himself stands in the midst of them.] Peace be to you. (Peace to you!—Peace be upon you.)

FIRST VOICE: He bade the women on the way to the grave, who were plunged in grief, to rejoice; but now, having brought about peace by the Blood of the Cross, He came in His own Person to bestow it. Peace is the fruit of justice. Only when the injustice of sin against God had been requited could there be an affirmation of true peace. Peace also implies order, the subordination of the body to the soul, of the senses to reason, and of the creature to the Creator. Isaias said there was no peace to the wicked because they are at enmity with themselves, with one another, and with God.

[The GROUP *is affrighted.*]

SECOND VOICE: The Apostles believed at first that they had seen a Spirit; despite the words of the women, the testimony of the disciples of Emmaus, the empty sepulchre, the angelical vision, and the recital of Peter of his interview with the Risen One. His Presence, they admitted to themselves, could be accounted for in no natural way, since the doors were barred.
They were terrified and affrighted and supposed that they had seen a spirit.

JESUS: Why are you troubled? And why do thoughts arise in your hearts? (What, are you dismayed? Where do these surmises in your hearts come from?)

SECOND VOICE: Jesus reproved them for their unbelief. He upbraided them for their unbelief and hardness of heart because they had not believed those who had seen Him after He had risen.

JESUS: Behold my hands and my feet, that it is I myself: handle

376

me, and see; for a spirit has not flesh and bones, as you see that I have. (Touch Me, and look; a Spirit has not flesh and bones, as you see that I have.—It is I myself; touch me and you will see that I am not fleshless spirit.) [*He shows them His hands and His feet.*]

SECOND VOICE: He showed them His hands and His feet, which had been pierced with nails on the Cross, then His side, which had been opened with a lance.

JESUS: It is I, myself; touch me and you will see that I am not fleshless spirit.

THE GROUP: [*They touch the Body of* CHRIST.] It is He, it is He! [*They cry joyfully, and again become afraid.*]

SECOND VOICE: And, touching Him, they immediately believed.

FIRST VOICE: It was by His wounds that He would be recognized. It was not that the cruel wounds were to be reminder of the cruelty of men, but rather that by pain and sorrow, Redemption had been wrought. If the scars had been removed, men would have forgotten that there was a sacrifice, and that He was both Priest and Victim. His argument was that the Body that He showed them was the same that was born of the Virgin Mary, nailed to the Cross and laid in a grave by Joseph of Arimathea.

These nail prints, this pierced side, these were the unmistakable scars of battle against sin and evil. As many a soldier looks upon the wounds he received in battle not as disfigurement, but as a trophy of honor, so He wore His wounds to prove that love was stronger than death. After the Ascension these scars would become as oratorical mouths of intercession before the Heavenly Father, scars that He would bear on the last day to judge the living and the dead.

If men had been left to themselves to form their own conception of the risen Christ, they never would have represented Him with the signs and remnants of His shame and agony on earth. Had He risen with no memorials of His Passion, men might have doubted Him with the passing of time. He bore on His Person the memorial of His Redemption.

SECOND VOICE: They rejoiced, seeing the Master. And yet they still did not believe but wondered (They were still doubtful and bewildered with joy). That is to say they thought the reality, to which they all were eyewitnesses, too good, too glorious, to be true.

It was not a phantom that they were seeing. To some extent they believed in the Resurrection, and that belief gave them joy; but the joy was so great they could hardly believe it. At first they were too frightened to believe; now they were too joyful to believe.

JESUS: <u>Have you here any meat?</u>

[**The GROUP** *gives Him a piece of a broiled fish, and some honeycomb. He takes it and eats before them.*]

SECOND VOICE: This was to further assure them that He was no shadowy form, no immaterial being of tenuous substance, but a living Personage with bodily organs, internal as well as outward.

And the eating of the fish was real to them, as they later told "We did eat and drink with Him after He rose from the dead." First, "the burning heart," then hearing, then vision, then touch, and finally taste. These were the steps passed by them in which their bodies (experience) touched the Body of the Risen.

But Jesus Christ would not rest until He had completely satisfied their senses. Eating with them would be the strongest proof of His Resurrection. Thus He would convince them that it was the same living Body they had seen and touched and felt; but it was at the same time a Body that was glorified.

JESUS: <u>These are the words that I spoke to you while I was yet with you, that all things must be fulfilled which were written in the law of Moses, and in the prophets, and in the psalms concerning me.</u>

SECOND VOICE: Then opened He their understanding, that they might understand the Scriptures.

JESUS: <u>Thus it is written, and thus it behooved Christ to suffer, and to rise from the dead the third day: and that repentance and remission of sins should be preached in His name among all nations, beginning at Jerusalem. And you are witnesses of these things.</u>

SECOND VOICE: These unquestionable evidences of their Visitant's corporeality calmed and made rational the minds of the disciples; and now that they were composed and receptive the Lord reminded them that all things that had happened to Him were in accordance with what He had told them while He had lived among them. In His divine presence their understanding was quickened and enlarged so that they

378

comprehended as never before the Scriptures—the Law of Moses, the books of the prophets and the psalms—concerning Him.

JESUS: And, behold, I send the promise of my Father upon you: but tarry you in the city of Jerusalem, until you be endued with power from on high.
Peace be to you: as my Father has sent me, even so send I you.

SECOND VOICE: He gives them his blessing and points to their authority.

FIRST VOICE: The first salutation of peace was when they were frightened; now that they were filled with the joy of believing, the second salutation of peace had reference to the world. He was praying not only for those that would be His representatives upon earth but for everyone throughout history who would believe in Him.

Thus the night of the Last Supper, before going to His death, He was concerned about His mission to the world after His Crucifixion—a mission into the world that had rejected Him. Now, after the Resurrection, He reiterated the same idea to His Apostles, the twelve stones of the foundation of this city of God. His mission and their mission were one. As Jesus was sent and through His suffering entered into glory, so now He bequeathed to them His share of the Cross and, after that, His glory.

JESUS: [He breathes on them.] Receive the Holy Spirit.

FIRST VOICE: Then Jesus breathed on them as He conferred some power of the Holy Spirit. Now that the Apostles had learned to lisp the alphabet of Redemption, He breathed on them as a sign and an earnest of what was to come. It was but a cloud that would precede the plenteous rain; better still, it was the breath of the Spirit's influence and a foretelling of the rushing wind of Pentecost. As He had breathed into Adam the breath of natural life, so now He breathed into His Apostles, the foundation of His Church, the breath of spiritual life. As man became the image of God in virtue of the soul that was breathed into him, so now they became the image of Christ as the power of the Spirit was breathed into them.

Thus there was a new creation as the first fruit of the Redemption. As He breathed on them, He gave them the Holy Spirit, which made them no longer servants, but sons. Three times the Holy Spirit is mentioned with some external sign; as a dove at Jesus' baptism betokening

379

His innocence and Divine Sonship; as fiery tongues on the day of Pentecost as a sign of the Spirit's power to convert the world; and as the breath of the risen Christ with all of its regenerative power.

This was the Spirit, which was to be received by those who learned to believe in Him. He was already in His state of glory, for He was bestowing the Spirit. He was now associating the Apostles with the life of His Resurrection; at Pentecost, He would associate them with His Ascension.

JESUS: <u>Whose sins you remit, they are remitted to them; and whose sins you retain, they are retained.</u>
(When you forgive men's sins, they are forgiven, when you hold them bound, they are held bound.)

FIRST VOICE: Next He conferred upon them the power of forgiving sins. There was to be a distinction between sins that the Apostles would forgive and sins they would not forgive. God would continue to forgive sins through man. His appointed ministers were to be the instruments of His forgiveness, as His own human nature was the instrument of His Divinity in purchasing forgiveness.

[<u>JESUS</u> disappears.]

SECOND VOICE: And again He suddenly disappeared, just as soon as they began to recognize Him.

Scene 13

THE UPPER ROOM—ONE WEEK LATER

SECOND VOICE: The first appearance of Jesus Christ in the Upper Room was to only ten of the Apostles; Thomas was not present. Thomas, one of the twelve, was not with them when Jesus came because of his unbelief. He had been too frightened even to meet with the other ten. And after eight days (on the next Sunday) again His disciples were within, and Thomas with them.

THE DISCIPLES: We have seen the Lord.

SECOND VOICE: They scolded him for being elsewhere than the upper room. Thomas was informed of what the others had witnessed, but was unconvinced. He did not wish to believe what the others had told him. This statement failed to awaken an echo of faith in his heart.

THOMAS: Except I shall see in His hands the print of the nails, and put my finger into the print of the nails, and thrust my hand into his side, I will not believe.
(Until I have seen the mark of the nails on His Hands, until I have put my finger into the mark of the nails, and put my hands into His side, you will never make me believe.)

SECOND VOICE: He regarded the reported manifestations as a series of visions. When the disciples came to tell him about the resurrection of Christ from the dead, he did not believe it. He thought the disciples had been deceived. Thomas's doubts arose, for the most part, from his despondency and from the depressing influence of sorrow and isolation; for he was a man apart from his fellows. Sometimes a man who misses a meeting misses much.

FIRST VOICE: Thomas did not say he refused to believe, but that he was unable to believe until he had some experiential proof of the Resurrection, in spite of their testimony that they had seen the risen Lord. Thomas did not refuse to believe; he refused to believe without evidence. He was skeptical.

His, however, was not the frivolous skepticism of indifference or hostility to truth; he wanted knowledge in order to have faith. It was unlike the self-wise who want knowledge against faith. He openly demanded proof for the incredible stories they told him. Thomas frames for us the world's intermittent cry of bewilderment. Jesus had ignominiously died. What had *that* achieved? To Thomas, death was no victory; it was terrible defeat. Little wonder he wanted evidence. Who, in his right mind, would have asked for anything else?

His attitude of skepticism commends itself to the world. Our whole modern structure of learning rests on a perverse and mischievous habit of mind.

Thomas is congenial and mentally akin to us. The way in which he goes off alone with his trouble and tries to fight it out by himself; his refusal to let himself be influenced in his opinions by what other people say because he prefers to be free to make up his mind for himself; his manner of standing up, with a certain obstinate defiance, for his own principles and conditions.

We are told that "Jesus lives; Jesus is victor." Yes, but can we seriously believe it? Does he really live? Does he, who vanquished death, leave his followers in terror and continue to give his enemies a free hand even now?

We may find like Thomas in the end our faith is only a delusion, which may give us a feeling of strength and security but which fades away like mist in the moment of disillusionment.

Jesus has risen? Jesus lives? Jesus is the Lord? The facts tell a different story, both to Thomas and to us: Jesus does not show Himself; He remains hidden; He does not help us out of our distress. Thomas was supposed to believe that they had really seen Him, to believe in spite of all the facts and against all reason. He needed comfort, in truth, and was well aware how greatly he needed it. But he also knew, and therein he remained incorruptibly honest, that no human word could give him certainty and strength, and that faith, in the sense of certainty and sustaining strength, never lies within human power, however strong our longing and however great our love may be.

We learn from Thomas that faith must be able to say: "I am certain." Otherwise it is not faith. And thus faith needs the living Lord Himself, because no other person can give us such certainty. Faith very frequently languishes and degenerates because we do not dare to go the whole way, refusing to give in until we have been convinced or reconvinced.

JESUS: [He comes suddenly, the doors being shut, and stands in their midst.] Peace be upon you.

SECOND VOICE: For the third time He gave this salutation. Was this an apparition, as many claimed, and yet He speaks?

FIRST VOICE: But we feel that Thomas is going too far and asking too much and that by delivering this ultimatum and speaking in this brutal manner he is pronouncing his own doom. Now, whatever we may think about it, the Lord Jesus Christ takes a different attitude. He knows that with Thomas the trouble comes from wanting to believe and yet not being able to believe. He knows that here there is an unsatisfied longing for peace and certainty, a longing so agonizing and so deep that only He Himself can help, and He does help. He Himself steps into the midst of His troubled and terrified disciples with the greeting, "Peace be with you!"

JESUS: Reach hither your finger, and behold my hands; and reach hither your hand, and thrust it into my side; and be not faithless, but believing. (Let Me have your finger; see, here are My hands. Let Me have your hand; put it into My side. Cease your doubting, and believe.)

382

SECOND VOICE: Thus Jesus singled out Thomas. The rebuking words to Thomas—to be doubting no longer—also contained an exhortation to believe and to shake off his gloom, which was his besetting sin.

FIRST VOICE: Immediately upon speaking of peace, the Divine Savior treated the subject on which peace rested, namely, His death and Resurrection. Thomas had asked for a proof based on the senses or the faculties that belong to the animal kingdom; and a proof of the senses would be given him.

Jesus knew of the skeptical words Thomas had spoken to the other Apostles—another proof of His Omniscience.

[**THOMAS** *does as he is told. He puts his hand into the wound of His side. He puts a finger in the nail holes of His hand.*]

FIRST VOICE: Then the way was opened for Thomas to believe. He heard Jesus' own word, he beheld the crucified Jesus alive again, he saw the marks of the nails and put his hand into Jesus' side, and knew—knew for certain—that he could and must believe, for Christ himself has said to him, "Be not faithless, but believing."

One can face life joyously and undismayed and can refuse to be afraid of anything.

THOMAS: [*He throws himself on his knees.*] My Lord and my God.

FIRST VOICE: The skeptical mind of Thomas was instantly cleansed, his doubting heart was purified and a conviction of the glorious truth flooded his soul. He acknowledged Christ's deity. Thomas was no longer disobedient to the heavenly vision. The doubter was so convinced by positive proof that he became a worshiper. Immediately, all of Thomas's doubts vanished.

Thomas gathered up all of the doubts of a depressed humanity to have them healed by the acknowledgment of Christ's deity. These words not only mean that Thomas has seen and known, has grasped and held Jesus; they express grateful praise and adoration; they show that Thomas has been gripped and held by Christ, that is, that he has a certain, yea, a living faith which stays and upholds him.

Thomas was an honest doubter; he accepted the light when it came to him. And as soon as he was convinced, he immediately acknowledged the Lord. The light that they had seen blinded them spiritually. The people could not have seen Him. God showed Him openly *not to all the people*, but to witnesses chosen before God. A healthy man is a man of this world and therefore cannot see the other world. In the "appearances" of the Resurrected is the first indication of a new existence. "Behold, I make all things new."

For those who saw Jesus, the chief thing was not the "immortality of the soul" but the "resurrection of the body." There would have been no reason for Jesus to have lived, died, and been resurrected if there was not doubt that the body could be resurrected. Here is exactly the proof that he has power over death and life.

If Christ had not conquered death physically, had not risen in the flesh, then "Christ died in vain, and your faith is vain."

JESUS: <u>Thomas, because you have seen me, you have believed: blessed are they that have not seen, and yet have believed</u> (blessed are they who, having not seen, believe). (You have learned to believe, Thomas, because you have seen Me. Blessed are those who have not seen, and yet have learned to believe.)

FIRST VOICE: Unseeing faith has a magical quality that overrules all things. He rebuked Thomas that he had not recognized the truth earlier.

There are some who will not believe even when they see, such as Pharaoh; others believe only when they see. Above both these types the Lord God placed those who had not seen and yet believes. If Thomas had believed through the testimony of his fellow disciples, his faith in Christ would have been greater. But he wanted the additional testimony of the senses.

The future believers must accept the fact of the Resurrection from those who had been with Him. Their faith would have to be of the highest type. They would not be able to demand the full evidence of sensible proof. Faith will not be dependent upon our seeing. And they will be more blessed because they will not have seen Him. Their believing will not be dependent upon their eyes and senses. It is possible to believe without seeing, but not without His living and life-creating presence, not without the Holy Spirit. And that is why it is quite impossible to do without Jesus' word. For it is through His word—and through His word alone—that the spirit works. "The Holy Spirit has called me by the gospel." But you cannot do without prayer, you must ask for the Holy Spirit and the Heavenly Father will give it.

Then we will prove that "tribulation teaches us to heed the word"; affliction will teach us to pray.

He revealed Himself to them as in the days of His first miracle, but

384

this time with even more power, conclusively matching His Glory against the offence of the Cross itself—and His disciples believed in Him. This was the greatest miracle.

A survival of His spirit would not have been enough. His disciples had to see Him; only in this way could the shame and offence of the Cross be redeemed. Miracles are only necessary until the moment when men's eyes are opened to the secret beauty of the Son of God and its power becomes evident.

The Apostles were now happy men but they were to be far happier when they fully understood the mystery of Redemption and so lived in it, and even had their throats cut for the reality of the Resurrection.

Scene 14

THE SEACOAST IN GALILEE

SECOND VOICE: After the events of the Passover week in Jerusalem, the Apostles returned again to their former haunts and abodes, and particularly to the Sea of Galilee, so full of tender memories. The Twelve were sorrowful and wept, and each one went back to his own house (to Galilee). They had been advised that the Lord would meet them there both by the angel at the sepulchre and the risen Christ Himself. They deferred their departure until after the week following the Resurrection, and then, once again in their native province, they awaited further developments.

Galilee would now be the scene of the Lord's last miracle, as it was the scene of His first, when He turned water into wine. On the first occasion, there was "no wine"; on this last occasion there were "no fish." In both, the Lord uttered a command: at Cana, to fill the waterpots; in Galilee, to cast the nets into the sea. Both resulted in a full supply.

DISCIPLES: [JOHN, SIMON PETER, ANDREW, THOMAS, NATHANAEL OF CANA *and* LEVI *are standing in a small group by the Sea of Galilee in the dawn. This is the Gennesaret lake—Sea of Tiberias—not far from Capernaum.*]

SECOND VOICE: The Disciples stand in a small group by the Sea of Galilee in the dawn, following the disruption of the fellowship by the death of the leader.

PETER: I go a-fishing.

DISCIPLES: We also go with you.
[*They go forth and enter into a ship immediately.*]

SECOND VOICE: They embarked on a fishing boat and though they toiled through the night, the net had been drawn in empty after every cast. As morning approached, they drew near the land, disappointed and disheartened. But when the morning was now come, Jesus stood on the shore.

[<u>JESUS</u> <u>stands on the shore.</u>]

SECOND VOICE: The disciples knew not that it was Jesus. He was on the shore and they were on the sea. They were near enough to address Him.

JESUS: [<u>He is near enough to the boat to converse with them.</u>] <u>Children, have you any meat?</u>
(Have you caught anything, friends, to season your bread with?)

THE DISCIPLES: No.

JESUS: <u>Cast the net on the right side of the ship, and you shall find.</u> (Cast to the right of the boat, and you will have a catch.)
[*They cast the net on the right side of the ship. They are not able to draw it in for the multitude of fishes.*]

SECOND VOICE: They did as directed and the result was so surprising as to appear to them miraculous. It aroused memories of that other remarkable draught of fishes. Then Jesus was in the boat, now as Jesus Christ He was on the shore. The tossings of life were over.

JOHN: [*Says to* PETER.] It is the Lord. Peter, it is the Lord!

FIRST VOICE: A stranger told them to cast down their nets on the right side. They caught so many fish that John suddenly understood. In this miraculous draught of fishes they were made strong. John was the first to recognize the risen Savior on the shore.

[*When* **PETER** *hears that, he girts his fisher's coat to him (for he is naked) and casts himself into the sea. The others leave the vessel and enter a small boat* *in which they row to shore, towing the heavily laden net. They are not far from land, being about two hundred cubits.*]

SECOND VOICE: Peter sprang into the sea, the sooner to reach land and prostrate himself at his Master's feet. Naked as he was in the boat, he cast a coat about him, forgot personal comfort, abandoned human companionship, and eagerly swam the hundred yards to the Master. John had the greater spiritual discernment, Peter the quicker action.
[*As soon then as they reach the land, they see a fire of coals there, and fish laid broiling thereon, and bread.*]

SECOND VOICE: He was there, upon the shore. It was indeed He. Some embers were smoking.

JESUS: <u>Bring of the fish which you have now caught.</u>

[**PETER** *goes up and draws the net to land full of great fishes, a hundred and fifty and three.*] (Peter dashed into the shallows and dragged the net to shore.)

SECOND VOICE: Peter drew the net to land full of great fishes, a hundred and fifty and three. And even though there were so many, yet the net was not broken. The Apostles understood that this great catch symbolized the faithful who would ultimately be brought to the barque of Peter.

JESUS: <u>Come and dine.</u>

SECOND VOICE: And none of the disciples dared ask him, "Who are you?" knowing that it was the Lord.

JESUS: [<u>There is about JESUS an awe-inspiring and restraining demeanor. JESUS then comes, and takes bread, and gives to them, and fish likewise.</u>]

SECOND VOICE: As the Host at the meal, He divided and distributed the bread and fish.

FIRST VOICE: The Son of God was preparing a meal for his poor fishermen; it must have reminded them of the bread and fishes Jesus had multiplied when He announced Himself as the Bread of Life.

JESUS: [When they had dined, He says to SIMON PETER.] Simon, son of Jonas, love you me more than these? (Do you care for Me more than these others)?

FIRST VOICE: He clearly reminded Peter of what had happened earlier when Peter had said he would never be like other men.

The query was: "Do you love Me with that truly supernatural love, the mark of a chief shepherd?" Peter had once presumed on the greatness of His love, telling His Master the night of the Last Supper than even though all others would be offended and scandalized in Him, yet he would not deny. The Lord thus reminded Peter of his past as a natural man, but especially of his fall or denial. He had been living by nature rather than grace.

The word of Peter's answer implied a rather natural emotion. Peter missed the full significance of the Lord's words about the highest kind of love, a supernatural love.

PETER: Yes, Lord; you know that I love you.

SECOND VOICE: No longer did Peter have sufficient confidence in Himself to say "I."

JESUS: Feed My lambs.

FIRST VOICE: Having made love the condition of service to Him, He now told Peter, "Feed My lambs." The man who had fallen most deeply and learned most thoroughly his own weakness was certainly the best qualified for strengthening the weak and feeding the lambs.

JESUS: [The second time.] Simon, son of Jonas, love you me?

PETER: Yea, Lord; you know that I love you.

FIRST VOICE: Peter left out the affirmation of love but conceded omniscience and a knowledge by Divine vision to the Lord.

JESUS: Feed my sheep. [The third time.]

SECOND VOICE: Thrice repeated was the appointment of Peter as the vicar of Christ on earth. Peter's denial had not changed the Divine decree making him the Rock of the Church; for the Savior continued the second and third question. This commission was an assurance of the

Lord's confidence, and of the reality of Peter's presidency among the apostles.

JESUS: Simon, son of Jonas, love you me?

FIRST VOICE: Jesus proposed to substitute love for fear.

SECOND VOICE: The question wrung Peter's heart, coupled as it was with the reminder of his bold but undependable protestation at the Last Supper that "though all men shall be offended because of you, yet will I never be offended." And yet at the trial he had denied Jesus.

Three times this dialogue passed back and forth on the shore of the lake. Peter was grieved because He said to him the third time, "Love you me?" Three times had he denied Him, and three times was he to hear from Him, "Love you me?"—that was why he was grieved.

Peter was pained at this reiteration, thinking perhaps that the Lord mistrusted him; but as he had three times denied, so now was he given opportunity for a triple confession.

No word was said of what had taken place. All that He did to remind Peter of his denial was to ask him three separate times, "Love you me?"

FIRST VOICE: Here came the *victory for love*. When doubt and fear strove in later days for dominance, Peter would use the formula given him by the seaside. The confession of love must precede the bestowing of authority; authority without love is tyranny.

JESUS: "Truly, truly, I say to you, when you were young, you gird yourself, and walked wherever you would: but when you shall be old, you shall stretch forth your hands, and another shall gird you, and carry you where you would not. (Believe me when I tell you this; as a young man, you would gird yourself and walk where you had the will to go, but when you have grown old, you will stretch out your hands and another shall gird you, and carry you where you go, not of your own will.)

FIRST VOICE: Impulsive and self-willed though he was in the days of his youth, yet in his old age Peter would glorify the Master by a death on the Cross. From Pentecost on, Peter was led where he would not go. He was obliged to leave the Holy City, where imprisonment and the sword awaited him.

The Lord so spoke signifying the death by which Peter should find a place among the martyrs. The analogy points to crucifixion, this being the death by which Peter sealed his testimony of the Christ. As Peter went step by step down the ladder of humiliation, step by step the Lord followed him with the assurance of the work for which he was destined. To Peter He had given the keys and the function of the doorkeeper. The Savior's function as the visible Shepherd over the visible flock was drawing to an end. He transferred that function to the head shepherd before withdrawing His visible Presence to the Throne of Heaven where He would be the invisible Head and Shepherd.

He now, having commissioned Peter with full authority to rule over His lambs and sheep, foretold that Peter himself would die upon the Cross. He was saying to Peter: "You will have a Cross like the Cross to which they nailed Me, and from which you would have prevented Me from entering into My glory. Now you must learn what it really means to love. My love is a vestibule to death. Because I loved you, they have killed Me; for your love of Me, they will kill you. I once said that the Good Shepherd would give up His life for His sheep; now you are My shepherd in My place; you will, therefore, receive the same reward for your labors as I have received—crossbeams, four nails, and then life eternal.

The other is the man of perdition, who opposes and exalts himself above all that is called God. He is called the "opposite Christ," Antichrist. And Peter conquered his "falling away" and became the "stone" on which the Church would be built. And the gates of hell shall not prevail against it.

JESUS: You shall have more to bear than all the others; follow you me.

SECOND VOICE: The friendly eyes of Jesus saw faults.

PETER: [*Turns about and sees* JOHN *following.* PETER *looks backward.* JOHN *follows as* JESUS *draws apart from the others on the shore.* JESUS *moves off a little way and Peter follows Him; and* JOHN *a little after him.*] Lord, and what shall this man do?

SECOND VOICE: Peter wished to peer into the future as to his companion's fate—was John also to die for the faith?

JESUS: If I will that he tarry till I come, what is that to you? Follow you me.

SECOND VOICE: Then went this saying abroad among the brethren, that that Disciple should not die: yet Jesus said not to him, He shall not die; but, "If I will that he tarry till I come, what is that to you?"

FIRST VOICE: Jesus uttered those mysterious words which were to make the other Disciples believe that John would not know death. It was an admonition to Peter to look to his own course of duty, and to follow the Master, wherever the road should lead. This was said to all mankind.

[<u>JESUS</u> vanishes again.]

Scene 15

ON A MOUNTAIN IN GALILEE

SECOND VOICE: Then the eleven disciples went away into Galilee, into a mountain where Jesus had appointed them. Jesus had designated a mountain in Galilee whereon He would meet the Apostles. And now the eleven disciples took their journey into Galilee to the mountain where Jesus had bidden them meet Him.

This was the Mount of Beatitudes. Here the beginning of the Message and the end join.

THE DISCIPLES: [*When they see Him, they worship Him and bow down before Him.*]

SECOND VOICE: And when they saw him, they worshipped him: but some doubted. Others beside the Apostles were present. They were unconvinced of the actual corporeality of the resurrected Christ.

JESUS: <u>[Comes and speaks to them.] All power is given to me in heaven and in earth.</u>

FIRST VOICE: He affirmed His absolute Godship. This was a power that He had merited by His Passion and His death and which was foretold by Daniel, who saw in a prophetic vision the Son of man having everlasting dominion and glory. The power that was given to Him was foretold in Genesis, namely, that He who was the seed of a woman would bruise the serpent's head. The kingdoms of the earth which Satan promised Him if He would be a political savior were now declared to be His own. His authority extended over the earth, all souls having been bought by His Blood. This authority as the Son of man extended not only on earth but also in heaven. His words combined the Resurrection and the Ascension; as the Resurrection gave Him power upon earth conquering both its sins and its death, so the Ascension gives Him power in heaven to act as mediator between God and man.

JESUS: <u>Go you therefore, and teach all nations, baptizing them in the name of the Father, and of the Son, and of the Holy Ghost: teaching them to observe all things whatever I have commanded you.</u> (You, therefore, must go out, making disciples of all nations, and baptizing them in the name of the Father and of the Son, and of the Holy Ghost, teaching them in the name of the Father and of the Son, and of the Holy Ghost, teaching them to observe all the commandments which I have given you.—Go you into all the world and preach the gospel to every creature.)
<u>He that believes and is baptized shall be saved, but he that believes not shall be damned. And these signs shall follow them that believe; in my name shall they cast out devils; they shall speak with new tongues; they shall take up serpents; and if they drink any deadly thing, it shall not hurt them; they shall lay hands on the sick, and they shall recover.</u>

FIRST VOICE: His authority was supreme, and those who were commissioned by Him were to minister in His name, and by a power such as no man could give or take away. If all authority was given to Him in heaven and on earth, then He had the right to delegate that authority to whomever He pleased.
If this commission were given solely for the lifespan of the Apostles, it is evident that they could not possibly go to all nations. The dynamism or current that was passed into the Apostles under the headship of Peter was to continue until Christ's Second Coming. That day the propagation of the faith came into being.
They were now to go to Jew and to Gentile, bond and free, to mankind at large, of whatever nation, country, or tongue. Salvation, through faith in Jesus the Christ, followed by repentance and baptism, was to be freely offered to all; the rejection of the offer thenceforth would bring condemnation.
Signs and miracles were promised to "follow them that believe," thus confirming their faith in the power divine; but no intimation was given that such manifestations were to precede belief, as baits to catch the credulous wonderseeker.
Nor were they merely to teach; for He who gave the commission

was not just a teacher. They were to make disciples in every nation; and discipleship implied surrender of heart and will to the Divine Master. The power of His redemptive Cross would be in vain unless His servants used it to incorporate other human natures unto Himself. As Mary gave Him the human nature which was now glorified in His Person, so men were to give their human natures to Him, dying as He died, in order that they might enter into glory.

This incorporation to Himself was to be initiated by baptism. Unless a man be born of water and the Holy Spirit he could not enter into the Kingdom of God. As being born of the flesh made a man flesh, so being born of the Spirit would make him a participant of His Divine nature.

JESUS: <u>And lo, I am with you always, even to the end of the world. Amen</u>. (I am with you all through the days that are coming, until the consummation of the world.)

FIRST VOICE: This was another last word to mankind: that He is to be with them always, to the very end, shows that it would not be as a physical presence that He would come back to them, but as a spiritual presence. His living presence would be with us, in our hearts, in guidance, sympathy, companionship and counsel. He attempted to clear up in the minds of the Apostles any doubt concerning His Presence with them.

Scene 16

THE MOUNTAIN IN JERUSALEM

SECOND VOICE: Before the expiration of the forty days, the Apostles returned again to Jerusalem, where the risen Christ had previously appeared to them. It was the old, familiar resort on the Mount of Olives.

FIRST VOICE: There He made it clear that His companionship with them was past; His influence would now be in heaven.

JESUS: <u>[He enlightens their minds, to make them understand the Scriptures.] Now all that was written of Me in the law of Moses, and in the prophets, and in the psalms, must be fulfilled</u>.

FIRST VOICE: But before taking leave, He reiterated the importance of prophecy and history. No one before was ever preannounced; but He was, and the more they would search the Old Testament the more they would understand. From now on, the Church was to draw from its treasury of the Law, the prophets, and the Psalms all that referred to Him.

A new light made all things appear different from what they were before; they looked different in the light of the Resurrection from what they had been in the previous darkness. It takes more than the light of the sun to read Moses and the prophets and the Psalms; some interior illumination, which is inseparable from goodwill and love, is also required. Several times Jesus told His own autobiography, and in each instance without exception it referred to the atonement He would make between God and man.

JESUS: So it was written, and so it was fitting that Christ should suffer, and should rise again from the dead on the third day.

FIRST VOICE: He now summarized His life for the last time, repeating that the Old Testament referred to Him as the suffering but conquering Servant. It was not His Sermon on the Mount that He would have remembered, but His Cross. There would have been no Gospel had there been no Cross; and the death on the Cross would have been useless for the removal of human guilt if He had not risen from the dead. He said it behooved Him to suffer because He had to show the evil of Sin, and evil is most manifest in the Crucifixion of Goodness. Having been defeated in that, it could never be victorious again.

Goodness in the face of evil must suffer, for when love meets sin, it will be crucified. A God who wears His Sacred Heart upon His sleeve, as the Lord did when He became man, must be prepared to have human daws peck at it. But at the same time, Goodness used that very suffering as a condition of overcoming evil. Goodness took all the anger, wrath, and hate, and pleaded: "Forgive"; it took life and offered it for another. Hence to Him it was expedient that He suffer in order to enter glory. Evil, conquered in its full armor and in the moment of its monumental momentum, might in the future win some battles, but it would never win the war.

No hope could be given to a wounded world by a Confucius, Buddha, or even a Christ who taught goodness and then rotted in the grave. No healing can be brought to broken wings by a humanism, which is brotherhood without tears; or by a gentle Christ who has no source of knowledge distinct from any other teacher, and Who, in the end like

394

them, could not burst the fetters of death, nor prove that truth crushed to earth may rise again.

The law He gave was clear: life is a struggle; unless there is a Cross in our lives, there will never be an empty tomb; unless there is the crown of thorns, there will never be the halo of light; unless there is a Good Friday, there will never be an Easter Sunday.

When He said: "I have conquered the world," He did not mean His followers would be immune from woes, pain, sorrow, and crucifixion. He gave no peace which promised a banishment from strife; for God hates peace in those who are destined for war. What the Resurrection offered was not immunity from evil in the physical world, but immunity from sin in the soul.

Now He told the Apostles that His life was a model for all of His followers; they were encouraged to take the worst this life had to offer with courage and serenity. No talisman was He to profess as security from trials; rather as a Captain He went into battle in order to inspire men to transfigure some of life's greatest pains into the richest gains of the spiritual life. It was the Cross of Christ that raised the questions of life; it was the Resurrection that answered them. Not the feminine but the virile Christ is He Who unfurls before an evil world the pledge of victory in His own Body—the scar-spangled banner of Salvation.

JESUS: Repentance and remission of sins should be preached in his name to all nations, beginning at Jerusalem. Of this, you are the witnesses.

FIRST VOICE: After having spoken His own autobiography, Christ wrote the biography of all whom He redeemed; the fruits of His Cross must now be applied to all peoples and all nations.

The last sermon Christ preached before ascending into heaven was the theme of His first. Repentance was to be the burden of the New Testament teaching. Repentance is linked up with the application of the Redemption won on Calvary. Repentance implied a turning away from sin and a turning to God. Now in His farewell discourse before the Ascension, He bade the world repent. This preaching of repentance was to begin at Jerusalem. The Lord's commands were to go out from Sion, His word from Jerusalem.

The Divine order to begin preaching Redemption in Jerusalem was a mark of His great compassion; for He was directing the Apostles to go to those who had falsely accused Him and tell them that He was their Advocate; that He would plead their cause from on high; and finally assure them that, though they scourged Him, through His stripes they would be healed.

JESUS: Behold, I am sending down upon you the gift which was promised by My Father; you must wait in the city, until you are clothed with power from on high. [He adds.] For John truly baptized with water; but you shall be baptized with the Holy Ghost not many days hence.

FIRST VOICE: He assured the Apostles anew that the promise of the Father would be realized in the coming of the Holy Ghost. Having finished His own autobiography, Jesus reminded them again of the Spirit that He promised the night of the Last Supper and fulfilled partly when He breathed on them and gave them the power to forgive sins.

Thus He promised a manifest increase of the Spirit beyond a breathing; in fact it would be a "power from on high." But to receive it, they must wait ten days after His Ascension. This power would enable them to proclaim the Redemption.

As He began His public life with the descent of the Holy Spirit, so they were to begin their mission to the world. The Spirit would come to them after their obedience to tarry in Jerusalem as they abided in prayer. When that power would come, they were to be witnesses not to His miracles alone or His prophecies or His moral commands, but to His Person. As on the Mount of the Beatitudes He reaffirmed that there is no doctrine apart from His Person.

THE DISCIPLES: Lord, will you at this time restore again the kingdom to Israel? (Lord, do You mean to restore the dominion to Israel here and now?)

SECOND VOICE: They were still imbued with their conception of the kingdom of God as an earthly establishment of power and dominion. The Apostles had not understood the nature of this power (spirit); for to them it meant a kind of restoration of Israel.

JESUS: It is not for you to know the times or the seasons, which the Father has put in his own power. But you shall receive power, after that the Holy Ghost is come upon you: and you shall be witnesses to me both in Jerusalem, and in all Judea, and in Samaria, and to the uttermost part of the earth.

FIRST VOICE: They were still thinking in the old terms of a political Messias, and of making Jerusalem what Caesar had presently made Rome. But He warned that it was not for them to know the times of the seasons; a faith in a bright future was not to prompt a presumptuous curiosity. In all things they must wait upon God. The present is the exclusive object of apostolic duty; as regards the future, some will reap where they did not sow.

Power they would have, but not power to restore Israel; it would be a power over living souls to channel into them the forgiveness and grace stored up in the reservoir of Calvary.

They wanted an earthly kingdom; He spoke of a spiritual one. They wanted a return of the old things; He told them they would be "witnesses" of a new thing. And to be a witness meant to be a martyr. The power of His Spirit was consonant with human weakness. They could be humanly weak as Paul was in his preaching but full of power because of the Spirit. They were bound by the idea of a nation: Israel; He included the world in His vision.

Their new power would be a gift; it would not be developed from oneself.

Scene 17

MOUNT OLIVET AT BETHANY—THE ASCENSION

FIRST VOICE: The physical reanimation was just for a short time. It had to be to confirm the prophets and to show that death had been conquered.

Now that the repeated appearances had freed the Disciples from all doubt as to the actual resurrection of their Master, the story of the open tomb had lost its significance. But the slander that the Disciples had come by night and stolen the body would not die down and the story must be preserved to meet it.

The risen Christ is absolutely demanded to explain the sudden shift in the feeling of the Disciples, one day mourning and weeping, in fear, disillusioned, the next going forth joyfully to danger and death, and always preaching as the one absolute dogma of the new faith the belief in the Resurrection. The appearances would cease when Jesus ascended to heaven.

Throughout the forty days following His resurrection, the Lord manifested Himself at intervals to the Apostles, to some individually and to all as a body, and instructed them in "the things pertaining to the kingdom of God. And these things were put into writing and made a matter of record that you might believe that Jesus is the Christ, the Son of God; and that believing you might have life through His name."

For those forty days after His Resurrection, Jesus Christ was preparing His Apostles to bear the loss of His Presence through the gain of the Comforter who was to come.

He gave out laws and prepared the structure for His Mystical Body, the Church. Elias fasted forty days before the restoration of the Law; and now for forty days the risen Savior laid the pillars of His Church, and the new Law of the Gospel. But the forties were about to end, and the Apostles were bidden to wait upon the fiftieth day—the day of Jubilee.

SECOND VOICE: Jesus Christ led them out as far as Bethany, which was to be the scene of the last adieu; not in Galilee but in Jerusalem, where He had suffered, would take place His return to His Heavenly Father. The Ascension took place on Mount Olivet, at the base of which is Bethany.

He led His Apostles out through Bethany, which meant passing through Gethsemane and the very spot where He wept over Jerusalem!

JESUS: [Lifts up His hands, and blesses them.] May God be with you.

FIRST VOICE: His sacrifice being completed, as He was about to ascend to His heavenly throne, He raised His hands bearing the imprint of nails. That gesture would be one of the last recollections the Apostles would have, save one. The hands were raised first to heaven and then pulled downward to earth as if to draw down its blessings on men. Pierced hands best distribute benediction. After showing that all prophecies were fulfilled in Him, He prepared to enter the heavenly sanctuary. Hands that held the sceptre of authority in heaven and on earth now gave the final blessing.

JESUS: [And while yet He speaks, He rises from their midst, and they look upon Him as He ascends until a cloud receives Him out of their sight. And even as He blesses them He parts from them, and is carried up into heaven.]

SECOND VOICE: Not as from a throne, but from a mountain elevated above the garden with the twisted olive trees crimsoned with His Blood, did He give the final manifestation of His Divine power!

FIRST VOICE: His heart was not embittered by His Cross, for the Ascension was the fruit of His Crucifixion. As He said, it was fitting that

He suffer in order to enter into His glory.

And He is seated now at the right Hand of God. There was a parting, and there will be the meeting. The Lord's Ascension was accomplished; it was truly a literal departure of a material Being as His resurrection had been an actual return of His spirit to His own corporeal body, theretofore dead.

In the Ascension the Savior did not lay aside the garment of flesh with which He had been clothes; for His human nature would be the pattern of the future glory of other human natures, which would become incorporated in Him through a sharing of His life. Intrinsic and deep was the relation between His Incarnation and His Ascension. The Incarnation, or the assuming of a human nature, made it possible for Him to suffer and redeem. The Ascension exalted into glory that same human nature that was humbled to the death.

A coronation upon the earth, instead of an Ascension into heaven, would have confined men's thoughts of Him to the earth. But the Ascension would cause men's minds and hearts to rise above the earth. In relation to Himself, it was fitting that the human nature which He took as the instrument for teaching, and governing, and sanctifying, should partake of glory as it shared in shame. It was very hard to believe that He, who was the Man of Sorrows and acquainted with grief, was the beloved Son in whom the Father was well pleased. It was difficult to believe that He, who did not come down from a Cross, could ascend into heaven, or that the momentary glory that shone about Him on the Mount of Transfiguration was a permanent possession. The Ascension put all such doubts away by introducing His human nature into intimate and eternal communion with God.

TWO ANGELS: [*While the Apostles stand gazing steadfastly upward, two personages, clothes in white apparel, appear by them. They speak to the* ELEVEN.] You men of Galilee, why stand you gazing up into heaven? This same Jesus, which is taken up from you into heaven, shall so come in like manner as you have seen him go into heaven.

FIRST VOICE: The glorious promise is that Jesus the Christ, the same Being who ascended from Olivet, shall return, descending from the heavens, in similar material form and substance.

They had mocked Him as a Prophet, a King and as a Priest. By the Ascension His triple office of Teacher, King, and Priest was vindicated. But the vindication would be complete when He would come in justice as the Judge of men in the human nature which He took from men. No one to be judged could complain that God knows not the trials to which humans are subject. His very appearance as the Son of man would prove that He had fought the same battles as men and endured the same temptations as those standing at His bar of justice. His judgment would immediately find an echo in hearts.

Another reason for the Ascension was that He might plead in heaven to His Father with a human nature common to the rest of men. He could now, as it were, show the scars of His glory not only as trophies of victory but also as emblems of intercession.

While in heaven, He would be not only an Advocate of men with the Father but He would also send the Holy Spirit as man's Advocate with Him. The Christ at the right hand of the Father would represent humanity before the Father's throne; the Holy Spirit abiding with the faithful would represent in them the Christ who went to the Father. In the Ascension, Christ took our necessities to the Father; thanks to the Spirit, Christ the Redeemer would be brought into the hearts of all who would believe in Him.

The Ascension would give Christ the right to intercede powerfully for mortals: "We can claim a great High Priest, and One who has passed right up through the heavens, Jesus, the Son of God. It was not as if our High Priest was incapable of feeling for us in our humiliations; He has been through every trial, fashioned as we are, only sinless."

[The DISCIPLES *bow down to worship Him. They start to go their way toward Jerusalem.*]

SECOND VOICE: And they went back to Jerusalem full of joy, where they spent their time continually in the temple, praising and blessing God. They there awaited the coming of the Comforter.

FIRST VOICE: Had Christ remained on earth, sight would have taken the place of faith. In heaven, there will be no faith because His followers will see; there will be no hope, because they will possess; but there will be love, for love endures forever! His leave-taking of the earth combined the Cross and the Crown that governed the smallest detail of His life.